# Conflict Management and Problem Solving

To
Timothy John Sandole,
his generation
and all who follow

In Memoriam
Adrian S. Fisher
Gilbert G. Pompa

# Conflict Management and Problem Solving: Interpersonal to International Applications

*Edited by*
Dennis J.D. Sandole and Ingrid Sandole-Staroste

Foreword by Kenneth E. Boulding

NEW YORK UNIVERSITY PRESS
Washington Square, New York

First published in the USA in 1987 by
NEW YORK UNIVERSITY PRESS
Washington Square,
New York, NY 10003

**Library of Congress Cataloging-in-Publication Data**
Conflict management and problem solving.
Bibliography: p.
Includes index.
1. Conflict management. 2. Problem solving.
I. Sandole, Dennis J.D., 1941- . II. Sandole-Staroste, Ingrid,
1948- .
HD42.C65 1987 658.4 87-11072

ISBN 0-8147-7866-6

# Contents

# Foreword

*Kenneth E. Boulding*

The present situation of the human race can be compared to a tribe living on a mesa surrounded by cliffs. There is plenty of food and resources on the top of the mesa, although some concern exists about a population explosion. At the moment, however, the tribe has been divided into two parts, each led by a vociferous leader. These leaders are determined to run a race and the only objective of each leader is to be ahead of the other. On the mesa, however, every race is towards a cliff, and the great question is whether the race can be stopped before they go over the cliff with most of their followers. There seems to be no way of building a fence at the edge of the cliff, so the only hope is persuading both the leaders and their followers to slow down, camp out, and think about what they are doing. If there must be a race let it be a race to a garden, a race to produce where everybody will be better off. This book is an important step in that direction.

Both conflict and conflict management have always been with us. Some conflicts are well managed and lead to situations in which everyone is better off. Some are badly managed and lead to situations in which either everyone is worse off or someone is a little better off and someone else much worse off. This is a negative-sum game. The skill in conflict management has to be learned. Some of it is learned in the family and in the ordinary experience of life, in what might be called 'folk knowledge'. The human race, however, is capable of another kind of knowledge called 'scholarly knowledge', which is the product of people who specialize in the art of increasing knowledge. Scholarly knowledge has given us the nuclear weapon that has made conflict infinitely more dangerous than it ever was before, especially in terms of international conflict. The folk knowledge that guides many of the world leaders is not adequate to deal with this problem.

It is not surprising, therefore, that there is a strong movement towards the increase in scholarly knowledge and conflict management, of which this book and the remarkable program at George Mason University, which gives a Master of Science in Conflict Management, are important parts. I taught a class in this program in the fall of 1985 and look back on it as perhaps the most exciting class I ever taught in my more than fifty years of teaching. The age range of the students was about twenty to seventy and I think a good deal of internal learning took place between the younger and the older members. The variety of life experiences in the class also added to the learning process. About a quarter of the class came from something like a military background; another were peace activists; another quarter, environmentalists; another quarter, unclassifiable. I think we all learned from each other. This book, likewise, could be described as a 'learning discourse' in which a great variety of people with different life experiences participated in a common effort towards understanding, in a scholarly environment, this crucial and yet very difficult and complex problem of conflict management.

Something that emerges very clearly from this volume is the complexity of conflict and its management. It is often very hard to identify even the parties to conflict and still harder to identify what the conflicts are all about. The folk knowledge of conflict is apt to overlook this complexity, to assume that we know who the parties are, who is benefited and who is injured by particular decisions, what people's values really are, and so on. It is the business of the scholar to take folk knowledge, much of which actually is quite valuable but parts of which may be misleading, and to build on it the knowledge that comes out of the scholarly methods of research, testing, and theory.

One of the problems that emerges from this volume is the importance of the organizational structure in determining whether conflicts will be well or badly managed. One of the tragedies of the world is that it is much easier to create organizations which are specialized in the pursuit of conflict, such as the Department of Defense, the CIA, and so on, which cannot justify their existence without conflict, and which, therefore, have a positive interest in failing to manage it and in making it costly. There is even an element of this problem in the law and in diplomacy, though these institutions are directed a little more towards conflict management. What is striking in the modern era is that, no doubt because of the enormous increase in the danger and cost of conflict, a new profession of conflict managers is developing and producing professional associations and conferences. Professionalism has its dangers as well as its virtues, as some of the contributors point out, but it is a child of complexity and there is no question about the complexity of conflict.

The editors and the authors are to be wholly congratulated on this volume. The editing is brilliant. Converting spoken language into written language is a rare skill which the editors have achieved remarkably well. This book will be useful in teaching, and one hopes it will spread a little scholarly knowledge into the minds of the powerful. Like all scholarly knowledge, it is incomplete: as an economist I must confess I find it a little weak on economic conflict and economics is not well represented in the authors, but that will come. The book stands as an introduction to a rapidly developing field.

The French call the study of conflict 'polemologie', which is hard to translate into English. Like all studies of the real world, it has to be interdisciplinary. This is not easy within the context of university life as universities tend to be loose federations of departments. Nevertheless, what is happening here is that an interdiscipline is becoming disciplined and this is very important. If unilateral national defense does not destroy us, as it may do, our great grandchildren may look back from a peaceful world in which there is genuine national security instead of the universal insecurity that unilateral national defense creates. They may look back on this book as an important step towards that better world which is in the human potential to achieve.

Kenneth E. Boulding
Institute of Behavioral Science
University of Colorado, Boulder
January 3, 1987

# (i)  Introduction

*Bryant Wedge*

This volume is an outcome of multiple convergences. There came an historic moment in the age-old story of managing human conflicts when scholarship and practice seemed suddenly to begin to flow together to the enrichment of both. Similarly, different intellectual disciplines found common purpose in the analysis of conflict and alternative means to its resolution: sociology, psychology, law, communication science, anthropology, management, politics and international relations among them. Practitioners ranging from family mediators through labor and management specialists to high-level diplomats began to find relevance in each other's procedures and experience, and multidisciplinary networks began to form in the 1970s. Finally, new institutional bases were formed, in universities, in association with overburdened court systems, in the federal and state governments and as free-standing centers.

The most important development was a movement in the United States Congress to establish a United States Academy of Peace and Conflict Resolution, starting in 1975, a movement supported by a public campaign that gave focus and legitimacy to the emerging field. This eventuated in the establishment of the United States Institute of Peace which began operations in 1986.

This background provided the context for the chapters of this book; by bringing together representatives of both academe and practice in a common forum, we hoped to explore the degree of coherence and convergence that appeared to be developing. Powerful confirmation of the converging tendency was provided by the fact that every contributor invited to speak accepted with alacrity, whether professor or official, lawyer or negotiator. The outcome so far exceeded our expectations that the Center for Conflict Resolution at George Mason University decided to support the immense labor of transcribing, editing and correcting relatively informal lecture presentations; again, the contributors responded nobly to our requests for approval and permission to include their excellent pieces. The Eugene and Agnes Meyer Foundation assisted with the costs while the editors, Dennis J.D. Sandole and Ingrid Sandole-Staroste, performed creative miracles of synthesis.

Having touched on the macroscopic emergence of what can fairly be regarded as a new professional field—it has even spawned the Society of Professionals in Dispute Resolution (SPIDR)—it may be useful to comment on the immediate setting at George Mason University.

As the relatively young State University of Northern Virginia, the President and Trustees are committed to innovation and the development of excellence in public affairs. When they became aware of the Peace Academy idea in 1980, the University invited Henry Barringer, a former Foreign Service Officer, and me, a psychiatrist turned international mediator, to explore the possibilities of establishing a conflict resolution program.

Strong faculty support from several disciplines provided a basis to propose a master of science degree program which was approved by the Virginia Council on Higher Education in October, 1980. As we prepared the curriculum and enrolled students to commence studies in the Fall of 1982, we initiated the lecture series on which this book is based.

The series was designed to test out the mix and fit of subjects and the philosophy and purpose of the program. In particular, we sought to bring practitioners and program managers together with scholars and researchers; we found substantial compatability with respect to central methods and purposes. There were, of course, differences of emphasis and some healthy disagreements, but we did discover that diverse approaches also shared central core concepts and that the exchanges which took place stimulated and enriched each separate mode of approach to analysis and resolution of human conflict.

A second major purpose was to expose interested persons to the ideas of the field, actually an exercise in communication. Here, too, we were gratified to discover a high level of interest and receptivity. The field, including relatively new concepts and procedures, is communicable. Some of the 50 to 70 attendees remained to become our students; others provided the kind of moral and material support that such a new enterprise requires.

Finally, another unanticipated outcome of this experiment in presenting a quite novel set of ideas was the growth of networks of common interest among institutions and practitioners. Ten years earlier, such a combination of diverse resources in conflict problem solving could not have been brought together. Nothing is more powerful than an idea whose time has come; we can fairly conclude on the strength of this volume that the science-based profession of conflict management represents such a powerful idea.

# (ii) Introduction

*Dennis J.D. Sandole*

## Prologue

Few of us would probably have the patience to endure a 'prophet of doom', a 'scare-tactic merchant' who, in pursuit of some private agenda, wanted to dazzle us with 'worst-case' assessments of various aspects of the Great Human Drama. Yet there are negative aspects of human experience, some of which are increasing in frequency or severity (or both), which clearly require attention and efforts toward creative management, if not outright elimination.

We read and hear much these days about spousal and child abuse, drug-related violence, teenage suicide, community violence, terrorism, the nuclear arms race, civil and international warfare, nuclear proliferation, the militarization of space, and so on. Each of these is a dramatic, extreme manifestation of what I call 'manifest conflict processes' (MCPs): situations in which at least two actors or their representatives try to pursue their perceptions of mutually incompatible goals by undermining, directly or otherwise, the goal-seeking capability of one another (Sandole, 1980, 1986). Each is also an example of one particular, pervasive approach to conflict management.

What is important about conflict is not its occurrence as such, but how parties attempt to deal with it. Morton Deutsch (1973), for instance, tells us that there are basically two orientations to conflict management: *competitive* and *cooperative*. Competitive processes are associated with 'zero sum' thinking and adversarial behavior, while cooperative processes are associated with 'positive sum' thinking and collaborative behavior.[1] Though the two orientations can certainly be viewed as polar opposites, a continuum can also be seen to exist between them. For instance, with competitive on one end and cooperative on the other, we can have use of deadly force (actual or threatened), litigation/adjudication, arbitration, conciliation, traditional mediation, facilitated problem solving and unfacilitated problem solving ('integrative/collaborative negotiation').

Deadly force, litigation and arbitration are intended, in descending order of severity, to impose solutions; in John Burton's (1986) framework, to 'settle' rather than 'resolve' conflicts. Conciliation, traditional mediation, facilitated and unfacilitated problem solving, on the other hand, all involve, in ascending order of parties' ownership of process and outcome, efforts to resolve rather than settle conflicts.

A third party is necessarily involved in each of these with the possible exception of deadly force, and the definite exception of integrative/collaborative negotiation (unfacilitated problem solving). The adjudicator or judge imposes a solution which is implemented in accordance with legal statute; the arbitrator hands down a decision which may or may not be binding on the parties; the conciliator endeavors to bring the parties together for negotiation; the traditional mediator may have them together or may be shuttling back and forth, to assist them in reaching a compromise; and the facilitator assists the parties in moving toward problem-solving processes and integrative outcomes. In integrative/collaborative negotiation, the parties attempt to do this on their own. Deadly force may involve a third party (for example, a professional assassin) but clearly the parties can do this for themselves as well (Lebanon, Northern Ireland, Sri Lanka, and so on).

'Conflict management' as expressed here is synonymous with 'conflict regulation' (Wehr, 1979), more comprehensive than 'conflict intervention' (Laue, 1982) which focuses on third party activities, and more comprehensive than 'conflict resolution' (Burton, 1986) which may or may not be the end result of conflict management processes. Cooperative processes of conflict management are associated with 'alternative dispute resolution' (ADR) (Ray, 1982). Conflict management as expressed here is part of conflict and peace studies (CAPS) which also includes conflict analysis, peace research, peace education, and peace action.

The cooperative processes of conflict management are concerned with preventing conflicts from exploding into what Anatol Rapoport (1960) calls 'fights', what I call 'aggressive manifest conflict processes' (AMCPs) (Sandole, 1980, 1986), where the parties or their representatives try to pursue their perceptions of mutually incompatible goals by physically damaging or destroying the property and high-value symbols (for example, heirlooms, flags, national treasures, and so on) of one another; and/or psychologically or physically injuring, destroying or otherwise forcibly eliminating one another.

The competitive processes are clearly associated with 'fights', with AMCPs, either as antecedents, consequences or both; this capability to be either 'chicken' or 'egg' or both indicates their potential for transforming conflicts into self-sustaining violent systems. It is the fights and competitive processes associated with them that we tend to read and hear about.

This volume is concerned primarily with cooperative processes. It examines conflict dynamics as well as negotiation and third party behavior on the assumption that we must know something about the nature of conflict, especially violent conflict, before we can deal effectively with it: intellectually, emotionally, and behaviorally.

## Genesis of the volume

As Bryant Wedge indicated in his introduction, this volume is the result of lectures given at George Mason University under the aegis of the Center for Conflict Resolution. Most were given during a thirteen-week 'Pro-seminar in Conflict and Conflict Management' in spring 1982 which was open to the public as well as to graduate students for credit. The remainder (which form the basis of Chapter 13) were given in March 1981 for a select group of University, governmental and other persons interested in conflict management.

The lectures were commissioned to highlight the newly created Center for Conflict Resolution, the Master's Program in Conflict Management that George Mason University was about to launch and the field of conflict management in general. A related objective was to provide support, by example, for the United

States Academy of Peace and Conflict Resolution which was then being debated by the US Congress.[2]

Each lecture was characterized by a main presentation followed by discussants and comments from the audience. The main speakers and discussants were professionally involved in conflict management as theorists, researchers, and/or practitioners or were otherwise interested in family and divorce mediation, community relations, environmental mediation, labor–management relations, hostage negotiation and international relations. They were lawyers, psychologists, intelligence officers, sociologists, law enforcement officers, psychiatrists, diplomats, mediators, negotiators and others. They came from academe, government, business and nonprofit organizations.

As Bryant Wedge and Henry Barringer—then co-directors of the Center for Conflict Resolution—were developing the 1982 series, it occurred to me that the lineup of speakers and discussants, together with those from 1981, represented a unique combination of roles, perspectives and experiences that could form the basis of an equally unique volume in conflict management. Wedge and Barringer agreed that it was an excellent idea but the Center was commissioning oral presentations, not written papers. For my idea to be fruitfully developed, therefore, the presentations would have to be tape-recorded; someone would have to transcribe the tapes; someone else, or perhaps the transcriber, would have to edit the transcriptions into something approaching the 'written word'; the presenters would have to be contacted and their permission to publish secured, and so on.

Having made the bold suggestion, I was then given the opportunity to practice what I seemed to be preaching—to accept the responsibility for transforming lectures into published volume. Henry Barringer either did the tape-recording himself or arranged for it to be done. He and Bryant Wedge made funds available for the services of my co-editor, Ingrid Sandole-Staroste. Over a period of four years of 'spare time', Ingrid transcribed all the tapes and together she and I edited the transcriptions into written 'reconstructions'.

All presenters indicated interest in the project and gave permission to proceed. Manuscripts were sent out with invitations to add, delete or otherwise change titles and bibliographies as well as exposition. I indicated to the presenters that I would mention in my introductory chapter that all of the presentations had originally been given orally, in part because I wanted to encourage them to retain, as they reviewed their manuscripts, the sense of exchange, of 'stimulus and response' between main speakers, discussants and members of the audience that was part of the original presentations. Most presenters made changes of varying degrees, including updates, while some rewrote their manuscripts completely. Significantly, all but two returned their manuscripts with permission to publish.

Each chapter begins with the 'stimulus'—what was originally the main presentation—followed by the 'response'—the critiques, elaborations and general comments of discussants. Responses to audience questions and comments have been integrated into the text at various points. The occasional dialog between presenter and discussant has been incorporated into the text as well.

## Conflict management: generic theory, research and practice

In Chapter 1, James Laue (The 'Emergence and Institutionalization of Third Party Roles in Conflict') conducts a wide-ranging tour of the field as it applies to all levels, specifying definitions of relevant terms and examining the historical development of the field with the 'maturing of dispute resolution in America'. Against this background, he discusses conflict intervention, specifically his topology of conflict intervention roles. The comprehensiveness of Laue's overall discussion is such that he effectively provides an overview of the entire volume.

Joseph Scimecca ('Conflict Resolution: The Basis for Social Control or Social Change?') addresses a point raised by James Laue: that conflict intervention is not a neutral process, but instead alters the distribution of power among the parties. He also argues that the distribution of power should be altered to the extent that the relatively less powerful parties are empowered.

Arnold Sherman ('Continuing Issues in the Management of Conflict') discusses some issues that arise from James Laue's presentation which are also relevant to other presentations in the volume, for example, what are the criteria of successful intervention?

In Chapter 2, Morton Deutsch ('A Theoretical Perspective on Conflict and Conflict Resolution') discusses the functions of conflict but also the pathologies typically associated with conflict, including some social-psychological processes associated with the development of self-perpetuating, vicious cycles. He also discusses the characteristics, determinants and consequences of the subject of his own long-term theoretical and empirical work: cooperative versus competitive processes of conflict resolution.

Dan Druckman ('New Directions for a Social Psychology of Conflict') addresses the contributions social psychology has made and can make to a further understanding of conflict and conflict resolution processes.

Maire Dugan ('Intervenor Roles and Conflict Pathologies') looks at two aspects of Morton Deutsch's presentation, conflict pathologies and trust building, as they apply to conflict intervenors.

In Chapter 3 Dean Pruitt ('Creative Approaches to Negotiation') discusses a number of conflict situations in which negotiations could take place. He examines some possible outcomes of negotiation, one of which, integrative agreements, is synonymous with win-win, problem-solving approaches to conflict management. He also discusses types of integrative agreements and how they can be achieved.

Larry Ray ('Trends Toward Alternative Dispute Resolution') looks at the development of neighborhood justice and community centers as part of the overall alternative dispute resolution (ADR) movement in the United States. He also looks at the role that the American Bar Association's Special Committee on Dispute Resolution has played in this development.

While Larry Ray looks at Dean Pruitt's analysis as it applies to the community level, Ralph K. White ('Deterrence and Tension Reduction') does so for the international level, where he also makes recommendations for an overall policy of prudent deterrence and tension reduction between the superpowers (a discussion he continues in Chapter 11).

In Chapter 4, Thomas Colosi ('A Model for Negotiation and Mediation') presents a model of negotiation and mediation developed from his own experiences as a practitioner. The model encompasses various types of negotiation, tri- and multilateral as well as bilateral relationships, and various kinds of third party roles. He also indicates how third parties should behave as well as how certain kinds of negotiators actually do behave.

David McGaffey ('Negotiation and Mediation: A Diplomat's Perspective') discusses his experiences as a United States Foreign Service Officer, negotiator and instructor in negotiation, against the background of Tom Colosi's presentation.

## Conflict management: interpersonal to international levels

In Chapter 5, Lawrence Gaughan ('Divorce and Family Mediation') draws upon his experiences as a lawyer and mediator to discuss the various dimensions of family mediation, especially separation and divorce mediation. Among the items he discusses are the emotional aspects involved in separation and divorce and, in part because of these, the importance of professionalism on the part of the mediator. Part of this professionalism is that mediators themselves must have some sense of why they respond to conflict situations the way they do.

Elizabeth Koopman ('Family Mediation: A Developmental Perspective on the Field') examines some myths which have prevented, and are preventing, the field of family dispute resolution from moving ahead as much as it could. She also makes some observations about the current status of various aspects of the field and addresses some issues which may be critical during the next ten years or so.

In Chapter 6 Gilbert Pompa ('The Community Relations Service') discusses the Community Relations Service (CRS) of the United States Department of Justice: why the CRS came into existence; its history during the past twenty years; the stages through which it goes in attempting to resolve community disputes; the range of interventions open to it; its objectives; and the qualities it desires in its intervenors. Pompa also discusses the dangers under which CRS intervenors often work and the various consequences of doing their work in a total absence of publicity.

Charles Bethel ('Dispute Resolution in Prison Settings') discusses some of the work he has been involved in with the Center for Community Justice in Washington, DC, designing and implementing dispute resolution programs in some of the prisons where the Community Relations Service has also been active.

Joseph Gittler ('Questioning the Questionable') raises some questions that are implicit in Gilbert Pompa's presentation that, like Arnold Sherman's questions in Chapter 1, apply to conflict management in general—for example, what rationale do third parties have for intervening in disputes, and what ethical notions are associated with the various kinds of intervention?

In Chapter 7 Ethan Smith ('Environmental Conflict Management') discusses the genesis of environmental conflict management in the United States, the unique characteristics of environmental conflict, the processes that might be undertaken in its management, outcomes of environmental conflict and the strategies that could lead to those outcomes.

Bruce Dotson ('Issues from the Practice of Environmental Mediation') discusses the work that he and his colleagues have been doing at the Institute for Environmental Negotiation, University of Virginia, on intergovernmental questions regarding the environment, land use and development.

Roger Richman ('Environmental Mediation: An Alternative Dispute Settlement System') looks at some of the reasons why environmental mediation is more likely than the courts to move parties 'away from purely competitive bargaining toward consideration of a wider range of positions and options than they originally were willing to consider'.

In Chapter 8 Harold Davis ('Managing Labor–Management Relations: A More Complete Approach') argues that members of the labor–management community in the United States should view recent economic and labor–management problems as an opportunity to reassess their relationship and to move away from a win-lose orientation toward a problem-solving one.

Kenneth Kovach ('New Directions in Labor Relations') provides some historical background to the development of labor–management relations in the United States. He also argues that if anything will lead to a reduction of labor–management conflict in the US it will be what has done so for parts of Europe: codetermination.

In Chapter 9 Conrad Hassel ('Terrorism and Hostage Negotiation') discusses the problems surrounding the definition of terrorism; that terrorism is not really a problem in the United States (though it is a problem for Americans abroad); the relationship between terrorism and the media; the kind of person who becomes a terrorist (left or right); the 'Stockholm Syndrome'; hostage negotiations; and the various kinds of hostage-taker.

Arnold Sherman ('"Terrorists" versus "Freedom Fighters": The Implications of Alternative Constructions of Reality') discusses some points raised by Conrad Hassel, particularly the absence of a commonly accepted definition of terrorism and some reasons for and implications of this state of affairs.

Robert Clark ('Insurgents Are Not Crazy or Irrational—They Are Different!') discusses some problems with the argument that it is important that insurgent actions fail, and are seen to fail by the insurgents themselves, in order that such actions are not repeated in the future.

Irwin Greenberg ('Terrorism: Making the Response Fit the Act') argues in favor of making responses to terrorism fit the nature of the act.

## Conflict management: the international level

In Chapter 10 Adrian Fisher ('East–West Negotiations') discusses international negotiations, particularly those involving the United States and the Soviet Union, in some of which he has been involved as an official representative of the United States. He looks at various problems within negotiating teams, between the teams and the authorities they represent, between nations and their allies and between the negotiating nations themselves. He also discusses the prospects for progress in the various negotiations involving the United States and the Soviet Union.

Bryant Wedge ('A Marginal Contribution to a Safer World') discusses the role he played in one of the situations Adrian Fisher was involved in: the Limited Test Ban Treaty.

Alex Gliksman ('The Other Side of Negotiations') argues that sometimes nations are not serious about the subjects addressed by their negotiations. He cites as examples the United States and the Soviet Union during the Mutual and Balanced Force Reduction (MBFR) Talks and Conference on Security and Cooperation in Europe (CSCE).

Jonathan Dean ('The Pragmatic View') responds to some points raised by Adrian Fisher, for example, the tendency for governmental security analysts to think in terms of the 'worst case'. He also argues that there is 'no ideal arms control, but only the pragmatic approach. We do what can be done, what is possible.' Further, he advances a number of reasons for arms control in Europe.

In 'Towards a New Rationality' I discuss two aspects of international negotiations raised by Adrian Fisher: the worst case and bargaining chip orientations to conflict management. I comment also on Fisher's reference to rationality, distinguishing between what Fisher apparently had in mind, a win-win kind of rationality and the rationality of conventional wisdom: win-lose. I argue that the latter, together with worst cases and bargaining chips, contributes to violent conflict worldwide.

In Chapter 11 Ralph K. White ('Preventing Nuclear War') discusses some reasons for the view that a nuclear war will not occur but also why there is a 50–50 chance that one will occur between now and the year 2000. He also expands upon his earlier discussion from Chapter 3, indicating how effective deterrence and tension reduction can be simultaneously pursued.

Willard Matthias ('Perceptions of the "Enemy" in United States Foreign Policy') discusses a number of 'devil theory' myths and misconceptions underlying American policy toward the Soviet Union. He also discusses what has gone wrong in the American intelligence community and what keeps Cold War proclivities alive in the United States.

Dean Pruitt ('A National Case of Jitters') argues that a number of American reactions to the Soviet Union have been overreactions. He suggests some reasons for and implications of these as well as some ways for avoiding them in the future.

In Chapter 12 Willard Matthias ('Surviving in the Post-Detente World') discusses the initiation and termination of the United States–Soviet Union period of détente during 1972–7. Specifically, he examines superpower relations, particularly the American contribution, arguing in effect that American policy toward the Soviet Union is counterproductive and self-defeating. He also indicates how the United States should remedy this state of affairs.

Leo Hecht ('What Makes the Russians Tick?') comments on Soviet history, thinking, perceptions, behavior and objectives regarding relations with other states, particularly the United States.

In Chapter 13 John Burton ('International Conflict Resolution and Problem Solving') argues that if the superpowers genuinely want to solve the problems that concern them both, then, in addition to the power-politics approaches they tend to use, which are associated with win-lose outcomes, they must also encourage the use of problem-solving approaches which are associated with win-win outcomes. He also argues that an effective problem-solving approach must rest upon unchallengeable epistemological, theoretical and applied foundations and that the

Conflict Management Program at George Mason University should be comprised of such foundations.

Michael Banks ('Four Conceptions of Peace') examines the contribution an academic program in conflict management could make toward alleviating global problems. Specifically, he examines four competing conceptions of 'peace' and their implications for such programs: peace as (1) harmony, (2) order, (3) justice, and (4) conflict management. He looks at the first three and, like Kenneth Waltz in *Man, the State, and War* (1959), indicates that any one of these alone is insufficient. He concludes by arguing in favor of the fourth conception, which views peace not as a condition but as a process, a dynamic state of affairs in which the essential properties arise from how we do things, not what we do.

A.J.R. Groom ('Problem Solving: Some Lessons from Europe') comments on some European experiences that have relevance for the Conflict Management Program at George Mason University.

## Conflict management: generic theory, research, and practice revisited

In Chapter 14 Bryant Wedge ('Conflict Management: The State of the Art') discusses the stages through which conflicts at all levels pass, as well as the context within which conflicts occur: change accompanied by perceptual and behavioral lag. Against this background, he mentions what has been a theme throughout the volume: 'resolution, even of serious and violent conflicts, becomes possible because the parties are encouraged to reanalyze and reassess whether the opponent is really so much of an "enemy".' He also looks at some changes which may be indicative of 'paradigm shifts' in the way people think about conflict and conflict management.

In 'Conflict Management: Elements of Generic Theory and Process' I argue that people with different beliefs, values, and expectations effectively live in 'different worlds'. One result of this is that they talk 'past each other'. The more that they do, the more they may experience frustration and hostility. The frustration–hostility nexus at any level can escalate over time into self-perpetuating violent conflict systems. I discuss some reasons why the parties themselves may never see the role they play in the development, maintenance and escalation of such systems.

## Recapitulation and conclusion

This volume deals with conflict dynamics and cooperative processes of conflict management—negotiation, mediation, facilitation, problem solving, and conflict resolution—in general (Parts I and IV) and at specific levels (Parts II and III).

It is, in a sense, a data-set for members of a field whose definition is being stretched to include social movement as well a 'metadiscipline' and profession. It should be mined for all it is worth, to further advance the field and those 'paradigm shifts' from competitive to cooperative modes of conflict management to move us further along toward some sense of 'self-actualization'(Maslow, 1954) and, perhaps, away from the prospect of 'globicide' (Wedge and Sandole, 1982).

**Notes**

1. In strict game-theoretical terms, 'zero sum' is the outcome of conflict situations where one party's gain is identical to another's loss (for example, +5 + -5 = 0). 'Positive sum', on the other hand, is the outcome of conflicts where both (or all) parties gain (+5 + +5 = +10). Less strictly, 'zero sum' refers to situations where parties think and act in terms of 'win-lose' outcomes (without the losses and gains necessarily being identical); whereas 'positive sum' suggests situations where parties think and act in terms of 'win-win' outcomes (without the respective gains necessarily being identical).

2. As Bryant Wege has indicated in his introduction, the US Academy of Peace and Conflict Resolution emerged from the Congress as the US Institute of Peace. It was established through the US Institute of Peace Act, which was signed into law in October 1984. Its purpose is to: serve the people and the Government through the widest possible range of education and training, basic and applied research opportunities, and peace information services on the means to promote international peace and the resolution of conflicts among the nations and peoples of the world without recourse to violence (*US Institute of Peace Act*, Section 1702(b)).

**Bibliography**

Burton, J.W. (1986), 'The Theory of Conflict Resolution'. *Current Research on Peace and Violence*, (Special Issue on Conflict and Conflict Resolution, (ed.) J. Käkönen), **IX**, no. 3, pp. 125–30

Deutsch, M. (1973), *The Resolution of Conflict: Constructive and Destructive Processes*; New Haven and London, Yale University Press.

Laue, J.H. (1982), 'Ethical Considerations in Choosing Intervention Roles'. *Peace and Change* (Special Issue on Conflict Resolution, M.A. Dugan (ed.)), **VIII**, no. 2–3, pp. 29–41.

Maslow, A.H. (1954), *Motivation and Personality*, New York, Harper and Brothers.

Ray, L. (1982), 'The Alternative Dispute Resolution Movement'. *Peace and Change*, (Special Issue on Conflict Resolution, (ed.) M.A. Dugan), **VIII**, no 2–3, pp. 117–28.

Rapoport, A. (1960), *Fights, Games, and Debates*, Ann Arbor, University of Michigan Press.

Sandole, D.J.D. (1980), 'Economic Conditions and Conflict Processes' in *Models of Political Economy*, P. Whiteley (ed.) Beverly Hills and London, Sage.

Sandole, D.J.D. (1986), 'Traditional Approaches to Conflict Management: Short-Term Gains vs. Long-Term Costs'. *Current Research on Peace and Violence*, (Special Issue on Conflict and Conflict Resolution, (ed.) J. Käkönen), **IX**, no. 3, pp. 119–24.

*US Institute of Peace Act* (1984), *Statutes at Large*, **98**.

Waltz, K.N. (1959), *Man, the State and War: A Theoretical Analysis*, New York. Columbia University Press.

Wedge, B. and D.J.D. Sandole (1982), 'Conflict Management: A New Venture into Professionalization'. *Peace and Change* (Special Issue on Conflict Resolution, M.A. Dugan (ed.)), **VIII**, no. 2–3, pp. 129–38.

Wehr, P. (1979), *Conflict Regulation*, Boulder, Westview Press.

# Acknowledgements

A number of people have assisted in the completion of this volume. At George Mason University, Mary Blackwell, Sandra Slater, May Thompson and Brenda Wallace of Office Support Services translated typed first drafts into word-processed copies. Dan Skripkar, of Design and Publications, arranged for the preparation of camera-ready copies of diagrams that appear in some of the chapters. At Frances Pinter's, the efforts of Sharon Kelly and Adèle Linderholm have ensured that the volume reads more like the written than the 'nearly' written word. Without my co-editor and life-partner Ingrid Sandole-Staroste, the volume would never have surfaced, and without the infinite tolerance of our son Timothy, it would never have been completed. Needless to say, without the presenters there would have been no volume at all. It is with sadness and regret that I report that two of them have since died: Adrian Fisher (March 1983) and Gilbert Pompa (April 1986). Finally, if Bryant Wedge and Henry Barringer had not organized the lectures of 1981 and 1982, the idea for producing this kind of volume might never have developed.

# Part I: Conflict Management: Generic Theory, Research, and Practice

# 1(i) The emergence and institutionalization of third party roles in conflict

*James Laue*

After a gestation period of several decades, the role of the third party has emerged in the 1980s as a central concept in the study of conflicts and conflict resolution. Experiences in labor–management relations, international conflict, racial and community disputes, court diversion and other arenas have convinced practitioners and scholars that the third-party role is useful and deserving of some degree of institutionalization.

To understand the emergence of third-party roles, we need to analyze three areas. The first involves important definitions and the background and scope of the field of conflict intervention. Then some comments about the development of the field of conflict intervention are in order, followed by an analysis of the variety of third-party intervention roles.

## Definitions and background

Let us look initially at *conflict*. Conflict is a natural and inevitable part of all human social relationships. Conflict occurs at all levels of society—intrapsychic, interpersonal, intragroup, intergroup, intranational and international. At all levels of human social systems, conflict is ubiquitous. Conflict is not deviant, pathological, or sick behavior *per se*. Traditionally, scholars and policy makers have tended to view conflict as an unusual occurrence in the social system—an example of disequilibrium that needs to be returned to a homeostatic state. Some see conflict as the opposite of order (see Wehr, 1979 and Schellenberg, 1982).

Rather than see deviance, sickness or pathology in conflict, we should examine the level, the intensity, the type, the object of conflict and the way it is handled. It is important to understand that conflict is not the opposite of order. Conflict is highly patterned; the field of conflict analysis allows us to predict some of the stages that conflicts in various systems' levels will go through. There is, then, an orderliness in conflict, although conflict can become disorderly. And it can be a very helpful and useful part of society.

Conflict may be defined, then, as escalated, natural competition between two or more parties about scarce resources, power and prestige. Parties in conflict believe they have incompatible goals, and their aim is to neutralize, gain advantage over, injure or destroy one another.

Within this framework, violence could be defined as a form of severely escalated conflict. Virtually all forms of violence are pathological; indeed violence generally hurts weaker parties more than it does stronger parties. The edge between natural, regulated competition and escalated conflict with violence is a precarious spot—for the analyst or third party as well as the protagonist in conflict.

*Third party* is a term of social science analysis, not mathematical literalism. It does not mean literally the third party in a situation in which there are two other parties. First and second parties have a direct interest or direct stake in the conflict and its outcomes. The third party is one with less directly at stake. The third party certainly has something at stake (reputation or professionalism, for example) but will not be affected by the allocation of resources, the exercise of power, the determination of new rules or the other types of outcomes which may take place as conflict is processed. The third party stands on a different base.

A *role* is a set of behaviors associated with a status. A status is a position in the social structure which carries rights as well as obligations. Role is the behavioral component—the acting out of the behavior associated with a given status. The concept of role implies that behavior is patterned, understandable and largely predictable.

The concept of role is focal in understanding how human social behavior is organized. To understand any conflict situation, the first step always should be a role analysis of every party to determine who has what at stake, what reference groups and membership groups are involved, what pressures and strains are pushing on the parties for particular kinds of behavior, the parties' perceptions of their goals and power and the goals and power of the other parties, etc.

*Resolution* is another term which requires definition; it is only one goal that one might have for conflict, although many assume it is the only legitimate approach. Conflict is never solved; we talk of conflict resolution, not conflict solution. Individual conflict incidents or episodes may be solved—they may move on to a termination which may or may not represent the interests of all the parties involved. Whether family or international disputes or anything in between, conflict incidents may be solved, but conflict *per se* is never solved. Each solution creates, in a Hegelian sense, a new plateau or a new synthesis against which the next conflict scenario is played. Society never 'solves' conflict totally. Conflict incidents or episodes are solved and then re-solved and re-solved.

When conflict resolution mechanisms are working smoothly, all the parties with a stake have adequate representation in the forum and can bargain toward a win-win outcome that satisfies at least some of their needs. If a good resolution to the conflict is achieved, the outcome 'sticks' and contributes to the ability of the system to resolve other conflicts as they arise, rather than allowing them to fester.

Conflict 'resolution' implies that there is joint participation of the parties in reaching the outcome. There also is an assumption that the outcome is—at least to some extent—satisfactory for all the parties involved. They are willing to live with it, or with parts of it or to live with the procedure established by the resolution process to resolve other conflicts. In this regard, it is appropriate that the Camp David agreements were called 'accords' rather than a 'solution' or 'settlement', for they established a framework for continuing the discussion regarding peace and peacemaking in the Middle East. Resolution, then, implies at least these two elements: the idea that the outcome is jointly determined and the achievement of at least some degree of satisfaction for the parties concerned.

But resolution is not the only thing one might 'do' about conflict. What we do about any specific conflict depends on what our status is, what our role is in the situation, who we are as a party and what we perceive our interests to be. The idea that conflict should be resolved is somewhere in the middle of a rough continuum ranging from repression on the right to instigation or agitation on the left.

I receive a newsletter from a Quaker project in Pennsylvania called *A Friendly Agitator*—a nice twist on the relationship of conflict to social change and justice. Generally, those in power would like to keep the system the way it is. They view conflict as a disruption in the system, and as a possible threat to the current organization of power and resources. Parties with this orientation seek to suppress conflict when it occurs. Those in power want to get conflict out of the way, perhaps get around the table and mediate it quickly and get on with business as usual. They are status-quo-oriented. Those with less power tend to be change-oriented, and will more likely be interested in instigating or agitating conflict. There is a range of other possible orientations in between, and one of the major approaches is conflict *management*. Conflict management is popular now, especially in business schools. The role of an organizational manager or adminis- trator is to manage day-to-day conflict in the allocation of scarce resources. Conflict *regulation* also is in vogue in the literature. But who will manage or regulate conflict?

I prefer an approach that allows the parties with the most at stake to be assisted in working through the conflict in their own interest. Persons who use the language of conflict management and conflict regulation argue that they want to increase the abilities of parties to manage or self-regulate their conflicts themselves because if conflicts escalate, external agents or agencies will step in and try to bring the conflict within their own definitions of acceptable boundaries of social control. Then the parties with much at stake really will lose.

Whenever I do pre-workshop questionnaires with people on how they handle conflict, a dominant response is 'ignore it'. Such people believe that if they can just ignore it, after a little while it will go away. Strikingly, if we examine a number of approaches to the racial disorders of the 1960s in the United States, many police departments took a variant of that position: contain it, ignore it as much as possible and hope it will pass. This is a typical way many of us deal with conflict. Once we recognize that conflict is patterned, we understand that it occurs in stages, eventually leading to some kind of termination. Hence, in many situations, individuals and organizations are willing to 'hang back' and hope that conflict will disappear or run its course quickly and painlessly.

In 1965, I was in Natchez, Mississippi, during a racial crisis, assessing the work of Community Relations Service (CRS) field representatives. The president of the local branch of the National Association for the Advancement of Colored People (NAACP) had been the victim of a bombing. The black community had mounted a boycott of the downtown shopping area that cut business by 75 per cent. I interviewed black and white leaders, and I asked the white leaders, 'What are you going to do to prevent this sort of thing from happening again?' Their answer was, 'Nothing. It is a fluke. The colored people got out of line. It won't happen again. We can handle that. We will tough it through. We won't do anything because we think we can weather it if it happens again, and we are hoping and praying and predicting that it won't happen again.'

Accordingly, there is a range of orientations that one could take toward a conflict—ignore, study, agitate, regulate, manage, instigate, repress, or forget it. Conflict resolution is only one approach, representing a value position—not a neutral stance—on how one will approach conflict.

What is meant by *intervention*? The main thrust of my work while moving back and forth between the roles of activist, academic, commissioner and mediator has been an attempt to develop a discipline of community conflict intervention. 'Conflict intervention' occurs when an outside or semi-outside party self-consciously enters into a conflict situation with the objective of influencing the conflict in a direction the intervenor defines as desirable. All intervention alters the power configuration among the parties, thus all conflict intervention is advocacy. There are no neutrals.

I discovered many years ago when working on this issue of values and neutrality that the parties in conflict are very, very smart. They probably think much harder about their conflict than the intervenor because they are living with it and know they must live with the outcomes in a way the intervenor generally does not have to do. Parties do not expect strict neutrality from intervenors. They do expect judiciousness—that they can trust the intervenor, that they can rely on that person's judgment, that they can trust the intervenor to carry to the other party what they could not themselves carry because they would lose too much face.

In my view there are two typical types of advocacy: party advocacy and outcome advocacy. The best example of a party advocate is a lawyer who operates within the adversarial system. The assumption is that in litigation one needs to have strong advocacy for one's party to make the framework and the rules work for the benefit of that party. 'My party, right or wrong' makes the system work. Another traditional form of advocacy is outcome advocacy or policy advocacy, in which one works on behalf of a particular outcome (the Equal Rights Amendment or a national land use policy, for example) rather than for a specific party.

A third type of advocacy emerging in conflict intervention roles is process advocacy, a good description of what mediation is about. The mediator's base is not in any of the parties, *per se*, nor is it in any particular or specific outcome of the parties in conflict. Instead it is based in the process, in a belief that the right kind of process will lead to outcomes which are relatively satisfactory to the parties and therefore will stick—in contrast to one party leaving the field, or a party simply terminating the conflict through superior power or other types of unilateral or force-based methods.

## Development of the field of conflict intervention

This entire volume suggests that we are dealing with an important social innovation. How do social inventions and innovations take place? How do we know when one is occurring? We know that when new roles emerge they become legitimated and people become socialized in them, and society recognizes them by forming institutions and institutional supports.

The field of conflict intervention is not yet a social science or a discipline or a profession, although various publications have referred to 'peace science' or the 'science of conflict'. The Commission on Proposals for the National Academy of Peace and Conflict Resolution said in its final report:

While the Commission believes it fortunate that peace is neither fully professionalized nor a single discipline, the Commission has established that peace studies is a distinct and definable field of learning for three reasons: it has a literature, courses of study, and professional organizations; it has some well-defined assumptions and definitions, and a variety of research methodologies; and it has a strong applied component in the practice of conflict intervention. The Commission finds that peace is a legitimate field of learning that encompasses rigorous interdisciplinary research, education, and training directed toward [ the acquisition of] peacemaking expertise (United States Department of Education, 1981, pp. 119–20).

Accordingly, in the view of the Commission charged with determining the feasibility of establishing a United States institution devoted to studying, teaching, and researching conflict resolution and peacemaking, there is a new approach requiring attention in the national interest. It is not yet a fully developed scientific field or discipline, but an embryonic field worthy of further study and systematization.

Some of the sources of the emergence of conflict intervention now may be assessed (see Laue, 1981). A major source is the social sciences in general, and Marxist sociology or philosophy in particular, for which conflict is the driving dynamic of society, and about which societies are constantly making various adjustments in their institutions. In addition, political science, the sociology of the military small-group dynamics, and other fields are important sources for the intellectual emergence of conflict intervention as a field.

Another source is the development of collective bargaining in the structure of labor–management relations in the United States. Collective bargaining represents the application of a nonlitigational, noncoercive model in a particular arena where the two major protagonists need one another. They are both institutionalized, they are both powerful. They both have the ability to sanction one another, although that was not always true. When labor achieved enough relative power and both parties realized that they had to live together for either to prosper, a set of mechanisms emerged called collective bargaining. And now it is enshrined in law to help make it work.

A third source is the field of international relations and the development of peace research. The literature in the field of peace research is derived from the history of warfare and international relations, the anthropology of human conflict, the study of state diplomacy, studies of human aggression and a range of related topics.

A very important source of the emergence of conflict intervention as a field in the United States has been the racial history of this country—specifically the way the nation's institutions responded to the sit-in movement, the Freedom Rides and the urban racial disorders of the 1960s.

In addition, the litigational system itself has helped spawn a number of alternatives to litigation which are quicker, less adversarial, cheaper and involve the parties more in representing their own interests and finding their own solutions.

There have been several waves of conflict intervention innovations in the United States. The three traditional institutional practices for dealing with social conflict in the United States are (a) the political process itself (a formalized way to deal with representation, the allocation of scarce resources, etc.), (b) legitimated force (police or other law enforcement agencies) and (c) litigation. There are many reasons why litigation is an inappropriate way for dealing with social conflict. We are the most litigious society in the world. In contrast, in China the mediation system works with individuals throughout the social structure, helping to ease conflict resolution over scarce resources and conflicting norms—an informal infrastructure which we do not have in the United States. And I recall a description of the obligation pressed at some points in ancient China: if one were in a dispute with another party or another family and came to believe that winning would psychologically injure or destroy the other party or would cause great loss of face, then it became the first party's obligation to lose. How different from our win-lose, highly competitive orientation in the United States.

But in this context, a series of experiences in various types of conflicts has led to the establishment of a field of third-party conflict intervention. The emergence of formal diplomacy in the United States and other countries has moved to a new level in recent decades with two important technological developments—good transportation and electronic communication—which made it possible to develop the League of Nations and the United Nations, and eventually spurred such activities as Henry Kissinger's shuttle diplomacy in the Middle East in 1974 and Jimmy Carter's Camp David mediation. The book edited by Jeffrey Rubin, *Dynamics of Third Party Intervention: Kissinger and the Middle East*, is a series of essays about how third-party intervention has worked in international affairs, much of it facilitated by jet planes, electronic communication, and, of course, highly skilled individuals (Rubin, 1981; see also Carter, 1985 and Quandt, 1986).

The labor–management difficulties of the 1920s and 1930s led to institutionalization of the collective bargaining process, supported by the National Labor Relations Act and a variety of organizations. The formation of the Federal Mediation and Conciliation Service in 1947 marked the formal commitment of the federal government to third-party settlement of disputes in an important sector of American society.

The civil rights movement and racial disorders of the 1960s spawned the Community Relations Service (CRS). It was established under the 1964 Civil Rights Act to mediate and conciliate racial disputes, difficulties and disagreements related to discrimination. The CRS has lasted for some twenty years as an approach to nonlitigated conflict resolution in the field of race relations in the United States. The American Arbitration Association and the Institute for Mediation and Conflict Resolution in New York City also established racial dispute and community dispute resolution programs for mediation and conciliation in the late 1960s, as a direct response to racial conflicts in the United States.

A later wave in the 1970s brought the application of these mediation and conciliation innovations to environmental disputes. Environmental conflicts differ from racial disputes, where there usually is an in-party and an out-party, and where it usually is clear who has the guns and the goods and who does not, and who has the power and who does not. Environmental disputes generally represent more power symmetry, but do not lend themselves to win-win outcomes as readily, say, as a social service program in which one bargains back and forth on benefits, numbers of units of service, etc. In environmental disputes, the dam either goes there or it does not; the highway goes there or it does not. Finding ways to convert such situations into win-win processes is likely to be difficult.

Still other innovations in conflict intervention have occurred in the criminal justice system. In the 1960s and 1970s there has been greater use of inmate grievance procedures, rooted in conciliation and mediation techniques. Court diversion projects and police–community relations training are another application. The Family Crisis Intervention Unit of the New York City Police Department is one of the premier units in the field. Their work dramatically reduced the number of officers killed while intervening in family crises, and increased the ability of line officers to assist in the resolution of such disputes. The development of hostage negotiation teams by police departments and national governments is another example.

An interesting additional wave in the 1970s was the growth of grass-roots or community-based dispute settlement. Many 'neighbourhood dispute centers' are sponsored by the local bar association or as an adjunct to the court system. Others began as spouse-abuse programs or store-front service centers, some in churches, some by Quaker or Mennonite agencies and others as public agency programs.

The 1960s saw the development of intervenors who had a national focus. They formed a kind of flying squad who, like the CRS, could go into cities on request and deal with racial conflicts. By the late 1970s, however, the field was coming back to the grass-roots approach described above. The idea of dealing with little neighbor-to-neighbor squabbles or family difficulties or other disputes in easily accessible store-front centers caught on. An important distinction needs to be made between what may be called 'professional' and 'community-based' approaches to such localized disputes. Most of the more than 400 programs now existing in the United States are sponsored by local bar associations or the court system, and are staffed by lawyers and other professionals, many of whom volunteer their time and services. But there is a growing interest and experimentation in resolving such disputes as an integral part of the day-to-day interaction in the neighborhood, with residents rather than outside professionals or volunteers serving as third parties. The Community Boards in San Francisco offer the best example. In this program, residents hear their neighbors' disputes on location. using a process which assumes (a) that the expression of conflict in this setting is more important than its actual resolution, and (b) that good conflict resolution is a function of a healthy and well organized community—not of the work of highly trained outside professionals.

Most of the developments noted above have taken place in the context of the traditional use of conflict intervention in the United States: techniques applied in reaction to a specific conflict or crisis, when the parties already may be trying to find a way out of a difficult situation. I believe that one of the most important innovations in the field is the recent application of conflict resolution techniques in a proactive, planning or policy formation mode. The emergence of the labor–management committee in collective bargaining is a good example. They meet not at contract time but between the contracts, trying to build relationships and getting a feel for what the positions are on all sides in an attempt to avoid a crisis at contract time. The Urban Coalition of New York City uses 'developmental mediation', in which they try to bring together for regular meetings all the parties who have a stake in a particular issue. Their focus is the public school system where unions, teachers, administrators, parents and students get together and work toward common goals in advance of the next crisis. There are several coal and oil industry mediation boards which meet regularly to try to deal with conflicts before crises erupt. These activities represent one of the best ways to prepare for conflicts and crises: to build interpersonal capital between disputants in low-conflict periods so they can expend that capital in times of intense disputes.

The Negotiated Investment Strategy (NIS) is perhaps the best example of a policy mediation experiment. In 1978 the Kettering Foundation convinced the White House urban policy staff to make the Federal Regional Council available to represent the federal position in structured negotiations about the future of three cities in the Midwest Region: Gary, St. Paul, and Columbus. The three mayors and the governors of their states (Indiana, Minnesota, and Ohio, respectively) also chose teams of negotiators. The private sector was to be involved through the local government team. All parties were asked to agree upon a mediator from a national list compiled by the Foundation. The three mediations took place in 1979 and 1980, lasting from four to eight months. The objective was a written agreement about the policy on future investments for each city.

I was fortunate to have been chosen as mediator for the Gary NIS. It had been said that an agreement there would be impossible. Gary had a black, Democratic, White House connected mayor, Richard Hatcher, who was president-elect of the United States Conference of Mayors—in a white, conservative, Republican state. When I asked the Hatcher administration to name their closest connection in Indianapolis, they laughed, and said, 'US Steel's tax division has a better relationship with the state government than we do!' They were right.

We worked for eight months in Gary and emerged in December 1980 with a document signed by the Federal Regional Council, the Governor of Indiana, the Mayor of Gary and the mediator, with a supporting letter from the US Steel Regional Vice President in Chicago and from the Reagan administration transition team. The document did not have the force of law, but it has provided the framework since that time for cooperative joint planning and implementation between the city, the state, and US Steel. A number of agreements also were produced in St. Paul and Columbus (see Barry *et al.*, 1982).

I think that this approach is important because it moves us beyond the use of third parties only in reaction to specific conflicts or crises, towards proactive uses, trying to deal with conflict in a way that gets all the parties with a stake to the table before a crisis occurs.

Beyond all of these specific applications lies another indication of the maturing of dispute resolution in America: the formation of a number of associations and umbrella organizations to advance the interests of practitioners and the field. The Consortium on Peace Research, Education and Development (COPRED) was established in 1970 by college, university, and free-standing peace and conflict studies programs. COPRED has approximately 100 institutional members today. Many colleges and universities not involved in COPRED have developed programs of instruction in negotiation, especially in law schools and business schools.

In the mid-1970s, the Society of Professionals in Dispute Resolution was formed, and now has a membership of more than 1,300, ranging from family and divorce mediators to arbitrators and public policy intervenors. The National Institute for Dispute Resolution (NIDR) was formed in 1982 to nurture growth and innovations in the field with grants and contracts. With the Hewlett Foundation, NIDR has become the major funder in the field in the United States.

Another indicator of the growth and institutionalization of the field of dispute resolution is the National Conference on Peacemaking and Conflict Resolution (NCPCR). Consciously aimed at a broad audience of practitioners, scholars, activists, students and policy makers, the initial conference attracted 250 to the University of Georgia in March 1983, then 600 to the University of Missouri-St. Louis in September 1984, and 900 to Denver in June 1986. The hundreds of papers and workshops—and their level of technical specificity—further attest to the maturity of the field.

Dozens of books, hundreds of articles in major journals, and several new journals have appeared since 1980 as the new field's literature grows. Added to the three-decades-old *Journal of Conflict Resolution* have been the *Negotiation Journal*, the *Mediation Quarterly*, the *Missouri Journal of Dispute Settlement*, and COPRED's quarterly, *Peace and Change*. In coverage of the St. Louis NCPCR in 1984, the *Chronicle of Higher Education* referred to the emergence of a new interdisciplinary field of scholarship, and analyzed some of its connections to the traditional academic disciplines (Winkler, 1984).

## Conflict intervention roles

From these experiences have emerged at least five analytically distinct roles for conflict intervenors. They are the subject of this final section. There are three conditions that must be met if third-party intervention is to be effective. One condition is a willingness to negotiate on the part of the parties. Unless all the parties are willing to enter into some form of negotiation, no intervention can occur, even if a judge orders it. The second condition is the availability of a forum that is agreeable to the parties involved—literally the right place with the right conditions, the right convenor, the right setting, the appropriate relationship to the outside media, a clear view of how parties shall relate to their constituencies, etc. The third condition concerns the credibility of the intervenor. The intervenor must find that Archimedean piece of ground on which to stand with the parties, i.e., literally have the 'standing' or legitimacy with the parties so they will allow that individual to assist in the dispute.

There are a number of ways to analyze intervention roles. One may view roles in terms of the system levels of disputes. For instance, different roles may be required for family disputes, group disputes, community disputes, neighbourhood disputes, intranational disputes or international disputes. Another approach would be to categorize intervention roles in light of the issue of the dispute, whether environmental, welfare, school segregation, racial, community or international. Another framework could begin with the skills of the intervenor. Still another would first analyze the nature and relative power of the parties. Intervenors' roles vary depending on who the parties are, what kind of power they have to affect one another and, indeed, whether parties allow an intervenor into a situation at all. Other approaches could include examining the base of the intervenor (the organizational affiliation, the source of salary, etc.) or the intervenor's personality attributes.

All these approaches reflect variables that one may take into account in considering different types of intervention roles. My major point is that there are definable, analytically distinct intervention roles that cut across all the other variables of personality, skills, type of issue, system level of the dispute, etc. These roles are based, in my view, predominantly on an intervenor's base and credibility—for whom does the intervenor work, who pays the intervenor to be there, and consequently what are the structured expectations for behavior of the intervenor in that role? What are the organizational sanctions to which the intervenor may be vulnerable? What kind of peer pressure exists?

With these questions in mind, let us consider a basic in-party/out-party dispute. Most disputes, of course, do not contain only two parties. But, on any particular conflict issue, it always is possible to find a party or cluster of parties who owns or controls the decision-making process regarding the resources at stake and who, in the dynamic of that situation, must be defined as the in-party. And we can find others who must be defined as out-parties because they do not have as much power or leverage as they would like, or they are not part of the forum for deciding on an issue of concern to them.

In a basic two-party dispute, there are five derivable roles (see Figure 1.1). First is the role of *activist*, one who is in, and almost of, one of the parties and who works extremely closely with the parties. For example, in a tenant–landlord dispute, an activist would be one of the tenants who lives in the housing project and is a leader of the tenant organization, organizing the tenants against the in-party. In this case, the in-party would be the landlord and the cluster of persons and institutions around him. Activists are rooted in their organizational base, in their leadership of their party and in their relationship with the other parties.

At the next level out from the center of the dispute is the role of *advocate*. A typical advocate role for an out-party is a community organizer, or a tenant advocate or legal advocate; this role is different from that of the tenant who lives in the project and will continue to live there when the dispute is over. A typical in-party advocate would be a corporate lawyer or management consultant. Many management consultants do not see themselves as advocates but rather as organizational technicians. But they are indeed advocating for certain values and parties within the organization—usually the owners, administrators or professionals.

Note that in Figure 1.1, the lines of the advocates overlap. This area of overlap represents negotiation. The lines of the activist are purposely not overlapped. True activists are not too conciliatory; they do not eagerly search for areas of negotiation. An activist generally plays a harder game. But advocates are able to reach out, and are expected by the parties to do so.

The third type of role is based in neither of the parties, but in the process. The *mediator* is concerned with the parties, with other intervenors and with the interaction between them. The mediator's ultimate advocacy is for process rather than for any of the parties *per se*, or any particular outcomes which they might be pursuing. Note the distinction between the mediator and the advocate. Many American diplomats would say that they are mediators interested in conflict resolution. But structurally they are advocates. Their job is to represent the interests of the United States government. That is quite a different position from

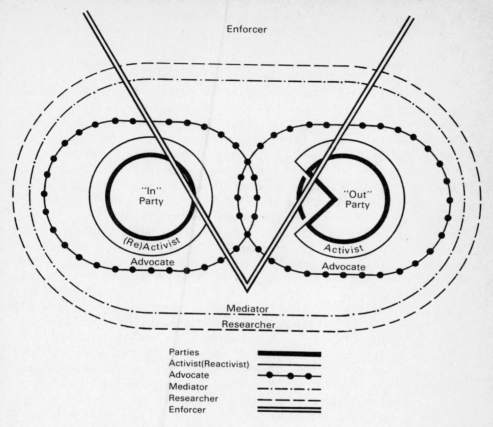

Parties  ▬▬▬▬▬
Activist(Reactivist)  ─────
Advocate  ●━●━●
Mediator  ─·─·─·─
Researcher  ── ── ──
Enforcer  ══════

*Adapted from Laue and Cormick (1978, p. 212).

**Figure 1.1.** Conflict Intervenor Roles*

that of a mediator, whose base is in neither party *per se* but whose goal is to help develop a process in which all the parties can achieve at least some of their goals without injuring or destroying the other party.

The further out one moves in the diagram in Figure 1.1 the less intense is the relationship to the parties and the issues at stake. Consequently, the next role ring is called the *researcher*. Examples include a journalist, a social science researcher or a crisis observation team. The Bar Associations in Washington and New York have developed observation teams for political demonstrations whose role is to record objectively the interaction between police and demonstrators.

Even the researcher is not neutral, as a group of psychiatrists attending a professional meeting in Washington in 1971 discovered. Demonstrators were marching to the Pentagon to put daisies in rifle barrels, and the psychiatrists, interested in moving from the couch to social relevance in the streets, were there observing—they thought in a clear, objective, neutral researcher role. But some of the psychiatrists eventually were subpoenaed because they might have observations in their notes about persons who were alleged to have committed punishable offenses.

Consciously or not, the instant an intervenor sets foot in a conflict situation, the power configuration is altered and the intervenor is likely to be used by the parties for their ends. In-parties often try to use third parties to gather intelligence on the natives, and experienced natives may use researchers to determine how the organizational structure works and what levers they can pull. While in a technical sense the role of researcher may be objective or neutral, once he or she engages in a conflict situation, the configuration of power in that situation is altered.

The final role is the *enforcer*. Arbitrators, judges and police are enforcers. Unlike the mediator who does not have the formal power to sanction the parties, but is present because the parties are willing to let that person into the conflict to help facilitate the negotiation process toward settlement, the enforcer actually has formal power to sanction either or all of the parties. The power of arbitrators and judges is well understood. In a street conflict, the police have arbitrary enforcement power to end the incident summarily through the use of force. Another example is a funding agency. In intense conflict between service providers and service recipients, a funding agency may say, 'Work it out, or we will rescind the funding'. It is rare to find in a major community dispute any party who could act as an enforcer because no single party generally has enough power or networks to be able to sanction all the parties. Mayor Richard Daley in Chicago came closest to providing an exception to that observation.

The characteristics and implications of the five intervention roles deserve further exploration. For instance, what kind of authority, in a Weberian sense, does each of these roles have? What is the ultimate value orientation of each? Can intervenors move from role to role in a conflict situation? If one first enters a given conflict situation as an advocate for one side or the other, it is difficult to become a mediator, or to have credibility as a judge or arbitrator in that situation, or be seen as an objective researcher. On the other hand, if one starts as a researcher, there may be a higher degree of role flexibility. A judicious and objective researcher in a particular community probably could move to any of the other roles and become accepted in them—but then perhaps be unable to return to the original role.

Another question concerns power. Intervenors must take care not to be entrapped in the unfair processes bred by power disparities between parties. Why is there so little call from out-parties or powerless parties for conflict resolution or peacemaking? They want power, justice and change. Conflict resolution usually is advocated by establishment parties who believe that peace—or at least order—is good.

## The future

I have argued that a field of conflict intervention or third-party behavior has emerged, and has begun the process of institutionalization. With that development goes new theories, practice strategies and techniques, the creation of new social roles, new training and socialization processes, the emergence of new occupations and the recruitment of persons into those jobs, new organizations, a literature, etc.

But with development and institutionalization also may come the ravages of success—professionalization, bureaucratization, practitioners primarily serving themselves instead of their clients, competition and the emergence of a market-driven mentality. Conflict intervention is at a critical stage, perhaps moving through a stormy adolescence and on the verge of a creative and innovative adulthood—or a stagnated, profit-oriented, business-as-usual approach to people and problems.

Whether the field of conflict intervention can escape the predictable ravages of success depends very much on whether its advocates can practice the values of consensus and win-win problem solving that they preach more than the competitive and win-lose values Western society teaches. Only holding the further development of third-party behavior to the highest standards of peacemaking itself will make the field unpredictably humane, cooperative and constructive.

## Bibliography

Berry, D.E., J.E. Kunde and C.M. Moore (1982), 'The Negotiated Investment Strategy: Improving Intergovernmental Effectiveness by Improving Intergroup Relations', *Journal of Intergroup Relations*, **X**, no. 2, pp. 42–57.

Carter, J. (1985), *The Blood of Abraham: Insights into the Middle East*, Boston, Houghton Mifflin.

Laue, J.H. (1981), 'Conflict Intervention' in *Handbook of Applied Sociology*, M.E. Olsen and M. Micklin (eds), New York, Praeger.

Laue, J.H. and G. Cormick (1978), 'The Ethics of Intervention in Community Disputes' in *The Ethics of Social Intervention*, G. Barmant, H. Kelman and D. Warwick (eds), New York, Halsted Press.

Quandt, W.B. (1986), *Camp David: Peacemaking and Politics*, Washington, DC, Brookings Institution.

Rubin, J. (ed.) (1981), *Dynamics of Third Party Intervention: Kissinger and the Middle East*, New York, Praeger.

Schellenberg, J.A. (1982), *The Science of Conflict*, Oxford and New York, Oxford University Press.

United States Department of Education (1981), *To Establish the United States Academy of Peace.* Report of the Commission on Proposals for the National Academy of Peace and Conflict Resolution to the President of the United States and the Senate and House of Representatives of the United States Congress. Washington, DC, US Government Printing Office.

Wehr, P. (1979), *Conflict Regulation*, Boulder, Westview Press.

Winkler, K.J. (1984), 'Interdisciplinary Field Seeks Understanding of Origin and Resolution of Conflicts', *The Chronicle of Higher Education*, 17 October, pp. 5–6.

# 1 (ii) Conflict resolution: the basis for social control or social change?

*Joseph A. Scimecca*

My first exposure to Jim Laue was through an article he wrote in *Peace and Change* in 1982 entitled 'Ethical Considerations in Choosing Intervention Roles' where he wrote of the importance of empowerment in the mediation process. At the time, I believed and still do that the notion of empowerment is a staple of any conflict theory worthy of the name as well as being one of the most important, if not *the* most important, idea within the field of conflict resolution.

In Laue's contribution to this volume, he expands upon his earlier line of reasoning, arguing in particular that there are no neutrals in the conflict resolution process, that all intervenors alter the power configurations between disputing parties, and that this alteration should be one of empowerment of the powerless. In so doing Laue presents a major argument against a charge that has been leveled against the emerging field of conflict resolution—that it is a form of social control.

As an emerging profession, the potential for the use of conflict resolution as a means of social control is obvious. However, in what follows, I will argue that far from being just another form of social control, conflict resolution can be a viable mechanism for social change. Before presenting this argument, a brief review of the concept of 'social control', or what is usually referred to as the 'social control thesis', is necessary in order to set the parameters of my argument.

Briefly stated, the 'social control thesis' holds that the history of modern society can be seen as the assertion of social control over activities once left to individuals or families. During the first stages of the industrial revolution, capitalists took production out of the household and collectivized it in the factory. They then proceeded to appropriate the workers' skills and technical knowledge by means of 'scientific management'. Finally, they extended control over the workers' private lives as well, through such professions as doctors, psychiatrists, teachers, child guidance experts and other specialties whose implicit role was to generate a socialization process which would insure loyalty to the status quo (Lasch, 1977). To this can be added the new professional: the conflict manager.

How, then, is this argument countered? As I stated before, Laue, in his analysis of the development and institutionalization of the third-party mediator, offers a counter-argument to the social control thesis. If we agree with Laue, conflict resolution differs from other social movements and attempts at professionalization in that it is based on a framework which is by definition anti-status quo. If the third-party role is one of non-neutrality, a non-neutrality based on the principle of empowerment, then the major premise of conflict management, the notion that the techniques are neutral, is rendered suspect.

Let us examine this in more detail. The most widely used conflict resolution process involves the use of a third-party mediator. The mediator is expected to be neutral. Training as a mediator varies anywhere from twelve-hour workshops to the two-year full-time graduate program at George Mason University. Obviously, as an educator, I believe that the former does not adequately train people, giving them only specific techniques without the necessary tools of diagnosis. Indeed, this is what leads me to focus upon the relationship between social change and professional training. Someone who goes through a twelve-hour workshop simply cannot know what he is doing and is therefore unaware of the potential harm he might inflict on one or more of the parties to a dispute.

It is in this unexamined neutrality position that the danger of co-optation, of conflict resolution becoming an agency of social control, manifests itself. With some notable exceptions (Jim Laue being the most famous), very few professional mediators challenge this role of neutrality. By introducing the notion of 'empowerment' (the giving of power to the powerless), a basis for social change is created. It is here that the strongest argument against the co-optation of conflict management can be made. Only a thorough grounding in conflict theory with its concomitant emphasis upon the role of power and powerlessness can show the mediator that without introducing empowerment into the process one is simply supporting the status quo. To resolve a conflict without being able to diagnose the power relations of the situation can do more harm than good.

Bercovitch (1984, p. 22) has summarized what a successful conflict resolution entails and it is worth repeating:

A successful resolution demands a change in symptoms and underlying causes; in behavior and perceptions. It demands abandoning power-oriented strategies which treat symptoms only, and embracing a participatory, analytical, and non-coercive approach which provides for the release of pent-up feelings and brings to the surface underlying values, motives, and perceptions. By its very nature, conflict resolution is a much more demanding and complex undertaking. Being so demanding and complex, the parties concerned may lack adequate knowledge, motivation, or experience to achieve this outcome.

Conflict resolution thus must be seen as a learning process, a learning process for all parties, based on a thorough grounding in conflict theory and empowerment. This is why a professionalism, which combines the theoretical with the practical, is so necessary. Practitioners must be armed with a knowledge base and theoreticians must develop processes that work. At present what we have are inadequately trained practitioners who are divorced from any real theoretical conception of conflict, from any substantive knowledge base. The conflict theory of Marx (1932; 1964), Weber (1921; 1968), Dahrendorf (1969), Collins (1975) is nowhere to be seen or at best is only given lip service by practitioners. Hard analytical reasoning is conspicuous by its absence.

Professionals trained in conflict theory must come to see through the naïveté that a mediation process is neutral. By understanding conflict theory they can become aware that anything neutral introduced into an unequal system, in the end, supports the group in power.

Conflict theory explains human behavior in terms of self-interest and the perpetuation of the social order by the organized coercion of certain groups over other groups. Although social conflict takes several different forms, what is crucial for understanding social behavior is the degree to which people are in positions to control others and how this is related to the accumulation of wealth, power and status.

The notion of empowerment, the giving of power to less powerful disputants in a conflict, has tremendous implications both for the resolution of conflict and for social change. In essence, conflict resolution professionals who advocate empowerment are not supporting the status quo, they are literally changing it.

The logical question to ask is why someone would give up power. The answer is that probably he would not. However, two important things occur when a conflict manager talks about empowerment. Once empowerment has been introduced, the more powerful party is put on the defensive, and an offensive weapon is also given to the less powerful party—knowledge about the structural determinants of his position.

Furthermore, if there really are skills of conflict resolution (and I believe there are), the conflict manager initially controls these skills and can direct the process toward social change to conditions that can lead to freedom, justice and autonomy. This is particularly important on the interpersonal level. One of the things we know about conflict is that human beings are constitutionally unable to live constantly in a conflict situation; it is just too unpleasant and takes too much of a toll on the individual. The introduction of empowerment into the equation, then, is unlike stress management which simply deals with the symptoms and not the problem; the former simply teaches people to live in an unequal power relationship. Stress management, at best, is a form of socialization for conformity, whereas conflict resolution, which speaks of empowerment before even attempting to intervene or mediate in a situation, provides the basis for a structural analysis.

By introducing empowerment, the conflict manager is offering an education in sociological analysis. In effect, he or she is showing that conflicts are rarely individual problems but are instead structural. I am not talking of social control but its opposite, personal control on the individual level; people can be in charge of their own destinies, but to do so they must change social structures. Such a position holds that individuals can truly make history. History may be made behind individuals' backs as Marx claimed, but it is not made behind everyone's back. Conflict resolution based on empowerment can help people to turn around and shape both their lives and the history of their society.

Of course, conflict resolution can be a means of social control, but it has not been so far and it does not necessarily have to be co-opted. The potential of the conflict resolution movement is simply too great to mouth the 'cynicism' of the social control thesis. For if those of us who believe in conflict resolution are right, what we are talking about is no less than having our children grow up in an environment devoid of the threat of the horrors of nuclear war, where they can truly develop as free and autonomous human beings.

In short, I see the movement toward the professionalism of conflict resolution not as a form of social control but as a radical attempt to change the status quo and in the process reduce violent, debilitating conflict. Conflict resolution, far from being a means of social control, can help to usher real peace into our lives.

**Bibliography**

Bercovitch, J. (1984), *Social Conflicts and Third Parties*, Boulder, Westview Press.

Collins, R. (1975), *Conflict Sociology*, New York, Academic Press.

Dahrendorf, R. (1969), *Class and Class Conflict in Industrial Society*, Stanford, Stanford University Press.

Lasch, C. (1977), *Haven in a Heartless World*, New York, Basic Books.

Laue, J.H. (1982), 'Ethical Considerations in Choosing Intervention Roles', *Peace and Change* (Special Issue on Conflict Resolution, M.A. Dugan (ed.)), **VIII**, no. 2–3, pp. 29–41.

Marx, K. (1932; 1964), *The Economic and Philosophical Manuscripts of 1844*, D. Struick (ed.), New York, International Publishers.

Weber, M. (1921; 1968), *Economy and Society*, Totowa, Bedminster Press.

# 1(iii) Continuing issues in the management of conflict

*Arnold Sherman*

My interest in conflict management comes from two sources. Firstly, as an individual I am concerned about many of the conflicts which exist today and secondly, as a sociologist, I am interested in the theories of conflict and conflict management. In terms of Jim Laue's classification, I am perhaps closest to a researcher and in terms of the models provided by others, my interests may lie in the area of fact finding.

Several hundred years ago, Montesquieu said that theories that hoped to eliminate conflict in society were mistaken. These theories were based solely on assumptions about the nature of the individual. Conflict theory based only on the nature of the individual can lead to the view that to the extent to which human nature is perfectable social problems can be eliminated. He argued that many sources of crime and conflict were in society, and we would be well advised to recognize that crime, disorder, conflict—being caused by society—cannot be eliminated and cannot always be resolved. At best conflict can, perhaps, be moderated, but sometimes this cannot be achieved.

Later Louis Coser (1967) and others suggested that not only can conflict not be eliminated in the social world but, there are many types of conflicts, some of which are very beneficial. While today we recognize that some conflicts are decidedly useful, there are others we would like to eliminate.

The 'law of the hammer' says that if we give a child a hammer then everything the child sees needs hammering. The corollary of that is if we give an adult a theory everything that the adult sees is fitted into the theory. In conflict management we have an ideal type, the case where a facilitator helps all parties reach a solution in which the pie is increased and everybody wins. I would urge caution, however, against total faith in one theory, one discipline or one technique. The good workman has many tools and he uses the ones which work best in each situation. He does not use a hammer on everything. The kinds of disputes best looked at by negotiation and mediation remain, in my mind at least, an open question. There may be some cases where mediation and negotiation are not possible, and it would be important to know those parameters.

The case has been made that mediation and negotiation are techniques whose time has come. We see support growing, a body of literature emerging, a number of courses developing and growing, degree programs emerging and a profession being born. But this is not the first time this has happened. In the late-nineteenth century, for example, Anthony Platt (1977) tells us that a social movement began which led to the first juvenile court in the United States being set up in Chicago in 1899. Today that court, and the principle of 'super' parent upon which it stands, has been found wanting and is being dismantled.

There are then a number of hard questions which need to be addressed. Many of them have been raised, but raising an issue is not the same as dealing with it. While the sections of the book identify some of the issues, they do not resolve them.

In the movie *Mondo Cane* (Italy, 1963) there is a story about a fishing village. The village is set next to a lagoon in which there is a coral reef. Fisherfolk can bury their dead in the land or in the sea, in the tradition of fisherfolk around the world. These are the two choices they have. Making that decision is a basic part of the beliefs, rituals and whole social organization of such societies. These people decided to bury their dead in the sea, but the bodies were cut up by the coral reef. Subsequently, the blood attracted sharks turning them into flesh eaters. Then if a fisherman was out fishing and perhaps cut his finger, the blood might attract sharks which could tip the boat and devour him. In such cases, the villagers would organize retribution parties. They would hunt down a shark, and force a poisonous sea urchin down its throat, allowing it to swim to a rather unpleasant death.

What would our reaction be? It is easy for an outside observer, for a fact finder, perhaps, to say, 'that is an easy one: do not bury people in the coral reefs'. Yet such a change in social practice is not taken lightly for it may disrupt the entire way of life in the village. Changes like that are going on all across the world. The international political economy, for instance, has been undergoing a constant transformation for the last four or five hundred years with peasants being turned into wage laborers. With these transformations, the subsistence skills of a relatively beneficial life are lost.

Sometimes the history of events is quite long. In 1869 the Suez Canal opened, leading to a series of events which would culminate in the Mau-Mau revolution of 1952–56. Involved here was a very simple thing—the British needed to protect the change in the geopolitical world. In order to do that they needed to protect the headwaters of the Nile so they needed a railroad from it to the nearest seaport in Mombasa. The British thought that this construction and concurrent colonial administration should be self-financing. They therefore instituted a series of laws and poll taxes which slowly drove the people off the land, brought them into the city and converted them into wage laborers. However, one should be clear that an understanding of what was happening between 1952 and 1956 in Kenya is impossible without first acquiring a serious, social political history of the series of events, misconceptions and misinterpretations that led up to that point. That is not something one can obtain simply by going in and talking to the parties at any particular moment. Similarly, the Civil Rights Movement in the United States cannot be understood unless one understands how it is related to the crops and cotton economy of the 1920s. Again one cannot simply go in, talk to the parties and necessarily find all the external variables that are operating. Another basic issue to be dealt with is the nature of the link between individual psychology and social and historical forces.

In general, then, we have a number of questions. What is a fact? Can facts only be obtained from participants? What are the varieties of fact finding? When are they useful? What does one do if beliefs which are false from one perspective are essential for the survival of a particular social system? If one reason we are concerned with creating new methods for settling conflicts is to make the world safe, then we must be concerned with serious threats. One which is very real is the proliferation of peasant social movements which use increasingly sophisticated, relatively cheap, off-the-shelf weaponry in wars of national liberation.

Analyses of the role of Britain with the Kikuyu and the Mau-Mau uprising suggest that a policy of treating terrorism as a crime is likely to backfire. Indeed, the whole pattern of attempting to treat social problems as crimes and then attempting to control the problems by arresting and punishing the perpetrators has failed and continues to fail.

I am not sure that negotiation is the first step that is needed to solve problems of that magnitude. There is a certain kind of social analysis and demystification that has to take place first. This is important. One of the places where mediators are most urgently needed is the criminal justice system. Yet it is likely that if a movement in the criminal justice system occurs on an *ad hoc* basis, Gresham's *Law of Comptency* will allow the less qualified to drive out the more qualified.

What is a science? Science can be built from case studies, as Laue has suggested, but for this to work there has to be a built-in process for collecting cases and for knowing what is successful under various circumstances. Yet some argue that the requirements of anonymity preclude the creation of a public data base for the profession of dispute management. Therefore no record of what works, or does not work, under a variety of circumstances, is ever created. Without such case collection, all we have are individuals saying 'this works for me'.

Years ago, when I was with the Office for Probation in New York, I talked to a senior probation officer who was near the end of his career. His metaphor for thirty-five years of experience working with a variety of children was, 'my professional life was like throwing darts over a screen at a target I could not see. I do not know what happened to those kids. I have no record of what worked and what did not work. I just know what I thought worked. And on reflection, that was not good enough.'

There are other models of science. Some scholars, such as my colleague Joseph Gittler, suggest that science can integrate theory and findings; this is a different model of science from one that starts with case collection. We need to be clear about these differences and their implications for different types of practice. This leads us to the next question. What is a profession? Is it tied to science or not? If so, what kind of science? Laue argued that conflict intervention is not yet a science, but is becoming one. What does all that mean? And where does it take us? What, in fact, is the relationship between knowing and doing? How do we obtain facts? What is the participant's version? What is the fact-finder's version? What conflicts of a serious nature are outside the parameters of successful intervention, negotiation and mediation? How do we know that it is possible to intervene successfully?

Without addressing these issues systematically, we are likely to produce practitioners who succumb to the law of the hammer, and a profession which fails to add to our knowledge. By addressing these issues, there is a better chance of building systematic analysis which will provide practical, useful and effective knowledge.

## Bibliography

Anderson-Sherman, A. (1982), 'The Social Construction of "Terrorism" ' in *Rethinking Criminology*, H.E. Pepinsky (ed.), Beverly Hills and London, Sage Publications.

Anderson-Sherman, A. and D. McAdam (1982), 'American Black Insurgency and the World-Economy: A Political Process Model' in *Ascent and Decline in the World-System*, E. Friedman (ed.), Beverly Hills and London, Sage Publications.

Coser, L.A. (1967), *Continuities in the Study of Social Conflict*, New York, Free Press.

Italy (1963), *Mondo Cane*, documentary film directed by Gualtierro Jacopetti.

Montesquieu, Baron de (1748) *The Spirit of the Laws* trans. by Thomas Nugent (1962), New York, Hafner Press.

Platt, A.M. (1977), *The Child Savers: The Invention of Delinquency*, 2nd Edition, Chicago, University of Chicago Press.

# 2(i) A theoretical perspective on conflict and conflict resolution

*Morton Deutsch*

A British political scientist, John Burton (1972), has said that conflict is like sex. It is an important and pervasive aspect of life. It should be enjoyed and should occur with a reasonable degree of frequency. After conflict is over, people should feel better as a result. Such is my own orientation to conflict.

For the most part social scientists have given conflict a bad reputation by linking it with psychopathology, social disorder and war. The psychological utopias of psychoanalytic theory with its emphasis on the pleasure principle, field theory with its stress on tension reduction and dissonance theory with its preoccupation with dissonance reduction would appear to be a conflict-free existence. Yet it is apparent that most people seek out conflict in their everyday life, in competitive sports, games, by going to theaters, by watching television and in the teasing interplay of intimate encounters. Fortunately, no one has to face the prospect of a conflict-free existence. Conflict can neither be eliminated nor even suppressed for long. The social and scientific issue is not how to eliminate or prevent conflict, but rather how to have lively controversy instead of deadly quarrels.

Conflict has many positive functions. It prevents stagnation, it stimulates interest and curiosity. It is the medium through which problems can be aired and solutions arrived at. It is the root of personal and social change. And conflict is often part of the process of testing and assessing oneself. As such it may be highly enjoyable as one experiences the pleasure of the full and active use of one's capacities. In addition, conflicts demarcate groups from one another and help establish group and personal identities.

I stress the positive functions of conflict and I have by no means provided an exhaustive listing because, as I have indicated, conflict is often cast in the role of villain, as though conflict *per se* is the cause of our individual and social problems. There are problems which arise from conflict, when conflict takes a pathological course. Initially, I want to describe a number of typical pathologies of conflict. On such pathology is conflict avoidance; a second typical pathology is premature conflict resolution; a third is excessive involvement in conflict and a fourth is position rigidification.

*Conflict avoidance* is expressed in the denial of conflict and in the suppression of awareness of the conflict, as well as in the shying away from dealing with the issues in conflict. Occasionally, it is useful to avoid conflict. Sometimes the issues in conflict will disappear with the passage of time or a change of circumstances. For instance, if a co-worker is temporarily irritable because of a situation unrelated to work, perhaps it is best simply to avoid getting entangled with him or her. There are also conflicts that are not likely to be resolved successfully if they are confronted. Often such conflicts are best handled by mutual recognition that they are to be avoided. For example, if a wife detests her husband's best friend, it may be best if both spouses can agree that they will avoid situations in which all three are together, and will avoid attempts to change each other's opinions in this matter.

Generally, however, conflict avoidance has harmful consequences. A conflict does not disappear, it festers underneath the surface and has many indirect effects. It can be debilitating as energy is expended to prevent the conflict from surfacing and can lead to a state of irritability as the tensions associated with the conflict go unresolved. It can also lead to distortions in one's perceptions and behavior as one engages in various tactics and maneuvers to deceive oneself and the other that no conflict exists between them.

Psychoanalysts have provided a description of such tactics and maneuvers in their cataloguing of defense mechanisms. For example, any or all of the following tactics may be used: displacement, in which the conflict is displaced onto other issues. Thus, a husband and wife who avoid confronting their conflicts over the giving and receiving of affection may displace their conflict onto financial matters. Who is being stingy? Who is demanding too much? There may be reaction-formation, in which attitudes and behaviors are expressed which are opposite to those involved in the conflict. Instead of confronting someone with whom one has a conflict, one acts in an overly pleasant, ingratiating way as though there were no issues between oneself and the other. Of course, if we see somebody who is being excessively friendly, we have reason to raise some questions.

Another defense mechanism is identification with the aggressor. Here a person goes beyond being unduly friendly toward another and assumes the other's viewpoint. An identification is made with the other's position, thus denying the validity of one's own self-interest. We see this happening very frequently with children in relation to parents, children facing very authoritarian parents who are very strict and harsh in their discipline. The children may want to rebel against their parents but find that that is very threatening and frightening. To prevent themselves from rebelling they take on the attitudes of their parents toward themselves and act towards themselves in the same critical, negative, judgmental way that the parents may manifest. The children are identifying with their aggressive parents as a way of preventing themselves from engaging in conflict with them.

Rationalization is, of course, a chief mechanism of avoidance. All kinds of seemingly good rationales and reasons are developed as to why the conflict is not to be confronted. 'It is not a good time to approach the other.' 'I am too tired.' 'The situation is not right.' The rationales are pseudo-rationales. The real motivation is the desire to avoid the anxiety associated with the fantasy of conflict.

A second typical form of pathology is *premature conflict resolution*. Sometimes the tension associated with conflict leads to premature resolution, so that the conflicting parties come to an agreement before they have adequately explored the issues involved in their conflict. The typical result is that the agreement will not last long. It will break down as soon as the realities reveal its superficial nature. This very often happens, for example, in divorce negotiations where a couple may find that the process is so stressful emotionally that they want to get out of it. Consequently, they may jump into an agreement about custodial rights, visitation, alimony and so on, which does not take into account either of their realities.

As a typical consequence, that kind of agreement usually breaks down and the couple end up in the divorce court trying to work out a new agreement.

A third kind of pathology is *excessive involvement in conflict*. Paradoxically, the tension associated with conflict sometimes leads people to be excessively involved in and preoccupied with conflict—in a sense, to become conflict prone. Some people seem to master their conflict anxiety by seeking out conflict. Their constant involvement in conflict serves to reassure them that they are not afraid of conflict.

There are many typical fears and irrational anxieties associated with conflict and in my clinical work I have found that these irrational anxieties are usually connected with unconscious or semiconscious fantasies that the conflict will get out of control. There is either the sense that one will become helpless in relation to the fantasied violence from the other party, or that one will be unable to control one's own aggressive and evil impulses and destroy the other. There is often an alternation between the fantasies: a sense of our own omnipotence with the other's helplessness or of their omnipotence with our helplessness, either of which may stir a good deal of anxiety.

A fourth typical pathology that results from the anxieties associated with conflict is *rigidification*. People start to have a kind of tunnel vision with regard to the issues in conflict. They see only a limited range of possibilities for resolving the conflict. They lose their creative potential for conceiving a range of options which might make the conflict a constructive experience in which both sides might profit. Rigidification and tunnel vision are often associated with excessive anxiety.

There are other forms of conflict pathology which are particularly relevant to conflicts which become self-perpetuating vicious cycles; these conflicts escalate. That is, there is some evidence that the parties are involved in a pathological conflict when the conflict gets detached from its originating causes which may even have been forgotten or may no longer be relevant after the conflict starts escalating; the conflict becomes more powerful than any of its initiating causes.

There are a number of typical social-psychological processes associated with the development of self-perpetuating vicious cycles in conflict. One of these is *autistic hostility*. In the course of many conflicts, negative feelings towards the other person may develop. As a consequence communication may be broken off. If contact is broken, we no longer have the opportunity to experience the other, to learn, for example, about possible misunderstandings. We may not have perceived the other correctly. In other words we are maintaining our view of the other autistically, through our own psychological processes rather than through our actual experience with the other.

Let me provide a personal example. I have an autistic hostility towards coffee. I do not know why but this has been the case for as long as I can remember and it was not worth spending money on psychoanalysis to try to find out why. But my autistic hostility is such that I never have contact with coffee. I never have the opportunity to experience that coffee might be different from my view of it. Thus my hostility towards coffee is maintained without any contact with it and that is a process which is very typical in self-perpetuating conflicts. We break off communication with the other in a way which leaves us with no opportunity to change our negative attitudes.

Another social-psychological mechanism involved in perpetuating conflict is the *self-fulfilling prophecy.* A negative self-fulfilling prophecy begins when we have a negative attitude towards another party as a result of some experience we think we have had, or some misunderstanding we have had. We assume the other will have a negative attitude towards us and so we engage in behavior which is negative towards the other. The other party experiences our coldness, our indifference and reacts to us in a cold and indifferent way, thereby fulfilling our expectations. We are engaged in a process whereby the behavior that we initiate towards the other confirms our original expectations, because it elicits from the other a behavior that we originally thought the other was going to engage in.

Let me illustrate again with a personal example. I have not only autistic hostility but a self-fulfilling prophecy towards coffee. Recently I thought I would try to break through my autistic hostility and imbibe some coffee, but I approached the drink with very negative expectations. My expectations could not affect the coffee, but it could affect the way I perceived the coffee. So, when I tried to drink it, I gagged and immediately spat it out. My expectations were shaping my perceptions of the coffee in such a way that my perceptions led to a confirmation of my expectations. So, sometimes a self-fulfilling prophecy goes beyond leading to behavior that elicits reactions from the other that confirm our expectations. It may even warp perceptions.

There is an important point here. In almost any extended, protracted conflict between two parties, both sides are always right. The other *is* hostile, the other *has* negative feelings: 'He doesn't like me; he is treating me badly.' And both sides would be right in their perceptions because they have set up a vicious, mutually confirming expectation. Each is treating the other badly because it feels that the other deserves to be treated badly because the other treats it badly and so on.

A third kind of process that leads to the self-perpetuation of conflict is *commitment processes.* In the course of conflict, people tend to get invested in the conflict. They get invested in particular positions that they have taken and in certain beliefs about the other that they have developed. It is difficult to give these up and it is sometimes a matter of pride not to give up these investments as a party may feel it is yielding or losing self-esteem.

In personal relations the investments are very heavily psychological. We can see in intergroup or international relations how commitments and investments can lead to the perpetuation of conflict. In Soviet and American relations, for instance, there is no question that the military-industrial complex plays a very strong role in determining government policies. There is no doubt that generals in the Soviet Union, as in the United States, prefer large defense budgets to small ones, to have more troops rather than fewer troops and to have more money committed to research and development for new weapons rather than less. In the United States if the Pentagon wants to close down a military base in a local congressman's district, that congressman will start to protest, even though he may be for peace and a limited, reasonable defense budget. The unions and businesses in that local district will also start to protest because of commitments and investments that are very difficult to change.

It is my experience, as a therapist, that one of the most important problems in psychotherapy is abandoning a commitment to the familiar, even though experience has shown that it does not work. Patients may learn that the defenses, the interpersonal tactics and strategies that they employ typically produce failure and depression, but at least they know what the effects of those defenses are; they are uncertain about what the effects of other tactics would be. It is one of the difficult problems to help them over the hurdle of giving up the familiar, albeit painful, in order that they can face the unfamiliar which may be quite rewarding. This is another kind of process which leads to the perpetuation of conflicts—the commitments one makes to the positions, the attitudes, the beliefs, the resources, the skills, the techniques, and the defenses that one has invested in a conflict process.

Thus far I have discussed some aspects of the pathology of conflict. I want now to turn my attention to the question that my theoretical and empirical work on conflict has focused on for many years (Deutsch, 1973). The question is, what determines whether a conflict will take a constructive or destructive course? Its answer involves two steps. The first is that a constructive process of conflict resolution can be identified with a cooperative social process: it has the same social-psychological characteristics as a cooperative process. A destructive process of conflict resolution, on the other hand, typically has the social and psychological characteristics of a competitive process. The second part of its answer is that successful cooperation tends to breed the conditions for further cooperation, while competition tends to breed the conditions for further competition.

In a conflict situation that has not yet already taken a strongly determined course the typical effects of a cooperative process will move conflict resolution into a constructive mode. The typical effects of a competitive process will move conflict resolution into a destructive course. Years ago, when I was studying at MIT, at the Research Center for Group Dynamics, my doctoral dissertation was concerned with the effects of cooperative and competitive processes. I started out with an interest in characterizing the nature of cooperative and competitive proceses, an interest in what were the typical effects of such processes. I developed a theory about the effects of such processes which has also turned out to be a theory of conflict resolution. The major idea of this theory as it applies to conflict resolution is that the typical effects of a cooperative process will induce cooperation and will induce constructive processes of conflict resolution and so on.

Some might say that this sounds so self-evident, that when we are cooperative this will engender cooperation, and when we are competitive, this will engender competitiveness. Is there nothing more to it than this? Those who would ask that might have a mistaken notion of science. The purpose of science is to come up with simple ideas which proliferate into a lot of detailed implications. The idea I have just expressed is simple, but if we think about it in a detailed way it has a wide range of implications. For instance, let us look at the typical effects of cooperation and compare these with competition in terms of what happens in communication. As a result of good cooperation communication tends to be relatively full and relatively open. People are attentive to one another, they are waiting to respond, to make helpful suggestions and to generally cooperate. They have no desire to mislead, misrepresent or falsely communicate.

On the other hand, the typical effect of a competitive process on communication is that it tends to interfere with communication. In some sense, there is no real reason to communicate because we think the other is not going to believe us; our interests are opposed, so why should we tell the truth. The typical result in competitive interaction is that communication becomes less frequent. Another typical effect is that people try to mislead one another; they misinform. In knowing that the other is trying to mislead them, people try to get their information indirectly, for example, through espionage techniques.

If we want to induce a constructive process of conflict resolution, we need to have a communication process that is more like the kind of communication that takes place in a cooperative context. Such a context is where people feel free to talk openly and fully, where they are attentive and responsive to one another and where they have no particular interest in misleading the other. If we want to produce a destructive conflict, on the other hand, we can also do that. Suppose we were in military intelligence and we wanted to instigate a destructive process within an adversary group, then we would want to disrupt and confound their communications. We would want to make their communications very noisy, so that people would start to misunderstand one another. Once they started to misinterpret one another, they would start to develop negative attitudes as a consequence of the poor communication.

Another typical difference between cooperative and competitive processes in terms of effects is the way we try to influence people. In the cooperative process we are interested in persuasion in having the other person see the position that we are advocating and to see it in a way that is acceptable. In a competitive process, on the other hand, we feel that such persuasion is unlikely to occur. Hence, we have to rely on the techniques of intimidation, coercion, threat and stronger power to force the other into a position we want. If we introduce weapons or tactics of coercion and intimidation into a conflict, these will tend to move that process towards a competitive and destructive course of interaction, while tactics of persuasion which are aimed at convincing the other will generally result in a cooperative process of interaction.

Another typical difference in the two kinds of processes is that in a cooperative process we have a positive interest in the power of the other. The stronger the other who is cooperating with us, the more resources it has, and the more intelligent and effective it is, then the better off we are. We are, therefore, interested in enhancing the power of the other. By comparison, in a competitive process, we are interested in increasing the differences between ourselves and the other's powers so that we become better able to intimidate the other. If we can induce a situation where people are oriented towards enhancing one another's power, then we will have a constructive process of conflict resolution. If we induce the opposite situation where people are oriented towards increasing the power differences, then we will have a destructive process of conflict resolution.

A typical result of cooperation is that one tends to see the other person as being similar to oneself with regard to basic values and orientations. A typical result of a competitive process, on the other hand, is that one sees the other as being different from and opposed to oneself. The differences between oneself and the other are accentuated rather than reduced. If we want to increase the destructiveness of a conflict, then we have to increase the size of a conflict making the issues in conflict seem large and terribly important, of vital significance to the parties. But if we want to increase the likelihood of a constructive conflict resolution then we have to help the parties reduce the definition of what is at stake so that it is not world-shaking, so that it involves relatively specific, small issues that are here and now, issues that do not necessarily determine precedence for history.

Clearly, friendly attitudes which are more typical of cooperative processes are more likely to lead to a constructive process, and hostile attitudes are more likely to lead to a destructive process. I could go on listing a lot of the specifics, but what I want to do is put forward the general idea that the typical effects of a cooperative process tend to induce cooperation, while the typical effects of a competitive process tend to induce competition.

I have done research on many of these issues, most of which has been conducted in the laboratory. But some of my students are more adventurous than I. They go out in the field and do investigations of conflict resolution in marriage or studies of the divorcing process or of other field situations. Here I will discuss briefly two types of laboratory studies we have done to give some idea of the experimental research that can be carried out in this area.

Figure 2.1 is a simple representation of a classic situation which has been

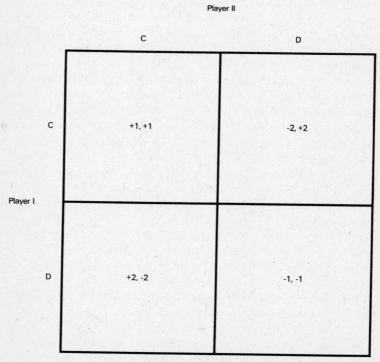

**Figure 2.1.** Prisoner's dilemma

identified in social science literature as the 'Prisoner's Dilemma Game.' It was a label that a mathematical game theorist gave to the situation (see Tucker and Wolfe, 1957). In Tucker's illustration there are two prisoners and a district attorney. The district attorney sets up a situation in which the two prisoners, who had been joint partners in crime, would 'squeal' on one another. I will illustrate it not in that way, but in other ways.

The Prisoner's Dilemma does not have to be a two-person game, nor a two-choice game, but in its simplest form, it is a two-person and a two-choice game. It is a situation in which what happens is determined not only by what one party does but also by what the other party does. Technically, it is a situation of interdependent behavior, interdependent choice, interdependent decision, where the outcomes for one party are the result of what both parties do.

In the game illustrated in Figure 2.1, the two players each have a choice between pressing a button labeled $C$ and pressing a button labeled $D$. The situation is such that if one player presses $D$ when the other player presses $C$, the player who presses $D$ wins, in this example, $2.00. If both players press $D$, then they both lose, but only $1.00 rather than $2.00. If they both press $C$, then they both win. If we look at the matrix of this game it is clear that in some sense it would be rational to choose $D$. The player would then win the most that he could, $2.00 rather than $1.00. Alternatively, he could lose the least that he could, $1.00 rather than $2.00. But if both players press $D$, they both end up in the $DD$ cell; they both lose, which does not appear to be too rational. On the other hand, if they both press $C$ they would both win, which does appear rational. But there is a basic problem here. That is, a player will only press $C$ if he trusts the other player, if he feels that the other player will be trustworthy and also press $C$. He in turn, can only press $C$ if he is willing to be trustworthy in relation to the other's trust. Without the condition of mutual trust there is no basis for truly rational behavior.

The Prisoner's Dilemma poses a dilemma not only for prisoners, but also for theories of society which are based on a purely individualistic notion of rationality. Such a notion says that if everybody simply pursues his or her own rational, immediate gains, then through the 'invisible hand' of the market, the social order will produce not only individual gain but social gain as well. There are many situations like the Prisoner's Dilemma which challenge that basic assumption. For instance, in the context of an arms race, $C$ means to cooperate and disarm, while $D$ means to arm. Now each side, in a sense, would be better off if it were armed and the other side was disarmed. But each side would be worse off if it were armed and paying the cost of heavy armaments, than if both had arrived at a mutual arms control agreement and reduced their arms. But they cannot do this unless there is some confidence on the part of each that if it engages in a process of limiting its weapons production, limiting its research, and so on, it will not be exploited by the other side.

The basis of mutual trust does not necessarily have to be character. Most trust in advanced, complex societies is not based upon character since we do not actually know most of the people we are trusting. We do not know the character of the mailman who might throw our valuable letters into a garbage can. We do not know the character of the driver who is on the same road, who might be crazy and might hit us. We have to engage in so many routine actions throughout our day, based not upon trust in the character of the other, but trust in social arrangements and structures which make other persons predictably trustworthy.

I have done a good deal of research with the Prisoner's Dilemma which supports in general the basic theory of conflict resolution that I mentioned earlier. That is, if we can increase any of the factors that tend to elicit cooperation, then we get greater readiness to engage in mutual trust. If we increase any of the factors that enhance competitiveness, then we get a greater tendency to choose D, with the consequent loss to both parties.

Another game that I have used in a good deal of research is a simple bargaining game. In this bargaining game I create two trucking firms, Acme and Bolt. Each firm gets paid for carrying a load of merchandise from a starting point to a finishing point. They get paid a constant sum, $1.00, minus a variable cost for each trip. The cost is a function of how long it takes in time to make the trip. The longer it takes in seconds the more it costs them and if it takes too long, they lose money on the trip. Each has two routes to his finishing point. One route, an alternative road is so time consuming that to use it would result in a loss of money; the other route is a short main road, in the middle of which is a section which is only one lane wide. As shown in Figure 2.2, Acme and Bolt both need to pass over this section. And the problem they face here is who is going to go through first and who is going to back up?

I have done many experiments with this game, but I will disucss only two—one

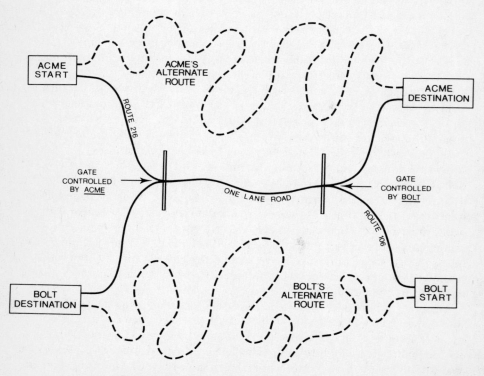

**Figure 2.2.** A simple bargaining game

set of experiments that relates to arms control and the other that relates to issue control. In the 'arms control' experiments, we introduced weapons, that is gates, which one player could use to prevent the other from going to its destination on the main route. In one such experiment, one condition involved both players having these weapons; in another condition, only Acme had the weapon; and in a third condition, neither player had a weapon. The results are rather strong in demonstrating that when both players have weapons, they do badly. They do badly on the first trial and they do badly over the series of twenty trials that we run. They also do not seem to learn very much. Where one player has a weapon, they start out doing badly, though not as badly as in the situation where both have weapons, but about halfway through, they learn to deal with the situation. Where neither player has a weapon, they start out not doing as well as they can, but they quickly learn how to coordinate and get up to a maximum.

Let us look in more detail at the results with a one-weapon situation. Of course, both players have weapons in a sense. The player without recourse to a gate can simply sit on the main path and prevent the other from going through. He can block, he can be obstinate, he can obstruct. It may cost him a lot to do it. What happens in the one-gate situation is that the person who has the weapon can withdraw usage of the weapon without appearing to be intimidating because in a sense the other seems to be in a weaker position. After a while he does withdraw use. But the results indicate that the person who has the weapon does better than the person who does not have the weapon.

But if we compare the one-weapon situation to the two-weapon situation, the players in a two-weapon situation do worse than a player without a weapon facing somebody who possesses one. Hence, if there is only one weapon available, the advantage lies with the weapon holder. But each may be better off if neither had the weapon because, having the weapon, players tend to use threats and intimidating tactics which the other may resist. It may cost the other to resist but it costs the threatener as a consequence of this resistance and prevents perhaps an easier, cooperative resolution. Consequently, arms control is important.

'Issue control' is also important. We can increase or decrease the size of the issue at stake, for instance, in an experiment like the simple bargaining one. If we increase the size of the differences in outcome between the parties, controlling for everything else, then we tend to make the conflict much more difficult to resolve. In such a situation, the players tend to use weapons more frequently, they come to deadlocks more frequently and they end up with worse outcomes than when the size of the differences between them is smaller.

To use an example from international relations, during the Cuban missile crisis in 1962 there was a time when it seemed that Khrushchev and Kennedy were defining the conflict as one between the 'Free World and Communism'. That kind of conflict is essentially not negotiable. Presumably, Kennedy would not negotiate away the 'Free World' nor would Khrushchev negotiate away the communist one. When, at the suggestion of several people, they started redefining the conflict as the location of seventy-two weapons systems, the size of the conflict shrunk. The issue of where seventy-two weapons are located is a much easier conflict to handle than the differences between Communism and the 'Free World'.

In personal relations we see this happening all the time. Sometimes a husband

and wife want to watch different programs on television at a given time but they only have one TV set. At first it may be a conflict about which program they are going to watch. It may then escalate into, 'I never get my way, you are always selfish!' And it may then escalate into, 'You are selfish and your family is selfish' and so on. As it starts to develop in that way and grows in size, it is obviously much more difficult to resolve than when the conflict is simply defined in terms of, 'what program do we watch now?'

It is often the case in parent and child relations for parents to define conflicts with children in ways which expand the scope of the issue enormously—for instance, by saying, 'you are a bad child', in response to specific behavior. Specific behavior which is expressed at a given time and place, is much easier to withdraw from than one's whole personality. It is not an uncommon conflict for a woman in a department store to have a problem about purchasing a dress. The problem may concern the dress, not as an economic issue, but as a symbol of 'self as a woman'. If it becomes that—the definition of self—which is involved in making the decision, then there may be great difficulty in dealing with the issue. But if the situation is narrowed down to a specific choice, about a specific dress, it is much easier to manage. Part of the process of managing conflict is not only helping people to get threats and intimidation out of the conflict process, but also helping them to define conflicts in terms of the issues involved, making them more negotiable and more manageable.

Let me end by summarizing the implications of the theoretical and empirical work that my students and I have done in the area of conflict. In brief, if one wants to create the conditions for a destructive process of conflict resolution, one would introduce into the conflict the typical characteristics and effects of a competitive process: poor communication; coercive tactics; suspicion; the perception of basic differences in values; an orientation to increasing the power differences; challenges to the legitimacy of the parties and so forth. On the other hand, if one wants to create the conditions for a constructive process of conflict resolution, one would introduce into the conflict the typical effects of a coopertive process: good communication; the perception of similarity in beliefs and values; full acceptance of one another's legitimacy; problem-centered negotiations; mutual trust and confidence; information-sharing and so forth.

However, bargaining and conflict resolution do not always take a constructive course. When the conflict takes a destructive course, third parties can play a role in regulating, aborting or undoing a malignant process of conflict resolution. What framework can guide a third person who seeks to intervene therapeutically if negotiations are deadlocked or unproductive because of misunderstandings, faulty communications, the development of hostile attitudes or the inability to discover a mutually satisfying solution? I suggest that such a framework is implicit in the idea that I have described earlier. The third party seeks to produce a constructive conflict resolution process by creating the conditions which characterize an effective cooperative problem-solving process: these conditions are the typical effects of a successful cooperative process.

# Bibliography

Burton, J.W. (1972), *World Society*, London and New York, Cambridge University Press.

Deutsch, M. (1973), *The Resolution of Conflict: Constructive and Destructive Processes*, New Haven and London, Yale University Press.

Deutsch, M. (1985), *Distributive Justice: A Social Psychological Perspective*, New Haven and London, Yale University Press.

Tucker, A.W. and P. Wolfe, (eds), (1957), *Contributions to the Theory of Games*, vol. III, *Annals of Mathematic Studies*, no. 39, Princeton, Princeton University Press.

# 2(ii) New directions for a social psychology of conflict

*Daniel Druckman*

My earlier work was concerned with developing programs of research on conflict, primarily in laboratory settings, but since coming to Washington, I have been tempted by the complex problems of international negotiations in the real world. Hence, I began to develop projects on that topic. Reflecting on the differences between my laboratory and field experiences, I have noticed some interesting, if not remarkable, differences which tell me, for instance, that our theories of conflict resolution are largely conditioned by the things that we observe. If we spend a lot of time in the laboratory studying interpersonal conflict, then we are likely to develop a particular kind of theory, like the one that Morton Deutsch (1973) has developed. If we spend a lot of time looking at international negotiations, then we will develop a different kind of theoretical structure. These differences are important, even though we use a similar language to refer to the processes.

My understanding of progress in social psychology differs from that of Morton Deutsch. His view is largely an *inside* view of conflict; it concerns a psychodynamic understanding of conflict reduction. My view of conflict tends to be an *outside* view. I think that context is important, that the type of setting really makes a difference. Large structures and institutions are the primary, though not the exclusive, determinants of conflict resolution processes and behaviors that we observe and build theories about. I believe that Morton Deutsch is sympathetic to this, though he does not emphasize it as much as I do.

My comments are organized into four general categories. These are categories that Morton Deutsch used in a recent paper (1980) where he evaluates the progress of social psychology in the area of conflict resolution. The categories are methodology, conceptual progress, empirical regularities or empirical progress, and applications.

## Methods

Let us start with methodology. Laboratory experimentation has been the primary mode among social psychologists for observing conflict behavior. In recent years, I have been advocating a more elaborate approach, one not divorced from experimentation, but which includes more complicated gaming structures. These are experimental simulations and even more involved constructions, such as attempts to reproduce whole systems, like international relations. In fact, I was essentially introduced to conflict in my graduate work at Northwestern University through the study of processes and perceptions in the Inter-Nation Simulation (INS) (Druckman, 1968). But in addition to this, we can increase our understanding of conflict through systematic case studies. I do not mean simply describing instances of conflict, but developing a system using concepts similar to the ones that Morton Deutsch talked about, and systematically superimposing these on complicated cases such as the SALT talks, the Mutual and Balanced Force Reduction talks, the Intermediate-Range Nuclear Forces talks—wherever we are interested in the phenomenon of conflict. There has been too little of that kind of work done in social psychology.

Also, and this takes advantage of both strategies, I see some value in developing parallel methodologies for studying conflict in the laboratory and in the field. We can use the same kinds of techniques in both settings. For instance, content analysis can be used to study strategies of bargaining in the laboratory and in the international setting. Parallel studies tell us something about the generality of the results that we obtain in the laboratory—the extent to which they are similar or different from what we observe in the field. In my own work, I have found some interesting differences which I will discuss shortly.

Four research strategies illustrate how an investigator can take advantage of laboratory and field methodologies. The first involves bringing 'critical' aspects of the real world into the laboratory. Referred to as experimental simulation, this is the most popular approach to the study of interpersonal conflict. The second strategy consists of bringing the analytical rigor of systematic laboratory research to the real world. This is illustrated by the few studies that have attempted to superimpose general dimensions upon case studies of negotiation (e.g., Haskel, 1974). The analytical challenge posed by this strategy is that of attaining a match between the dimensions and the case. The third strategy involves moving between the laboratory and the real world, using labortory and field materials to complement one another. By employing content-analysis categories that can be used in several settings, the technology of experimentation is brought into closer contact with the case-study literature on negotiation (the work of Hopmann and Walcott, 1977, is the best example). The fourth strategy is deductive; it emphasizes model building. The model is regarded as an integrative device that organizes 'part-processes' of negotiation (a first step in this direction is illustrated in Druckman, 1977). The iterative process of model development and adjustment serves to refine our image, producing a better representation of the phenomenon. Further discussion of these strategies can be found in Druckman (1983).

## Concepts

The second category concerns conceptual progress. A number of issues with social-psychological implications have not been adequately addressed by social psychologists. The most important of these, it seems to me, is that of linkages between microprocesses (e.g., interpersonal relations, communication, and social learning) and macro phenomena (e.g., the structure of institutions or the structure of regional systems). Similar concepts are being used by scholars in international relations and in social psychology. One of these, interdependence, has been central to Deutsch's experimentation. It is also central to recent thinking about complex relations between nations within regions. But what is the difference between the levels and how do they link up? Influence processes and exchange processes describe relationships between nations, as well as relationships between people. To understand how the process of conflict moves between collaboration and conflict requires an understanding of exchange processes and attempts to exert influence.

In a chapter on regional politics (Druckman, 1980), I tried to characterize regional systems simply as cooperative, conflictual or as undergoing transformation. I labeled some ten regions around the world and speculated on the kinds of negotiations that we see in regional conferences and found that it seemed plausible to suggest a relationship between a cooperative regional system (e.g., the European Community, or the United States, Mexico and Canada) and cognitive conflicts. I also found it plausible to suggest that there is a relationship between competitive systems and conflicts where the intention is to increase, rather than decrease, the differences in power; that is, to give one party a power advantage over the other. Thirdly, there seemed to be a relationship between regions undergoing transformation and the willingness of negotiators to address values. It is important to include ideologies or values in the deliberations as a prerequisite to changing the nature of the system.

In all of this work, I have been trying to find out whether there is a relationship between social-psychological phenomena, that is, people and their behavior, and the implications of that for a system of nations. This is a very complicated idea and I am not sure that I am satisfied with my progress in this regard. In any case, it is an issue that social psychologists have largely avoided.

Another conceptual concern is the difference or similarity between bargaining processes as studied with trucking game paradigms or Prisoner's Dilemma situations and the phenomena with which I have been dealing recently, namely international negotiations. In this regard, in another paper (Druckman, 1983), I tried to indicate seven areas where there are differences between negotiating processes. The contrast is between bargaining theory and international negotiations. The purpose of bargaining, generally in the laboratory, is to achieve some sort of mutually satisfactory understanding or agreement. The purpose of many international negotiations that I have observed is not to achieve agreement, but instead to produce what we refer to as 'side effects', effects not pertaining to agreement *per se*, but which allow the parties to keep talking. For example, with regard to arms or troop reduction talks, it is important to keep talking to avoid unilateral reductions. The United States, for instance, can thus avoid making a decision to implement reductions on its own. The idea here is that if we are talking to reduce in conjunction with an adversary, and if that goes on for years, no decision is going to be made. If no decision is going to be made, that suits the purposes of those opposed to unilateral arms reductions. This is one kind of side effect which propels negotiations, quite apart from the objective of achieving an agreement and such talks often last for years with no apparent progress.

Another dimension of difference is the nature of the bargaining dynamic. In our laboratory work compromise or concession-making is the essence of the negotiating process. In the real world, however, concessions are only one aspect of negotiations, in fact, just a small stage in an extended process which includes debates and other kinds of exchanges which have little to do with movements in positions. Positions are usually difficult to define.

In our laboratory experiments, preferences are typically imposed upon the participants. We can pinpoint them, we know where the participants stand on a particular issue. In international negotiations, however, preferences are usually not stable; they tend to emerge during the process. They are built up from the bottom, in the same way as our theories often evolve. They are built up as a result of experience, as a result of what we are observing and exchanging; it is a dynamic situation.

Relating back to conceptual problems associated with system-individual linkages in the laboratory, we rarely pay much attention to the broader context. If we were analysts in international relations, it would become apparent that context is intertwined with process; the two cannot be separated. Most investigators recognize the limitations of work that ignores contextual factors: for example the nature of a region, or cultural assumptions about negotiations. Clearly, complexity makes for differences; laboratory work attempts to avoid such complexity. There, the focus of analysis is on a few issues, on a bilateral structure, usually two parties, and relatively brief sessions. In the real world of international negotiations there is a focus on packages of issues, on multilateral, bureaucratic and domestic structures that have a strong influence on progress, and also on chronologies that can, as in the cases I have analyzed, extend to ten years.

Perhaps relating more to methodology than to concept, in our experimental work we emphasize similarities from one session to another. We call the sessions 'replications' and perform statistical analysis on them. The political scientists who have looked at various negotiations have treated them as cases. They have emphasized differences between them, thus creating problems for comparative work. I have been trying to persuade my colleagues in political science to develop conceptual systems that would permit comparative work, even though their cases are very complex. Similarly, I have been trying to persuade my social psychologist colleagues to notice the kinds of differences that I am talking about here and build stronger, more realistic models of the phenomena that I seem to be observing.

## Empirical Regularities

Are there empirical regularities that transcend situations? Given what I have already said, there might appear to be none. But it is my view that there are at least two kinds of conflict processes which might indeed transcend situations. The first of these is represented by a dynamic equilibrium model. This model, which is different from Deutsch's self-generating spirals, indicates that there are phases of high intensity conflicts and phases of low intensity conflicts. Depending on where we are in terms of the model, there are factors, such as ideological differences, which exacerbate and escalate the intensity of conflict, and factors, such as schisms, coalitions and cross-cutting interests, which can moderate the intensity of conflict.

The intensity of conflicts results from both the extent to which the parties are polarized and the extent to which mediational mechanisms are present and operative. The more polarized the parties are at any point in time, and the fewer mediational mechanisms operating, the more intense the conflict and vice versa. When the two forces operate simultaneously, the conflict is kept at a tolerable level. This pattern resembles a balancing mechanism, alternating between an intensifying influence and a moderating influence on the conflict. When changes are taken into account, the pattern takes the form of a dynamic equilibrium model. Such a model has been proposed elsewhere (Druckman and Zechmeister, 1973) as a conceptualization of the interplay between interests and ideologies in political decision-making.

The second kind of empirical regularity that might transcend situations is represented in what I refer to as a threshold-adjustment model—a model originally suggested by an economist, Coddington (1968). Common in the literature on conflict is the notion of action-reaction processes. I propose that, again, things are more complicated than that. In a sense it is action-reaction but action with a delay that is, another party does not react very quickly. What he is really doing most of the time is monitoring, following what the other party is doing. He is noticing differences in size of concessions, if these are the primary object of the game, or noticing differences in toughness when postures are the object of the game. When he notices a large difference between the two parties, he adjusts, and the adjustment is usually upward. That is, he adjusts toward getting tougher and making fewer concessions, toward closing the gap, or 'the window of vulnerability'.

The adjustment seems to be made when the size of the difference between the teams approaches a threshold value: in other words, when it is noticed. The negotiators use information about the other's behavior to create a synchronous pattern such that they do the same thing at the same time. We have observed this in several negotiations. Similar results were obtained in analyses of early and late test-ban talks and in the SALT context. Soviet concessions were found to be related positively to the harder American position in the previous round as measured by the *differences* in concession rates. (See the review of findings presented by Druckman (1983) and Jensen's article on SALT (1984).) My recent work on military base rights negotiations confirmed this pattern in terms of rhetoric: the softer team (usually the American) adjusted its rhetoric in the direction of harder statements when it noticed a gap in postures (Druckman, 1986). Taken together, the evidence suggests that threshold adjustment may be a better model of responsiveness than simple models of reciprocity (e.g., Bartos, 1974). It captures more subtle features of the bargaining process, including both monitoring and decisions, as well as concessions and rhetoric.

## Applications

Finally, we turn to Deutsch's last category: applications. Essentially the question he is asking is, have the results of social-psychological research thus far been used in some meaningful ways? Though my answer is slightly different from his, I remain optimistic. It is my view that there have been few direct, self-conscious applications of the nonobvious findings that Deutsch talks about in his 1980 paper (e.g., the advantages of ignorance, disadvantages of toughness). However, I think there may have been some important indirect contributions made by social psychology. These consist of new ways of thinking about processes and an enhanced sensitivity by those trained as social psychologists to the impact we have on others and the impact they have on us. This is very important. If we are going to apply ideas related to the analysis of conflict processes, we need to become more experiential as well as empirical. That is, in addition to presenting our findings, we must find ways, not only to communicate our findings but that also enable others to experience the phenomena themselves, whether as subjects in experiments or as participants in workshops.

With regard to conflict resolution, it is the case as I mentioned before, that resolution or agreement is not a goal of all parties in conflict. There are side effects and 'clients' are usually less interested in negotiating about a conflict whose resolution is clearly not to their advantage. Therefore, the destructive aspects of conflict seem often to be emphasized more than the constructive aspects. The challenge for applied social psychologists is to change that state of affairs.

One promising application that builds on social-psychological concepts is the problem-solving workshop. Viewed by some as an integrative device, workshops draw on developments in several areas. Literature on conflict resolution and theories of intergroup relations, group process and regional politics contribute ideas that are used by workshop designers. If these were combined creatively, the resulting synthesis could produce desired perceptual changes. More often, however, the application is eclectic, due largely to the exploratory aspects of the approach. The exploratory motif stems from the fact that the technique itself is still evolving. This is true of each of the several variants on the general approach. Each is open to change, extension and recombination, as Kelman (1977) notes in his review of the 'technique'. The format provides exciting opportunities for innovation at the juncture between theory and application. Such opportunities have been exploited in recent years, most notably in the area of international conflict resolution.

Finally, the government invests a lot of money in research of one sort or another, but often the investment is in tools rather than an understanding of processes. That is, the government seems to be investing in technologies for organizing information and in computer systems for better processing of data. Though there are social-psychological implications in this kind of investment, it does not constitute analyses of problem-solving or conflict processes. These are useful tools that can help an international negotiator to organize packages of issues and perhaps come up with a solution, but they are not the whole story, even though they are often treated as such.

To conclude, what I have been arguing here is not that experimental social psychology lacks significant achievements, but that we as social psychologists ought to strive to extend the domain that we cover and the types of issues that we address. Working collaboratively with investigators from other social science disciplines is one approach. Organizing our research in a cumulative fashion through centers for research on conflict resolution is another.

## Bibliography

Bartos, O.J. (1974), *Process and Outcome of Negotiations*, New York, Columbia University Press.

Coddington, A. (1968), *Theories of the Bargaining Process*, Chicago, Aldine.

Deutsch, M. (1973), *The Resolution of Conflict*, New Haven & London, Yale University Press.

Deutsch, M. (1980), 'Fifty Years of Conflict' in *Retrospectives on Social Psychology*, L. Festinger (ed.), Oxford and New York, Oxford University Press.

Druckman, D. (1968), 'Ethnocentrism in the Inter-Nation Simulation', *Journal of Conflict Resolution*, **12**, pp. 45–68.

Druckman, D. (1977), *Negotiations: Social-Psychological Perspectives*, Beverly Hills and London, Sage.

Druckman, D. (1980), 'Social-Psychological Factors in Regional Politics' in *Comparative Regional Systems*, W.J. Feld & G. Boyd (eds.), Oxford and New York, Pergamon.

Druckman, D. (1983), 'Social Psychology and International Negotiations: Processes and Influences' in *Advances in Applied Social Psychology*. R.F. Kidd and M.J. Saks (eds.), Hillsdale, New Jersey, Lawrence Erlbaum.

Druckman, D. (1986), 'Stages, Turning Points, and Crises: Negotiating Military Base Rights, Spain and the United States', *Journal on Conflict Resolution*, **30**, pp. 327–60.

Druckman, D. and K. Zechmeister (1973), 'Conflict of Interest and Value Dissensus: Propositions in the Sociology of Conflict', *Human Relations*, **26**, pp. 449–66.

Haskel, B.G. (1974), 'Disparities, Strategies, and Opportunity Costs: The Example of Scandinavian Economic Market Negotiations', *International Studies Quarterly*, **18**, pp. 3–30.

Hopmann, P.T. and C.D. Walcott (1977), 'The Impact of External Stresses and Tensions on Negotiations', in *Negotiations: Social-Psychological Perspectives*, D. Druckman (ed.), Beverly Hills and London, Sage.

Jensen, L. (1984), 'Negotiating Strategic Arms Control, 1969–1979', *Journal of Conflict Resolution*, **28**, pp. 535–59.

Kelman, H.C. (1977), 'the Problem-Solving Workshop in Conflict Resolution' in *Unofficial Diplomats*, M.R. Berman and J.E. Johnson (ed.), New York, Columbia University Press.

# 2(iii) Intervenor roles and conflict pathologies

*Maire A. Dugan*

In this section I propose to explore two general areas relating to Morton Deutsch's chapter. The first draws upon his discussion of conflict functions and pathologies and how this relates to an intervenor's choice of roles, a topic also explored in greater depth in James Laue's contribution to this series (see Chapter 1 (i)). The other area addresses the goals of intervenors as they enter disputes, particularly in light of the issue of trust, which is, as Deutsch points out, of crucial importance in determining the constructive or destructive tendencies of a conflict.

Before proceeding, I want to make one observation. Deutsch's discussion of conflict—its functions, pathologies and promise—is focused on the behaviors of the conflicting parties themselves. My brief discussion here will have more to do with third parties and their potential in helping parties to reduce the pathological aspects of conflict and make constructive use of its positive functions.

My starting point is Deutsch's recognition of premature conflict resolution and conflict avoidance as pathological responses to conflict. These two general categories are often highly related in that a primary reason why parties resolve conflict before dealing adequately with the issues in conflict is that they are uncomfortable with conflict and wish to avoid it. Even those who, like myself, spend much of their professional lives discussing the positive functions of interpersonal and social conflict, are often the victims of these pathologies. When I find myself in a conflict situation, I am uncomfortable, I want to relieve this discontent by terminating the conflict. I have a resulting strong impulse to avoid the conflict or to settle it right away, most likely prematurely. Furthermore, as Deutsch has pointed out, this type of strategy is dangerously common not only on interpersonal levels, but at institutional, community and international ones as well.

One way of approaching this problem is to develop and test models for analyzing conflict which allow for distinguishing appropriate times for resolving versus not resolving a conflict. The analytical model I find most helpful in this regard has been developed by Adam Curle (Curle, 1971; Curle and Dugan, 1982). In Curle's model it is possible to understand when a conflict is not only not ready to be resolved but needs in fact to be accentuated.

There are two primary variables in Curle's model—balance and awareness, the interplay of which affects both when and how an intervenor appropriately enters a conflict situation. The basic principle I derive from this model is that generating awareness of the conflict and some balance between the parties relative to the conflict precedes making peace within the relationship. 'Balance' refers to the distribution of power within the relationship. In a balanced relationship, each party is more or less equal in power relative to the relationship, or relative to the conflict within the relationship. The parties are not necessarily symmetrical; that would require a degree of similarity that is rare. The sources of power may be different for each party. One party, for example, may rely on wealth and control of material resources as its source of power, while the other may rely on strength of numbers and the possibility of withdrawal of support. Labor–management conflict is an example of this and because the parties are both empowered to take action, the nature of the relationship should continue to change and move forward in a peaceful fashion.

While lack of awareness can be a problem in both balanced and unbalanced situations—for peers in a balanced relationship and for both the weaker and stronger parties in an unbalanced relationship—what I am particularly concerned with is the weaker party in an unbalanced relationship. Here the party may have been downtrodden to such an extent that its members have come to incorporate their inferior status as part of their self-image. As a result, they may have come to believe that their status is deserved, that they can do nothing to change it, and/or that the relative opulence of the stronger party is not related to their own misery. Unless the weaker party perceives that it has the right to fair treatment and that its misery is a byproduct of the other party's favored position, then very little can be done to change the situation. That is, very little can be done to change the nature of the relationship, to bring about a solution that would not only minimize overt physical violence but also move toward a just distribution of resources.

Curle believes that until we get to the situation where both balance and awareness are relatively high, mediation is inappropriate (see Figure 2.3). In a situation of low balance and low awareness, educational and *not* resolution efforts are required. Where awareness has increased as a result of educational efforts, but where the balance is still fairly low, then some form of confrontation is needed. In this case, the preference would be for nonviolent forms of confrontation, rather than physical, violent forms. When this confrontation has produced some level of balance, only then is it appropriate for the intervenor to act as a mediator in an attempt to solve the conflict. Up to this point, the function is to make the conflict manifest, to make all parties aware of it and to create a degree of empowerment. In this way, the parties to the conflict can come together in a relatively balanced way to generate a solution to whatever the problem is. To relate this to James Laue's (1982) work, the more appropriate roles for a conflict intervenor to play at these early stages are those of activist and advocate rather than mediator or conciliator. Their concern should be not only to avoid the pathology of a premature settlement, but beyond this to help the parties to make the conflict more visible and understood.

Another way of looking at appropriate roles for an intervenor to take is to focus on goals. Deutsch's research suggests a goal of reducing the size of the conflict issue, at least in terms of perception, from an insoluble level e.g., 'The Free World versus Communism' to a manageable one, e.g., 'where to place seventy-two weapons systems'. Here it would be an intervenor's role to help parties redefine their issues. One strategy for doing this is Roger Fisher's (1964) method of fractionating conflict. Redefining issues, as well as encouraging cooperative rather than competitive behavior—persuasion as opposed to intimidation and threat, open communication as opposed to misinformation and rumor—is an appropriate role for Laue's mediator or whose goal is a 'jointly determined, win/win resolution involving all stakeholders' (1982, p. 33).

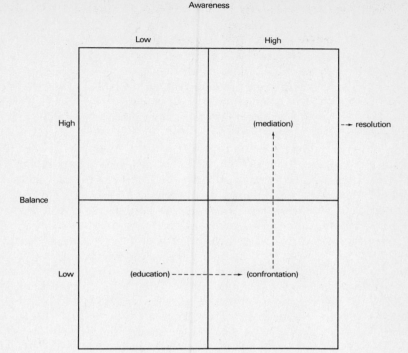

**Figure 2.3.** Balance-awareness relationships

A different set of goals would emerge in a situation where, for example, an ethnic or racial minority is differentially deprived of community services, despite numerous studies of neighborhood conditions and requests for action. In this case, if the neighborhood constituency itself is sufficiently aware of the problem and organized to tackle it, the politics of protest and confrontation is the appropriate strategy and an intervenor who focused on mediative techniques, such as conciliatory behavior and fractionating conflict, would be out of place. Once, however, the power balance has been addressed and the community leaders are willing to engage in real bargaining with the formerly disenfranchised neighborhood group, the conciliatory intervention role becomes even more important. This is because, as one moves from confrontation to bargaining tactics, the negative feelings and distrust which have been heightened during the confrontation stage must be delicately handled and redirected so that constructive problem solving can occur.

One of the mediator's most difficult tasks in this regard is trust building, the first stage of which is opening up lines of communication. There are several ways in which intervenors can help parties overcome the stumbling block which distrust poses to constructive conflict processes. I will mention three. One is to provide parties sufficient protection from each other: mutual trust is not a requisite for a workable solution; trust for the intervention process and/or the intervenor may be sufficient. A second is for the intervenor to allow for and encourage, where appropriate, a transference of trust from the process and the third party to mutual respect and trust between the parties. As Party A, I may begin by distrusting Party B because of his dishonesty, underhandedness and so on. If, however, I see him engaging in open and honest communication with the intervenor, whom I trust, I may begin to allow for the possibility that he is not always dishonest. This slight repositioning of my trust level regarding Party B may pave the way for a gradual and continuing change.

A third way to build trust is for a conflict party to break directly into the self-perpetuating conflict spiral and redirect it. This can be done by engaging in a behavior antithetical to what the other party would expect i.e., challenging the other side to reassess its self-fulfilling prophecy and giving it a chance to respond in a way which interferes with one's own self-fulfilling prophecy. Looking at a very complicated conflict, such as that between the United States and the Soviet Union, we can get a quick, oversimplified idea of what this might mean. One side, say the United States, might decide to make a conciliatory move toward the other. This move need not and probably should not endanger its own security but should be invitational in encouraging a cooperative response by the other side. If this reverse spiral maintains its direction and energy, then perhaps by the 'umpteenth' move, each side will be engaging in behavior toward the other which earlier would have endangered its security. This trust-building strategy is in fact an oversimplified summary of Charles Osgood's (1962) Graduated and Reciprocated Initiative in Tension-Reduction (GRIT).

Few of us have the opportunity to consult on trust building between the United States and the Soviet Union, but the principle remains the same regardless of where a conflict lies on the continuum between interpersonal and international. The capacity to challenge those perceptions which play into the continuation and escalation of conflict is based upon communication contacts which can facilitate the building of trust. Otherwise, Party B is likely to be suspicious even of the most purely conciliatory action on Party A's part. This then becomes a very important role for the intervenor: to identify where and how communications can be transmitted, to help suggest or evaluate alternative options for action, to help parties interpret and respond to conciliatory efforts by the other, all so that each side can be conciliatory while not endangering its own position of security.

In conclusion, while it is not only possible but appropriate to train people in how to avoid pathological responses to conflict in order that they may be able to approach future conflicts more constructively, this may be too late if they have already engaged in pathological behavior. In this case, the role of the third party may well be crucial in salvaging the possibility of a durable win/win outcome. It is, therefore, most important that the appropriate intervention role is chosen.

**Bibliography**

Curle, A. (1971), *Making Peace*, London, Tavistock Publications.

Curle, A. and M.A. Dugan (1982), 'Peacemaking: Stages and Sequence' in *Peace and Change* (Special Issue on Conflict Resolution, M.A. Dugan (ed.)), **VII**, no. 2–3, pp. 19–28.

Fisher, R. (1964), 'Fractionating Conflict' in *International Conflict and Behavioral Science: The Craigville Papers*, R. Fisher (ed.), New York, Basic Books.

Laue, J.H. (1982), 'Ethical Considerations in Choosing Intervention Roles' in *Peace and Change*, op.cit., pp. 29–41.

Osgood, C.E. (1962), *An Alternative to War or Surrender*, Urbana, University of Illinois Press.

# 3(i)  Creative approaches to negotiation

*Dean G. Pruitt*

Negotiation is a discussion aimed at resolving a perceived divergence of interests. In this section only the two-party case is covered, although of course negotiation often involves many parties.

Interests are all the motives that can underlie a proposal—all the goals, values, perceived costs and so on. Interests are divergent when the means available for achieving X's interests frustrate Y, and/or the means available for achieving Y's interests frustrate X. It is possible to talk about interests being divergent in reality, but I think it is much more important to talk about psychological divergence, the perception that my interests are opposed to yours. Conflict arises when somebody *perceives* that his or her interests are opposed to another's, though they might not actually be opposed.

I want to illustrate perceived divergence of interests with some rather homely examples. Let me first of all say how the accompanying diagrams work. In Figure 3.1, there are two parties: management and labor. The abscissa is the value to management. The further out the abscissa, the more valuable is an option to management. The ordinate is the value to labor. The further out, the more valuable it is to labor. In that space are points which refer to the options or alternatives that are known at the time which people have been able to conceptualize. In this case we are dealing with a hypothetical wage negotiation involving the possibility of a $0.50, $0.75, $1.00, $1.25 or a $1.50 raise. A $0.50 raise is highly valuable to management and hence is near the end of the management dimension, but it does not have much value for labor, and hence is rather down towards zero for labor. Quite the opposite can be said about a $1.50 raise—this has high value for labor and low value for management. Then there is something in the middle, a $1.00 raise, which has moderate value for both management and labor. If we drew the coordinates of that point, we would see that it is roughly in the middle of both axes.

In Figure 3.2, a husband wants to take his vacation in the mountains and his wife wants to take hers at the seashore. In this case there are only two apparent options and there is no middle ground.

Figure 3.3 represents a professor who asks his head of department for some time off. He wants to take a semester off to write a book, and the head does not want him to do so.

Figure 3.4 illustrates a situation that actually happened to me. A carpenter came to my house because I had some ceiling work to be done. After he had inspected the house and told me what was needed, he said: 'Well, I will charge you twenty-five dollars for making an estimate.' He said that the reason he charged the fee was because so many people, once they received money from their insurance company, would simply do the work themselves. His perception was that there were two options: either the carpenter does the work or the client does the work. If

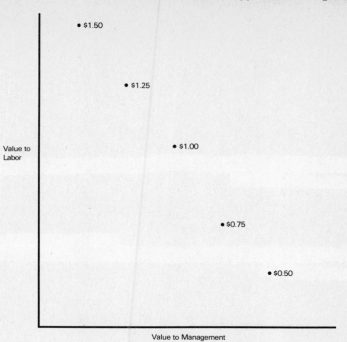

**Figure 3.1** Prospective wage raises

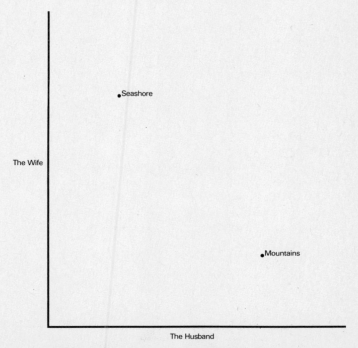

**Figure 3.2** Prospective vacation venues

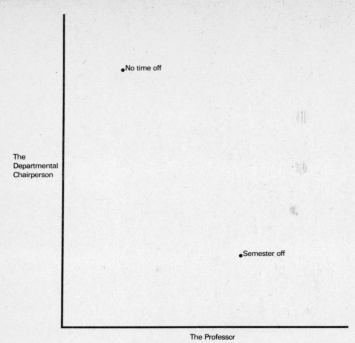

**Figure 3.3** Time off for a professor

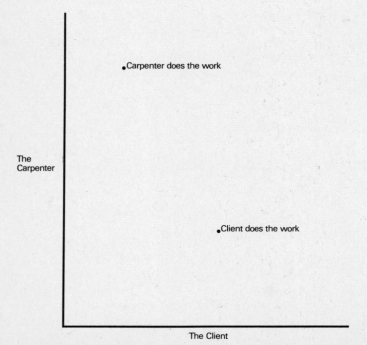

**Figure 3.4** The carpenter and client: divergence of interest

the carpenter does the work that is very good for the carpenter but not for the client. The opposite is true if the client does the work. It turned out that he had totally misperceived the situation, which was more like that in Figure 3.5.

These diagrams illustrate a number of ways that a conflict can start which could lead to bargaining. In Figure 3.1, it is a matter of exchange: work for money. In Figure 3.2 it is a joint decision about how two parties are to proceed. If agreement is not reached there will be no vacation together. In Figures 3.3 and 3.4 the conflict arises when one party tries to influence the other, to push the other into some action.

Regardless of how the divergence of interest arises negotiation can always take place. Whenever we talk about a divergence of interest, we are negotiating. Negotiation is frequently much more complex than these simple examples. We often find many, many issues. For example, in international negotiations there may be a thousand or two thousand issues. Furthermore, if the negotiators are doing their jobs properly the issues will constantly change. Some people might object that the kind of analysis presented here which deals with a single issue or small group of issues reduces negotiation to absurdly small proportions. I would have to agree that things are often much more complicated, but this type of analysis can be extended to the more complicated case.

Negotiation is important because it is an efficient way to resolve controversies. When we use words, we can make fine discriminations and project ahead sharply. Other methods, such as fist-fights, are usually less effective for resolving controversies. Furthermore, negotiation is non-escalatory. As long as people are talking with one another they are unlikely to fight. Even if there is no progress in the negotiation it is often desirable to keep it going in order to prevent a more severe controversy from erupting.

In the first part of my analysis I am going to discuss possible outcomes from negotiation. Following that, I plan to discuss some of the mechanisms by which these outcomes can be developed. Finally, I shall discuss some of the different approaches that negotiators can take.

## Negotiation outcomes

Some possible negotiation outcomes are (1) no contest, (2) no agreement, (3) capitulation, (4) compromise and (5) integrative agreement. Actors may, as a result of an initial discussion, discover that there really is no issue. One would hope that this will often happen. This was clearly the case with the carpenter who came to my home. From his viewpoint there was a divergence of interest as indicated in Figure 3.4. Either he did the work in which case he was happy, or I did the work in which case I was happy. As soon as he mentioned this, I said something like this: 'You've got it all wrong. Actually if you do the work I will be very happy because I'm all thumbs at carpentry. If I have to do the work we are both going to suffer.' There was a convergence of interest from my viewpoint, as indicated in Figure 3.5 not a divergence of interest. There is no real conflict in a case like that, conflict only exists in the long run if both parties see a divergence of interest.

Let us now discuss the situations where there really is a conflict. Another major outcome could be no agreement, relations could break off. Agreement has to be

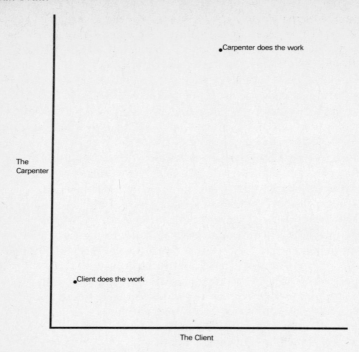

**Figure 3.5** The carpenter and client: convergence of interest

seen as having some sort of value in the graphs along with the options that are under consideration. If a party is rational he should only be willing to consider those options that are better for him than no agreement. If both parties are rational and there is some option that is better than no agreement for both of them it should be possible to reach agreement.

Let us assume that a strike would constitute no agreement in a labor–management situation. Let us say that, from the viewpoint of management, a strike would be as bad as a $1.35 raise and, from the viewpoint of labor, a strike would be as bad as getting only $0.65. From a logical viewpoint it should be possible to reach agreement on one of these three options. If people can keep their wits about them, and talk clearly and concede reasonably, agreement should be reached. However, there is no guarantee of an agreement even when it is logically possible. There are two reasons for this. One is that in the course of defending their interests, negotiators often become committed to their proposals. For example, in asking for a $1.25 raise labor may say, 'we are going to insist on $1.25 and we will not budge from this position. That is our bottom-line.' Such a statement is called a positional commitment. Instead of rationally taking $0.65 as their lower limit, labor may now very well insist on $1.25 as their lower limit because they have become boxed into this position. If management insists on $0.75, it would be rational for labor to accept this figure. But they may not be able to do so because they have become committed to a higher one. This is one way in which negotiators can fail to reach agreement, even though it is theoretically possible to do so.

Positional commitments that are made publicly tend to be especially problematical. They upset one's sense of a minimally acceptable position. Earlier this century, Woodrow Wilson said that international diplomacy should consist of 'open agreements openly made'. I do not think that is right. Rather what we need are open agreements *privately* reached. This is because when we make a public statement about where we stand, we become committed to this position and often cannot extricate ourselves. It then becomes impossible to reach agreement.

Another way in which actors can fail to reach agreement when there are viable alternatives is if one party concedes so slowly that the other concludes that the former's limit is too high. In other words, if management starts at $0.65 and concedes very slowly, labor might conclude that management's bottom line is out of reach. Labor might then conclude that there are no viable options, and decide to break off negotiation.

There are many different kinds of bargaining situations, and in some cases it may be in a party's interests that there be no agreement. For example, if the status quo is in one party's interest, then that party is better off not bargaining, unless the other party arranges for the status quo to seem unpalatable. An example of this might be the parties in Figure 3.3. If, from the viewpoint of the head, no time off is preferable to the professor having a semester off, and if this is the status quo, then it is in the head's interests for there to be no agreement. Indeed the head is likely to try to avoid negotiation altogether. Frequently in a case like this, we will find the other party (e.g., the professor) engaging in the use of threats.

What such threats do is make failure to reach agreement less palatable to the party who benefits from the status quo. This is one of the most common functions of threats. Perhaps the professor will hint around or say, 'Well, you know, if I do not get the semester off, I am going to be kind of wooden. I am not going to be able to work very much anymore because I am so tired.' Or he may harass the head by coming in again and again. His aim is to make no agreement (the status quo) seem less and less valuable to the head, hoping the latter will begin to say, 'Boy, if I do not reach some sort of agreement with him, he is going to be a pest. If I stick to my guns, he won't do any work and I am going to end up in bad shape.'

The same thing essentially was happening with the carpenter in Figure 3.4. Having concluded that we had a severe divergence of interests, he was trying to threaten me with a charge of twenty-five dollars. Since the status quo allows the client to do the work, he was trying to make this option seem less palatable to me.

A third possible outcome of negotiation is capitulation—one side gives in. This is not particularly interesting theoretically, so I want to go on to a fourth, which is compromise. A compromise involves movement by both parties on an obvious dimension to some middle ground. The potential for compromise is easy to see in Figure 3.1. If I start at $1.50 and the other party starts at $0.50, we would be compromising if we reached agreement at $1.00 or $0.75 or $1.25.

Let us return to the situation of the seashore and the mountains (Figure 3.2). How can we move to a compromise there? It will require us to invent a new alternative, but this is likely to be fairly simple. If it is a two-week vacation, we might decide on one week at the seashore and one in the mountains—or perhaps ten days in one place, and four days in another. Compromises are usually obvious.

Compromises are often reasonable as agreements, but they are usually not outstanding. Indeed they are often rather shoddy in comparison to integrative agreements, our next topic. Nevertheless, there are many forces pushing people toward compromise. One such force is that a formula like a week at the seashore and a week in the mountains satisfies strong social norms of fairness, e.g., the norm of equal outcome and the norm of equal concession. Furthermore, being easy to find, compromises are appealing to people who do not like conflict. Such people concede too rapidly and hence often fail to discover the integrative options in the situation.

An integrative option is one that reconciles both parties' interests so that both are satisfied. A possibility in the husband-wife case would be the following: suppose each of them could arrange for a four-week vacation. The husband could then get his two weeks in the mountains and the wife her two weeks at the seashore. Both would be getting exactly what they want, which is a much better agreement than a compromise.

The carpenter and the client do not require an integrative agreement because there really was no divergence of interests. But let us consider the case of the professor and the head. Suppose that the professor wants time off from his courses, while the head is concerned about staffing a major curriculum committee which meets twice a week. If those are the two parties' underlying interests, then there is a possible integrative solution: the professor gets course relief in exchange for serving on the curriculum committee. This is all right for the head, though it is not quite as good as having the professor there all the time. It is also all right for the professor, though not quite as good as having the whole semester off. It is not a bad arrangement for the two of them.

Perhaps the best example that contrasts a compromise with an integrative agreement concerns two girls arguing about an orange. They argue and argue, and nearly come to blows. Finally one of them proposes a compromise: 'Let's split it fifty-fifty between us.' She gets a knife and cuts the orange in half, and the other chooses one of the pieces. The first girl then takes her half and squeezes it for the juice. The other peels her half, and puts the rind into a cake, throwing the pulp away. A compromise of this kind is certainly fair to both parties but it misses out on the potential in the situation. A more integrative option is possible, namely that one girl gets all the peel, and the other gets all the pulp. That would be 100 per cent effective in achieving their goals.

## Achieving integrative agreements

How can integrative agreements be achieved? How can compromises that are so often available be avoided? When we have an example like the above, it seems obvious that we should worry about this issue because an integrative agreement makes both parties happier, and it satisfies our notions of 'the greatest good for the greatest number'. There are several additional arguments for trying to achieve an integrative agreement. One is that it is frequently not possible to reach agreement unless an integrative option can be discovered. This is true when the negotiators' limits are so high that no compromise is possible. Suppose that in the example shown in Figure 3.1, labor feels it must get $1.25 or higher and management feels it must get $0.85 or lower. In this case, no compromise is possible. The parties are not going to reach agreement unless some sort of integrative option can be discovered. It might seem in the case of money that there is no way to find an integrative agreement, that we are limited to this single dimension. But it is amazing what people can do with a little thought.

For example, management may find that by putting in a small amount of money, they can buy a health insurance plan that is very valuable to labor. Accordingly, the combination of, say, a \$0.75 raise plus an insurance plan might be an option that both parties can accept. This would be an integrative option in the sense of reconciling the two parties' strongest interests.

In addition, it is important to develop integrative agreements because they are likely to be more lasting. Compromises are more likely to become unraveled over time because they are typically closer to the parties' limits. Today an agreement on one week at the seashore and one week at the mountains might be acceptable, but tomorrow one party might think better of this arrangement, and discussion again ensues. But two weeks in the mountains and two weeks at the seashore might be so good for both parties that neither would be likely to reopen the issue.

Integrative agreements also strengthen relationships and improve the chances of finding subsequent integrative agreements. They make people more attuned to one another's interests and make the process more hopeful the next time around. It is my impression that many more integrative agreements are potentially available than most people realize. People tend to be fairly pessimistic about conflict. They easily gain the impression that they are engaged in a win-lose struggle. Consequently, they do not think in integrative terms, but integrative potential is nevertheless present in most situations. In our dealings with the Soviet Union, for example, if we were just willing to say, 'maybe there are ways in which we can both be satisfied', we would be off and moving toward a more hopeful world.

## A typology of integrative agreements

One of my objectives in this discussion is to present a typology of integrative agreements. A knowledge of this typology allows a negotiator or mediator to try one possible agreement after another until one works. I distinguish five types of agreements: (1) broadening the pie, (2) nonspecific compensation, (3) logrolling, (4) cost-cutting (specific compensation) and (5) bridging.

Integrative agreements can be developed by anyone associated with a controversy, including either of the parties involved or a third party, e.g., a mediator. I shall call a person who is trying to develop an integrative solution a 'problem solver'.

In addition to describing the various types of integrative agreements, I am also going to discuss certain refocusing questions that problem solvers need to ask in order to move toward achieving these agreements. Further, I shall discuss the kind of information that is required in order to achieve each kind of agreement. It is not always possible to achieve every kind of agreement, but asking the right questions and getting the right information helps.

The first type of the integrative agreements, *broadening the pie*, allows both parties to get exactly what they are asking for. The secret is to increase the size of the disputed resource. For example, the solution I mentioned in Figure 3.2

involves broadening the pie. If the husband and wife can get four weeks of vacation, two in the mountains and two at the seashore, they will no longer have a controversy. Such solutions are useful whenever the main issue is one of resources. Of course, if the husband hates the seashore and the wife hates the mountains, then the problem is not one of tight resources but of preferences and broadening the pie will not work. Another example comes from Follett (1940). Two milk companies fight as to who is going to unload first onto a loading platform. Milk spoils rapidly, so there is an advantage to being first. Then finally, somebody thinks of widening the platform so that both can unload the milk simultaneously—in effect, broadening the pie.

The refocusing questions here are: how can both get what they want? Does the conflict hinge on a resource shortage? How can this critical resource be expanded? Information requirements here are very, very slim. Broadening the pie requires no analysis of the interests underlying the demands that people are making. We simply accept their demands and ask how both sets of demands can be achieved.

The second type of integrative agreement, *nonspecific compensation*, occurs when one party gets what it wants and the other is paid for its losses, paid for its costs. The compensation is nonspecific in the sense that the payment is in some unrelated coin. For example, with regard to the couple and the mountains versus the seashore, suppose the husband proposes to the wife, 'If you go with me to the mountains, then you get a fur coat at Christmas'. Or the wife can propose to the husband, 'If you go with me to the seashore, then I will agree to go bowling with you on Tuesdays'. It is simply a matter of buying the other party off, compensating it for its expenses. It is perhaps the most common of all integrative agreements.

I have already provided an example of nonspecific compensation in the case of management and labor. Management gets what it wants with a $0.75 raise, but provides labor with compensation in the form of a hospitalization plan. The critical information needed here is the nature of some interest that is important for one of the parties. It is also important to know how much the party that does not achieve its wishes is 'hurting' from the other's proposal, so as to calibrate the extent of compensation required.

*Logrolling* is closely related to nonspecific compensation. This kind of solution is potentially useful whenever parties have a complex agenda involving many issues. In such circumstances, they often can find several issues that can be traded off against one another. For example, consider a negotiation between labor and management involving a number of issues including wages and hospitalization. If wages are more important to management and hospitalization more important to labor, then the parties have the potential for a horse-trade, for a logrolling agreement involving lower wages and higher hospitalization. The kinds of questions to ask in a situation like this are: what are party X's priorities among those issues—which are the most important issues, which are the next most important issues, which are the least important? What are party Y's priorities among these issues? If we can find out about priorities then we have the possibility of a trade-off. X can offer to give away things that are of low priority to it, and Y can offer to give away things that are of low priority to it. Logrolling solutions are possible whenever the parties have nonoverlapping (i.e., complementary) preferences among the issues under consideration.

I have developed a negotiation task with logrolling potential for use in laboratory situations (Pruitt, 1981; Pruitt and Carnevale, 1982). It is a buyer–seller task in which television sets and typewriters are under consideration. The buyer (a large department store) gets very good profits from the television sets and the seller (a manufacturer of small appliances) gets very good profits from the typewriters. If they can agree to a high price on the one and a low price on the other product, both parties will end up rather well. The information required in order to find such a trade-off is simply the nature of the two parties' priorities among the issues. It is not necessary to understand anything about underlying interests or hidden issues. One need not know why typewriters are important to one party and television sets are important to the other. We just simply have to know which issues are most important for each party.

This bring us to the last two types of integrative agreements, cost-cutting and bridging. These have much more complicated information requirements than the other three types because they require parties to analyze the interests, the values and goals underlying their overt demands. *Cost-cutting* (or specific compensation, which is the same sort of thing) involves one party getting what it wants and the other party's costs being reduced so that he or she does not worry about the first party's success. For example, to return to our case of the seashore and the mountains, let us assume that the wife interviews the husband and says, 'What do you not like about the seashore? Or what do you like about the mountains?' She does this to find out about the interests that underlie his position. Suppose the husband says, 'What I hate about the seashore is all those people, all that noise. The mountains, on the other hand, are really calm.' Now, if the wife can arrange to get a house at the seashore with a very quiet inner courtyard, then the husband might be willing to go to the seashore because he could sit in the courtyard while the wife goes out into the hustle and bustle. In this solution, the wife gets her way and the husband's costs are reduced to the point where he can agree to her proposal.

The refocusing questions that have to be asked in order to get at a cost-cutting solution are, in the first instance: what bothers you about my proposal? What is it that you like about your own, that you have to give up in going over to mine? And then, how can these costs be prevented or how can these costs be repaid?

The information requirements for cost-cutting are rather formidable because it is usually necessary to have very specific information about just what interests underlie one party's proposals. It is often not easy to get that kind of information. For one thing, people often do not know exactly why they feel as they do. The husband in our example may know full well that he does not like the seashore and that he likes the mountains, but he may not be at all clear why he has these preferences.

Quite often our preferences, our demands on other people, are based simply on our past raw experiences. The husband has been to the seashore and he did not like it. He has been to the mountains and he did like it. He cannot articulate what the reasons are. It is amazing how often this is the case. Research in labor–management negotiations (Balke, Hammond and Meyer, 1973) provides examples of people who were unable to say why they were putting forward a particular proposal, even though they felt very strongly about it. Similarly, it may be hard for one party to articulate what it is that it likes or dislikes about the other's proposal. In such cases, it is easier to broaden the pie, or for one party to compensate the other in a nonspecific way, than to engage in cost-cutting. But through careful interviewing, it may still be possible to come up with a decent understanding of underlying interests.

Also people are sometimes afraid to reveal the nature of their true interests. When we reveal something about ourselves, about our motives or values, we may be giving other people a handle on ourselves. They may learn how to threaten us or may become capable of committing themselves to a position that barely satisfies our limit. For this reason, then, we may be rather reluctant to say just what it is that we want. Consequently, others may find it difficult to figure out how to cut our costs.

The fifth kind of integrative agreement, *bridging*, usually requires analysis of both parties' interests. The needs, values and perceived costs underlying their demands are first assessed, and then a new alternative is identified that satisfies both sets of interests. Bridging is not like broadening the pie, where attempts are made to satisfy the two parties' demands. It is rather a matter of satisfying the interests that produce the demands. Let us return again to our case of the mountains and the seashore. The problem solver in this situation—be it husband, wife or a person who is trying to mediate—might find out that what the husband likes about the mountains is fishing, and what the wife likes about the seashore is that she can relax on a sandy beach and go swimming. If these constitute the pair of interests underlying the overt preferences, then it might be possible to find an island resort in which there is good fishing and also a lovely beach with excellent swimming and sunning facilities. Such a solution might very well be far better than a compromise.

A possible bridging solution for the case of the professor and the head of department has already been outlined. The professor wants a semester off. Somebody, perhaps a colleague, interviews him and concludes that he wants this benefit in order to have time to write a book. The head, on the other hand, is mainly concerned that the professor not drop out of a sensitive committee assignment. In this case, a bridging proposal might be that the professor takes time off but comes into the office a few hours per week to attend the committee meetings.

The process of developing a bridging proposal often goes through several stages. The first stage involves seeking information about the goals the parties are after and what costs they are trying to avoid. Then questions are raised about how these goals can be achieved and these costs avoided on both sides. The problem-solver can work with that agenda for a while, but suppose success is not forthcoming. What then? The second stage then would be to ask about the nature of the interests underlying these interests. What are the goals, values and perceived costs underlying those already revealed? If there is no solution at this level, a tertiary level can be examined, and so on until a bridging solution is developed.

The point is to examine the interests underlying the interests to a depth that allows development of a bridge between the parties. For instance, Figure 3.6 exhibits the interest tree for a son who wants to buy a motorcycle and a set of values espoused by his father who does not want him to do so. The opening

|  | Son | Father |
|---|---|---|
| **Initial Positions:** | Motorcycle | No motorcycle |
| **Interest Level I:** | Noise | No noise |
| **Interest Level II:** | Attention in the neighborhood | Live unobtrusively |
| **Interest Level III:** | Self-Esteem | OK |

**Figure 3.6** An interest tree

situation is shown in the top row. There is a clear-cut divergence of interest here because there are only two options under discussion. The son wants the motorcycle and the father does not. Let us assume that the mother, acting as mediator, interviews both of them. She asks her son, 'Why do you want the motorcycle?' He says, 'I love noise'. So she asks her husband, 'Why don't you want him to have a motorcycle?' He says, 'I hate noise'. This is not going to work; there is no way of integrating these positions.

Again the mother interviews the boy. She asks, 'Why do you like noise?' He says, 'I want to get attention in the neighborhood. I want to be a big man here. People pay no attention to me.' But the boy's father is still not impressed. He prefers to live a private life in which he does not attract attention. Consequently, there is no solution at this level either.

Now the mother digs deeper and finds that the boy's root interest is self-esteem, a sense of accomplishment, of being somebody. At this level, there are many possible solutions that will not be opposed by the father e.g., going out for basketball at school.

In short, a bridging solution is often developed by moving down one or both parties' interest tree(s) until a level is found at which there is no incompatibility between their preferences. If this procedure fails and no solution comes up, then the problem solver must get one or both parties to relax some of their interests. This means encouraging them to find priorities among their goals and values and then trying to satisfy those that are most important.

Returning to the case of the seashore and the mountains, perhaps the problem solver determines that the husband wants fishing, hunting and mountain vistas, and that the wife wants sunning, swimming and the sea air. A search for priorities might reveal that mountain vistas are least important for the husband and the sea air least important for the wife. It may then be possible to find a resort that satisfies the remaining values—hunting, fishing, sunning, and swimming. If not, additional prioritizing will be in order.

We cannot rule out compromise as a basis for solution in such cases. It may be necessary for our married couple to accept a week at the seashore and a week in the mountains. But they should try first to find an integrative solution because this will benefit them both more and only turn to compromise as a last resort. Unfortunately, compromise is often the first rather than the last resort in such discussions.

Sometimes, when the problem solver moves down an interest tree, he or she comes upon a dichotomy that appears more opposed than it really is. On careful analysis, the opposition disappears. Examples of such dichotomies can be seen in Figure 3.7, which is based on Fisher and Ury (1981). It is worth studying this list because if one knows about these contrasts beforehand, they can be more easily recognized.

An example of the appearance-substance dichotomy can be found in a controversy that Kissinger mediated in the Middle East after the 1973 war between Israel and Egypt (Golan, 1976). Israel had surrounded the Egyptian Army, and negotiations were under way about control of a road on which this army relied for food and supplies. It was important to the Israelis that no arms or new recruits go down this road. Against this background, Israel proposed that it station troops along the road to man check-points so that all vehicles coming down the road could be searched. Egypt refused, and the two sides seemed to be at loggerheads. Kissinger then came in, talked to both parties, and concluded that the controversy was largely a matter of appearance versus substance. What the Israelis wanted was a search of the vehicles, that was substance. What Sadat (Egypt's president) wanted was the appearance, in the eyes of the news media, that the road was in Egyptian or neutral hands.

Accordingly, Kissinger proposed that Israeli soldiers should be taken off the road and that the check-points be manned by UN soldiers, who were strictly instructed not to allow any military material to get through. This solution was satisfactory to both parties: it satisfied Israeli substantive concerns and Sadat's concern with appearances.

Another dichotomy is immediate versus delayed. This played a role in a controversy in the town where I work, Buffalo, New York. The disputants were motormen and the bus company. The motormen wanted a large raise and the company would not allow it. The mayor came in and mediated the case. He looked at some of the interests underlying the two positions and discovered that the company was refusing to give the raise because it did not have sufficient money that year, a temporary situation. Given that the motormen's main concern was to set a precedent so that they would have the raise in the future, the mayor proposed that the motormen get part of their raise that year and the remaining part the following year, in a two-year contract. That way, the company could pay what

| | | |
|---|---|---|
| Appearance | vs. | Substance |
| Immediate | vs. | Delayed |
| Precedent | vs. | A particular case |
| Economic | vs. | Political |
| Internal | vs. | External |
| Issues | vs. | Relationships |
| Progress | vs. | Respect for tradition |
| Symbolic | vs. | Practical |
| Politics | vs. | Welfare |

**Figure 3.7** Dichotomies which are not really contrary to each other

they were immediately able to pay and the union would have the guarantee of the full raise in perpetuity thereafter.

Another dichotomy is encountered when the problem solver discovers that one party is concerned about precedent while the other wants to solve a particular case. A possible formula in such a situation is for one party to agree to the other's request in the particular case at hand but for this to be seen as an exception that does not set a precedent for the future.

What I have just done is listed five kinds of integrative agreements, and discussed the procedures that might be used in arriving at them. I want now to take some time to discuss three possible approaches to negotiation: the win-lose, lose-win and win-win approaches.

## Approaches to negotiation

The win-lose approach is when a party engages in positional bargaining. That party endorses a forward demand and stands firm on this demand, using competitive tactics to get its way, such as threats and positional commitments. Win-lose bargaining is the best known kind; it is the common stereotype of negotiation. A win-lose approach can sometimes lead to agreement. But it more often encourages win-lose behavior on the other side, producing a stalemate and failure to reach agreement.

Furthermore, a win-lose stance makes it difficult to move toward problem solving i.e., toward integrative agreements. The parties become rigid with respect to their positions, making it difficult to analyze the interests underlying those positions.

The lose-win orientation is one in which a party tries to serve the other party's needs. This approach often results from a fear of conflict and produces an aspiration collapse. Sometimes both sides have a lose-win orientation, and aspirations collapse simultaneously. In this case, the parties will end up with a compromise.

The win-win or problem-solving approach involves efforts to find an integrative solution. A useful guideline for a disputant who takes this approach is to be firm yet flexible and conciliatory. To be firm means that the party is concerned about its own interests, keeping its aspirations high and not conceding easily on its basic concerns. And yet it is also necessary to be flexible with regard to the means for achieving these interests, being willing to experiment with various ways for achieving them. Being conciliatory means being concerned about the other party's interests.

A firm but flexible and conciliatory stance is likely to result in the kind of creative thinking that is needed to find an integrative solution. But that is not the only reason for adopting it. Another, and perhaps equally important, rationale is that the adoption of such a policy is likely to wean the other party over to a win-win orientation as well. I once saw a license-plate that said, 'Courtesy is catching'. I would argue that problem solving is catching as well. The point is that we need to wean the other party away from a win-lose approach. If we are firm about our major interests and make clear that we cannot be budged from them, then the other party will not be so hopeful about forcing us to concede.

Consequently, a win-lose approach will not look so good to that party. On the other hand, if we show a lot of flexibility and indicate a concern about the other party's interests, we give the other an incentive for taking a win-win approach. The other sees the possibility that problem solving will pay off, that a satisfactory solution will emerge from cooperation. In technical terms, it strengthens the perceived integrative potential (Pruitt, 1983) for the other.

In summary, I am arguing that a win-win approach is good not only for developing integrative solutions but also because it encourages the other party to take the same approach.

## Bibliography

Balke, W.M., K.R. Hammond and G.D. Meyer (1973), 'An Alternate Approach to Labor–Management Relations', *Administrative Science Quarterly*, **18**, pp. 311–27.

Fisher, R. and W. Ury (1981), *Getting to Yes: Negotiating Agreement Without Giving In*, Boston, Houghton Mifflin.

Follett, M.P. (1940), 'Constructive Conflict' in *Dynamic Administration: The Collected Papers of Mary Parker Follett*, H.C. Metcalf and L. Urwick (eds), New York, Harper.

Golan, M. (1976), *The Secret Conversations of Henry Kissinger*, New York, Quadrangle.

Pruitt, D.G. (1981), *Negotiation Behavior*, New York, Academic Press.

Pruitt, D.G. (1983), 'Strategic Choice in Negotiation', *American Behavioral Scientist*, **27**, pp. 167–94.

Pruitt, D.G. and P.J.D. Carnevale (1982), 'The Development of Integrative Agreements' in *Cooperation and Helping Behavior*, V.J. Derlega and J. Grzelak (eds), New York, Academic Press.

# 3(ii) Trends toward alternative dispute resolution

*Larry Ray*

Over the past several years I have participated in or observed hundreds of mediations which might readily be classified into the categories designated by Dean Pruitt. For instance, not long ago I was in Chicago at the Neighborhood Justice Center, observing a mediation session between a sixteen-year-old boy and a thirty-year-old man. The conflict involved a car, the boy thinking that the man had transferred ownership of the car to him. Consequently, the boy had taken the car, started to fix it up and put a few new parts in it when the police apprehended him. At that point, he found out that the transfer evidently had not been completed. During the mediation session the boy pursued the return of some of the parts he had put in the car. At the end the man agreed to pay the boy to finish fixing the car and also for the parts. This was a creative solution as both of them seemingly left happier than when they arrived.

A case occurred at a local mediation center in northern California involving a dispute between a painter and an elderly woman. The woman's husband had just died, and she was trying to cope, for the first time, with all the difficulties associated with home ownership. In this instance, she had had the house painted and subsequently was absolutely certain that she had been victimized by the painter. She indicated that she had wanted her home painted a certain shade of beige, but that he had painted it using differing shades on various sides of the building. The painter insisted that this was not the case. What we did at the mediation session was to visit the home and walk around. For my part I could see no difference in the coloring on the different sides of the house. At the end of that session the painter had not agreed to repaint any of the sides of the house. Instead he suggested that her spouting needed to be replaced; and in coming to some type of agreement, he agreed to repair all the spouting. Again, both parties apparently were a lot happier than before.

In some contrast to that situation was a mediation session I attended in New York City. In that case, a woman had brought an assault charge against her boyfriend. Evidently, they had been living together for several years and had separated. There seemed to be some property disagreements as well as some type of aggressive contact during the final split-up. Five minutes into the mediation session, the woman completely broke down and revealed that she was pregnant. This reduced the significance of all the other issues, the property, and so on, and suddenly her boyfriend wanted her to move back in and begin the relationship all over again.

All the above mediation sessions can be looked at in terms of the categories suggested by Dean Pruitt. If all users of mediation programs, including mediators themselves, would take the time to understand these categories, the mediation process might well be improved. Indeed, the whole process of public education is, I think, one of the major problem areas to have been uncovered by most of the mediation programs throughout the United States. For example, there is the issue of compromise. During the four years I worked in the Prosecutor's Office in Columbus, Ohio, a number of people would come into the office each day to file what they perceived to be a criminal charge. In each case we would explain that they had the option of mediation, which was basically voluntary. Usually their response was, 'Are you expecting me to compromise?' Compromise did have negative overtones for most of the individuals—if mediation involved compromising, then they wanted nothing to do with it. Most of these people, as they came through the Prosecutor's Office, reflected the average citizen's approach to problem solving. They usually underestimated their own problem-solving skills, but overestimated those of others. Hence, when individuals came into the Prosecutor's Office, they thought that we could achieve instant results. When we explained the system to them, that it was not how it was portrayed on television, and it was not how it was portrayed in the newspaper, then they began to operate on a more realistic basis.

The American Bar Association (ABA) has created the Special Committee on Dispute Resolution (formerly the Special Committee on Alternative Means of Dispute Resolution, and earlier the Special Committee on Resolution of Minor Disputes). The Committee has existed since 1976, largely at a rather low-key level. It was based initially in Miami and then subsequently moved to Washington, DC. The overall goal of the Committee is to promote alternative means of dispute resolution in any way we can, either within or outside the legal system. In view of our budget our scope is necessarily limited. We began with three basic activities. One is to run a clearing house for information. In this regard, we are trying to obtain information on every ongoing alternative dispute resolution program as well as listings of different organizations and individuals who express an interest in such information. In this way, for example, if someone wants to start a juvenile mediation program, they can call us and we can then indicate to them how many juvenile mediation programs we know of throughout the country. We can provide them with names and addresses and help them out in that manner. Our second area of concern is publications: we produce a quarterly newsletter as well as a directory (e.g. 1981, 1986-7) listing a number of minor dispute mediation programs and other publications. Third, we are trying to provide technical assistance, on-site or off-site.

Basically the Committee started by waiting in the office until contacted by others and then responding. But then the ABA president David Brink made alternative dispute resolution his number-one priority, as a result of which there has been solid funding for the Committee. Hence, we can concentrate on other things. It has also resulted in more publicity. In fact, in the April 1982 issue of the *ABA Journal*, the 'President's Page' was devoted to alternative dispute resolution. There was also Chief Justice Warren Burger's state of the judiciary speech to the ABA in January 1982 in Chicago which revolved around alternative means of dispute resolution (Burger, 1982).

Accordingly, it does indeed seem that within the legal system, among the heads of the legal system, and throughout the country in general, there is an alternative dispute resolution movement. Purely in terms of minor dispute resolution programs, in 1971 there were about three neighborhood-type justice or mediation centers; in 1977 there were twenty or thirty; in Spring 1982 there were some 180 and in the Summer of 1986, there were approximately 350 of these centers.

Among some of the leaders of the neighborhood justice and community mediation centers, I sense a wistful looking back to the days when justices of the peace or other community leaders helped to resolve these disputes, but I hope that we are looking ahead rather than looking back, looking ahead to the point of trying to have the parties themselves assume these methods of resolving disputes.

Working within the legal system, it did not come as a surprise to me that the ABA created the Committee because lawyers involved in plea-bargaining and/or in settling cases out of court have already been doing alternative dispute resolution, even if the procedures were not being identified as such. They may not be using certain terms familiar to some of us, but they are nevertheless using the alternative approaches. In fact, the worst thing we can do, is go into the community and say that we have designed or created a new kind of mediation. Invariably, there would be hundreds of social workers, psychologists, lawyers, political leaders and the police saying, 'well, we are already doing that'. And to some degree that would probably be true.

I am frequently asked why the ABA is involved in alternative dispute resolution. In the Columbus, Ohio mediation program, we rarely encountered any resistance from attorneys; all the judges and all the attorneys were basically in favor of it. But as I have gone about the country, speaking at different bar associations, and helping them to get programs, I have encountered, much to my surprise, some resistance. For instance, when a mediation program was started in Waterbury, Connecticut, I went before the bar and one of the first questions they asked about the director was, 'Is he an attorney?' This seemed to me to have no relevance at all. And even though I was there giving support to the ABA, I was nevertheless viewed as an outsider. I was seen as a part of 'this ABA', which comes up with a lot of different policies which Waterbury attorneys do not necessarily have to obey.

On the other hand I have seen bar associations playing major if not leading roles in establishing alternative dispute resolution programs. The best example of this may be the Houston Bar Association which basically started the Houston Neighborhood Justice Center. Subsequently, the Texas bar promoted legislation to make available solid funding for community mediation programs throughout the state of Texas. Indeed, although I have experienced some resistance, in most cases bar associations are supportive of alternative dispute settlement.

I think they are in favor because like the ABA, they have an investment within the legal system; they want to see the legal system flow and flow well. According to interviews and talks with many people who have been a part of the legal system, it is not flowing that well. And apparently mediation, arbitration and other types of alternative programs do indeed help the system to flow a little better.

## Bibliography

Brink, D.R. (1982), 'President's Page: Improving Our Justice System Through Alternatives', *American Bar Association Journal*, **68**, April, p. 384.

Burger, Chief Justice W.E. (1982), 'Isn't There A Better Way?' Address to the ABA Midyear Meetings, Chicago, 24 January in *American Bar Association Journal*, **68**, March, pp. 274–7.

*Dispute Resolution Program Directory, 1981*, Washington, DC, ABA Special Committee on Alternative Means of Dispute Resolution.

*Dispute Resolution Program Directory, 1986–1987*, Washington, DC, ABA Special Committee on Dispute Resolution.

*Dispute Resolution: Quarterly Information Update of the Special Committee on Dispute Resolution*, Washington, DC, ABA Special Committee on Dispute Resolution.

# 3(iii) Deterrence and tension reduction

*Ralph K. White*

The basic concepts which can be applied in conflict management and problem solving are useful in many different areas, for example in husband-wife relationships; in labor-management disputes; in any relationship between a subordinate and a boss; in neighborhood justice situations; in relationships between the Third World and our Western countries and between parents and children. But incomparably more important than any of these, in my judgement, is the application of these concepts to the prevention of the extinction of the human species.

The *New Yorker* published a series of three articles in February 1982 by Jonathan Schell, articles which were subsequently published as the book, *The Fate of the Earth*. Schell's thesis—and it sounds trite but the way he presents it is not trite at all—is that nuclear war could in a matter of minutes extinguish not only most of the human race but most of all living things, or at least start them on an irrevocable downward path. I had never before felt so deeply the urgency of preventing the human race from an extinction that could occur in moments and would be nearly total. Schell represents this eloquently, fervently but very solidly with all of the scientific information that he has at his fingertips to back it up. For example, the title of the first of the three articles is 'A Republic of Insects and Grass.' His thesis is that the resistance to death by radiation is much higher among insects and plants than, let us say, among birds or mammals, including, of course, man. We are one of the most vulnerable species and if a nuclear attack ever took place, the most evolved parts of the ecosphere—trees, flowers, birds, mammals and of course people—would disappear sooner or later, and probably sooner.

This raises some very interesting questions that I, for one, had not previously confronted. One is the ethical problem. For example, do we have a right to continue to avoid renouncing any first use of nuclear weapons? We Americans have not even done that: we have not even said that we would not be the first to use nuclear weapons. This is the most obvious initial step, I think, in preventing nuclear war. Do we have the right not to take that obvious initial step, considering that it is not just we who might conceivably, at some future time, have to choose between being 'red or dead'? This is, of course, a very misleading way to put the formula. In any case, it is not just we who now have to choose, that is, to choose between taking some remote chance of becoming 'red' and a near certain chance of being dead. For, in the latter case, it would not only be we who are dead, but generations, a thousand generations of human beings which might exist after us but would not, if we made that choice. Do we have the right to inflict death not only on all future generations, but also on the 88 percent of the world that is neither in the Soviet Union nor in the United States? Is it our right to inflict this kind of total extinction on the forthcoming generations and most of the human race that lives today?

This sounds as if there were some simple solution and I am not going to say that there is a simple solution. It is as complicated as all of Dean Pruitt's diagrams, and probably a good deal more so. That is what I want to discuss here, as a matter of fact. It seems to me that if people have not been motivated to try to solve this problem using all the conceptual tools that Dean Pruitt and others have discussed, then they should read Jonathan Schell (1982).

Do these conceptual tools apply to the international level? There are some very encouraging signs. One is that all five of the scholars I can think of who have done the best work in this field of integrative agreements or integrative problem solving have been interested in applying their work to the international level and have made a good deal of progress in applying it to that level. Dean Pruitt is one of them. His book, *Negotiation Behavior* (1981), tells a great deal more about the application of his work to international affairs than he has indicated here in his presentation. Another is Bryant Wedge who has done a great deal on the international level (for example, 1970, 1971, 1974). There is also Roger Fisher, co-author (with William Ury) of *Getting to Yes: Negotiating Agreement Without Giving In* (1981), and his answers are very much like those of Dean Pruitt and Bryant Wedge. The very title of this book, not just the main title but also the sub-title, gives the impression of toughness combined with reasonableness—perhaps strength but a nonthreatening strength—that Roger Fisher and many others are interested in.

A fourth outstanding figure in this field, in my judgement, is Robert Jervis. Though he has not directly contributed to reasonableness on the international level as Fisher has, he has analyzed the sources of misperception—national misperception—in his book, *Perception and Misperception in International Politics* (1976). It is the most complicated, and the most challenging of any of the books I have seen even more so than Dean Pruitt's book. But these are the two scholars whom I would put at the top as proof that this is not just a field for dillettantes or people who respond viscerally instead of analytically. This is a field that has developed by now a very complicated set of facts—relevant facts—and integrative theory. Jervis is outstanding because the development of creative solutions is a problem of perception on both sides, and that is his specialty. Then there is Morton Deutsch whose book, *The Resolution of Conflict: Constructive and Destructive Processes* (1973), is a real landmark, a real masterpiece.

These five all agree essentially with the principles we have been presented with here. They say it in different words. For example, Dean Pruitt talks about firmness and flexibility or firmness and concilation, the tough side and the reasonable side. Roger Fisher talks about negotiating agreement, which is the reasonable side, but without giving in, which is the tough side. Jervis presents two models of interaction between nations—what he calls the deterrence model and the spiral model. The deterrence model enjoins toughness; we should be strong enough and firm enough so the other party cannot walk all over us. The spiral model is, in a way, the opposite. It is the old idea of a conflict spiral. If one side is unreasonable and arms more than it should, then the other side gets less reasonable and arms more than it should. The process goes back and forth until an explosion, perhaps a tremendous war, ensues. What Jervis does is not to opt for one or the other anymore than Pruitt or Wedge or Fisher do. He analyzes, in great detail, under what circumstances deterrence is more important and more realistic, and under what circumstances the danger of a spiral is a more important consideration.

Deutsch's terms are similar. He uses the term deterrence for the threatening side of the picture and the term nonpunitive strategy for the reasonable, nonthreatening side. He presents data that indicate that the nonpunitive strategy in laboratory games is more often effective in arriving at a solution that helps both sides—a win-win solution. With regard to what he calls the deterrent strategy, I think a better term would be punitive deterrence. We need deterrence, but not the punitive kind, not the kind that says, 'if you hurt me, I will hurt you more. And I am strong enough to do it.' There are nonthreatening kinds of strength that imply, 'if you attack me, then you will be in trouble. But if you do not attack me, then you will not be in trouble at all'—reassurance along with deterrence.

How does all this apply at present, given the philosophy of the Reagan Administration? I would like to present my terms and some concrete examples, not as firm, concrete answers—knowing exactly when to emphasize deterrence and when to emphasize the more conciliatory, reassuring side of national policy—but, given the urgency and the danger of the extinction of the human species, as food for thought.

My terms are deterrence and tension reduction. In international affairs, tension reduction is part of a gradual process, not a single agreement that we can arrive at tomorrow or next year. It is a long, continuous process of gradual reduction of tension between the opposing sides in an acute conflict, such as the conflict between the United States and the Soviet Union, or the conflict between the Arabs and the Israelis. How can we, over the years, gradually reduce tension, along with maintaining enough deterrence to put in the mind of our opponent a wholesome fear of the costs he would incur if he attacked us?

With regard to deterrence and tension reduction, there are a few things to think about. Though these are just my ideas, I believe they represent something of a consensus among people who have studied these problems most, in detail. Under *prudent* deterrence, there are three items. There is, first of all, a need for a relatively invulnerable, nuclear second-strike capability, so that an opponent will not be tempted to make a first-strike against us. The first strike is the terrible humanity-extinguishing thing that we want to deter. If we can have a relatively invulnerable second-strike capability so that the opponent knows that his cities will be devastated if he does that kind of thing to us first, then we will have made progress. Secondly, there should be a concentration on defensive weapons, when such is possible. The long-range bomber is not a defensive weapon. Fighter planes that may knock down the bomber before it gets to its target are a defensive weapon. Minefields are an essentially defensive weapon and it is good that Western Europe have many of these to deter the Soviet Union from attacking. Antitank weapons, of which we have a great many in Western Europe, fortunately, are essentially a defensive weapon. Thirdly there is a need for collective deterrence via a world federation. This is what the World Federalists have been talking about all along as the only basic solution. According to them, everybody who does not want war can band together to deter the one country that might want it.

But if measures of this sort, that is, those designed to promote deterrence, are not combined with tension reduction, then they are likely to be worse than useless. They promote war, they are all in the field of frightening the opponent, and fear alone is not a solid basis for peace. Unless they are combined with tension reduction, they will not be effective.

Accordingly, I have come up with three possible, important forms of tension reduction which we can pursue right now, the Reagan Administration permitting. The first is something which I have already mentioned—the renunciation and denunciation of any first use of nuclear weapons, including tactical and theatre nuclear forces (TNF). We are now, more or less, trying to force TNF on Western Europe. It seems to me that we should totally renounce the first use of *even* tactical weapons. If we do not, the implication is that if there were a clear-cut Soviet (conventional) attack on Western Europe, which I do not think they have any intention of launching, the danger in our using tactical nuclear weapons in response, as we are apparently planning to do, is that the other side is also perfectly capable of using tactical nuclear weapons. However, there is no clear line here. Once the firebreak between non-nuclear and nuclear weapons is crossed, there is no clear way to stop until we arrive at the destruction and extinction of the human species.

Secondly, under tension reduction, and there is likely to be plenty of controversy on this, there should be a drastic reduction of nuclear weapons and the means of their delivery: the various kinds of missiles (for example, Pershing II and cruise missiles), bombers, etc. A drastic reduction of nuclear weapons and the means of their delivery, by agreement with the Soviet Union if possible, but unilaterally if necessary. It is that important. A drastic reduction down to the level required for an adequate second-strike capability. This means primarily that submarines should be retained. Submarines are the hardest systems to destroy in a first-strike.

Finally, number three: we should scrupulously avoid intervening in the affairs of any other country, at least when there has been no clear, unambiguous aggression by the forces of the major opponent. I am not saying that Chamberlain was right to appease Hitler at Munich. There are times when we have to stand up and fight, when aggression is clear, but not when it is ambiguous as it was in Vietnam. If we could set that plainly as one of our cardinal principles, I do not think that the Soviet Union would have the kind of paranoid fear of the United States that I think they currently have.

## Bibliography

Deutsch, M. (1973), *The Resolution of Conflict: Constructive and Destructive Processes*, New Haven, Yale University Press.

Fisher, R. and W. Ury (1981), *Getting to Yes: Negotiating Agreement Without Giving In*, Boston, Houghton Mifflin.

Jervis, R. (1976), *Perception and Misperception in International Politics*, Princeton, Princeton University Press.

Pruitt, D.G. (1981), *Negotiation Behavior*, New York, Academic Press.

Schell, J. (1982), *The Fate of the Earth*, New York, Knopf.

Wedge, B. (1970), 'Communication Analysis and Comprehensive Diplomacy', *Social Education*, **XXXIV**, no. 1, pp 19–27.

Wedge, B. (1971), 'A Psychiatric Model for Intercession in Violent Intergroup Conflict', *Australian and New Zealand Journal of Psychiatry*, 5, pp. 84–100. Revised for *The Journal of Applied Behaviorial Science,* 7, no. 6, pp. 733–61.

Wedge, B. (1974), 'Citizen Conciliation: A Program for National and International Conflict Resolution', in *Social Psychiatry*, I, J.H. Masserman and J.J. Schwab (eds.), New York, Grune & Stratton.

# 4(i)  A model for negotiation and mediation*

*Thomas Colosi*

Editors' note
* This is a slightly altered version of Thomas Colosi's 'A Model for Negotiation and Mediation', which appears in *International Negotiation: Art and Science*, edited by Diane B. Bendahmane and John W. McDonald, Jr., Washington, DC, the Foreign Service Institute, Center for the Study of Foreign Affairs, US Department of State, 1984. We have included it here, with the permission of the author and publisher, because it parallels closely his presentation during the lecture series which gave rise to the present volume.

There is a great deal of negotiating going on domestically and internationally, and those who know how to negotiate well are usually richly rewarded. However, we still do not teach the principles, theory, process and skills of negotiation in our society. We do not teach it in our secondary schools or schools of government. Our business and law schools are just beginning to teach the subject in a meaningful way.

Although we do not teach negotiation with any uniformity, practitioners such as those contributing to this book provide various and sundry groups with education and training in the negotiation process. For example, in addition to the Foreign Service Institute, I work with the American Society of Association Executives, a very prestigious group of people who manage a range of associations, from those that distribute medical supplies to those that make truck vehicle bodies. It is the private sector personified. Large law firms also have expressed needs for training in negotiation. I have trained forty-five attorneys from a firm in Washington, DC, to give them a better idea about the arts and skills of negotiation. Similarly those involved in school desegregation disputes, native American land takeovers, land use or environmental disputes, prison disputes and so on are beginning to note a greater need for training in negotiation.

The model for training these groups, which I am about to describe, was developed through much trial and error. As a practitioner, I believe that that is probably the approach I am most comfortable with. The model now used links the articulated need for training and the subtle and complex world of negotiation.

## Common confusions about the negotiation process

The process of negotiation often is confused with other decision-making processes such as litigation. Many people have a perception of how the litigation process works, and they conduct themselves in the negotiating process as they believe people should conduct themselves in the litigation process. As a result, they are far too adversarial and argumentative, thereby creating unnecessary problems for themselves.

A second confusion is the belief that the essence of negotiation is extremely complex when in reality it is quite simple and very human. The negotiation process provides the parties or disputants an opportunity to exchange promises and commitments through which they will resolve their differences and reach an agreement. Trust is the key to the success of any negotiation. Groups and individuals will not exchange promises or commitments that they really expect to see fulfilled with groups or individuals that they do not trust. When trust is low, communication is low. When communication is low, mutual education cannot take place, and education is the most constructive thing that can take place in any negotiation.

The third confusion is the idea that negotiation is a simple process. It is generally assumed that if you are not the spokesperson, you take a few notes, make a few comments, caucus, and the negotiations somehow go forward. The model I have developed helps communicate some of the concepts, and shows the complexity of the negotiating process. Here the model is somewhat simplified for the sake of clarity. Over the years (and with several modifications), it has shown itself to be valuable in transmitting both the fundamental and some of the more complex elements of the processes of negotiation and mediation. This model has been expanded successfully from bilateral relationships (commercial transactions, labor–management relationships) to trilateral relationships (as in prisons and partnerships with three principals) to multilateral relationships (environmental, community and international disputes) and expanded further to include various neutral third-party involvement such as conciliation, mediation, fact finding and arbitration.

## The conventional perception of bilateral negotiation

Negotiations are typically depicted as involving one entity sitting across a bargaining table from a second. One side presents its demands or proposals to the other, and a discussion or debate follows. Counterproposals and compromises are offered. When the offers are eventually accepted on both sides of the table, the dispute is settled and an agreement is signed.

Within this 'horizontal bargaining ' model, all the interesting and relevant action is presumed to occur back and forth between the two sides. The model also

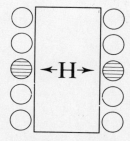

**Figure 4.1.** Horizontal (H) bargaining

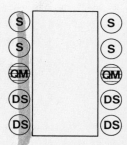

**Figure 4.2.** The three components of negotiating teams: stabilizers (S), destabilizers (DS), and quasi-mediators (QM)

assumes that both sides are monolithic, even if represented by bargaining teams. The way in which the participants are billed—labor versus management, prisoners versus guards, environmentalists versus industry, nation versus nation—assumes that all team members share a common goal, common objectives and the same set of demands, agree on a strategy for handling the opposition and have come to the table with equal enthusiasm for the negotiating process.

Unfortunately the conventional model of negotiation obscures much of the richness and complexity of the bargaining process. In actual practice, bargaining teams are seldom monolithic. Team members often have conflicting goals, strategies, objectives, tactics, perceptions, assumptions and values. In order to have an effective negotiation, some sort of consensus must develop internally before agreement can be reached with the opposite team, which should be going through the same consensus-building process.

### Stabilizers, destabilizers and quasi-mediators

Within each team, members usually hold quite different attitudes. Some want to settle at any cost. They may be called 'stabilizers'. They seek agreement with the other side to avoid the disruptive consequences of nonsettlement. Depending on the context of the case, stabilizers see nonsettlement as reverting to lengthy, expensive or disruptive alternatives such as litigation, strikes, demonstrations, riots and wars. These people usually understand negotiation to be a stabilizing process and bring others to the negotiation table in the hope that nonsettlement could be avoided. A second general type, the 'destabilizers', do not particularly like the negotiation process. Destabilizers tend to disagree with most of the proposals of their own team and all of the counterproposals of the other side. They would rather see the dispute settled by adjudication or by disruption through raw contests of will and power than by compromise on a given position. The terms that the destabilizers would accept are far more stringent than those acceptable to the stabilizers. In the middle on each team there is a third type, the 'quasi-mediators', who play several roles. They are usually spokespersons charged with responsibility for the success of the effort. To those sitting across the table they may simply look like other negotiators, but within their own team they often act as mediators between the faction of stabilizers and the faction of destabilizers.

### Horizontal, internal and vertical negotiations

Relatively little true negotiating goes on horizontally across the table. Instead, speeches are made, symbols and platitudes are thrown out, emotions are displayed and some signaling occurs. If the communication is healthy, the two teams use the contact time constructively to educate each other on each other's position and rationale across the table. Except for this opportunity to educate and to learn, however, all of this may be less important than the activity going on internally within the negotiation team.

A team is rarely independent of a larger constituency. It is at the negotiating table because it has been sent there to accomplish something. In the context of private sector labor negotiation, for example, management's vertical hierarchy is the company's leadership; for the union's bargaining committee, it is the international union and, usually, ultimately the membership who must vote to decide on a proposed contract. There are almost always important negotiations that take place between a team and its vertical hierarchy at one point or another in the negotiation process.

The negotiating team members are continually being re-educated through the horizontal negotiations occurring at or near the negotiating table. Thus, they are frequently far more advanced in their thinking than are their constituents or the final decision-makers back home in the vertical hierarchy. The resulting gap can be a dangerous trap for all concerned. Part of the art and skill of being a negotiator is recognizing how far from the constituents the bargaining team has moved. Negotiators must also know when and how to go back to educate their own constituents. In the same way, spokespersons or quasi-mediators must continually recognize just how far they are or have moved from the stabilizers and destabilizers on their own team. They must not get so far ahead of the parade that they can no longer hear the music.

Sometimes the vertical hierarchy will tell negotiators what they should achieve at the negotiating table, but after several sessions with the other side the negotiators may come to believe that they simply cannot deliver what was asked. It is within this context that negotiation between the team and its own vertical hierarchy takes place.

## Internal team negotiations

Resolution of differences between the stabilizers and destabilizers is a prerequisite for effective negotiation with the other side, as well as for reaching accommodation with the teams's own vertical hierarchy. When a team is considering making an offer, for example, the stabilizers will probably want to present a generous package while the destabilizers may not want to offer anything. The quasi-mediator must begin to explore with the stabilizers why the concessions might be excessive and probably unacceptable to the team's vertical hierarchy and to discuss with the destabilizers why the proposal may be good and why the team should not be so rigid, since the costs of nonsettlement may be unacceptable. Much like a neutral third-party mediator, the quasi-mediator may choose to meet jointly and separately with the stabilizers and nonstabilizers.

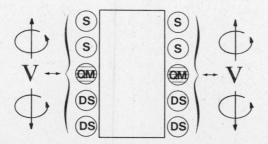

**Figure 4.3.** Vertical (V) bargaining

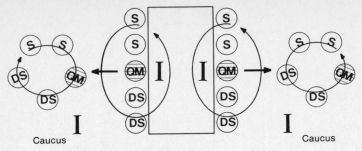

**Figure 4.4.**Internal (I) bargaining

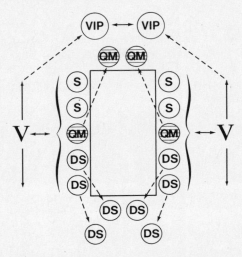

**Figure 4.5.** Shadow (S) bargaining

It is easy to see why internal negotiation tends to be far more extensive than the horizontal negotiation that goes on between the two teams across the table. Each proposal and counterproposal that has been brought up will be discussed and perhaps debated during the internal team negotiations. Unfortunately, if the team is not well disciplined, this discussion may take place at the table for all to see.

**Shadow negotiations**

Sometimes members of the two teams may meet privately to get things moving. This may prove successful because the negotiators can dispense with the kind of 'posturing' that characterizes across-the-table sessions. 'Shadow bargaining', however, may also prove to be self-defeating: whether authorized by fellow team members or not, their outcomes may be rejected by the vertical hierarchies.

**Multi-party negotiation**

The most important difference between two- and multi-party negotiation is that the latter opens up the possibility of various configurations or partial agreement.

For example, if there are three parties —A, B and C—they may come to full agreement or no agreement, but they also may be able to forge alternative side deals. Any two parties may strike a deal that disregards the interests of the third party. Were A negotiating with just one other party, it could simply weigh any proposed settlement against the consequences of nonagreement. Here, however, A must also compare a possible settlement involving both B and C with the advantages of different agreements with B alone or C alone.

Moving from three parties to four, five and beyond increases exponentially the number of theoretical alliances, the opportunities for partial agreements and subsequent problems that may flow from a lack of full consensus. Even when the particular circumstances of a given case make some theoretical alliances unlikely, it should be clear that communication and fact gathering become progressively more difficult as the number of negotiators increases, necessary as they may be. Indeed, the complexity is even greater than might at first be apparent. Some coalitions may hold for the entire negotiation, but often alliances shift with various issues or over time as events, personalities and loyalties change. Full consensus building among multiple adversaries is always a most difficult and delicate balancing act.

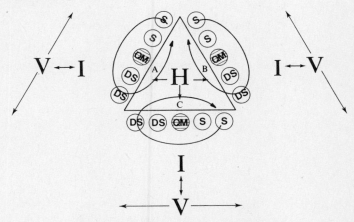

**Figure 4.6.** Trilateral bargaining

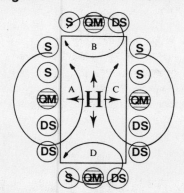

**Figure 4.7.** Quadrilateral bargaining

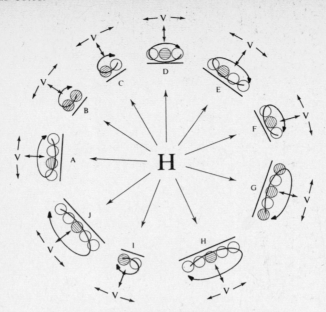

**Figure 4.8.** Multilateral bargaining

Finally, the presence of so many parties at the table usually will mean that there is much more business to transact. The important education process, described earlier, is more difficult and usually requires much more time, as the negotiators at the table have the additional burden of carrying far more information back through their various vertical hierarchies, each of which has its own decision-making process. It is not unusual for multilateral disputes to take months, even years, to settle.

## Quasi-mediators and mediators

Up to this point no outside, neutral third party has been introduced to the core model of negotiation. Outside mediators enter disputes for a very specific reason: to fill a trust vacuum that exists when an impasse is reached among and within the parties. The quasi-mediator and mediator play separate yet related roles, although both use the creation and maintenance of doubts to move other negotiators closer to settlement. The quasi-mediator, like the other negotiators, has personal, organizational and institutional stakes in the outcome of the negotiation process. The truly neutral mediator does not. The quasi-mediator also has some power to make decisions about substantive and procedural issues. Whatever power the mediator might enjoy is procedural if the parties are in agreement with the process and judgments of the mediator.

## Role of the mediator

The third-party neutral mediator's first job is to obtain the trust of all parties. This is not an end in itself, but a means (a temporary one at that) toward larger objectives. Mediators win trust principally by carefully demonstrating by both obvious and subtle behavior that they are truly neutral.

There are a number of techniques that mediators may use to demonstrate their neutrality and win the parties' trust. Mediators must, for example, listen and not say very much in a joint conference and in early caucuses; likewise, they cannot reveal their emotions and personal attitudes. Taking care to express only positive or neutral opinions of the groups involved in the dispute is one important approach. Mediators must avoid giving any impression that they would 'bad-mouth' any party behind its back. They should listen to any party's ideas with an open mind not merely to obtain a comprehensive view of the problem, but to set an example by showing that there is little risk in entertaining other points of view. Mediators should emphasize they are participating only to help the parties, and that they have absolutely no decision-making authority regarding the substance of the issues. Mediators must also assure the parties that their conversations will be held in strict confidence.

Mediators may also be able to use other processes for gaining trust. For example, parties who are leery about entering mediation nevertheless may be willing to engage in third-party fact finding. Viewed narrowly, fact finding is a process for gathering information for the purpose of better understanding and organizing the issues, positions and rationale in a dispute, and giving advice about possible settlement areas. In fact finding, unlike arbitration, the parties are not bound by a fact finder's recommendations. Experienced mediators, however, see broader potential in fact finding. Disputants who initially would have refused to mediate might engage in fact finding because each party is secure in its perception and analysis of the 'facts'. After some informal fact finding and some careful prodding by the mediator, they might agree to come to the table with the mediator.

The process of enhancing trust in the mediator is not without risk. Inexperienced mediators frequently feel somehow empowered by the confidence and acceptance that the disputants may quickly show toward them. Mediators must keep in mind, however, that their perception of power often flows from the parties' need to fill the trust vacuum. Furthermore, their perceived power is only an early and temporary phenomenon in a developmental process that should ideally lead to the empowerment of the negotiators themselves through the help of the mediator.

Having obtained the parties' trust, the mediator must next work to transfer it from himself to the negotiation process. The parties must be shown that it is the negotiation process that is the way through their problem. They must understand the process before they can value it. Specifically, they must become comfortable with the negotiation process, experiment with it and use it to achieve actual successes. In the early stages of a dispute the best kind of intervenors often will avoid substantive issues, and instead concentrate on procedural matters as they work to educate the parties about negotiation and mediation. The parties should know that mediation is available if wanted, but they should not move into mediation until they really need it.

Because negotiating skills are not taught in our society to any great extent, there is very poor understanding about how the negotiation process works. As a result, many people do not trust the negotiation process *per se*. Indeed, the concept of trusting a process is not even part of conventional thinking. People tend to concentrate instead on whether or not another party should be trusted. When there is a trust vacuum, however, this orientation creates a major problem: it may be too big a leap from no trust to trust in another person. Some interim step is needed.

Once the interim steps have been taken, once there is trust in the mediator and in the negotiation process, the professional mediator must work very hard to transfer that trust to the parties themselves. This can occur in two ways. First, the mediator acts as a 'role model', showing the parties the importance of listening and showing respect for other people's opinions and limitations. The mediator helps the negotiators create an environment where it is safe to trust the other party by encouraging the negotiators to develop a statement of a mutual goal. Second, trust is established among the parties through practice. The preliminary stages of negotiation involve some cooperation among the parties in relatively simple process decisions. These may involve minor procedural matters, what we might call 'housekeeping issues', yet over time they provide a shared experience that allows the parties slowly to develop a more trusting relationship, one that is essential when high-stakes issues are approached.

The core model of negotiation presented here does contemplate an outside, third-party mediator when necessary, though, as was stressed, some of the negotiators themselves may perform important mediating functions. Quasi-mediators may work within their team or between a team and its vertical hierarchy to try to build agreement. In cases where there is enough trust among the parties to allow these sorts of exchanges, there may be no overriding need for an outside, third-party mediator. Where trust is lacking, however, such a mediator can help generate it.

Mediation is simply an extension of the negotiation process. Effective mediators rely on the same tools that effective negotiators use: the creation and maintenance of doubt. In some instances, of course, neutral outside mediators may be able to use this approach more effectively than the parties actually included in the dispute. When one negotiator questions another negotiator's views, the statement may be dismissed out of hand as being self-serving. Because neutral, outside mediators are perceived as having no stake in the terms of the settlement, they may well be more successful in getting disputants to re-examine a position. By and large, of course, it is not the mediator's role to tell disputants that they are wrong, but it is certainly proper for the mediator (much like the negotiator) to try to convince the parties to think through all the possible consequences of the stand they have taken. This sort of probing, thorough questioning almost always leads to the creation of doubts.

### The mediator's capacity to raise and maintain doubts

Effective mediators create and maintain doubts by raising questions about alternatives and implications that the negotiators may not have considered or fully appreciated. Like any good negotiator they avoid flat statements. If, for instance, a mediator wants a negotiator to think about the reaction of the negotiator's superiors to a certain proposal, the mediator is better off asking,

'What would your boss say?' rather than declaring, 'Your boss would not support you on that'. The same axiom would apply in a situation where a mediator and negotiator are discussing a negotiator's decision to leave the multilateral negotiating table. Assuming that the negotiators are using full consensus in their decision-making process, the mediator might privately say to the reluctant negotiator, 'The other parties might come to some decision in your absence. Have you considered the implications of your not being present to veto decisions that would hurt your side?' The use of questions rather than statements gives negotiators more room to respond and more freedom to consider what the mediator is saying. It also allows the mediator to play a more neutral, *laissez-faire* role as declarations tend to be more leading and value-loaded than questions. The negotiators are thus subtly encouraged to take maximum responsibility in the negotiation process.

As noted earlier, most important negotiating takes place in the internal team caucuses. As a consequence, this usually is where the mediator is most active as well. Private meetings are usually the best forum for the mediator to raise doubts, so it is here that most probing will be done.

During horizontal (across-the-table) negotiations, assuming the atmosphere is conducive, each team tries to educate the other about their respective positions and rationale. The negotiators try to raise new doubts in the minds of their counterparts. As a result, a new set of assumptions and proposals may become plausible. (New issues and problems may arise, as well.) In this phase of negotiation, the stabilizers and destabilizers tend to open up to each other in the caucuses when these new concerns are discussed. If the quasi-mediator is unable to create doubts in the destabilizer's mind, an outside, neutral mediator may be enlisted before the team resorts to autocratic decision making or internal disciplinary measures to bring the dissenter along. Committed to stability, which is represented by settlement, the mediator concentrates on internal team negotiating and similarly tries to raise doubts about the viability of nonsettlement in the minds of the destabilizers. Sometimes the emphasis is less on outcomes and more on process. If the destabilizer does not trust the negotiation process, the mediator must raise doubts about the viability of competing process alternatives.

## Parties who will not settle

It should be noted that a few disturbances on a negotiating team may be healthy, as they assure to some extent that the stabilizers and quasi-mediators will be forced to consider the negative aspects of a potential settlement. However, what can a mediator do if an entire team is comprised of destabilizers?

Some negotiators enter the process quite willingly and demonstrate a strong commitment to meeting with the other side to discuss the issues. They may spend days huddling with their counterparts, caucusing among themselves and reporting back to their constituents. Yet in spite of all this activity, these negotiators are more committed to talking rather than to settling. For them negotiation may only be a device to stall for time. They may be waiting for the other side to exhaust its financial and/or other resources. They may have calculated that in time public opinion will shift in their favor. Time may be needed to prepare a lawsuit, launch a media campaign or use some other external pressure on the other side. It may simply be that these 'negotiators' prefer the status quo to any foreseeable alternative.

A group may privately know that it never wants to settle, or it may simply be buying some time to assess its priorities. Perhaps an organization may enter negotiations just to keep its future choices open; this is particularly likely if it has only begun to research the issues, hire staff and assemble resources. If negotiation is being forced while the hierarchy of an organization is still in flux, the negotiators at the table may have to stall until these lines of responsibility are more sharply defined. A negotiation team may simply believe that no settlement is possible, but it may desire to continue the negotiation process until its vertical hierarchy fully appreciates this fact and is prepared for the consequences. This is particularly important if an organization has much at stake in settlement, such as proving to its members its effectiveness in solving problems or in winning against adversaries.

How can a mediator tell when a team is using negotiations to gain time? Often, of course, it is as simple as asking. Mediators who have the trust of the team may find that negotiators will talk to them openly in caucuses about their expectations and intentions. The negotiators may be carrying out orders from their vertical hierarchy, instructions with which they may not entirely agree. In such a case, the negotiators may be searching for something to bring back to their constituents (the vertical hierarchy) which will convince them that settlement is superior to any competing strategy. The mediator's informal assessment of the case can be just such evidence. The negotiating team may be able to use the mediator's assessment to foster doubts among their own constituents in order to lessen their resistance to settlement.

There are cases, of course, when the negotiators are not candid about their desire to use the process to stall. The team may agree with the instructions of its vertical hierarchy, or it may have decided on its own to play for time. Negotiators who oppose settlement do not fully trust the activities of the mediator who is working hard for resolution.

How can the mediator penetrate the defenses of the negotiators to learn their aspirations? One technique is to test the negotiators with alternative proposals, asking them how they would respond to hypothetical offers. Because the negotiators can never be certain if the mediator is floating actual proposals from the other side, they may reveal hints about their real agenda. This is particularly true if the mediator dangles a very sweet sounding proposition. Experience as a negotiator usually helps a mediator recognize responses and intentions of the negotiators. The most important qualities of a mediator are the ability to listen and to analyze.

Mediators must always be extremely careful to emphasize that such offers are strictly hypothetical and should not be read as messages from the other side. There are three distinct dangers: erroneously raising the expectations of any of the negotiators, misrepresenting any side in any way and violating their own standing as neutrals. To be effective, mediators must avoid these pitfalls yet at the same time avoid appearing too tentative or coy if they are to plant the seeds of necessary doubts. The 'trial balloon' must have both plausibility and desirability. The negotiators who are examining it must be made to perceive that there is risk in ignoring what actually could be an attractive approach.

The mediator's approach of using reasonable hypotheticals serves different purposes at different stages of the negotiation. In the early stages, the mediator may properly interpret a negotiator's reluctance to discuss hypotheticals as revealing some lack of trust or even a lack of interest in settlement. It may take time before the parties are ready to disclose their true priorities to the mediator. If this reticence persists even as the final deadline approaches, however, the mediator may well be justified in doubting the negotiators' willingness to accept any settlement. Conceivably, the reticence could still be related to distrust of the mediator, but if that is the case, it may be time for someone else to fill that role or for the parties to bypass the mediator. (It is the negotiators who are responsible for making this decision.) A far more likely explanation for the negotiators' reluctance to respond to reasonable hypotheticals is that there may be simply no settlement that they are prepared to accept.

Once it has been determined that a team is negotiating just to buy time, a mediator faces a situation between the contending parties that is similar in many respects to the internal process that occurs within a team between stabilizers and destabilizers. The destabilizers are those who must be convinced by the quasi-mediator (and the stabilizers) to remain at the table, to listen to the message of the other teams, to consider their arguments, and ideally, to revise their positions to enable their negotiating team to offer deliverable proposals. The quasi-mediator first tries to raise doubts in the minds of the uncooperative team-mates about the consequences of nonsettlement. (What losses would be incurred: a strike, litigation, violence? Can the group afford such losses?)

A team dedicated to nonsettlement occupies the same position in horizontal negotiations as the destabilizer does within the team. It, too, may be uninterested in settlement. In this instance, however, it is the mediator rather than the quasi-mediator, who steps in. Although the person is different, the role is much the same. The mediator relies on the same basic technique of raising doubts about the team's decision to stall, probing to see if all the implications of nonsettlement have been evaluated.

In spite of the important parallels, there is at least one distinction between the two situations. In the case of an internal negotiation, a stubborn destabilizer may be overruled by whatever form of discipline the parent organization uses to control its members. The quasi-mediator and stabilizers, therefore, can control the internal team bargaining process if they can ultimately invoke the disciplinary machinery. (Again, in some instances a third-party neutral mediator may be called in by the quasi-mediator to help with the destabilizer on the team.) When it is used successfully, the team is able to negotiate across the table as an apparently monolithic force. By contrast, the neutral mediator has no such force to apply when working between two negotiating teams. What should such a mediator do when it is clear that an entire team is opposed to any agreement, even after the mediator has attempted to raise all possible doubts about that strategy, yet for some reason the team wants to prolong the negotiations? Does continuing to help such a team violate the mediator's own fundamental commitment to settlement?

Although the mediator is deeply committed to settlement, this commitment rests on an even more basic belief that settlement is in the interest of the negotiators. Yet if it becomes obvious that a party has carefully considered its position and has determined that settlement is not in its interest, then after appropriate probing the mediator ultimately must accept the party's own judgment.

In such instances, the mediator must decide whether or not to participate in a negotiating process that will not produce an agreement. One productive role that he might take on would be to help the parties develop and implement a process for managing an active conflict that they cannot bring to a close. The outside neutral may also let the parties know that he or she stands ready to continue to mediate. should conditions change enough, in the parties' minds, to warrant such an effort.

## The mediator's values

The mediator intervenes to help the parties reach some settlement. But what kind of settlement should the mediator be helping the parties to reach? Professional opinion is sharply divided on this issue. One group of practitioners and theorists contend that mediators have a professional obligation not simply to help the parties reach agreement, but to assure that the agreement is somehow a 'good' one. Those that emphasize the quality of agreements are particularly concerned that settlements are fair to the disputants, that they are efficient, that they are comprehensive with respect to the issues in contention and that they are not likely to fail (for example, see Laue, 1982).

Others contend that any settlement reached by the disputing parties is a 'good' settlement, and that a mediator should be concerned only with helping disputants to agree. Proponents of this view believe that mediators who attempt to make an agreement 'fair' on 'workable' necessarily must turn to their own system of values and that doing so constitutes an irresponsible imposition of personal objectives or values upon the wills of the disputants. Fairness and feasibility, it is argued, are inherently subjective commodities; mediators who try to impose their values and perceptions of what is fair and workable have gone far beyond their authority in my opinion.

This second group characterizes the mediator as value-free. 'Any settlement is a good settlement', they would say. To a large degree, the model of negotiation developed here is consistent with the view that settlement is paramount (also see Colosi, 1983).

At times, the mediator will feel that the negotiators may be moving toward a settlement but that it is not a 'good' one. To a limited extent a mediator may probe and question each negotiator's decision-making process but must cease raising doubts once satisfied that the negotiators have thought through the implications of their choice. Strictly speaking, even granting mediators this limited responsibility gives them some measure of influence in decision making as related to process choices but not choices in the substantive areas of dispute. So that this influence is not abused (and so that it does not compromise their neutrality), mediators always must remember that the negotiating process belongs to the negotiators.

## Conclusion

The bilateral model described here is based on the assumption that the negotiating process can be manged once better understood, that the groups who are going into a negotiation can sit down and establish an overall goal, develop an overarching strategy and set objectives and appropriate tactics along a time-line. I encourage scrutiny of this model and some of the concepts and theories that flow from it by the international community. This is a particularly difficult challenge because as more and more parties are added to the bilateral model the result is a complex multilateral model that must also be superimposed with multicultural and attendant national interests and language differences. The model has potential application whether the subject matter of negotiations is essentially political, economic or military. It is important to note, in addition, that this model is appropriate for analyzing the negotiations that occur among various federal agencies, as well as with private commercial interests, attendant to many international negotiations.

## Bibliography

Colosi, T.R. (1983), Foreword to *Ethical Issues in Dispute Resolution*, C. Gold (ed.), Washington, D.C., Society of Professionals in Dispute Resolution (SPIDR).

Laue, J.H. (1982), 'Ethical Considerations in Choosing Intervention Roles', *Peace and Change* (Special Issue on Conflict Resolution, M.A. Dugan (ed.)), **VIII**, no. 2–3, pp. 29–41.

# 4(ii) Negotiation and mediation: a diplomat's perspective

*David McGaffey*

As a diplomat, rather than a mediator, when I go abroad and deal with other nations, I am a party to the exchange representing the interests of the United States. I am, however, fascinated by the process of mediation, and I am hopeful that a way can be found to create some structures in support of a third party which disputants could recognize as a credible, potential mediator.

Lacking such recognition, the major role a third party can play is as an expert consultant, educating and guiding one interested party in the process and meaning of negotiation. I have found that the better each party to a negotiation understands the process, the better the chances of success. I do not, however, see any structure which can give a third party effective status as an independent mediator, standing between and assisting both parties concerned in an international dispute. Such has been attemped through the League of Nations and the United Nations, but does not really exist at present, nor do I have much hope that it will exist in the near future.

I am a negotiator, and I have been fairly successful in my work. I have been recognized as such and consequently, I have been asked by the State Department to find ways of teaching negotiation to other Foreign Service Officers. One of the ways that I have found is represented by the work of Tom Colosi. He brings to our studies a structure for analysis of the process of negotiation, and a language we can use to talk about the process. The structure of analysis is important, whether or not it is absolutely correct, because it gives us a means to test assumptions and hypotheses; a way to go beyond anecdotal evidence and look at the real world in a useful manner.

Language is very important because until we can agree on definitions of terms, we will not know what the other is talking about and the biggest obstacle to effective negotiation is a lack of understanding. Colosi refers to the negotiator's need to 'create doubts'. In my observations of the human condition, the experience of doubt is commonplace. When parties are negotiating, they attempt to arrange the best possible deal for themselves. But they may experience doubts about the validity of their own positions: they may be asking for too much or too little. In either case, they may try to overcome their doubt by demonstrating that they are absolutely sure of their position. The phrase 'creating doubts' does not convey this additional meaning; hence, there is a problem of language here.

Nevertheless, I agree with Colosi that the essence of negotiation is the creation of doubts. If two parties to a dispute have put forward positions which are very far apart, and each is convinced that it is right, then until doubts are created and experienced, there is little, if any chance of an agreement being found. But an additional element is the creation of confidence: giving one's opponents (as well as one's own team members) the confidence that the results of the negotiation are viable, that the outcome of the process will be beneficial to the other (as well as one's own) side.

The major function of the negotiator is to get an agreement, not with maximum possible benefit at the lowest possible cost, but maximum benefit consistent with an agreement that will endure over time. The trademark of a good negotiator, therefore, is being able to build, in the minds of the other side, the perception that they are getting the maximum possible at the minimum cost, regardless of what one's own side is getting. As Colosi has indicated, negotiation, at the United Nations or elsewhere, does not really take place across the negotiating table. Negotiation is a process of relationships between two or more parties: as soon as parties have a relationship, they have the beginning of negotiation. If through power, tricks, manipulation, force of argument or anything else, I, as a negotiator, manage to leave the table with a piece of paper which, either in fact or in perception, is unfavorable to the other side, then I have not negotiated an agreement, but soured a relationship.

During the events leading up to the downfall of the Shah of Iran I was United States Principal Officer in Isfahan, responsible for Central Iran, with approximately 18,000 foreign civilians (15,000 Americans and 3,000 Europeans) looking to me for protection. A situation occurred in Isfahan, long before it occurred in Tehran, where all central authority, all acknowledged authority, was effectively eclipsed by the emergence of seven 'committees', each with its own religious leader, students and unemployed young men who were armed, anxious, frightened, full of doubts and angry. They were angry because they thought that the likely results of their actions would be their own deaths. There was no transportation between Isfahan and the outside world. Bandits controlled the highways and the airports were closed as well. In that context I had the task of negotiating the safe withdrawal of those 18,000 foreigners. The first part of that task was to build up the confidence of those who held the actual power: those who held the assault rifles and guarded the roads. I built up their confidence to the extent that they felt they could talk to me and make decisions that were to their benefit. But once that task was completed and they made their demands, it was then my task to create doubts in their minds about those demands so that the outcome would be compatible with my set of interests.

As a representative of the United States government, I had to try to create a situation in which the United States would not be permanently blocked out of Iran. I cannot say that I was successful or that the United States was successful. Iran is a prime example of failure in negotiations, though not an absolute failure. Until his recent death, I still spoke by phone with the senior Ayatollah in Isfahan about once a month. I talked with many members of the various Iranian governments that emerged during the 444 days of the hostage crisis. I could talk to them almost in the role of a mediator because they saw me as being without power. I was, in fact, a negotiator: I was involved in the operation and had interests to defend. But I consciously cultivated the perception that I was powerless. I was, perhaps, a 'quasi-mediator'.

Among the concepts in Colosi's framework, the 'stabilizers' are those whose primary interest is in the getting an agreement, the 'destabilizers' are those whose primary focus is their own set of interests and the 'quasi-mediators' are the persons who attempt to use the stabilizers in the process of getting an agreement and to convince the destabilizers that their interests can and will be met through the agreement. The stabilizers can be very tough process negotiators. As part of their effort to secure an agreement, they can adopt the tricks, attitudes and the style of absolute toughness and sometimes that can be very successful. I have done it. On one occasion I railroaded an agreement through and when the dust settled, the people involved thought that they were better off than when we started. Stabilizers, however, can be a problem. They often assume the role of a mediator because they want an agreement and want everyone to be happy. They then become so interested, so focused on getting an agreement to all parties' satisfaction that they forget about their vertical hierarchy. While they are attempting to divorce themselves from interests and to deny power, their vertical hierarchy and team members continue to perceive them as negotiators. The resulting role uncertainty can be very disturbing.

The United States had some very talented people who worked for years on the Law of the Sea Conference. They met with hundreds of representatives of different governments and interests and attempted to come to an agreement which they thought would endure. But they ignored Washington and the political process in the United States. They came back after all those years of effort only to discover that someone had gotten close to Ronald Reagan with the message, 'This treaty is contrary to the spirit of free enterprise', and that was sufficient for the president to be against it. They had not made this most significant member of the vertical hierarchy a part of the process.

Though the above comments about the role confusion of stabilizers may suggest otherwise, the processes of mediation and negotiation are not separate and distinct. Every time a mediator interacts with any one party during a caucus, the relationships between the disputants, as well as their perceptions of relative power and of roles may change. The mediator in this instance is negotiating. On the other hand, a negotiator who is interested in defending his own interests may on occasion mediate between two members of his own team or indeed, between persons on both sides. The point is, mediation and negotiation are so intertwined that attempts to define them as separate processes will be exercises in semantics. That said, I still believe that Colosi's efforts to create a word-structure, a framework so that we can talk to each other meaningfully about what we do and how we can do it better, is something that we should all be involved in and should encourage. He once spoke to some senior diplomats and experienced negotiators, one of whom came to me and said, 'What Tom Colosi does not understand is that negotiation is an art. He is trying to "paint by numbers".' The next day I overheard that same person saying to one of his colleagues, 'When we get to Vienna, we must be careful of Tchevchenko: he is a real "destabilizer" type.'

I have lived, worked, and negotiated in many cultural settings and while the same processes are manifest in all cultures, they have different values. For instance, if we learn about the kind of negotiating that goes on among American middle-class, labor-union types and then try to apply it in a different cultural setting, even within the United States, without making adjustments for different cultural values, we may find ourselves 'trampled in the riot'.

Someone who had spent some time in Iran suggested to me that there the 'go-between' was a time-honored mechanism, whereas in the United States, there seemed to be a cultural preference for face-to-face confrontation and one-on-one negotiation I was asked whether the go-between role in Iran and elsewhere was similar to the mediator role as discussed above, or was there some difference?

In Iran there are many differences in the style of negotiation. The public negotiations across the table are designed to be an external education process. The parties get together to posture to their own sides and to prepare them for the agreement which has been reached before they sit down. This is what the parties aim for, though it does not always work out that way.

An important role is played in this process not by a mediator as we have been using the term here, but by a go-between. Each side selects someone to carry their messages to the other side, and it is usually not the same person. Such persons have some mediation role because they are seen to be disinterested in any particular issue, but they are also seen as representing the general interests of the parties. Very often go-betweens assume the role of arbitrators, in which case they have a great deal of power. For instance, a go-between hears the demands of one side, thinks about what he has heard, and then says something quite different to the other side. He returns to the first side and explains that he may have forgotten what exactly they had asked him to say, and then presents them with the gist of what he did in fact say, thereby presenting them with a *fait accompli*.

The go-between is usually an older, senior person and because he speaks for only one side, that side feels bound by what he said to the other side. This is power, and this is clearly not what we have in mind with a 'mediator'. It is more like a father attempting to arbitrate a dispute among his children.

Any framework or typology, such as that which Tom Colosi has presented in this chapter, must always be viewed and indeed used with cultural differences in mind, lest we err on the side of an extreme reductionism with perhaps extreme consequences.

mediators seen as effective when it is perceived they have no power or seem to be disinterested.

# Part II: Conflict Management: Interpersonal to International Levels

# 5(i) Divorce and family mediation

*Lawrence D. Gaughan*

Mediation is a fascinating field. Indeed, the general field of conflict resolution is one of the most intellectually challenging areas of inquiry in the contemporary world. I came into conflict resolution originally as a law school teacher of international law in the 1960s. Now I have come to believe that the families of people are more interesting than the family of nations. As a divorce mediator, I see microcosms of international conflict in my office every week.

The relationship between the theory and practice of divorce mediation interests me deeply. What is especially exciting about this new medium is that within a relatively brief period of five years or so, it has moved from a speculative 'good idea' into being a respectable and complex profession. In the course of its development, it has drawn on the more established fields of conflict resolution, such as international and labor relations, as well as academic disciplines such as social psychology.

The late O.J. (Jim') Coogler started doing divorce mediation back in 1974, putting together a system he called 'structured mediation'. In 1978, he described his system in a book called *Structured Mediation in Divorce Settlement*. Jim Coogler had a background as a transactional analysis therapist as well as a lawyer. His goal was to set up a completely new system for handling divorce settlements. Coogler did not trust lawyers or the legal system, and he really did not trust the spouses involved in a particular dispute either. Consequently, he put together a system of rules to maintain control over the entire process from start to finish; these are set forth in his book. The rules put everyone, at least theoretically, in a situation where they were required to take the mediation seriously. Courts and lawyers were kept at arm's length. His system is still widely used, even after his death, although by only a minority of mediators presently in practice.

As different people with varied professional backgrounds have entered the field of mediation, a variety of models have developed. Many mediators have found structured mediation to be excessively rigid and have discovered that quite often the couple (or their attorneys) refuse to accept such restrictions. As other models have developed, the field has experienced doctrinal differences as well as skirmishes over professional terrain.

What is family mediation? To answer the question, we need to make some distinctions. First, mediation generally is the use of a third party, the mediator, to assist the disputants through effective negotiation. Second, a mediator does not make binding decisions; that would be the role of an arbitrator. Third, whether a mediator even makes non-binding recommendations is controversial, not every mediator believes that to be an appropriate mediator function. Fourth, divorce mediation is only one form of family mediation; some of the other forms will be described later.

Nevertheless, divorce mediation accounts for most family mediation as it is presently practiced. Many mediators, including myself, prefer to use the more general term 'family mediation', not only because it is more inclusive, but also because it is less negative.

Another related term is 'conciliation'. This is the most ambiguous term in the field of conflict resolution because it is used in different ways. In international relations, it describes a situation where the third party not only actively assists in the dynamics of the negotiation between the disputants, but also is expected to make non-binding recommendations. On the other hand, in labor relations, one might describe conciliation as 'soft mediation', in that it means little more than encouraging the parties to get to the bargaining table. To a mental health professional, conciliation may be equated with saving a marriage. Family mediation may include either the international or labor relations definition, but it does not include reconciliation. That may be the job of some other professional, with the encouragement of the mediator, but it is not the mediator's role.

The primary focus of divorce mediation is to assist a separating or divorcing couple in reaching an enforceable agreement dealing with issues such as property division, support and custody. According to United States Census projections (US Dept. of Commerce, 1980, p.7), over 35 percent of couples in their late twenties who enter into first marriages will divorce, and an even higher percentage will separate at some point in their marriage. In second marriages, the divorce rate will be roughly 40 percent, and with each successive marriage, the rate is likely to be even higher.

A family mediator does not decide the substantive issues, and often does not even make non-binding recommendations. What the mediator does do is to organize the process of interaction in the couple, focusing them in an organized way on reaching the decisions that need to be made. The ability to expand creatively the possible options for settling a given point is one of the most important skills a mediator can have.

The best mediators usually prefer to respect the decisional autonomy of the couple. Sometimes this is difficult because the spouses may not have negotiated very effectively with each other during the course of their marriage. Even so, a good mediator can find ways of making their negotiations work just for the purpose of getting an agreement on matters such as their respective responsibilities toward children, transfers of funds for continuing support, and a fair division of the marital property. These are the principal tasks of divorce mediation. Again, the end result is a legally enforceable agreement.

Separation and divorce mediation are not the only areas of family mediation. The most extensive case in my personal experience was with a fifty-year old family corporation doing a business of over two million dollars per year. There were four branches of the family in the second generation, and immense tensions surfaced when they attempted to transfer the management of the corporation to the third generation. There were several dozen participants in the mediation, and it took over 120 hours to work through to a new management structure. I have also done mediations of antenuptial agreements, that is, the written agreements that some couples enter into before they marry. There have been cases of people who wanted a contract to live together without marriage, and I have also mediated in the situation of homosexual couples who were breaking up. Another kind of mediation is between spouses in their second marriage who are having difficulties in framing their wills so as to treat each other and their respective children fairly. It is common to mediate problems people have after their divorce, having to do with interpretation or enforcement of their agreement or court order, or with the desire of one or both parties to make changes in the agreement or order.

Even though there may be a separation or a divorce, a family does not cease to be a family, although it may be a quite different kind of family. The residences are in different places and the legal ties may be broken. But where there are children, and often even when there are not children, the family relationship goes on. What family mediation does, as it is conducted in a separation or divorce context, is to give each spouse a chance to honor the ending marital relationship by coming to a legal agreement to be fair to each other and to cooperate in the best interests of their children. There is nothing more fulfilling than to work and sweat with a couple through the mediation process, and then to see them leave knowing that, although they will never again live together as husband and wife, they can still respect each other and be friends, and continue to work together as parents of the same children.

The field of family mediation keeps on growing, but not by leaps and bounds. Unlike the more established fields of alternative dispute resolution, there is still not much of a track record of using mediation and arbitration in divorce settlements and other family legal disputes. Arbitration is used even less than mediation, even though it has probably been used more than mediation in many other areas of the law. In an arbitration, the third party makes a binding decision. In many respects, arbitration is nothing more than a different kind of court. It is often more informal and quicker than court proceedings, and is likely to be less expensive. In the field of divorce, attorneys are usually unfamiliar with arbitration, even more so than with mediation. So far, arbitration is expanding in use in divorce settlements at a slower rate than mediation. Both processes involve a change in the existing system, and systems changes take time to catch on.

One of the facets of divorce settlements is that emotions become intertwined with legal and practical issues. It is this which gives the field of divorce mediation some of its most difficult challenges. Ideally, an awareness of the emotional dimensions is helpful not only to mediators, but also to attorneys negotiating an agreement in the traditional adversarial format. Presently, the legal incidents of divorce in most cases continue to be settled by negotiations between attorneys, although mediation is encroaching on this traditional method of settlement. The final mode of reaching a decision is through litigation. Sometimes litigation is necessary even in the best of circumstances, since not every case can be decided by agreement.

Even with the advent of mediation, attorney-to-attorney negotiation will remain as a viable option for reaching an agreement. This can be a good system if the attorneys really desire to reach a cooperative settlement, rather than to engage in posturing and bombast at the client's expense. A lawyer who is also a mediator should be clear whether (and to what extent) a given case is appropriate for mediation or traditional attorney representation. For instance, if a case is one for an attorney, but mediation needs to be done, the lawyer–mediator may refer the client to another mediator; or if it is a mediation case, but legal work needs to be done, the clients may be referred to separate attorneys. The roles of mediator and attorney should never be mixed in a single case.

It is easy to theorize how the emotions of a marriage can be present in the room where mediation is being done. We visualize the conflict as being expressed in angry voices, insults, charges and counter-charges, expressions of blame and so forth. Actually, this kind of interaction occurs much less than one might expect. A far more usual situation is one where each party is able to negotiate with a workable level of effectiveness. When emotion is a problem, it often comes out in denial or withdrawal, or the inability to participate actively. Sometimes it is the seemingly quiet, calm people who can be the most rigid or overbearing. At times, one person may continually attempt to negotiate for the other. In short, the range of emotional reactions which a mediator sees is much more varied that one might hypothesize.

There are many different kinds of cases where one encounters an emotional roadblock to reaching a settlement. The strategy and tactics of mediation thus involve finding ways to work on the legal and practical issues that must be resolved. Even though the emotional level of the dispute must be transcended in order to reach an agreement, the mediator must obviously be aware of the emotional currents. One of the most difficult decisions a mediator has is whether to meet an emotional issue head-on or to find a way to bypass it.

Every mediation needs a structure, but it need not be as formal or as imposed as the Coogler method would require. There is always some initial session to start the mediation, explain the process, surface the issues and get some agreement on the timetable and agenda. Beyond this, there are clear differences among mediators. For example, some mediators almost never see members of a couple separately, while others frequently (perhaps routinely) use this procedure. 'Shuttle diplomacy' mediation, where the mediator uses the activist, even arm-twisting, methods of a labor mediator, may be the customary style of one mediator but anathema to another.

There is some 'bad' mediation being practiced, for example cases where the result is unfair to one party, the agreement is too simplistic or unjustifiably complicated, important issues are left unresolved or the openended or ambiguous nature of the agreement contains the seed of future disputes, practical issues such as taxes or cash flow are not dealt with or the emotional resolution is so neglected that one or both parties will find a reason not to sign. Another form of 'bad' mediation occurs when the mediator should not have taken the case in the first place, and where the only effect of the mediation is to increase the expense to the parties and delay the ultimate settlement, which finally takes place through court action or attorney negotiation.

There is also much effective mediation, leading to balanced settlements which are understood by the parties as fair, are reasonably in tune with what a court would otherwise do and are practical and workable. Among skilled and experienced mediators there may be a variety of valid approaches. It may not make much difference whether the mediator sees the couple separately on a frequent or infrequent basis, so long as what is done suits the mediator's style and skills. Some mediators try to insist that both spouses use a single lawyer at the end of the process, where ethics rules permit this, while others routinely recommend that each has a separate counsel. Similarly, a mediator may need written rules and procedures or may practice with few or none of these. The more experienced the mediator is, the more the mediation process may be influenced by the specifics of a given case rather than by any set of pre-existing rules.

What matters is that the mediator be a true professional. For me this means, first of all, that the mediator must have a relevant professional background, as well as specific training and supervised experience, appropriate to the variety and complexity of the field. Second, it is important that the mediator recognize this complexity, and be committed to a lifetime of learning through research and practice to develop the understanding and skills needed for the different kinds of cases. In this regard, the mediator should be dedicated to active participation in the theoretical development of the field, and the sound organization and continual restructuring of his/her clinical practice. Third, it is vital that the mediator have a sense of ethics and responsibility—a deep concern with the social mission of his/her practice. Simply put, the profession of family mediation is not just a satisfying avocation, a kind of sideline, but something that must be at the center of one's total professional growth and development.

Family mediation is a field which has both actual and potential social importance. The primary mission is and will remain, of course, to get fair, workable divorce settlement agreements. There is something else, however, that has definite social value. At the heart of mediation as a movement is the idea that a family does not cease to be a family upon parental separation or divorce, and that family members should take as much responsibility as possible for their own decisions when this happens. There is a recent book by the social historian, Christopher Lasch, *Haven in a Heartless World: The Family Besieged* (1979), in which he describes the harm which may be inflicted on families by professionals (such as divorce lawyers) who take over the responsibility for decisions that the family ought to make. Mediation keeps the responsibility where it should be, with the separating or divorcing spouses. The family is, after all, not just the basic unit of social interaction, but also a kind of 'ground level' governmental institution. Families have rules as well as social and emotional patterns, and they are a basic forum for many important decisions. With an intact family, we leave those rules and decisions, for the most part, to the family. Much harm has been done by our practice of doing this differently when, through lawyers and courts, the family is separated.

To understand how conflict arises in a separating or divorcing family, it is important to see how any conflict may generate an emotional response. There does not necessarily need to be a prior relationship. For example, suppose that I am at a subway station and a stranger comes up to me, waves a fist in my face, and says, 'Man, I really do not like your looks. You are one of the ugliest people I have ever seen. I do not like you at all.' At this point, we certainly have a conflict situation, one which could be dealt with in several different ways. I might try simply to avoid the situation: for example, I might reply with something like, 'I can understand what you're saying, it's a problem I've been struggling with all of my life', and just walk away. After all, this is a person with whom I am related only through the present conflict situation, but even if I do that, I will have a strong emotional response to the conflict situation in which I find myself. I may feel anger, fear, guilt, a desire to strike back and above all, anxiety, that emotion which perhaps drives all the other emotions. There is no way in which I can avoid an emotional response, even though the conflict situation was quickly terminated.

Conflict in a marriage can be far more extensive, because it arises between people who have had the most intimate form of relationship. When the conflict occurs, it unites the emotional reactions which generated the conflict situation with the emotional response which occurs when one perceives that one is in such a situation. In some ways this may be the same as a dispute between two countries, or between labor and management, but it is also different. To understand conflict around separation and divorce, one needs to be aware of the problems of conflict resolution in marriage itself.

Every intimate human relationship has as its focal point the tenuous balance between self and other. I am responsible for myself and I am the only person who can really be responsible for myself. However, I am also responsible to a special other person, my responsibility coming from our intimate human relationship. Somewhere in that relationship, if it is going to be successful, we must work out a delicate balance at the emotional level between being either too enmeshed with each other or too distant. If I am too enmeshed, I cannot distinguish myself adequately from the other person. I may come to confuse my needs and goals with those of the other, and when the other does something that affects me emotionally, I react. On the other hand, I may feel that I must maintain an artificial distance between myself and the other person, perhaps because I am unable to tolerate real intimacy.

Both the enmeshment and distance modes are deep emotional reactions to the relationship. If the structure of the relationship is rigid, there will not be an ability to negotiate a creative change. The pattern takes over; we are all creatures of habit. On the other hand, if there is not a sufficient pattern on which to base expectations, then everything may seem to be 'up for grabs'. Such issues of rigidity versus instability are also part of the emotional side of the relationship. In a sound relationship, we have at the core a kind of 'grounded' flexibility, balanced between enmeshment and distance and also between rigidity and instability. Put another way, the balance is between the inability to make long-term changes and excessive and unpredictable changes.

The fundamental variable is negotiation, regardless of whether our perspective is conflict resolution, social psychology or family therapy. Effective negotiation is a basic skill required in all workable human interactions. The job of the mediator is not to negotiate for the participants, except as a last resort, but to assist them in negotiating effectively with each other. In this regard, there is an excellent book by Roger Fisher, an international law professor, and William Ury, a psychologist. The book, entitled *Getting to Yes* (1981), may be, in my opinion, the single best book ever written on the subject of negotiation. As such, it is useful in understanding many different kinds of human interaction. It is useful to mediators, family law practitioners and therapists.

As a mediator, I have a need to try and understand the theory of negotiation. Negotiation is the human interaction I work with, and which I try to make work. If I have a couple in my office and they are insulting each other when they should be convincing each other, I may need to remind them of the object of their negotiation. I might say to a father, 'John, do you feel that Mary convinced you to give her custody of the children by telling you what a terrible father you are?' John might reply with something like, 'No way!' And I will then turn to Mary and say, 'Mary, you heard what John just said. Let me see if you can find a way to be more convincing. Remember, you have both said that you need the assistance of the other parent. Mary, you told me that you wanted John to play an important role in the children's lives. Therefore, why don't you start by telling John the things he does right?' Usually there will be some awkward starts in getting this process working, but ultimately, it does work out in most cases.

In order to make mediation succeed, the task at one level is keeping the negotiation at a productive level. In one sense, therefore, a mediator is an educator. The skill is to provide the education gently, without exceeding the boundaries of good counselling. One basic tool in facilitating the education process is an easel with a large sheet of paper and a marker. Indeed, this could be the most fundamental tool of all. It may be hard to imagine how this works, but if anyone has ever seen a couple who where shouting at each other but who quietened down when the mediator went over to the easel, they will understand. The mediator writes down the facts for each of the parties to look at, such as the positive skills that each admits the other possesses. Of course, this process has a hidden value assumption, which is that there are two good parents in the room, each of whom has something of value to offer the children. We can also tell them that one aspect of being a really good parent is to be able to recognize the positive skills of the other parent. Once the mediator has achieved this point, then the parties themselves can come up with the particulars. The mediator enters all items on the sheet of paper and somehow, nasty personal comments are not included. What we are doing is working through a more positive tone into a general spirit of cooperation and when the sessions is over, we have a permanent record. We then date the sheets of paper and place them in the file folder, where they can be taken out for review at a future session.

In those situations where the degree of emotional enmeshment or disengagement, rigidity or instability, gets in the way of good negotiation, what we are trying to do is to move the spouses somewhere into the flexible center between those four poles so that they can negotiate effectively with each other.

According to *Getting to Yes*, four points must be considered to make negotiation productive in a problem-solving sense. The first is to define the negotiation not as an adversarial or win-lose situation, but as a mutual-gain, genuine problem-solving experience. Essentially, all negotiation may be divided into two categories, problem-solving and adversarial. If we start off by defining the negotiation as being of the problem-solving kind, then we can really be concerned with the problem and not the emotional relationship of the participants. We are also careful to define the problem in such a way that in working out a solution, we can look at the underlying concerns of the disputants, and not just at their different positions.

The second step therefore is to identify those concerns, as distinguished from the positions. The natural tendency of people in a conflict situation is to take a position and hold to it, and the more directly they are challenged, the more they dig in. This is what basic psychology, including the concept of defense mechanisms as developed by Anna Freud (1967), teaches us. On the other hand, if we can talk in terms of concerns, then we can identify ways to meet the real goals of both sides in reaching a more creative solution. For example, a mother may be unwilling to agree to the legal status of joint custody because she wants to retain control over the choice of schools. It may be that this is her most basic concern, while it may not be very high on the father's list. The solution may be to define the joint legal custody so as to give the mother control over the choice of schools, perhaps limited by certain of the father's concerns, such as the cost of certain private schools. In other words, in many cases we can fine-tune the agreement to meet the concerns of both parties.

Thirdly, according to Fisher and Ury, a mediator looks for creative, practical options. The focus is on the problem, then the concerns, then the options. What are the various possible solutions? This ability to find workable options that give both parties much of what each wants is, more than anything else, the hallmark of a good mediator.

Finally, the mediator looks for some sort of objective criteria for deciding among the options. Often, this is nothing more than a shared idea that a particular option is fair or practical, or that it contains a number of the benefits that each party desired to achieve. For example, in a recent mediation, a high-level federal employee and his wife were arguing over her rights in his government retirement pension. He was fifty-six years old and planned to retire in five or six years, after he had completed thirty years of government service. She was forty-five years old. Because of the difference in their ages and the fact that the life expectancy of females is higher than that of males, it appeared that she might survive him for about the same number of years as he would expect to spend in retirement prior to his death. The basis of the agreement then became a tradeoff, whereby he agreed to maintain her as his sole and irrevocable survivor beneficiary, and she agreed that he could collect his full pension (less a 10 percent premium to maintain the survivor benefit option) while he lived. Each will probably do much better than if they had to split each of his pension checks when he received them, and he had not instituted the survivor benefit coverage for her.

As a mediator, I do not assume that a couple I am working with is going to be in a 'zero-sum game', that is, a situation where there is only a finite pie, so that if John takes a certain piece, then the amount that Mary receives is going to be reduced by exactly that amount. How does one get out of such a bind? Again, one way is through the use of creative, practical win-win options, such as the example involving survivor's benefits. The mediator facilitates a *substantive* solution that makes each party a winner.

The second basic way is through *process* approaches to the zero-sum game condition. Let us consider the case of a couple whose only real asset was their jointly owned residence, in which they had a rather substantial equity. In their particular jurisdiction, a divorce court had the discretion to divide the ownership as the judge saw fit; there was no rule that required it to be split down the middle. The question was, what share of the equity was each party going to get? Each of them had good reasons for arguing for more than a 50 percent share. By the time they came in for mediation, each had already spent approximately $5,000 in lawyer's fees. The mediator's job was to make them see that the cost of getting a court decision might well exceed the value of what they were fighting over. Once they were both convinced on that point, a compromise became possible.

When we speak of the process advantages of mediation, we are talking about potential because not every advantage is present in every mediation. Mediation has the potential to be less expensive, both individually and collectively, than either attorney-to-attorney negotiation or litigation. The potential for it to be quicker is very good. And there is also the potential to achieve a more flexible, more fine-tuned and ultimately more satisfactory solution. In other words, mediation provides more options, more alternatives to extricate the parties from a zero-sum game.

In many cases, the process advantages of mediation may be compared to the 'prisoner's dilemma game', in which a failure to cooperate always has collective costs. The parties to the prisoner's dilemma game may continue to hurt each other, whereas if they cooperate they can both do better in the long run. Cooperation is the only way to beat the system and mediation is usually the best means to promote cooperation.The mediator is constantly searching for both substantive and process alternatives to the zero-sum game, and means to educate both parties to the availability of the options.

One of the very important things that a mediator does is to facilitate the exchange of financial information. Usually, this is done through a form which covers property, income, expenses and liabilities. Such a form is good homework for the party filling it out, an appropriate and necessary disclosure to the other party and a means for the mediator to review the issues to be resolved. This exchange also permits the mediator to function on the basis of more accurate information and to use the easel effectively, rather than to be locked in by the competing arguments of the parties. The exchange of information also helps to balance the negotiating strengths of the spouses.

I mentioned earlier that the mediator controls the process. Part of controlling the process means managing the agenda. So, if there are two issues which are interdependent, the mediator may determine that it will be unproductive to work on issue B until issue A has been resolved. Or, the mediator may choose to focus on issue C, even if it is less important, because it is easier to resolve, just to show both parties that it really is possible for them to cooperate. For example, a couple may be fighting over money or property, but may be very much in agreement about the children. When the spouses find that they do not disagree over everything, that they really can reach some agreements, they may think, 'My God! It can be done! There are some things on which we actually can agree.'

Another element is focus. This, I think, is also very basic to understanding conflict resolution. When one is in a dispute, there is a human tendency to over-generalize the extent of the conflict. Earlier, I talked about some of the emotional dimensions of conflict. There is both the emotional relationship involved in the generation of the conflict, and the emotion of finding oneself in a conflict situation. A couple may in fact be arguing over two relatively small issues, but they may perceive their conflict as monstrous because of all of the emotional overlay that surrounds it. The mediator, often with the help of that 'priceless' easel, can help them to understand that their disagreement is actually rather narrow and, therefore, quite manageable. The mediator records all of the elements of their agreement, surfaces their concerns over the matters on which they apparently disagree and helps them find options which meet those mutual concerns.

Another technique is reframing. A mediator may use a certain choice of words to put a positive (or at least a manageable focus) on the issue. For example, a father may say to a mother, 'You spend a lot of time goofing off with the kids.' The mediator restates this as, 'What you are saying, I gather, is that she and the children are able to find time just to have fun together.' If the father accepts this, then it does not sound so bad. There are some obvious limits to reframing, relating mainly to the mediator's credibility. The mediator can reframe a conflict by looking at its creative potential, by using words that enable the parties to consider the positive options, but without stretching the words so far that the mediator's credibility is impugned. The task is to find the words with which one can take a negative thing, turn it around to a positive dimension and find a way to solve the problem.

Part of the experience of a mediator is derived from reflecting on how people react in conflict situations. In separation or divorce mediation, this requires an understanding of the divorce process as well as of conflict generally. People who go through a separation or divorce, experience something very much like the steps of death or dying as described by Elizabeth Kubler-Ross (1969). These stages include denial and disbelief, frantic attempts to bargain with the other spouse, anger (often mixed with guilt), frustration and difficulty in coping (perhaps culminating in depression) and finally an acceptance, a decision to get on with the rest of one's life. Each person goes through this process in somewhat different stages. During this difficult time some people, even people who are normally very nice, do some quite unlovely things. It is important for the mediator to recognize this as a comprehensible human phenomenon, to believe that it will pass, and not to lose sight of the fact that people are basically decent, and that in almost everyone, the emotional desire to resolve conflict is stronger (or at least as strong) as the emotional desire to sustain the conflict.

Finally, a mediator should remember how important it is for people to validate each other, to accept the humanity of people and to recognize the worth of others. It is also important not to be discouraged when these expectations are not always fulfilled.

Anyone in a conflict who wants a safeguard against reacting emotionally should assume that the position of their opponent is valid. Admittedly, this may seem to require a great leap of faith. What I mean by 'valid' is not that the other's position is necessarily correct, accurate or true. Rather, I mean to assume that it is rational and coherent, that there is some thought behind it and that it is taken in good faith. The point is, if I am in conflict with someone but can accept their point of view as valid, then I have a buffer against my own emotional responses: against anger, the need to strike back, to put the other person down, to retaliate, to get even or to adopt any other kind of defense mechanism. By avoiding these, I can give myself time to think and am less likely to do something which will further exacerbate the conflict.

But I must also accept that my own position is valid. If I accept that, then I am not going to go unnecessarily out of my way to accommodate the other person, to give in out of guilt, fear or just the simple desire to smooth things over. Accepting both my position and that of the other person as valid gives me a built-in buffer against rash action either way. If later on I find that the other's position was not taken in good faith, I can deal more calmly with the problem then because I have had time to think.

There is a scene in the motion picture, *Patton* (Twentieth Century Fox, 1970), in which General Patton meets a Russian general who offers him a toast through an interpreter. Patton looks at the interpreter and says, 'Tell him that he is a son of a bitch!' And the interpreter says, 'I cannot say that to him, sir'. Patton repeats the order, 'Tell him that he is a son of bitch!' So the interpreter finally, and very reluctantly, goes over and says something in Russian to the other general. The general responds in Russian. The interpreter turns apologetically to Patton and says, 'He says that you're a son of a bitch, too.' Patton raises his glass and says, 'Well, then, as one son of a bitch to another, let us drink.' That may be the 'bottom line'. If we cannot reach an agreement based upon trust, or even mutual interest or mutual needs, then at the very least we should do the next best thing, which is simply to recognize that we may have to deal with each other. We may even be in a situation where the conflict really is a zero-sum game and reconcile ourselves to dividing the pie. Even in this kind of case, however, it is better to explore mediation as a process for resolving the conflict than to assume that we must carry on the fight in more destructive ways.

For the future, the crucial issue is professionalism in family mediation. One final point on this: I do not think that one can be very successful in helping other people to resolve conflict unless we have a good sense of how we respond to conflict in our own lives. How do we deal with conflict when we are involved personally? Do we compete, in the sense that we have not only a need to be assertive (which can be positive), but to be aggressive as well? Do we feel a need to win? Are we adversarial, or are we more likely to concede a point if we are challenged? Do we push conflict under the table and withdraw from conflict situations? Or are we more likely to say (whether it fits the situation or not), 'Let's just split the difference?' Or are we genuinely skilled at problem solving, even when we are personally involved in the conflict? Do we really find ourselves being creative when we are challenged? If we can do that in our own lives, then perhaps we can help other people. To me, that is probably the most basic test of professionalism in mediation.

## Bibliography

Coogler, O.J. (1978), *Structured Mediation in Divorce Settlements: A Handbook for Martial Mediators*, Lexington, Massachusetts, Lexington Books.

Fisher, R. and W. Ury, (1981), *Getting to Yes: Negotiating Agreement Without Giving In*, Boston, Houghton, Mifflin.

Freud, A. (1967), *The Ego and the Mechanisms of Defense*, Revised Ed., London, Hogarth Press.

Kubler-Ross, E. (1969), *On Death and Dying*, New York, Macmillan.

Lasch, C. (1979), *Haven in a Heartless World: the Family Besieged*, New York, Basic Books.

Twentieth Century Fox (1970), *Patton*, motion picture film featuring George C. Scott and Karl Malden, and directed by Franklin J. Schaffner, Hollywood, California.

United States Department of Commerce, Bureau of the Census (1980), *Social Indicators III: Selected Data on Social Conditions and Trends in the United States*, Washington, DC, US Government Printing Office.

# 5(ii)  Family Mediation: a developmental perspective on the field

*Elizabeth Janssen Koopman*

## Introduction

Nineteen hundred eighty-six is an appropriate time for those interested in family dispute resolution to review a decade of cooperative conflict resolution applications to family problems, to assess the current *modus operandi* in the field, and to contemplate possible future issues which may be critical to the utility of this family service. Thus, for this book, the present commentary regarding family dispute resolution is presented in the following format: (1) the remarks of the 1982 George Mason University symposium; (2) some selected observations about the current status of service delivery, philosophy, education and research, particularly in the divorce mediation sector; and (3) the articulation of some issues of future concern and opportunity which may be critical during the next decade. While the family mediation movement is expanding in other nations, for example in Canada, Australia, New Zealand, and The Netherlands, this commentary focuses on developments in the United States.

## Family mediation: George Mason University Symposium, 1982

In his section Lawrence Gaughan mentioned or alluded to some issues that I would like to comment on. The first one is the whole area of professional integrity. In a developing profession, integrity is something that people will have to deal with. I take the position that there will ultimately have to be three distinct professions involved in providing services to families: (1) a family law profession, (2) a family mediation profession and (3) a family therapy profession.

I agree with people working in the field that mediation is going to go through a process akin to Anna Freud's (1958) description of adolescence, i.e. a 'transitory developmental disturbance'. I believe these developmental issues are going to be exciting and I think that out of that process, we are going to be defining some good services for people. This is one reason why I have enjoyed working with the Center for Conflict Resolution at George Mason University because ultimately the generic kinds of issues that we are dealing with here are the base line for the practice of family mediation. A family mediator draws upon the law, and understands the law; bargains in the shadow of the law; and has a knowledge of finance, the family system, child development and adult development, but the roots and the primary focus of family mediation should be grounded in generic conflict resolution.

I think that conflict resolution is a movement whose time has come. However, there are some barriers which are going to keep it from succeeding as quickly as it might. These in my opinion are associated with myths in the public mind. One of these myths is the view that conflict, by definition, involves a 'legitimate' party and an 'illegitimate' party and that the essence of resolving conflict is that the legitimate party wins and the illegitimate party loses. This assumption pervades the public mind and poses quite a problem for family mediators. The problem exists at other levels as well, for instance, in Northern Ireland and in the Falkland Islands dispute.

A real breakthrough in conflict resolution with families and in other relations occurs with the acknowledgment that in almost every conflict, there is a legitimate position on the part of both or all parties; that the conflict arises because of the incompatibility of two or more legitimate positions, not from the legitimacy or illegitimacy of those positions. When we look at mediation—and I speak from my own professional biases as an educator—we find that the function of the mediator is to educate the parties, to enable them to understand. This is especially true when we are dealing with issues that concern children. There is a legitimate parenting need and concern as well as a responsibility on the part of both parties and we try to resolve the overlapping but legitimate needs on both sides. Getting the parties to acknowledge that the other's position is legitimate, however, is difficult and will be problematic for persons who enter the field of conflict resolution.

Another myth is the view that life will or should be fair, but as many of us who have lived long enough to know, that it not always the case. Divorcing couples are not going to win everything: they are not going to have the same standard of living, families will be living in two households, and so on. I have never known a couple who have felt that everything was fair in the resolution or management of their conflict, but what mediators can do in any arena is come up with a viable, workable solution that parties can live with.

Other barriers to the successful development of family mediation have to do with the myths which the people in mediation are creating about the mediation process. I am deeply concerned about this. For instance, in *The Washington Post*, there was the headline, 'Divorce without Trauma—Go through Mediation'. This is false advertising; there is no divorce without trauma. Another headline was, 'Winning through Mediation'; this gets back to the equity and fairness issue. The idea here is that there is a win-lose situation and one is going to win if he/she opts for mediation. But mediation is not an issue of competition and winning, as we are led to believe is the case in other arenas of life. Another subtitle was, 'Divorce without Losses'. There is no such thing as divorce without losses. 'Divorce Mediation Will Help Everyone!' This is not true. Indeed, there are couples for whom I think therapists and attorneys would probably be in their best interests.

There is also the myth that mediation is fast and easy. Anybody who works in mediation knows that that is not necessarily true. It can be efficient and, hopefully, people will not be exploited but, it is not easy. As a matter of fact, mediation is in some ways more difficult. In the mediation process, we are asking the couples to work hard to reach solutions. In an adversarial attorney relationship, on the other hand, the parties are asking the attorney to work hard on their behalf.

One hopes that a couple in a divorce conflict can come up with solutions for themselves. This is a very important issue, that parties come up with solutions for themselves, but not by themselves. This is the essence, the power of mediati-on—the mediator facilitates the process to enable couples to do something for themselves, but not by themselves. Attorneys, on the other hand, tend to do something for the couple, but without the direct involvement of the couple. As we mature and grow, we have to do our growing for ourselves. We are very, very fortunate in life, however, when we have friends, family, therapists and colleagues who walk that path with us so that we do not have to do it alone. I think that principle is important in mediation.

There is another myth confronting family mediators—that divorce by definition means breaking up a family. When we realize that 55 percent of children born today are going to experience divorce and live in single-parent families, then we can appreciate Anna Freud's characterization of a 'transitory developmental disturbance', to changing and restructuring family patterns. There are certain groups of children, for instance, handicapped children, in which the divorce rate is 85 percent. In state schools, the general rule is that if the children in those classrooms come from divorced families, then that is not the exception. The 'Dick and Jane, and Puff and Spot' phenomenon is now only a pattern for 15 percent of American families. Our perception of what a family is, is very much out of date and it reflects upon how we feel about ourselves and how we feel about the divorce process.

Faced with those statistics and being in the field of human development, I would argue that we have to get over the myth of divorce as an aberrant phenomenon. It is a modal phenomenon, whether we like it or not. Divorce is a developmental task for people in our culture, no matter what their age. It is a developmental task of early childhood, of adolescence, of young adults, of mid-age and of old age. Not only do we see the divorce rates among the elderly increasing, but the elderly families are also carrying the brunt of their children's and grandchildren's divorces.

Dealing with divorce, my position is that divorce is a normal developmental task—in Anna Freud's terminology, it is transitory, it is developmental and by God, it is disturbing! I think these things can be dealt with if we are able to look at and deal with divorce in families in a positive way which focuses on the future and helps the parties to restructure their lives. When divorce happens, spousal relationships can be terminated, but parental roles can and should be maintained. This does not constitute breaking up families. At Catholic University I work with some of the priests to enable people, especially the clergy, to view mediation not as a way to help families break up, but as a way to help children maintain relationships with their parents, even though their parents are no longer living together. This is the great power of mediation: its contribution to child development, to helping to build and strengthen families and to adult development in the future. If we adopt that orientation to mediation, that is building future viable family roles and responsibilities, then we will be enhancing that manifold contribution.

## Family mediation: a 1986 perspective

From its informal and exploratory beginnings in the 1970s, the philosophy and practice of non-adversarial means of resolving family disputes have evolved into a variety of increasingly institutionalized and formalized modes of service delivery, the most common application being in decision-making regarding the issues surrounding marital dissolution.

At the present time, there is a great deal of heterogeneity in education, service delivery and goal and process conceptualizations in the field (Comeaux, 1983; Koopman and Hunt, 1983; Milne, 1983b; Pearson, Ring and Milne, 1983; Koopman, 1985a). The rich, and often confusing diversity in the field can be appreciated by describing some of the more common variations: (1) issues mediated, (2) service delivery setting, (3) professional backgrounds of the mediators and (4) goal and process conceptualizations.

Obviously, marital dissolution entails decision making regarding multiple and complex issues. Yet for family mediators these issues tend to group within three basic configurations:

(1)   Child custody and visitation only;
(2)   'All child-related issues': custody, visitation and child support;
(3)   Comprehensive dissolution issues: division of money and property; determination of spousal and child support; and articulation of child custody and visitation arrangements.

While the bulk of family mediation takes place in court-connected settings, both family service agency and private practice services are expanding. In court settings, mediators most commonly come from a social work or other mental health discipline. The clients are typically parents seeking judicial remedies for pre-or post-dissolution problems regarding their parental rights and responsibilities. These persons are either sent to mediation by judicial order, or the services of a court-employed mediator have been made available to them on a voluntary basis. While the issues mediated in this setting have typically been restricted to custody and visitation, this writer anticipates a trend toward the mediation of all 'child-related issues'. The 1984 federal legislation regarding child support guidelines and enforcement procedures (Williams, 1985), in conjunction with the benefits of greater decision-making coordination among interrelated issues, seem to be forces indicating a change toward the 'all child-related issues' configuration in court settings. The establishment of court services has typically come about via state legislation or by administrative rulings within individual jurisdictions (Comeaux, 1983). Free service delivery is typical, but in some jurisdictions there is a sliding scale free for services.

In family service settings, the mediator's primary professional background tends to be in a mental health discipline. Services in all three issue configurations are available. The comprehensive issue configuration is typical for spouses at a pre-dissolution stage. Post-divorce parenting conflicts are often addressed via one of the child issue configurations. Mediators may also be consulted regarding a single issue (most often a parenting issue) by referral from another professional such as a therapist or attorney. Fees for service are typically on a sliding scale basis. The private practice component of divorce mediation most commonly addresses the comprehensive issues of a martial dissolution. Recently, under the aegis of the American Bar Association's standards of practice (Bishop, 1983), an increasing number of attorneys are providing such mediation services to divorcing couples. Private practice mental health persons who engage in family mediation also most often address the comprehensive package of issues at the pre-divorce decree stage. Hourly fees are typical, and the addition of a mediation service as an adjunct to another predominant, professional practice, i.e. law or therapy, is the standard practice.

The greatest amount of diversity in the field is in the area of education and training (Folberg and Taylor, 1984). The specialized education and training of persons claiming to provide family mediation services ranges from none at all to those having extensive graduate-level academic training in the field. Fortunately, the proponents of the 'none at all' model are few in number, and while there is no absolute guarantee that more is better, educational issues are clearly linked to competency factors.

Decisions relating to (1) the determination of critical content areas and (2) the subsequent determination of the extent of coverage of those subject matters are basic to curriculum development. There is some, albeit limited, disagreement in the divorce mediation field regarding which are the essential content areas. It is the observation of this author that the disputants in the issue of content areas are predominantly those persons who closely and narrowly identify divorce mediation with their primary profession, 'individuals who . . . due to the seeming, though misleading, resemblance of the divorce mediator's role to their own professional role, make the casual assumption that they already possess the knowledge and skills to serve as a divorce mediator' (Koopman and Hunt, 1983, p. 31). Such persons take the position that 'solely a legal education/solely a clinical counseling education/or solely a negotiation/arbitration background' is needed for divorce mediation competencies. There is increasing evidence, however, gleaned from discussions at professional meetings, from reading the professional periodic literature, and currently from initial data analyses of a divorce mediation curriculum survey of professors in a variety of relevant graduate academic units in higher education (Koopman, Boskey and Gorman, 1984), of considerable agreement regarding the importance of a broad interdisciplinary knowledge base which incorporates subject matter regarding law, finance, family, adult and child development and conflict theory in addition to knowledge and skill in techniques of communication, negotiation, and mediation. [Koopman, 1985b, p.17.]

At the present time, in all three practice settings, the great majority of mediators have (1) a graduate degree in one professional discipline and (2) specialized workshop-type training, typically of three to five day duration, in divorce mediation. There is clearly a difference between a several-day workshop experience and a specialized graduate degree in any field, family mediation included. The extent to which this educational difference is translated into qualitative differences in service delivery remains to be researched:

Although research in the effectiveness of mediator skills and mediation processes is being developed, the research component of mediation education and training has been almost entirely overlooked. The importance of specific contents, the efficacy of particular pedagogical techniques, and the degree to which these and other variables are translated into quality service delivery remain unclear. It is apparent that progress is being made in articulating curricular contents and in experimenting with education strategies, yet these are only the first steps. Curricular consensus is not necessarily curricular adequacy, and much of the current thinking is still based on unexamined assumptions, untested theories and practices, and, perhaps, unfounded fears. It is now time for educators and trainers to scrutinize and evaluate the results of their efforts. Quality assurance depends on such research evaluations. [ Koopman, 1985a, p. 139 ]

Family mediation today remains a field in which there is either disagreement regarding goal and process conceptualizations or in which mediation skills, techniques, stages and so on are described, or even prescribed in a vacuum, without any discussion or clarification of these constructs. To some extent discrepant conceptualizations are a function of persons' professional predispositions derived from their primary professional discipline, for example law, labor relations, therapy and so on. For example: 'The goal of the final mediated agreement is to develop a settlement that is mutually satisfactory and that can be adhered to with confidence . . . . each side is usually angling for the best financial settlement' (Markowitz and Engram, 1983); 'The ultimate goal is an agreement that leaves no one a loser and that both parties are willing to abide by' (Blades, 1985); 'My job is to get the spouses to agree about the children, support, and property division. That they agree, not what they agree to, is my problem' (anonymous: personal communication, 1984).

Some persons have attempted to identify and address these conceptual issues:

While all mediators generally agree that the primary goal of divorce or post-divorce mediation is a comprehensive settlement of the dispute issues, there is considerably less agreement regarding the sub-goals of mediation. Within the overall context of reaching agreement, mediators often have four more specific goals: restructuring the marital relationship into a post-divorce relationship that can deal with the continuing parenting function in a civilized, businesslike manner; restructuring parent-child relationships both to adapt to the realities of the divorced family and to meet the needs of each family member; creating a model of problem solving and communication that will service the clients in their future dealings with each other; and facilitating the adjustment to divorce [Kelly, 1983, p. 35].

On the one hand, there are those who say the goal is to get an agreement. In contrast, there are those who say the goal is to create healthy, functioning, post-divorce families. Such discrepant conceptualizations become quite problematic. It is evident that as a teacher, my choice of fundamental knowledge bases and my determination of critical practitioner skills would be profoundly different when I define the goal of the process as an agreement and when I define the goal of the process as the creation of viable non-nuclear family patterns in the post-divorce period. Further, profoundly different criteria for evaluating the success of the mediation process emerge from these respective definitions of goal [Koopman, 1985c, p. 326].

In the opinion of this writer, for the practitioner, the educator and the researcher lack of conceptual consensus is far less problematic than lack of articulated and well understood goals and purposes. It is when researchers and practitioners describe 'success' in a vacuum of defined criterion variables or educators (and writers) prescribe recipes for mediator practices in an absence of goal-referenced '*raisons d'etre*', that concern is warranted. A recipe-book mentality of 'how to's', lacking theoretical and pragmatic conceptual foundations upon which to formulate the 'why to's' of practice, is one of the greatest problems in the family mediation field today.

A description of the current status of the family mediation field would be incomplete without reference to the status of research in the field. Because of the newness of the field, the large discrepancies among various conceptualizations of goals and processes, the varied backgrounds of practicing mediators and a relatively small pool of research subjects, and indeed researchers, the state of the art in family mediation research is primitive at this time. Distressingly, claims made for the efficacy of the practice are far more likely to be based on hopes rather than any type of documentation. Yet, a research component to the field has begun. Informal case studies and anecdotal data have been presented (Pearson, Ring and Milne, 1983; Saposnek, 1983); some client satisfaction studies have been undertaken (Bahr, 1981; Pearson and Thoennes, 1982, 1984); some research describing the mediation process has begun (Slaikeu, *et al.*, 1985; Pearson and Thoennes, 1984; Vanderkooi and Pearson, 1983; Donahue, Allen and Burrell, 1985). Limited studies regarding mediation outcomes have been conducted (Koopman, Hunt and Stafford, 1984; Pearson and Thoennes, 1984). Some research regarding the relationship of mediator characteristics and skills to mediation outcomes is underway (Folger and Bernard, 1985; Donahue, Allen and Burrell, 1985; Slaikeu *et al.*, 1985), and some research into the influence of client characteristics on the mediation process has been begun (Johnston, Campbell and Tall, 1985). The prospects and challenge of a fertile yet largely untilled field of research are quite apparent.

## Family mediation: the next decade

Of one thing we can be sure, the family mediation movement will be evolving within the context of a society experiencing massive change. Some of these changes will directly affect the nature of family mediation services, the issues and range of options available and the parties to the mediation process. The changes can be categorized as changes in family structures and economics, legal reforms and likely educational and professional developments in the family mediation field.

In the first category, of critical concern is the rapid increase in the percentages of American children born to unmarried mothers and fathers: in 1984, 26 percent of families with children under age eighteen were single-parent families, and over 50 percent of black children were living in single-parent homes (Norton and Glick, 1986). It is estimated that in some urban areas between 70 to 80 percent of children are born to unmarried parents, and the number of adolescent, unwed mothers, a very vulnerable population, has been increasing rapidly in all racial and social-economic groups. (Currently, over one-third of the family mediation cases in the Baltimore City Circuit Court involve conflicts between mothers and fathers who have never married.) At least 60 percent of American children born in this decade can expect to live in a single-parent home sometime during their lifetime. This prediction, in combination with the statistics revealing that close to 60 percent of children in one-parent families live below the poverty line, gives one sobering pause. The findings of Lenore Weitzman (1985) in her ten-year study of divorce in California, for example, that divorced women and their children suffered an immediate 73 percent drop in their standard of living while the former husbands experienced a 42 percent rise in theirs, describe problematic phenomena for divorce mediators, eschew the reality of vulnerable parties with unequal resources and may contribute to part of possible legal reforms in the near future.

In the area of legal reform, Public Law 98-378, the Child Support Enforcement Amendments of 1984, Title IV, subtitle B (Domestic Relations Tax Reform) of the Tax Reform Act of 1984, and the Retirement Equity Act of 1984 are already modifying standards and norms regarding alimony, property transfers, dependency exemptions, definitions of marital assets and child support (see Kolko, 1985). Family mediation, in which the parties do indeed 'bargain under the shadow of the law' (Mnookin and Kornhauser, 1979), will increasingly be influenced by state formulae for determinations of child support amounts; continuing legislation and court rulings regarding grandparental and unmarried fathers' rights are likely to bring in additional parties to decisions regarding child-related issues; and data such as those presented by Weitzman are very likely to prompt new definitions of marital property (e.g., value of potential career earnings and employment perquisites) and revised formulae for 'equitable' division of property and child support obligations. Thus the climate and context of family mediation practice will be anything but static.

In the area of educational and professional development, the increasing involvement of higher education in teaching, research and service in the field of mediation will impact upon the establishment of educational expectations (possibly influencing certification or licensure requirements), facilitate the development of service evaluation procedures and policies for accountability and contribute to greater clarity in the conceptualization of processes, goals and competency in the field. The willingness of academicians and of the academy to devote time and resources to these endeavors and the degree to which interdisciplinary cooperation transcends academic territoriality will be critical.

Within the contexts of the above societal changes, the following challenges will be pressing:

(1)   the need for competency and accountability;
(2)   the need for new knowledge generation, research and evaluation;
(3)   the need for providing access to quality services to all families, regardless of family structure or financial capacity;
(4)   the need for interprofessional cooperation and collaboration in order to best utilize all available professional expertise and resources for both education and service delivery.

The field of family mediation has not arrived; it must and will evolve and change. If this evolution is to proceed well there must be a broadly based cooperative effort for an ongoing process of careful scrutiny, rigorous testing, thoughtful criticism and well documented recommendations for improvement and change. If the 1970s were the era of 'hopping on the mediation bandwagon', surely the late 1980s and early 1990s must be the era for rolling up our professional sleeves and joining the disciplined and professional workforce. There is much to be done.

## Bibliography

Bahr, S.J. (1981), 'An Evaluation of Court Mediation: A Comparison in Divorce Cases with Children', *Journal of Family Issues*, 2, pp. 39–60.
Berg, A.G. (1983), 'The Attorney as Divorce Mediator', *Mediation Quarterly*, 2, pp. 21–8.
Bernard, S.E., J.P. Folger, H.R. Weingarten and Z.R. Zumeta, (1983), 'The

Neutral Mediator: Value Dilemmas in Divorce Mediation', *Mediation Quarterly*, **4**, pp. 61–74.

Binenfeld, F. (1983), *Child Custody Mediation: Techniques for Counselors, Attorneys and Parents*, Palo Alto, Science and Behavior Books.

Bishop, T.A. (1983), 'Mediation Standards: An Ethical Safety Net', *Mediation Quarterly*, **4**, pp. 5–18.

Bishop, T.A. (1984), 'The Standards of Practice for Family Mediators: An Individual Interpretation and Comments', *Family Law Quarterly*, **17**, pp. 461–8.

Blades, J. (1985), *Family Mediation: Cooperative Divorce Settlement*, Englewood Cliffs, Prentice-Hall.

Brown, D.G. (1982), 'Divorce and Family Mediation: History, Review, Future Directions', *Conciliation Courts Review*, **20**, pp. 1–44.

Burger, W. (1982), 'Isn't There a Better Way?' *American Bar Association Journal*, **68**, pp. 274–7.

Comeaux, E. (1983), 'A Guide to Implementing Divorce Mediation in the Public Sector', **21**, pp. 1–25.

Coogler, O.J. (1978), *Structured Mediation in Divorce Settlement: A Handbook for Marital Mediators*, Lexington, Lexington Books.

Coombs, R.M. (1984), 'Noncourt-Connected Mediation and Counseling in Child-Custody Disputes', *Family Law Quarterly*, **17**, no. 4, pp. 469–97.

Cornblatt, A.J. (1984), 'Matrimonial Mediation', *Journal of Family Law*, **23**, no.1, pp. 99–109.

Crouch, R.E. (1982), 'Divorce Mediation and Legal Ethics', *Family Law Quarterly*, **16**, no. 3, pp. 219–50.

Donohue, W.A., M. Allen and N. Burrell (1985), 'Communication Strategies in Mediation', *Mediation Quarterly*, **10**, pp. 75–90.

Folberg, J. and A. Taylor (1984), *Mediation: A Comprehensive Guide to Resolving Conflict Without Litigation*, San Francisco, Jossey-Bass.

Folberg, J. (1983), 'A Mediation Overview: History and Dimensions of Practice', *Mediation Quarterly*, **1**, pp. 3–14.

Folger, J.P. and S.E. Bernard (1985), 'Divorce Mediation: When Mediators Challenge the Divorcing Parties', *Mediation Quarterly*, **10**, pp. 5–24.

Freud, A. (1958), 'Adolescence'. *The Psychoanalytic Study of The Child*, **13**, pp. 255–78.

Furstenberg, F.F. and C.W. Nord (1985), 'Parenting Apart: Patterns of Childrearing After Marital Disruption', *Journal of Marriage and the Family*, **47**, no. 4, pp. 893–904.

Hansen, J.C. and S.C. Grebe (eds), (1985), *Divorce and Family Mediation*, Rockville, Aspen Systems Corporation.

*Harvard Law Review* (1984), 'Protecting Confidentiality in Mediation', **98**, pp. 441–59.

Haynes, J.M. (1982), 'A Conceptual Model of the Process of Family Mediation: Implications for Training', *American Journal of Family Therapy*, **10**, no. 4, pp. 5–16.

Haynes, J.M. (1981), *Divorce Mediation: A Practical Guide for Therapists and Counselors*, New York, Springer.

Irving, H.H. (1981), *Divorce Mediation: A Rational Alternative to the Adversary System*, New York, Universe Books.

Johnston, J.R., L.E.G. Campbell and M.C. Tall (1985), 'Impasses to the Resolution of Custody and Visitation Disputes', *The American Journal of Orthopsychiatry*, **55**, pp. 112–29.

Kelly, J.B. (1983), 'Mediation and Psychotherapy: Distinguishing the Differences', *Mediation Quarterly*, **1**, pp. 33–44.

Koch, M.A.P. and C.R. Lowery (1984), 'Evaluation of Mediation as an Alternative to Divorce Litigation', *Professional Psychology: Research and Practice*, **15**, no. 1, pp. 109–20.

Kolko, S.J. (1985), *Family Law Handbook*, Washington, DC, Bureau of National Affairs.

Koopman, E.J. (1985a), 'The Education and Training of Mediators' in *Divorce and Family Mediation*, J.C. Hansen and S.C. Grebe (eds), Rockville, Aspen Systems Corporation.

Koopman, E.J. (1985b), 'The Present and Future Role of Higher Education in Divorce Mediation: Problems and Promise in Teaching, Research, and Service', *Journal of Divorce*, **1–2**, pp. 15–32.

Koopman, E.J. (1985c), 'The Role of Higher Education in Family Dispute Resolution: Current Developments and Future Challenges', in *The Elements of Good Practice in Dispute Resolution*, C. Cutrona (ed.), Washington, DC, Society of Professionals in Dispute Resolution.

Koopman, E.J. and E.J. Hunt (1983), 'Divorce Mediation: Issues in Defining, Educating, and Implementing a New and Needed Profession', *Conciliation Courts Review*, **21**, pp. 25–37.

Koopman, E.J., E.J. Hunt and V. Stafford (1984), 'Child Related Agreements in Mediated and Non-mediated Divorce Settlements: A Preliminary Examination and Discussion of Implications', *Conciliation Courts Review*, **22**, no. 1, pp. 19–25.

Koopman, E.J., J. Boskey and K. Gorman (1984), 'Divorce Mediation Curriculum Survey: Preliminary Analyses', unpublished manuscript.

Lemmon, J.A. (1983), 'Divorce Mediation: Optimal Scope and Practice Issues', *Mediation Quarterly*, **1**, pp. 45–62.

Markowitz, J. and P. Engram (1983), 'Mediation in Labor Disputes and Divorces: A Comparative Analysis', *Mediation Quarterly*, **2**, pp. 67–78.

McIsaac, H. (1981), 'Mandatory Conciliation Custody/Visitation Matters: California's Bold Stroke', *Conciliation Courts Review*, **19**, no. 2, pp. 73–81.

McIsaac, H. (1983), 'Court-Connected Mediation', *Conciliation Courts Review*, **21**, pp. 49–59.

Meroney, A.E. (1979), 'Mediation and Arbitration of Separation and Divorce Agreements', *Wake Forest Law Review*, **15**, no. 4, pp. 467–86.

Milne, A.L. (1983a), 'The Development of Parameters of Practice for Divorce Mediation', *Mediation Quarterly*, **4**, pp. 49–60.

Milne, A.L. (1983b), 'Divorce Mediation: The State of the Art', *Mediation Quarterly*, **1**, pp. 15–31.

Milne, A.L. (1985), 'Mediation or Therapy—Which is It?' in *Divorce and Family Mediation*, J.C. Hansen and S.C. Grebe (eds), op.cit.

Mnookin, R.H. and L. Kornhauser (1979), 'Bargaining in the Shadow of the Law', *Yale Law Journal*, **88**, pp. 950–97.

Norton, A.J. and P.C. Glick (1986), 'One Parent Families: A Social and Economic Profile', *Family Relations*, **35**, pp. 9–17.

Pearson, J. and N. Thoennes (1982), 'Mediation and Divorce: The Benefits Outweigh the Costs', *Family Advocate*, **4**, pp. 26–32.

Pearson, J., M. Ring and A.L. Milne (1983), 'A Portrait of Divorce Mediation Services in the Public and Private Sector', *Conciliation Courts Review*, **21**, no. 1, pp. 1–24.

Pearson, J. and N. Thoennes (1984), 'Mediating and Litigating Custody Disputes: A Longitudinal Evaluation', *Family Law Quarterly*, **17**, no. 4, pp. 497–524.

Pruhs, A., M.L. Paulsen and W.R. Tysseling (1984), 'Divorce Mediation: The Politics of Integrating Clinicians', *American Journal of Orthopsychiatry*, **65**, no. 19, pp. 532–40.

Payne, J.D. and J. Dimock (1983), 'Legal and Psychiatric Approaches to Marriage Breakdown or Divorce', *Psychiatric Journal of the University of Ottawa*, **8**, no. 4, pp. 189–97.

Sacks, A.M. (1984), 'Legal Education and the Changing Role of Lawyers in Dispute Resolution', *Journal of Legal Education*, **34**, no. 2, pp. 237–44.

Sander, F.E.A. (1983), 'Family Mediation: Problems and Prospects', *Mediation Quarterly*, **2**, pp. 3–12.

Sander, F.E.A. (1984), *Mediation: An Annotated Bibliography*, Washington, DC, American Bar Association, Special Committee on Dispute Resolution.

Saposnek, D.T. (1983), *Mediating Child Custody Disputes: A Systematic Guide for Family Therapists, Court Counselors, Attorneys, and Judges*, San Francisco, Jossey-Bass.

Silberman, L. (1981), 'Professional Responsibility: Problems of Divorce Mediation', *Family Law Reporter*, **7**, no. 15, pp. 4001–11.

Slaikeu, K.A., J. Pearson, J. Luckett and F.C. Meyers (1985), 'Mediation Process Analysis: A Descriptive Coding System', *Mediation Quarterly*, **10**, pp. 44–74.

Spencer, J.M. and J.P. Zammit (1976), 'Mediation-Arbitration: A Proposal for Private Resolution of Disputes Between Divorced or Separated Parents', *Duke Law Journal*, **4**, pp. 911–39.

Stier, S. and N. Hamilton, 'Teaching Divorce Mediation: Creating a Better Fit Between Family Systems and the Legal System', *Albany Law Review*, **48**, no. 3, pp. 693–718.

Trombetta, D. (1981), 'Custody Evaluation and Custody Mediation: A Comparison of Two Dispute Interventions', *Conciliation Courts Review*, **19**, no. 1, pp. 13–20.

Vanderkooi, L. and J. Pearson (1983), 'Mediating Divorce Disputes: Mediator Behaviors, Styles, and Roles', *Family Relations*, **32**, no. 4, pp. 557–73.

Weitzman, L.J. (1985), *The Divorce Revolution: The Unexpected Social and Economic Consequences for Women and Children in America*, New York, The Free Press.

Williams, R. (1985), 'Child Support and the Costs of Rearing Children: Using Formulas to Set Adequate Awards', *Juvenile and Family Court Journal*, **36**, pp. 41–8.

# 6(i) The community relations service

*Gilbert G. Pompa*

I am a former practicing attorney, and became indirectly involved in the conflict intervention field. In 1963, I was chief prosecutor for the municipal courts for the city of San Antonio, Texas— when, without even knowing what mediation and conciliation were—I found that most of the work we were doing in that process consisted primarily of negotiating some sort of agreement between people. A sizable number of the disputes that came to our attention were actually settled without the filing of formal complaints which had to be prosecuted in court.

The same thing happened later when I left the municipal courts and served for four and a half years as chief of the Misdemeanor and Complaint Division for the Bexar County, Texas, District Attorney's Office in San Antonio. It became apparent that many of the complaints that came to our attention there could be handled by people with just a smattering of a legal background. Most of the people who came in to complain merely wanted to vent their anger and wanted some kind of satisfaction short of litigation. So I hired law students who could handle many of the walk-in complaints and we dealt with most of the cases that way.

It was this experience that prepared me for the kind of work that I eventually wound up doing at the Justice Department. (And in addition to a law degree, I also studied sociology as an undergraduate.)

It started one day, when I was told about an agency called the Community Relations Service (CRS). At the time I was still a prosecutor involved primarily in law enforcement. My informant said he was from the Justice Department, and I immediately assumed that CRS was an enforcement agency. I did not know what it was but it sounded very interesting. He said that he was on a recruiting mission and asked me whether I would be interested in applying for a consultancy position with the agency and the next thing I knew I was up in Washington being interviewed for the job. After about six months in the consulting role, I was offered a permanent position, which I accepted.

I started off at the bottom as a conciliator with CRS assigned to San Antonio in 1967. Two years later I was appointed Assistant Director and transferred to Washington. I was appointed Associate Director in 1971, Deputy Director in 1976, and was named Director of the CRS in 1978 by President Jimmy Carter. In 1982 I was re-appointed to the position by President Reagan.

What I shall attempt to do here is provide some sense of what we do in the Community Relations Service. I shall discuss the stages that typically characterize our efforts to resolve community conflicts and the range of strategies that are available to us. I shall also discuss the manner in which these stages are categorized, some of the factors that we consider when making determinations about whether or not to intervene, and the processes that we utilize once we have made a determination to intervene. Finally, I shall indicate the significance of conflict resolution in the context of civil rights compliance.

Let me begin by explaining what the Community Relations Service is. There are twenty-seven agencies within the Department of Justice. Probably some of the better known are the FBI, the Bureau of Prisons, the Immigration and Naturalization Service and the Marshals Service. Even though the CRS is one of the least known agencies we literally and significantly touch on the work of at least ten other agencies within the Department of Justice. For example, we may be drawn indirectly into some of the Indian cases that the Lands Division might be working on or we may work on police abuse cases or complaints that are eventually filed with and litigated by the Civil Rights Division. Or we may work on refugee and illegal alien issues which normally would be handled by the Immigration and Naturalization Service. In effect we are literally all over the map.

The agency was created under the 1964 Civil Rights Act, specifically, Title X of that act, Public Law 88-352. The concept of a conflict resolution agency, which eventually led to the creation of the Community Relations Service, was first advanced by the late Presiden Lyndon Johnson. As a United States Senator, he conceived the idea of a need for a voluntary, third-party intervener type of conflict-resolution process within the federal system. I believe there was also the fact that he believed strongly in the success of many of the Human Relations Commissions that were in existence at the time. He also foresaw the possibility of some very turbulent times coming up and the need for a voluntary compliance type of mechanism. In his introduction of the bill proposing a human relations type service in 1959 he stated, 'civil rights involves the idea of human under-standing and of human dignity. The outward manifestations of tolerance can be enforced by guns, clubs, and bayonets. But understanding does not exist until the people themselves will it to exist.'

That was the cornerstone of the development of the Community Relations Service. It took literally five years of debate in the Senate and the House before it eventually became Title X of the Civil Rights Act. Paraphrasing from the Act, the function of the CRS was

to provide assistance to communities and persons therein in resolving disputes, disagree-ments or difficulties relating to discriminatory practices based on race, color or national origin which impair the rights of persons in such communities. The Community Relations Service may offer its services whenever, in its judgment, peaceful relations among the citizens of the community involved are threatened; it may offer its services either upon its own motion or upon the request of an appropriate state or local official, or other interested persons. In providing conciliation assistance, the activities shall be conducted in confidence and without publicity.

There are three significant points to remember about this Act. First, it does not cover sex discrimination; we therefore do not get involved in issues involving allegations of sex discrimination. This is not the case with other agencies. The Equal Employment Opportunity Commission (EEOC), for instance, originally did not have sex discrimination in its mandate but when it was reenacted, sex discrimination was added. Title X has been so fragile for us in terms of survivability that no one wanted to tamper with it, so no one has ever introduced any legislation to insert sex discrimination in the mandate. Consequently, we still have no provision for handling sex discrimination complaints.

Second, the assistance to communities may come either through our own motion, or at the request of others. What this means is that we do not have to wait to be asked to go into a dispute. We can go in on our own if we determine that it is serious enough for us to intervene. And third, we operate under a confidentiality clause that prohibits us from divulging information obtained in confidence in the performance of our duties. And that is significant because we are not even supposed to divulge that information to members of Congress. In the legislative history of the Act, there were attempts by some Senators and Congressmen to insert a provision that would make us accessible to members of Congress in terms of some of the information that we would have obtained. As it eventually turned out, some of the people involved in framing the Act felt very strongly that we should not be permitted to do that because if we did, we would be politically compromised and could not do the job we were empowered to do.

The confidentiality aspect of the Act has never been tested. During the Wounded Knee trials the federal judge who presided was prepared to order us to testify as to our role during the conflict. We were prepared to resist. It would have been to our advantage to testify because some of the testimonies that were emerging were inconsistent with what I felt, or what I knew, had happened. So I would have welcomed the chance to testify. Eventually, the inconsistencies were clarified through other means without our having to give testimony. I shall return to the Wounded Knee case later on to clarify what I mean.

Originally, the CRS was located in the Department of Commerce for about a year. In 1965, it was transferred to the Department of Justice. Legislative history indicates that it was originally given life through the Department of Commerce because most of the activity that we were going to be handling involved inter-state commerce. Hence, it was felt that we should be empowered through the Inter-State Commerce Act. But recently I read a comment by Joseph Califano, who was Special Assistant to President Johnson at the time that the agency was created. He stated that the reason why the CRS was placed in the Department of Commerce was because they were afraid that if they put it in the Department of Justice, Senator Eastland of Mississippi, who was then Chairman of the Senate Judiciary Committee, would have blocked the legislation creating the Community Relations Service. In any case, over the years that I have served with the CRS, we have had some very good relations with Senator Eastland. So, I am sure that we were able to convince him that the agency was something that was truly needed in the South at the time.

When the agency came into existence, most of the staff were white and most of the work that we were doing involved voluntary compliance with the integration of public facilities, public accommodations and educational institutions in the South. We were primarily involved in voluntary integration of hotels, motels, public beaches, schools and universities. In essence, most of the activities that we were involved in were characterized as 'fire fighting' in nature. Our people were literally all over the South.

Shortly after that initial effort, we moved into the major civil disorders that occurred in the mid-sixties. Commencing with Watts (Los Angeles), then Detroit, Newark, Cleveland, Washington, and all in between—we were there to offer our services. By 1967 the agency began to expand; this included the integration of the staff with a large black component. Shortly after the Chicano farm workers' marches, we began to get the Hispanic reaction to some of the problems in California and Texas. Cesar Chavez was marching in Texas and he had already organized farm workers in California and catalyzed a series of confrontations that resulted in the need for the Community Relations Service to begin to integrate their staff with Hispanics. The agency's staff composition has been close to 43 percent black, about 20 percent Hispanic and the rest, white plus others.

In 1968, we began to look at the problems we were dealing with more in terms of the underlying causes as opposed to the fire-fighting role. We looked at some of the causes of the frustration that were producing some of these violent reactions that we were being drawn into, specifically riots. We isolated five key areas which we felt were the greatest source of frustration for minorities in the United States. The most important area was the administration-of-justice process: everything from brutality to lack of employment, to lack of inclusion in the process but more importantly, the way the process was perceived as working against minorities. The second area was education: allegations of disparity in the process, unequal treatment in terms of discipline, lower levels of educational attainment, etc. The third was lack of fair housing opportunity, inadequate living conditions. The fourth was economic development: the lack of access to opportunities to become involved in the American mainstream in terms of economic opportunities. And the fifth was communications: the lack of access to or participation in the media.

We took these five program areas and began to apply a new approach to each one by actually helping minorities into these areas. We developed what was known as the CRS 'Programmatic Approach' to the underlying causes of minority frustration. We committed 70 percent of our resources to this approach. We continued in that mode until about 1972, when the Office of Management and Budget decided that the type of assistance that we were providing in each of those areas could best be handled by other agencies that had specific responsibilities for those areas. Administration-of-justice issues would be handled by the Law Enforcement Assistance Administration (LEAA); education problems would be handled by the Department of Health, Education, and Welfare (HEW); housing problems would be handled by the Department of Housing and Urban Development (HUD); economic development problems would be handled by the Department of Labor; and communications would be left to the Federal Communications Commission (FCC). The CRS was to continue providing crisis response.

By 1972, we had shifted our whole emphasis to conflict resolution and crisis intervention. We began to retrain all our people in state-of-the-art techniques of conflict resolution, specifically in conciliation and mediation. At that time, we began to contract for training with organizations such as the National Center for Dispute Settlement and the American Arbitration Association and this has remained our mode since 1972. Although sometimes we still get involved in a limited amount of preventive work, most of our activities are now confined to crisis response.

I would like now to provide some idea of how we get involved in the kinds of disputes that we handle. Before we actually get involved in a dispute, several operational steps have to be taken. The first thing that we do when an incident comes to our attention is file an 'alert'. An alert is a formal entry in the office log, involving the assignment of a file case number. Alerts come to our attention at our regional field locations throughout the United States. Our headquarters office is located in Washington; our regional offices are located in Boston, New York, Philadelphia, Atlanta, Dallas, Kansas City, Chicago, Denver, San Francisco and Seattle. Our conciliators and mediators operate out of these regional offices, plus two temporary offices in Miami and Houston. Alerts come to us in various forms: through former contacts, the media and through people for whom we have handled cases.

Once a dispute comes to our attention, we subject it to a criteria check. In subjecting an incident to a criteria check, the first question that we want to answer is, is it jurisdictional for us? Is it a dispute or disagreement or some kind of difficulty relating to race, color, national origin? The dispute has to fall within that criterion or it will not go beyond that point. A phone call may clarify this. If the incident meets that criterion, then we check to see whether it has community-wide implications. And it must be potentially responsive to the CRS process; we must have resources available to handle it. That is, we must have a conciliator or mediator available to provide the service.

The reason why we employ these three criteria is that there are incidents happening all the time and we cannot respond to all of them. For example, some of the situations that do not meet our criteria are anti-war demonstrations which have no relation to race, color or national origin; labor disputes which are not race-related or ERA (Equal Rights Amendment) demonstrations. These are events which we might refer to somebody else, but we could not get involved in them ourselves because they are nonjurisdictional to our legislation.

We have made only one or two exceptions in the last twenty years. For example, we made an exception in the massive demonstration which took place during the anniversary of the Kent State killings. We were involved there because the President was asked to provide federal assistance to minimize the possibility of a broader conflict. I persuaded the Attorney General that, although it was nonjurisdictional for us, we could provide the assistance in the same manner that the National Guard is sometimes used in a nonintended role during a disaster, carrying out such tasks as shoring up dikes and other missions that are not really within their intended purpose. Our mediation and conciliation process could be used in this instance to help solve or prevent what might otherwise become a national emergency. The Kent State demonstrations were reaching the point of becoming a national emergency. The Attorney General accepted my suggestion.

Once a dispute has met the criteria for moving beyond the alert stage, the appropriate regional manager then authorizes a conciliator to move to the next level which is the assessment stage. An assessment can take anywhere from one hour to one week. Assessments can be made either by telephone, or on site. The questions to be answered during this stage are, first of all, is there actual violence taking place? Or is there a potential for violence? Is it something within our priority area? Priority areas for us include the use of deadly force by police, police-minority friction, education problems, or refugee–immigration issues.

How many people are affected? We need to know the importance of the regional and national implications of an incident that has been brought to our attention. But we also need to know who is making the referral. We tend to be a bit more responsive, for instance, if the president of the Urban League calls us from New York and says there is something that needs attention in Syracuse, than if an anonymous person were to call from Syracuse. The respect and credibility of the source is a determinant of whether or how we respond. Another determinant is the probable effectiveness of our involvement, assuming that we have the resources to intervene.

An incident does not have to meet all of these criteria, but it does have to meet some of them. In any case, once an incident passes the assessment test we are ready to intervene.

Some of the determinations to intervene are made quickly. Such a decision is one where the events are unfolding quickly. For example, a recent Haitian detention issue which resulted in a full-scale riot in Miami occurred on a Sunday afternoon and by Sunday night, we were on site. The fact that the Attorney General had made an inquiry on the matter meant that it had national implications. I put a team together and we were in the air two hours later. The same thing happened in the Miami riot of 1980. The Attorney General called, we flew down and we were on site while the riots were still going on.

While some assessments can be made immediately, others take a little longer. An example of one where we took our time, assessed the incident thoroughly, and moved in at our leisure was the planned march on Skokie, Illinois, by the American Nazi Party. In that incident, we had enough lead time to subject it to a close scrutiny in terms of all the possible implications involved. We had enough time to sit down, set goals and develop a strategy on how to deal with it. After receiving the information on the march, I made the determination to intervene. There was an initial question as to whether this incident fit our criteria, that is, whether the anticipated Jewish demonstration, protesting the march, fell within the jurisdictional definition of race, color or national origin. I made the decision to go in and we did.

Our primary objective in the Skokie case was to negotiate with the American Nazi Party a shift of their march away from Skokie, where over 10,000 people were prepared to confront them, to Marquette Park in Chicago, where the Chicago Police Department could better monitor the situation and prevent what could possibly have become a very violent confrontation. Skokie is a small town which did not have an adequate police department (in terms of size) and could not possibly have contained what potentionally might have happened. In the motion picture that was later made about the Skokie incident, there was no mention of the role of the Community Relations Service. But we were there, from the beginning to the end. At the end of the film, one could see that the march was shifted to Chicago but one was never told how or why. The reason was that our mediator negotiated the move from Skokie to Marquette Park. One of the reasons he succeeded was because the Nazis were allowed to shift their March from Skokie to Chicago in a face-saving manner.

The CRS tends not to receive any publicity because the techniques that we use in conflict resolution usually involve the empowerment of others while we stay in the background. We are the people who enter these situations and actually bring in the technical assistance that is needed to get people to negotiate, to get them to understand what issues they are really dealing with and not necessarily what they think they are dealing with. In doing that, we let others handle such things as the media. A spokesperson may be appointed to do that. We feed information to that person and in effect, help him or her to improve their side's negotiating posture to the point that when the conflict is over, they are the people who get all the publicity for having solved the problem. We slowly slip away.

It is unfortunate that we rarely receive credit for our work. I testified at one of our appropriation hearings in 1981, pointing out some of the good work we had been doing. Congressman O'Brien, a member of the Appropriations Subcommittee from Illinois, whose district includes Skokie, commented, 'if you guys are so good, how come you were not in Skokie?' I had to point out to him that we were. A similar thing happened with a Congressman from Massachusetts, who inquired, 'how come you did not get involved in the Boston desegregation controversy?' I said that we were. Unfortunately, it does us little good to do all these good deeds if Congress does not know about it. And they cannot know about it because we cannot do our work accompanied by publicity.

Sometimes information regarding our work does not even reach the Attorney General. I have served under thirteen Attorneys General thus far, and have found that the first inclination of most of them is to get rid of CRS. They usually do not know who we are or what we do. Eventually though, they turn around after examining the value of our process.

Once we get through the alert and assessment stages, we proceed to the intervention process itself, that is, conciliation and mediation. Obviously, we establish some objectives before we actually do this. The most obvious objective is the resolution of the dispute to the satisfaction of all parties. Sometimes we have to settle for less. The minimum contribution that we make to conflict resolution could be something as simple as a 'federal presence'. Federal presence is sometimes very important, particularly in small areas of the country where the only federal official that people usually see is the mailman. Let us imagine a situation involving a small-town police department in conflict with a minority community. We enter by virtue of our federal status as Justice Department officials and as such tend to freeze the situation in place immediately. The first thing that the local police chief or sheriff imagines is the possibility of an FBI investigation and subsequent negative publicity. It is this pause, this freezing of everything in place, that allows us to identify the issues that the parties involved are facing and begin to get the parties to communicate.

Some of the common objectives that we strive for in intervention are to prevent violence and loss of property, improve communication between the parties, surface the underlying causes of problems and try and move the parties from conciliation to formal mediation. If necessary we also provide training for police departments through our Office of Technical Assistance and Support. In 1978, following the killing over a sixteen-month period of eighteen Mexican-Americans held in custody by police in a particular Texas community, we were able to get some jurisdictions to accept training on the proper use of deadly force.

At this point, I think it is important to mention that within the general context of civil rights, there is a broader significance to our intervention in community disputes than the improvement of race relations. Because the kind of dispute that we undertake usually involves a conflict between the powerful on the one side and the powerless on the other, the indirect end-product that occurs through our intervention and the successful resolution of the case is a redistribution of power. What happens is that we usually have a dispute where the decision makers, that is the majority of the establishment, have reached the point where they have defined the situation to be one of crisis and when they have defined it as crisis, that becomes a power term for the other side, the powerless. In effect, a situation will have been defined by the majority in such a way that the minority has received a tool with which to negotiate. These crises can be indexed through demonstrations, boycotts, violence, threats of violence or threats of economic loss. When any of these occurs, the negotiating posture of the powerless is enhanced to such a point where one can intervene and begin to assist in negotiating a settlement of the issue which will generally be to the benefit of both sides but in particular, to the minority community; the outcome will be a redistribution of power.

For this reason, what is very important in our kind of work is a sense of timing. If one goes in too early, one may not achieve a settlement that will result in an equal payoff for both sides. If one does not achieve that, then the settlement will not be a lasting one. There will be dissatisfaction felt by the parties and the problem may start up again. For example, in the 1980 Miami riots, we tried over a period of time to involve the Dade County Metro Police in a series of symposiums on the use of force. We held one in St. Petersburg and another one in Fort Lauderdale. They were attended by most of the police jurisdictions from around those areas. Dade County did not attend. They did not have a crisis as far as they were concerned and took a very strong position that they did not have to be present. Our assessment had been that the city of Miami was definitely heading towards a riot.

I sent a report to the Attorney General two days before the riots began. There had been an intrusion into the home of a black. Nathaniel Lafleur by mistake. The police went into his house and physically attacked him. Then there was the indictment and conviction of a black school superintendent in Dade County and the assault and killing of Arthur McDuffie. McDuffie was on a motorcycle, pursued by police for a traffic violation. Eventually he was overtaken and beaten to death. In these three incidents involving blacks, one was beaten, one killed and a third indicted, prosecuted and convicted. Consequently, a perception developed in the black community that the administration-of-justice process worked when a black was the accused, but did not work when a black was the victim and sought redress. The situation came to a head when, after a trial of those accused of killing Arthur McDuffie, the five police officers in question were acquitted. On the day of the acquittal, a Saturday, 'all hell broke loose' in Miami.

I use the Miami riots as an example of how communities sometimes fail to define a developing volatile situation as a crisis. Immediately after the crisis Dade County became very amenable to negotiation, but it was too late. (Sometimes a crisis can be defined before a riot occurs. If a chief of police or mayor perceives the impending threat such as the one in Miami, we can assist in settling the dispute before it becomes an unmanageable problem.)

Another example of this was the Santa Fe prison incident where we were asked by a federal judge to assist in the resolution of a list of inmate grievances that had become the basis for a federal suit. We attempted to negotiate settlement of those issues for three months and although I feel we were making good progress, the American Civil Liberties Union (ACLU) convinced the prison administration that it would be best to litigate the issues instead of mediating them. Four months later, there was an eruption in the institution in which some thirty people were killed. I am not saying that we could necessarily have prevented that, but the issues which we were negotiating through mediation were the same issues that eventually reached a critical climax and exploded into a riot. I feel that the mediation process was providing a good outlet for the airing of grievances that was not available through litigation.

I want now to say something about the techniques that we use in our approach to conciliation and mediation. We use the skills of persuasion, knowledge of the dynamics of conflict and human behavior and technical information. These are the basics which other professionals in the field use. The major difference is that we sometimes take on certain types of conflicts under dangerous circumstances. Indeed, several of my men have been physically assaulted in the process of carrying out their assignments. James Laue, an expert in this business, was standing close to Martin Luther King when the latter was assassinated. At the time Laue was part of a CRS team that had been sent to Memphis to conciliate between the Southern Christian Leadership Conference (protesting on behalf of garbage workers) and the city of Memphis. Tommie Jones, then one of our mediators in Kansas City and now CRS Northeast Regional Director, was meeting with the court monitor for the Dayton, Ohio desegregation case when somebody walked in with a pistol and put five bullets into the gentleman and killed him. I was the chief negotiator between the Government and the American Indian Movement (AIM) during the occupation of Wounded Knee where three Indians were killed, one FBI agent wounded and one federal marshal shot and paralyzed for life during the conflict. It all happened during the time I was there. There is a distinct element of danger involved in the kind of work that we do.

I would like to use the Wounded Knee experience as an example of the conciliation process that we carry out. During the crisis four main negotiating sessions took place. Although we set up the negotiations, we did not handle the negotiations themselves. The personalities involved were sufficiently strong to conduct the negotiations themselves. The American Indian Movement had attorneys and the other side, which, of course, was the Justice Department, had their chief negotiator, Harlington Wood. He was then Assistant Attorney General of the United States and is now a Federal Appeals Judge in Chicago. The area where the occupation took place was wide open and barren. Both sides had established zones of occupation when we began negotiations. The government controlled an outside perimeter, the Indians controlled an inside perimeter and there was a kind of no-man's land there that we called the DMZ (demilitarized zone), where the first negotiations were held in a bus. The second negotiation session was held in a teepee also in the DMZ. The third negotiation session was held in a church inside the occupied area and the final session was held inside the AIM headquarters building where the issue was eventually settled.

We used the basic techniques of conciliation. Our first priority was to open communication between the parties. Our second goal was to give the disputants a chance to vent their anger and discuss their perceptions of the situation. In this case, the major issue concerned alleged violations of Indian treaty rights. The rationale for the occupation was supposedly to highlight and articulate the plight of Indians in the United States. By explaining that to the Government, we were facilitating the second goal, that is giving the disputing groups an opportunity to discuss their perceptions of the conflict.

The third goal was to identify and interpret the issues. As I have said, the basic issue in this case was treaty violations, but in the course of the occupation, while setting up negotiation sessions, we were drawn into other issues that also had to be dealt with by CRS: the issue of the hostages, the need for medical attention and the need for food within the occupied areas, as well as the fact that the Indians began to slaughter cattle that belonged to nearby farmers. We had to get involved in the resolution and interpretation of these satellite issues. The government eventually paid for the cattle and the Indians used the cattle for food. Another issue was the demand for amnesty for all people except the leaders involved at Wounded Knee.

Our fourth goal was to narrow the gap between the parties' perceptions and the facts; this was a major objective. In the Wounded Knee case, I was the only one who was privy to what was taking place on both sides; hence, I had the primary interpretive responsibility. On the one hand, I was a member of the government's command staff which was comprised of an Assistant Secretary of the Interior, an Assistant Attorney General of the United States, a brigadier general from the 82nd Airborne Division, the head of the Marshals Service, and two members of the hierarchy of the FBI. At the same time, I also had the responsibility for going into the occupied territory and sitting with the Indian leadership and listening to them articulate their demands.

Misperceptions were everywhere. The federal representatives were convinced that the Indians possessed better weaponry than they actually did. The government law enforcement personnel had M16 rifles, jets, helicopters, and so on and yet somehow, became convinced that the Indians had better equipment. I knew better because I was inside the occupied area daily. Now, how did I handle that? I am a conciliator, my job is not intelligence and I cannot compromise the confidentiality clause of Title X. The height of credibility in that case was to have the respect and trust of the Indians and at the same time, meet with the government forces without carrying intelligence, but convince them that the Indians did not have what the government forces thought they had. That situation had to be handled very delicately. Most of the weapons the Indians had were shotguns, 22-caliber weapons and some deer rifles. Though I could not report to the government forces exactly what the Indians had, I could clarify misperceptions by explaining that 'they do not have what you say they have'.

The misperceptions occurred on both sides. The Indians, for example, thought that the Government had tanks; in reality, the vehicles in question were armored personnel carriers. Consequently, I had to clarify to both sides what was really going on in the interest of keeping them from overreacting to each other. Part of my job was also to explain to the Indians how unrealistic some of their elaborate demands were. Eventually I was able to get them to scale down some of their demands, to be a bit more realistic and more acceptable to the government's interest in negotiating.

We had other problems to contend with during the occupation that impeded negotiations. There was internal friction on both sides. For instance, within the Indian group, there was constant posturing by various individuals which could have led to the development of factions, of splinter groups which could have ruined the negotiating capability of the Indians. We had to attempt, therefore, to keep the Indian group intact so that they could negotiate effectively. We had the same problem with the government side; for instance, one of the problems centered on whether the FBI or the Marshals Service were in charge of law enforcement activities. As the negotiator between those parties, trying to figure out who was really speaking for a particular position, I had to sort through all this. Positions varied every day. One day the government's position might be 'we are going to take them by force', or 'we had better not do it'. And then again, 'I think we should'. But 'women and children are in there', or 'if we use gas', and 'no, we cannot because we will get an overreaction'. The world media were there. All these factors were taken into consideration during the negotiating process. We had to let the government know that if they decided to do certain things, they would get a reaction that was going to put them in a bad light around the world. We had to negotiate against certain actions in order to minimize the possibility of a broader confrontation.

Our fifth objective was to identify resources that might be used in the resolution process. The Reverend John Adams, of the National Council of Churches, was a resource person at Wounded Knee. He was very important in the resolution process. He came in with other religious leaders who had a calming effect within the occupied territory. There were some people we had to keep out, for example Marlon Brando, Angela Davis and others who were not cleared for entry because we felt that they would not have a calming effect on the situation.

Our sixth objective at Wounded Knee was to explore options and alternatives. There were numerous proposals and counter-proposals discussed during the four negotiating sessions, ranging from amnesty to the reductions of charges for Dennis Banks and Russell Means, the two AIM leaders.

There were a lot of humorous incidents during the occupation. One of them concerned the negotiating session in the teepee. The Indians had demanded that the session be conducted in a teepee. We found a teepee but none of the Indians knew how to put one up. One of the US Marshals, a white, who was a boy scout leader, did; he put up the teepee for the Indians to negotiate in. Another incident occurred during one of our last negotiating sessions. Our entry into the occupied territory for the session was like something out of Hollywood. The Indians were lined up on horses with rifles as we drove in with two cars, white flags flying from the aerials and the government negotiator, Harlington Wood, inside one of the cars.

So much for our involvement at Wounded Knee. I would just add that AIM eventually agreed to surrender their arms to CRS.

The other primary area where we get involved is mediation. Mediation is the most formal process we undertake. The classic mediation for us—and one that is most typical–is the Port Arthur, Texas case that we handled a few years ago. A white police officer pursued and shot a black man who allegedly had shoplifted a ham. The black community reacted with three days of rioting. The city had been preparing for a big celebration, including a parade. It had just been voted the 'All American City of the United States'. Everyone was up in arms because the parade had been cancelled due to the threat of violence. One of our conciliators went in and froze the situation in place. He talked the city into negotiating with representatives of the National Association for the Advancement of Colored People (NAACP), the Urban League and every black leader in Port Arthur. We kept the situation cool while we brought in a CRS mediator. Within two weeks he came up with a written agreement in which the city adopted a firearms policy and an affirmative action plan, both of which were incorporated into a city ordinance.

The situation in Port Arthur had reached crisis proportions, the city's image was at stake, the parade had been cancelled and the whole world was preparing to look down on them. They were amenable to negotiations, so we went in and negotiated a settlement. That is the ultimate goal in mediation cases: to encourage people on both sides who have the authority to act to reach an agreement which is lasting enough to prevent a recurrence of the issue that caused the problem in the first place.

The CRS conciliator looks for six factors in determining whether or not a case should be referred to mediation. First, he/she tries to determine whether the issues are negotiable and can form the basis of a written agreement. Second, the rhetoric level of the dispute has to be sufficiently reduced to make it conducive for the parties to sit down and negotiate. Third, the situation must have already been defined by the majority of society as a crisis. Fourth, the protest leaders must be ready to end the confrontation before they can sit down and negotiate. Fifth, the protest group must be sufficiently representative of the minority community to sign a binding and lasting agreement. And sixth, the establishment negotiating team must have the authority to act.

The only other thing that I should mention about mediation is that a vast number of our cases are referrals from the Federal Judiciary. A few years ago, I made presentations before two different United States Federal Circuits to explain the Community Relations Service mediation process, and from that we got many referrals. Most have involved prison inmate grievances.

Let me discuss briefly the kinds of skills that we look for in the people we employ in the Community Relations Service. We have a 'gut feeling' for what kind of person fits into our type of work. There is no sure way we can tell, but after we have interviewed someone, we usually have a feel for whether or not he or she will fit into this kind of work. We have found that some people who are suited in general, are not suited specifically for some of the disputes that we handle. We have people in the agency who will absolutely refuse to take on a case which is dangerous, but we have even more people who will volunteer to go where the situation is dangerous.

It is interesting that at Wounded Knee, I felt very safe. Though the bullets were flying, I never felt afraid. To this day, I do not know why. When I went into Fort Wayne, Indiana, immediately after Urban League President Vernon Jordan was shot, for the first time I felt a little fear, and I do not know why. Perhaps I was not as afraid of the Indians as I was of an unknown assailant running around Fort Wayne. I also experienced some fear in Miami; we were there in the midst of the riots.

CRS people must be the type that can sit down with the governor in the morning and meet with the most militant representatives of a local community in the evening. They have to be excellent communicators and good listeners as well as energetic, imaginative, quick thinking and tolerant. Most important of all is that our people must be racially sensitive and be able to establish credibility. Credibility is one of the most important traits that we must have in our business. And it is interesting that most of the people with whom I have had contact over the years, and who have a lot of respect for us, will say, 'well, I cannot vouch for CRS, but I can vouch for Jim Johnson', or any particular CRS person. Our people earn credibility on a one-to-one basis. They cannot get it through the agency because there is a natural distrust of the Department of Justice in general by many of the groups with which we deal.

Our people must have, of course, a knowledge of community structure and organization, particularly of minority communities. They must have a good knowledge of the minority groups' cultural patterns and history. They have to know, for example, that within the Hispanic community in the United States there are differences. People tend to paint a homogenous picture of Hispanics in general—of Cubans, Puerto Ricans, Mexican-Americans and South Americans. In reality, we know that there are differences between Puerto Ricans and Cubans, between Puerto Ricans, Cubans and Mexican-Americans. The dominant Hispanic group is Mexican-Americans. And our CRS people have to know when not to use certain terms when dealing with Hispanic groups. We would not call a Puerto Rican a Chicano. And we would not call some Mexican-Americans Chicano either, because they resent it. Our people have to be sensitive to that and know how to deal with these groups and organizations in such a way that they do not ruin their credibility and perhaps, get themselves 'blown out of the water'. Credibility is our most effective weapon in negotiating.

# 6(ii) Dispute resolution in prison settings

*Charles Bethel*

The Center for Community Justice has been in existence now for about eleven years, setting some kind of modern-day record in Washington for small, nonprofit corporations. The Center is a group whose primary interest is the application of nonjudicial methods of dispute resolution, including mediation, to a variety of cases. These include interpersonal disputes, as well as disputes between individuals and larger institutions. The Center also operates a Community Mediation Center that is now connected with a governmental agency in the District of Columbia, and uses volunteer mediators to mediate between 900 and 1,000 cases a year, a number which is growing.

An area in which we have been involved for a long time, and which relates to some degree to the work of the Community Relations Service (CRS) is that of prison conflict and the resolution of disputes that arise in penal institutions, both local jails and state prison systems. We have been active in this field since 1972 and, for the last several years, have worked with a variety of state and local agencies around the country on the design and implementation of administrative remedies for inmate grievances. Why do we think this field is important? One of the reasons is that some of us have a background in law and in dealing with disputes which are litigated. Rather early on, it became quite clear to us that many of the problems and points of friction which occur inevitably within penal institutions, if not dealt with fairly, have the potential for festering and creating a climate that could help to produce some of the very unfortunate, very violent incidents that have occurred in correctional institutions over the last fifteen to twenty years. Attica is one example and New Mexico is another. Even if incidents of that magnitude do not arise, the costs are enormous in both mental and physical terms—in human terms, really—of not providing for an equitable way of responding to legitimate complaints within penal institutions. And the cost is borne by society at large in the form of security measures that may have to be taken. It is also borne quite heavily by those people whom we pay, not very well, to work in penal institutions.

We have had occasion to work in three of the institutions where the CRS had been involved: the Colorado State Prison at Canon City, Walla Walla in Washington State and Reidsville in Georgia. I have not been involved at Reidsville; that work is still going on, but I have spent some time in Canon City and in Walla Walla. In each of these cases, the work that we undertook followed work done by the CRS. This is really an example of the interdependent nature of so much work that goes on in dispute resolution. Our goal in the prison work that we do is to help people set up systems for resolving disputes which will work a little better, or at least be a good corollary to the entire range of informal systems that exist in any institution for responding to complaints. Unfortunately, if the systems are all informal, a lot depends upon the potential user's position of authority, power or coerciveness within the system. In effect, when we set up a formal system we are setting up a legal process. By legal, I mean a system that has rules that have to be adhered to by everybody involved. Rules that are written down can be passed along and do not depend on individuals to keep the system operating.

There are two components of the kind of model we have been working with. One is the idea that inmates and line staff members—that is custodial staff, treatment staff, people who are working with inmates day in and day out—ought to be involved in a process of responding to problems because those groups are the ones who have to live with the solutions or the lack of solutions. The second component is the idea that a grievance ought to be open to examination by someone outside the institution who is not beholden to the correctional structure. This may sound like a very radical idea, and it has been perceived by some people in that way. It does not necessarily mean that someone outside the system has to have the authority to order people to do certain things; the courts do that already. But there has to be, at least, the opportunity for an independent review of the problem. Incidentally, I am only pointing out the two areas that give people the most difficulty. And I am not talking only about prison administrators, but also about attorneys general, governors, politicians and inmates to some degree.

Perhaps the most important function of a complaint process within the penal setting is to give inmates the opportunity to vent their anger, to speak about their perceptions of the problem, and if there are individuals on the staff or administration side who are accused of wrongdoing, to give them a chance to put forward their perceptions as well. All this should be done in a particular setting, one that promises to an inmate a fair hearing and as proof that the inmate is being listened to, a formal written response to his problem should be provided, no matter how petty or ridiculous the problem may appear.

A system like this should also provide an opportunity for correcting misperceptions. One of the biggest benefits of any grievance process is simply that of providing information. Information says to an inmate, 'here is why something is done this way', as opposed to, 'that is the way it is; don't bother me'. And in the process of answering the why-question, it sometimes becomes apparent that the 'why' is not really good enough, and perhaps some changes have to be made.

It is extremely important to open up channels of communication between inmates and staff members and between inmates and the administration. Perhaps ironically, one of the biggest side benefits of a good grievance process within a prison is that, sometimes for the first time, it gives the lowly staff member an opportunity to express his or her views, and to say something to an administration which may not often listen to the person in the cell bloc who has to carry out decisions made higher up.

As with any dispute resolution process that begins with one relatively powerless party and another more powerful one, a permanent dispute resolution process in a prison setting does result in some change in the power relationship. Obviously, this can be perceived as a grave threat by those who hold the preponderance of power. One thing we should keep in mind—and this is true for political situations in general, including behavioral processes in prisons—is that it is always erroneous to think of one group as not having power and the other group as having power. Prisons are operated through a compact between the administrators, the guards and the inmates. And no institution, no prison, can run day-to-day without a tacit agreement that it is going to be allowed to continue to operate. When that basic compact breaks down, we have situations like Attica, New Mexico, and so on.

Empowerment obviously takes place within certain boundaries, because inmates are inmates and every facet of their lives is controlled or affected in some way by their position as inmates. I would, however, add one point to the idea of empowerment: that mediation, or a grievance procedure based in part upon mediation, also says to someone, 'you, perhaps for the first time, are going to be given an opportunity to affect the outcome of this dispute', but that carries with it the concomitant responsibility to be constructive. The process of getting people to accept, and to become part of a mediation process, or some other kind of dispute resolution process, is a two-way street. If they are the right people, then one has some chance of success.

In the process of working with staff and inmates, to develop a procedure which might work in a particular institution, we experience many of the same problems that one faces as a mediator or conciliator—for example are we dealing with the appropriate representatives of the various factions? Do they have the ability to deal, and to make decisions? Will the agreed-upon solution, in this case the design of a program, work?

Sometimes the success that we have in a dispute or in working out something like a grievance process, comes in surprising areas. I am thinking particularly about some experiences in Canon City in Colorado. In the same way that some of the actors in a dispute are not ready to sit down until they have agreed that a crisis is upon them, so some people in correctional institutions are not always excited about sitting down to design what they feel is an elaborate, time-consuming and costly process for responding to complaints unless they feel there is a crisis, or a sufficiently strong leader is able to say, 'you are going to have a crisis if you do not do what I tell you to do'. In that kind of atmosphere or when the cooperation is somewhat tentative, it is sometimes difficult to work on a program of dispute resolution, not to mention the individual disputes.

Canon City was an example of a heterogenous inmate population, a fact not clearly conveyed by the media. It is simply not true that all inmates are alike, anymore than it is true that all Hispanic people are alike. And in that case, there was at least a three-way division along racial lines. There was also a lot of resistance among inmate representatives to working together and to negotiating with the staff and administration about the program for responding to inmate complaints, and there was certainly a lot of resistance to working with staff members in the actual resolution of disputes. Of course, on their side, the staff members were more than sceptical; they were actually hostile to the idea of allowing inmates to be involved in the resolution of complaints brought by other inmates. However, once the grievance process was operating, the part which worked most successfully was the inmate–staff grievance committee. It had a very important role in the resolution of disputes. Part of the reason that it was successful was because, for the first time, people in both groups were actually given some real responsibility for coming up with constructive, creative solutions to very real problems. Unfortunately, in that situation the weakest part of the process was the professional administrators who were supposed to be doing certain things. It was their job but they were not quite so good at it.

All of this is to say that there is a lot of interconnection between attempts made to construct ongoing processes for responding to disputes either within institutions such as prisons, or disputes in communities or interpersonal disputes which arise again and again, disputes which do not have a forum or an outlet that is easily available and inexpensive.

As is the case in large-scale community disputes of the sort that CRS might handle, when we talk about conflict-management procedures, people always want to know what the costs and benefits are. Generally, it is often very hard to put a dollar-and-cents figure on this. We were asked to do an evaluation of a grievance process which has been in use for eight or nine years by the California Youth Authority (California's correctional system for juveniles). One of the things that impressed me was that all of the line staff and administrators with whom we talked had one thing to say about the difference in the institution before and after the procedure went into effect. This was the case, even though many of them did not particularly like the procedure and thought it was kind of a goldmine for the inmates: 'My own kids on the street don't have what the procedures authorize that we give these kids'. What the staff all said was that the number of violent incidents between resident and resident, and between resident and staff had markedly declined. In the institution which I visited, there was a decline from dozens of serious incidents (for example stabbings) per year to one incident in the last two years.

How do we measure that kind of thing? How do we measure an atmosphere? How do we measure the effect on someone who works in a place like that and is now less afraid of being physically injured on the job, or on the resident who is less afraid of an incident blowing up in which he will be unwillingly implicated? These are hard to measure, but in the area of dispute resolution, getting this kind of positive feedback is the pot of gold that is at the end of the rainbow. It is the experience of getting a few positive comments that makes us want to go on and go to work the next day, even if we do not always see the results that we would prefer to see.

# 6(iii) Questioning the questionable

*Joseph B. Gittler*

Throughout history, human thought and even more manifestly, human knowledge have been rooted in implicit, and less often in explicit questions. Socrates stands out as a prime example of moving by means of questions along the paths to ascertainable knowledge. Others—Aquinas, Spinoza, Newton, Einstein, Russell and Wittgenstein—have clearly recognized the role of questions as stepping stones to discovery and intellectual invention. When Einstein was asked how he came to his original idea of relativity, he is alleged to have replied, 'I questioned an axiom'.

It is this rationale that accounts for the rather curious title of my commentary on Gilbert Pompa's chapter. A number of questions arose as I read through it. My raising these questions is not to be construed as displeasure: asking questions is merely an instigative instrument for elucidating the perplexing and the puzzling.

One question that has always intrigued me about the endeavors of conciliators, negotiators and mediators is why do they conciliate and mediate? By this is not meant that they—we—should not mediate or conciliate conflict situations. Rather, I would ask, what rationale do we have for invoking these processes and procedures? Do the procedures imply an inherent and accepted 'good' and value in resolving conflict? If they do, what ethical norms and theories lie rooted in their *modus operandi*? If there are latent ethical assumptions, would it make for more profound and increased understanding of the procedures to delineate the assumptive theories explicitly? Once these theories and assumptions are presented, would it not be intellectually propitious to analyze the valid as well as the invalid aspects of the theories?

Similar questions lie behind the advent of legal enactments. The agency, Community Relations Service, was created under Title X of the 1964 Civil Rights Act. Although law and morality are not always coincident, all legal precepts are implicitly morally grounded. Would we obtain more understanding of the 1964 law if the ethics of inter-racial and inter-ethnic equality were examined?

Pompa states that 'in 1968 we [Community Relations Service personnel] began to look at the problems we were dealing with more in terms of the underlying causes . . . . We looked at some of the causes of the frustration' for minorities in the United States. He then proceeds to enumerate the areas that the people of the Community Relations Service 'felt' were the greatest source of frustration. Here I wondered what Pompa meant by causation. A crucial question in social research has always surrounded the definition of causation as well as the formulation of the design that would sustain 'an invariant relationship between variables'. I am concerned that much subjectivity and personal skills were primarily involved in the conciliation processes which he described. This is true of many conciliatory processes in situations of conflict management. I wonder, therefore, whether these procedures could and should have been analyzed, giving rise perhaps to a set of propositions governing a verifiable and objective *modus operandi* rather than on a priori conviction about workable skills. In verifiability lies increasing reliability.

# 7 (i) Environmental conflict management

*Ethan T. Smith*

I am with the United States Geological Survey, essentially a scientific unit within the Interior Department. A few years ago we carried out a research project in the rather ill-defined area of natural resource or environmental conflict management. We attempted to define the subject matter but found very little in the literature in the environmental field, so we tried to establish a theoretical framework, a base of information. We also attempted some case study work and became involved with educating federal employees about what environmental conflict management might mean to them. In this regard, we were fairly successful, conducting a series of workshops in environmental conflict management.

Though my perspective is that of the federal government, some of our activities overlap with those of state or community governments. Many of the cases we have examined are concerned with what happens when a corporation wants to develop a natural resource, for example to mine coal or drill for oil, which is quite different from a concern with noise-related or other local problems.

What is the genesis of environmental conflict management? During the middle and late 1960s, there was a focused development of, and upswing in, environmental consciousness in the United States. This led to much new legislation such as the National Environmental Policy Act, the Clean Air Act, the Clean Water Act and the Federal Lands Management Act. Consequently, it became relatively easy to pursue violators of the environment. This was an unwanted development for resource development firms as they saw their costs escalating. A question commonly asked was, 'How long does it take to get a simple permit?' The efficiency of the system was breaking down; time was stretching out. For instance, it takes about ten years for a steam electric generation plant to go on-line, which is a lot longer than it takes to build the plant.

Government analysts had been watching the time and, of course, the costs, which were escalating exponentially. It seemed to them that there must be a better way to do business, a more efficient way to develop resources in an environmentally conscientious fashion, but at the same time, to get the product out as well. If there is no oil, the lights will not burn. So we developed an inhouse response. In the process, we discovered that we were not in a unique position; we were trapped in something called the 'lateralization of power', a term coined, I believe, by Michael Doyle of Interaction Associates in San Francisco. What this means is that is is very easy to terminate certain operations, to 'throw sand in the works', but very difficult and expensive to achieve more positive goals.

The government's response in this case was a tiny fraction of a much larger effort going on in universities and companies around the country, to explore better ways to make decisions which is what this book is about.

Let me now discuss some characteristics which are unique to environmental conflicts. These can be categorized as people, procedure and substance-oriented.

With regard to *people*, environmental conflicts are usually characterized by many parties, up to twenty, in contrast to the labor-management model where there tend to be only two. The parties vary in their degree of organization. For instance, on the government side, there is a highly structured bureaucracy. Also, a large corporation and a citizen's group are very different with regard to power, goals and the manner in which they accomplish their goals. Furthermore, in environmental conflicts, we are dealing with the future. We are making decisions that are going to affect generations still to come, and we do not know how to represent their interests adequately. New parties may emerge, since there is no upper limit on how many can participate. Imagine, for instance, a conflict in mediation when suddenly some American Indians, who reside on a particular piece of land say, 'no one bothered to consult us on this and yet you are about to strip mine right where some of our sacred sites are'. The parties would have to go back to the beginning and start over again. There may be very strong ideological biases involved. We can see this in the names of some of the organizations, for example Friends of the Earth. The organizations represented in these conflicts tend to have some kind of value structure behind their positions. Often they do not talk to each other.

The *procedural* problems that often exist in these areas have to do with the fact that there may be no institutional dispute resolution procedures. Perhaps, in a given case, an agency may have a provision to hold a public hearing. Such hearings have been described as analogous to standing on a stage and painting a target on one's chest. And yet, that is the only mission that government organizations are legally empowered to undertake. Government organizations can do only what public law and regulations enable them to do, no matter what the preferences are of the government officials involved. There is no other institutionalized way of dealing with these problems. There may also be competition between different procedures, in part because environmental conflict management is a new field; there may also be confusion about how things will fit together. There is probably no way of ratifying or implementing an agreement once it has been made. We are very good in our society about 'up-front' goals. Once a problem has been 'solved', once it is off the front page, we turn our backs on it; it is never seen again unless it re-emerges as a crisis. There should be some mechanism for monitoring the texts of agreements, but often this is not provided for at all.

Concerning *substance*, the issues are frequently multiple, intertwined, complex—in a word, difficult to understand. It is not a simple case of a mine opening or not opening. Let us not forget those American Indians with their sacred areas. Also, facts may be incomplete or contradictory. Where do the parties obtain accurate data? Such are difficult to come by. We read in the newspapers that a river is polluted beyond redemption. What does that mean? How does one measure that? If it is measured, it is reported as a 'scientifically valid' observation in a language which is not well understood outside of a select community, and there is no procedure for that select community to tell others about it. No one has ever been given that job to do. Long range effects may be uncertain. We make a decision today, but what about the future? Again, what about those generations yet to come? Often scientists cannot answer such questions. This is clearly different from labor and management settling on a contract which is good for the next two years and which can be renegotiated. In an environmental case, unforeseen things may happen in the next two years, either for good or ill. Also, life-and-death decisions are common in the environmental field; they may also be irreversible. For instance, once a decision has been made to strip-mine a particular area, it may not be possible to reclaim the land.

What about the kinds of processes that might be undertaken in the situations we have been discussing? There are a number of them, beginning with the least structured and moving toward the most formal: fact-finding, conciliation, negotiation, facilitation, mediation and arbitration. We will discuss each briefly and then some of them in detail.

Fact-finding is perhaps one of the least labor-intensive types of processes that we can undertake. We have already said that frequently the facts are not well known. No one may have looked for them. A fact-finding analysis can be merely verifying what is true and documenting it. Many cases can be solved simply by removing the misperceptions of what is true in terms of the data, the parties' values and their relationships with other organizations.

About conciliation, let me briefly say, in terms of the definitions that we are using here, that it is an emotional, confusing approach. We now know that environmental conflicts are concerned with problems involving people, perhaps involving stereotypes: 'These people are going to plunder the land; those guys are a bunch of bubble-headed bureaucrats.' Often the object is to get the parties together to enable them to recognize each other as human beings, that they are not demons, and so on.

Negotiation is the next most structured approach. What the parties are trying to do in this case is both to educate and bargain with one another. Facilitation, often called cooperative problem solving, is one step further in the formal direction, primarily because that is the first time that the parties require someone from outside. We can do fact-finding, conciliation and negotiation ourselves if we are a party to one of these disputes, but once we get to facilitation, we need someone who is outside the dispute.

Then there is mediation where the the third party has even more power, and finally, arbitration where there is some kind of binding decision made. From the federal perspective, there is almost no authority to carry out binding arbitration in environmental cases. We are limited, therefore, to the less formal procedures, some of which I shall now discuss in more detail.

There are basically three categories of facts for the fact-finding process: people-oriented data, relationship-oriented data and substantive data. Concerning people, there are considerations such as: what are the interests of a particular group? What are 'interests'? An interest is something that a party has which is more important than the set of issues currently before the board. In labor/management it might be: 'I'm going to negotiate for a new salary structure for my union, but we have some good jobs there which we don't want to lose.' The environmental case is more global. A company that wants to enter a certain area and drill for oil may be drilling on public land, require permits to do so and need to build a road into the area. What do they really want? They would like to make a profit, but one thing for certain is that they do not want to lose the right to drill. That is much more important than individual issues.

Many aspects of people problems are oriented around the value structures of the parties to environmental issues. Is it more important to people to keep the lights burning or to save the whales? Usually those who work for different organizations do so because of equally held values. Many of us become involved with science and engineering, for instance, because we feel more comfortable with inanimate objects than we do with people; the former are easier to deal with than the latter. Such people feel much more comfortable with engineering-type answers to problems. Such basic value structures in people are not easy to change. The parties may also have very different sources of power: public law or personal competency.

Relationships is a difficult area, again because environmental conflict management is an N-party situation involving relationships between each pair of parties. The parties will have different histories of dialogue with each other. The status of each of these parties may be changing as well. For instance, for various economic and political reasons, the status of the relative power of the organizations in the environmental area may be less now than it was three years ago.

Substance, the third area of fact-finding, poses questions such as: 'Can we find the central issues? And the secondary issues as well?' Returning to the well-drilling example, how many wells does the company want to drill? What is the production of the well or wells? How do they get to the well? They may have to build a road to get to the well. What kind of road? What about erosion in the area? What about the problem of washout? Are there other companies relevant to the issue? Should they somehow share part of the costs? What about the Indians' sacred sites in the area?

Clearly, when we start to examine an environmental case, the list of issues can proliferate considerably, but that is secondary to examining the interests. We have already tried to determine what interests are. We are now discussing what issues are. What about the options available? Should there be one well, two wells, five wells, ten wells? Should we have a gravel surface road, or a paved road? Should one company pay for it, or all companies? What is the order of precedence of jurisdiction for the federal government, county government and all the other parties who would be involved? Have these options been fleshed out? Or has it degenerated into a name-calling contest? 'We have to build that well. Let 'em freeze in the dark.' That dates from 1973, when we were worried about the first oil embargo. 'Yeah! You are going to build that well over my dead body and all my lawyers too.' Or Ralph Nader's famous call to arms: 'sue the bastards!' Obviously, if people are engaging in that kind of dialogue, it is very unlikely that they have developed a dispassionate set of options.

Once the parties have obtained their facts, what do they do with them? There is a process called conflict management planning which involves the development of positions. What are the possible outcomes of environmental cases? The typical one is the win-lose outcome: somebody wins, somebody loses. That is the outcome we are most familiar with; somebody wins, somebody loses because one side has overwhelming power. The stakes are high. 'My God! and we are going to win this case.' We can hear the client talking to his lawyer, 'Go in and win.' This is the adversarial approach.

Impasse outcomes can develop when the parties are quite well balanced in power. One side cannot push the other off. The stakes may not be high enough for a real win-type situtation. Compromise outcomes are when everybody has to give something up in order to get part of what they want. Usually, neither party perceives itself as having the power to win totally. The stakes for winning are high, but perhaps not overwhelmingly high. Win-Win outcomes are the results that many of us are looking for. Can an outcome be achieved in which all sides feel as though their real interests have been met? Needless to say, this is difficult to achieve. But in any case, a win-win orientation means that the parties are not engaged in a power struggle; they are not in it to 'get the other guy'. Instead, they are interested in maintaining a positive relationship with the other parties. The stakes are high, not just for winning one particular situation, but for producing a solution that will be satisfactory now and in the future.

The various kinds of outcomes can be linked to different strategies, for instance competition, if the parties are aiming for the win-lose option. The flip-side of competition, accommodation, involves all parties giving in a little through negotiation, making concessions—the process we are most familiar with in labor-management relations. Avoiding the problem could lead to an impasse. For example, a federal agency may say, 'we prefer at this time to take no position on the issue of that well.' This sounds innocuous, but unless the relevant parties obtain some reaction from the agency (which might not even be the main agency), they cannot go forward. The whole process stops, and the agency has essentially cancelled itself out through its inaction. Finally, if the parties are lucky, they might try facilitation or cooperative problem solving, which is essentially the win-win option, building a consensus.

When fact-finding has been successful, we know the parties, their issues and their interests. We know that each of the parties has a number of gambits, like in a card game. The question then becomes: how do we put all this together into a framework? One way is through a negotiation framework for making tradeoffs. This involves each party developing its own strategy, its own 'negotiation table' and figuring out the tables of the other parties. 'Know your enemy.' The parties must be clear about their own interests, for example retaining their jobs, their union; continuing to drill on a particular piece of land, etc. These interests are not to be compromised. Then the various issues should be listed: number of wells, type of road, surface of the road, erosion control, Indian sacred areas, and so on. The next item is the development of positions. This is something that the parties do with 'crossed fingers' and the hope that each is guessing better than the others. Here the parties have to bracket the target on each issue; that is they have to determine their initial positions and then their 'bottom lines'. In the well-drilling case, for example, the company may want at least one well drilled on a particular property, but as their initial position, they may specify twenty wells, with the 'in-between bracket' constituting successive fallback positions (fifteen, ten, five).

What is the purpose of the initial position? Negotiation is an educational process. For education to be possible, most negotiators would prefer to face an experienced person across the table than someone who is new to the game. Why? If our opponents do not know the game, then we can defeat them. If they do not know the game, then they do not know its rules. They might be playing by one set, and we by another, or perhaps worse, we might be playing wholly different games. Let us recall the air traffic controllers' strike. They were not playing the same game as the government—a definite failure in negotiation strategy. In any case, if the drilling company and the government are playing the same game, then, when the former puts forward twenty wells as its initial position, the latter will have been 'educated' to an awareness that the company wants to drill some wells. The government will not know that the company would settle for one.

This is exactly how negotiation operates. And we wonder why disputes sometimes take years to get settled. This is very much like poker. The parties simply cannot reveal all their cards. Unfortunately most of the government people do not know how to play the game. We are not trained that way. Instead, we have been trained to turn the problem over to our office of the solicitor. We are permitted to do only what public law regulations say, i.e., there is no institutional forum for anything but adversarial procedures. This again is the reason why we have been researching environmental conflict management, conducting workshops to train government people in the field, and so on. Again, negotiation is the process that results in the compromise outcome. As we have already indicated, negotiation is not the only process and compromise is not the only outcome in environmental conflict management.

Facilitation or cooperative problem solving is another response to the need to try to make more efficient decisions. One part of the world where facilitation occurs a great deal these days is Japan. We often wonder why we cannot do things the way the Japanese do them, why we cannot build better cars, and so on. The Japanese take a long time to make any kind of a decision, and what they are doing essentially is cooperative problem solving. They may, however, have some cultural advantages over us in this regard. Still, there are some fine practitioners of facilitation in the United States, such as Interaction Associates in San Francisco, a base which we are trying to develop into a more pervasive American version of the Japanese experience.

In our scheme of things, facilitation represents the first occasion that parties to a conflict require a third party. The third party is a process person who does not enter into the substance of the situation. For example, keeping all the parties at meetings in line and making the final decision is the responsibility of the chairperson. This is usually too much for one person to do. Modern day managers spend somewhere between 60 to 80 percent of their time in such meetings. The time and money involved are not insignificant, but it is all very inefficient. Facilitation is an attempt to make meetings more efficient by ensuring that agendas are available, that the parties adhere to them, and so on.

Specifically, the facilitator provides for initial conciliation, a chance for the parties to ventilate their feelings, to determine that the other parties are not 'demons'. This may occur at a series of meetings held, say, every two months over a one-year period. Given that it can take ten years for a power plant to go on-line, a year of meetings might be a cheap solution.

The facilitator also assists in the development of a relevant definition of the problem. Although striving to remain clear of substance, the facilitator can ask of each party, 'Tell me, what are the issues as you see them?' This is especially relevant for the people in the 'back of the room' who do not say anything. They will come to meeting after meeting, representing, for instance, a county-level government, without ever uttering a word. The facilitatot has to draw them out.

Most importantly, he may have to restate the issues in language that everyone will accept. This is crucial because every group will use different words; semantics tend to be very slippery in conflict management. One approach to this is to write down all relevant developments. This may be done on a board at the front of the room or on a flip chart with a magic marker. Why? Research has shown that people absorb 10 percent of what they hear and 90 percent of what they see. If the parties are really lucky, the facilitator will help them to arrive at a decision. The classic book on this is *How to Make Meetings Work*, by Michael Doyle and David Straus of Interaction Associates.

The remaining procedure I want to consider is mediation. Mediation is one step further in the formal, structured direction. The mediator is similar to the facilitator except that he has more power: the mediator can get involved with the substance, and not just the process, of disputes. The parties may decide that they require a mediator because the number of issues is unmanageably large, they are poorly organized or there are so many of them that they are all in a perpetual wrangle instead of discussing the issues. In such a situation of deadlock, in the absence of institutionalized conflict management machinery, if the parties prefer not to go to court because they know that will cost them a lot of money, then a mediator is a cheap alternative to a lawyer or a judge. This is a very persuasive consideration.

What is unique about the mediator? He knows what all the negotiation tables are, and he is honor-bound not to reveal one party's strategies to another. Who is in a better position to discern where the solutions (if any) may lie? Since the parties cannot reveal their strategies to one another, the mediator is in a perfect position to make recommendations. Whether he is able to succeed or not, of course, is not always clear. People may change their negotiation tables; they may back off. Mediation does not—indeed, cannot—always work, but it does seem to be particularly relevant to the 60 to 70 percent of environmental cases that appear to be caused simply by misinformation. When it does succeed in these and other cases, the parties—and society at large—will have been spared the economic, psychic and other costs of an adversarial approach.

Environmental conflict management is a new field, an alternative to adversarial approaches. Although it is becoming more and more visible, a major problem is that there are very few mechanisms for making if work. This is certainly the case in government agencies.

## Bibliography

Alexander, T. (1978), 'A Promising Try at Environmental Détente for Coal', *Fortune*, 13 February, pp. 94–102.

Arnold, R. (1978), 'Loggers vs. Environmentalists—Friends?, *Logging Management*, February, pp. 16–19.

Bernstein, J.Z. (1970), 'Environmental Mediation', *EPA Journal*, November–December, pp. 30–1.

Carpenter, S.L. and W.J.D. Kennedy (1979), *Conflict Management: Its Application to Energy Disputes*, Boulder, ROMCOE (available from authors on request).

Clark, P.B. (1978), *Brayton Point: An Experiment in Collaborative Problem*

*Solving*, Boston, Clark-McGlennon Associates, Inc. (available from author on request).

Cormick, G.W. and L.K. Patton (1977), *Environmental Mediation: Defining the Process through Experience*, University of Washington, Seattle, Office of Environmental Mediation (available from authors on request).

Council on Environmental Quality (1978), 'National Environmental Policy Act: Implimentation of Procedural Provisions, Final Regulations', *Federal Register*, **43**, no. 230, pp. 55977–6007.

Doyle, M. and D. Straus (1976), *How to Make Meetings Work*, Chicago, Playboy Press.

Fanning, O. (1979), 'Environmental Mediation: The World's Newest Profession', *Environment*, **21**, no. 7, pp. 33–8.

Fradin, D.M. (1976), *The Moorehead Malt Plant Dispute, Report on Minnesota's First Environmental Mediation*, St. Paul, Environmental Balance Association of Minnesota.

Gladwin, T.N. (1978), *The Management of Environmental Conflict: A Survey of Research Opportunities and Priorities*, New York, New York University Graduate School of Business Administration, #78-09, (available from author on request).

Lake, L.M. (1977), 'Mediating Environmental Disputes', *Ekistics*, **44**, no. 262, pp. 164–70.

Lake, L.M. (1978), 'Environmental Mediation: An Effective Alternative?' Los Angeles, University of California (available from author on request).

Lake, L.M. (ed.), (1980), *Environmental Mediation: The Search for Consensus*, Boulder, Westview Press.

Margolin, S.V. (1979), *The Two Minute Mile*, Cambridge, Arthur D. Little, Inc., occasional paper (available from author on request).

Massachusetts Institute of Technology Environmental Impact Assessment Project and Clark-McGlennon Associates, Inc. (1978) (draft), *Guidelines to Identify, Manage, and Resolve Environmental Disputes*, Cambridge, Massachusetts Institute of Technology.

McCarthy, J.E. (1976), 'Resolving Environmental Conflicts', *Environmental Science and Technology*, **10**, no. 1, pp. 40–3.

McCloskey, M. (1977), *Environmental Conflicts: Why Aren't More Negotiated?*, San Francisco, Sierra Club.

New England River Basins Commission. (1979), *Power Plant Siting: Water and Related Land Resources: A Prospectus*, Boston, NERBC.

Nice, J. (1979), 'Stalemates Spawn New Breed: The Eco-Mediators', *High Country News*, **II**, no. 6, Lander, Wyoming.

Nicolau, G. (1978), *The Limits and Potential of Environmental Mediation*, New York, Institute for Mediation and Conflict Resolution.

O'Connor, D. (1978), 'Environmental Mediation: The State-of-the-Art', *EIA Review 2*, October, Cambridge, Laboratory of Architecture and Planning, Massachusetts Institute of Technology, pp. 9–17.

Patton, L.K. and G.W. Cormick (1977), *Mediation and the NEPA Process: The Interstate 90 Experience*, Seattle, Office of Environmental Mediation, University of Washington.

Resolve (1978), *Environmental Mediation: An Effective Alternative*, Palo Alto, Resolve.

Rivkin, M.D. (1977), *Negotiated Development: A Breakthrough in Environmental Controversies*, Washington, DC, The Conservation Foundation.

Rocky Mountain Center for the Environment (1978), *What ROMCOE Does*, Boulder, ROMCOE.

Straus, D.B. (1977), *Mediating Environmental, Energy and Economic Tradeoffs: A Case Study of the Search for Improved Tools for Facilitating the Process*, New York, American Arbitration Association.

Susskind, L. (1978), 'Viewpoint: It's Time to Shift Our Attention to Strategies for Resolving Environmental Disputes', *EIA Review 2*, October, Cambridge, Laboratory of Architecture and Planning, Massachusetts Institute of Technology, pp. 4–8.

Susskind, L. (1978), 'The Political Realities of Environmental Dispute Mediation', Cambridge, Massachusetts Institute of Technology, (available from author on request).

Urban Land Institute. (1979), *Conflict Resolution: Environmental Comment*, Washington, DC.

Vaughn, B. and L. Hunter (1978), *Selected Readings in Environmental Conflict Management*, Palo Alto, Resolve.

Wondolleck, J.M. (1979), 'Bargaining for the Environment: Compensation and Negotiation in the Energy Facility Siting Process', Unpublished thesis for Master of City Planning degree, Cambridge, Massachusetts Institute of Technology.

# 7 (ii) Issues from the practice of environmental mediation

*Bruce Dotson*

Ethan Smith's section deals with the process of environmental conflict analysis and resolution generally; I would like to try to particularize his comments by reference to the work in environmental land use and development issues that we do at the Institute for Environmental Negotiation.

But first, some preliminary comments. Our initial source of funding at the Institute was the Virginia Environmental Endowment. The Endowment, in turn, receives its funding from the fine that was levied by the federal courts against Allied Chemical in 1977 for the spill of Kepone in the James River. In this case, the federal judge imposing the fine gave Allied Chemical an opportunity to help determine how their money should be utilized. Allied's response, perhaps in the spirit of 'victim compensation', was to create an environmental fund where the money, the interest from $8 million, would be used on behalf of the environment. This exemplifies the kind of creative thinking that turns around traditional views and opens up new possibilities. Such a reformulation of a problem and its solution is made possible through negotiations.

Against the background provided by the other chapters in this book, environmental mediation may seem to be a very specialized or narrow topic. These are relative terms. To environmental mediators, we are ourselves a diverse group dealing with a broad range of substantive topics from a variety of consensus-seeking standpoints. At the Institute we work on issues regarding the environment, land use and development primarily at the state and local level, but we must frequently deal with the federal government. Our experience is that many issues are intergovernmental in nature. It is very hard to classify an issue only as a local issue or only a state or a federal issue because the implementation of a national program very often occurs at the state and local levels. Disputes can involve several local communities (for example a city, a town and a surrounding county), a state agency which is attempting to apply and enforce environmental regulations at the state level, plus federal regulations and federal grant-making programs.

Since all levels of government are involved in environmental conflict they can potentially be involved in its management. There seems to be the notion that governments are not supposed to fight among themselves. They are supposed to be serving the same purposes, essentially the public interest. Accordingly, governmental officials feel very uneasy when differences of opinion exist among them. This attitude, if I am correct that it exists, is consistent with Roger Fisher's (1981) notion that negotiation is possible where the disputing parties hold some interests in common although they diverge on others. Consequently, one of the prime areas for environmental mediation may be intergovernmental relations. In our experience, the intergovernmental area has been a very fruitful area of involvement.

We have been involved in a wide range of land-use disputes: for example disputes concerning the location of shopping centers, the expansion of a parking lot associated with a hospital, enlargement of a waste-disposal area, a boundary on a park, management issues associated with parklands and water resources, as well as health regulations dealing with septic systems at the state level. Stone quarries is a category of issue that has been called 'LULUs'—locally unwanted land uses. Since nobody wants a quarry next door, it is almost automatic that such site-specific issues generate controversy.

The initial thing that we do in any situation is to conduct an assessment of the conflict and the potential options for managing it. In Ethan Smith's terms, this is a fact-finding operation. We examine each of the parties, their relationships, and so on, then we construct what we think their negotiation tables might be, all in an effort to determine whether or not the situation is right for some kind of third-party intervention. In our experience—and this seems to be true of others as well—such intervention may be appropriate in only 10 to 25 percent of the cases. When a mediator does enter such situations, I am pleased to report that more often than not a satisfactory solution is developed.

Having mentioned several categories of activities let me indicate that we generally classify cases into the following groupings:

(1)   site-specific disputes (e.g., shopping-center development proposal);
(2)   interjurisdictional disputes (e.g., city-county annexation proceedings);
(3)   policy dialogues (e.g., consensus on policy about siting hazardous waste facilities);
(4)   interagency task forces (e.g., state ground-water protection strategy);
(5)   expanded public involvement activities (e.g., devising public participation/negotiation strategies);
(6)   conflict assessments (e.g., fact-finding about attitudes toward negotiations).

Gaining entry into a dispute is the most difficult situation for a third party. We are in the position, on the one hand, of wanting to promote mediation and negotiation as a process because we think they are viable alternatives that have not received sufficient consideration. On the other hand, we are neutral with respect to the substantive outcome of the dispute. This role duality creates some entry problems that have to be dealt with on a case-by-case basis. In general, however, there are several ways to gain entry. We have, in some cases, initiated the contact ourselves. We read the newspapers, become aware of a quarry or a housing dispute and then simply telephone the person whose name is mentioned and ask if we may send them a copy of our newsletter. There are some, however, who argue that if a potential third party initiates contact, this can be perceived as taking sides. Our policy is to demonstrate our neutrality once we are on the scene. We also conduct training sessions, convene conferences and bring in citizen activist leaders as part of our effort to educate the public and develop constituencies. At the present time, in contrast to when we started in 1981, we rarely have time to pursue projects based on newspaper leads.

Another way to gain entry is at the initiative of an interested party. More and more our cases come to us in this manner. Sometimes we are contacted by government officials or by other parties. It is noteworthy that if the parties themselves contact the third party, it is not usually to seek neutral assistance but because they perceive the person as helping their side achieve its objectives. The parties tend, therefore, even in seeking mediation, to reflect a win-lose mode. Another interesting observation is that in about 90 percent of the cases that have been brought to us, especially by officials, our intervention has been successful. There seems to be, therefore, a high correlation between being called in and successful intervention, but in general, entry remains a major problem for the third party.

Because of the entry problem, institutional support of third-party intervention can be very important. When the parties to a dispute know that mediation is part of the overall process that they have to go through, then they may be more willing to try it. This institutional prod may be just what it takes to trigger meaningful negotiations. We have also experienced situations, however, where we suspected that the negotiations were primarily a ritual to satisfy a requirement that negotiation be attempted. It is crucial that the parties feel they can potentially gain from negotiation in order to commit the necessary time and attention to the negotiation process.

There seems to be two schools of thought regarding the kind of training needed to be a successful third party. According to one, the third party is a person who is skilled primarily in meeting management and general conflict resolution procedures. This is the facilitator in Ethan Smith's terms. According to the other school, the third party is much more capable of achieving a successful outcome if he/she also knows something about the subject matter being mediated. Our leaning at the Institute is toward combining both process and substantive knowledge. We feel that because we are urban and environmental planners, our knowledge and experience very often enables us to move the parties to environmental and land-use disputes in constructive directions. For instance, when someone suggests a solution, we are familiar with its technical components. Consequently, we can raise questions that the parties had not previously considered; in this way, we can help them test the workability of ideas. We do not fill the role of expert, but we can help translate expertise in ways that are useful for problem solving.

I might add that this combination of substantive and process skills is something toward which agency personnel might aspire. If regulators and managers could think like mediators, many conflicts could be avoided. If there were more 'inside' mediators, there would be less need for outside mediators like the Institute. A potential problem for inside mediators, however, are situations in which the mediator's neutrality and credibility might be undermined. For instance, in a dispute involving a city as a party, a local planner employed by the city would clearly be very limited in terms of being able to claim neutrality. On the other hand, when the objective is fact-finding or finding someone simply to 'break the ice' and initiate communication, the neutrality *per se* is not the sole criterion. If, at more advanced stages, a truly neutral person were needed, then an outsider could be brought in. One of our experiences has been that in many disputes, one side is very well organized while the other side is not. We have spent a good deal of time with neighborhood groups simply to get them together to determine what their negotiating positions might be, what their alternatives are, how far they are willing to go, how much time they are willing to put into the effort, and so on. All of this may be necessary to get them to a point where they are ready to sit down and talk to the opposition. Again, that could be done very easily from an inside position within the neighborhood's own leadership.

Though environmental mediation is a specific part of conflict analysis and resolution generally, it comprises its own broad range of topics, some of which have been addressed in this section.

## Bibliography

Fisher, R. and W. Ury (1981), *Getting to Yes: Negotiating Agreement Without Giving In*, Boston, Houghton Mifflin.

# 7 (iii) Environmental mediation: an alternative dispute settlement system

*Roger Richman*

New conceptualizations of old problems are forced on us by the failure of traditional means for dealing with those problems. Such is the experience in the development of the emerging professional field of alternative dispute resolution, particularly in our subject, environment conflict management. The 'old' problems in this subject are created when our traditional dispute settlement systems encounter the conditions of environmental conflicts—conditions of issue complexity, multiple parties with stakes in the outcome, uncertain facts and inadequate data and, ultimately, of value conflicts that do not provide a basis for conflict resolution through the political process or through the reasoned judgment of the court system. The new approaches—environmental mediation and structured facilitation—offer means to address these problems as complements (but not as complete replacements) to the traditional public dispute settlement systems: the courts, administrative processes of public agencies and the political process.

My objective here is to explore some of the reasons underlying the introduction of mediation as an alternative to reliance on the courts to settle environmental disputes. I begin with a case study of the emergence of an environmental conflict, and then explore the reasons why the courts are unsuitable for resolving issues in environmental conflicts. A theoretical discussion of attributes of conflict outcomes is then presented, including a discussion of the way the institutional requirements of court systems limit the outcomes available to parties. As a final point, the potential roles for mediation as an alternative dispute settlement system, are described.

## Genesis of an environmental conflict

In North Carolina a few years ago I encountered a case where the United States Army Corps of Engineers found its proposed actions blocked by an environmental group. The Corps was responsible for maintaining the depth of an inlet from the Atlantic Ocean to the Intercoastal Waterway, a main shipping highway. The channel silted periodically and now required dredging. A local fishing industry in a nearby town depended on the dredging to maintain access to the open waters of the ocean.

The Corps of Engineers, following internal procedures, held a public hearing on the proposed dredging. The agency was, however, committed by its past experience and its mission to the dredging project. It was not neutral on whether or not the dredging should take place. The Corps' representatives were surprised to find much opposition at the public hearing. More than a hundred local residents attended and many made presentations against the dredging project. An environmental organization, the local chapter of the Izzak Walton League, a national sport fishing and environmental conservation group, had mobilized to fight the dredging project. Local leaders of the League contended that the dredging project would have negative environmental effects on the mouth of the White Oak River, a major natural feature in the area, and the site of two population centers, the towns of Cape Carteret and Swansboro. League members produced photos of the river in the 1930s, 1950s, and 1970s, and noted that the river's mouth had continually been silting as a result of the Corps' dredging of the inlet a few miles away. The League claimed that the Corps' actions were leading to the destruction of the river. They claimed that annual water flow was down, that the river was much shallower in the 1970s than it had been thirty years before and they forecast that the river would eventually stop flowing altogether and become a swamp—all because of the Corps' dredging activities. The League, one of whose members owned the local newspaper, intensively publicized its findings and created significant public opposition to the dredging project. Elected officials of the four local governments surrounding the river mouth sided with the environmentalists.

The conflict included the following parties: the Army Corps of Engineers; the local commercial fishing industry; the local chapter of the Izzak Walton League; and the mayors and county supervisors of four local governments concerned that their towns might no longer be riverfront communities. A state agency, the North Carolina Coastal Zone Management Agency, had an indirect interest in the conflict, but deferred to the local public officials' positions. The conflict was brought forth by the president of the local Izzak Walton League, an activist who took an adversarial stance toward the Corps. He had battled the Corps on another project in a different state years before and had won—the Corps had backed off—and he was convinced that he could do it again. However, the Corps had indicated that in this case a national interest was at stake in maintaining the open channel from the sea, and that despite the negative public hearing it would probably go ahead with the dredging.

The basic conflict was about values. As the environmentalists saw the issues, the conflict was about what was more important—maintaining a commercial route to the sea or preserving the natural river flow to avoid turning the river into a swamp. The conflict, significantly, was affected by the parties' interpretations of the sketchy scientific data available. While the Corps questioned whether its dredging really would make the river silt and become shallower, the environmentalists leaned heavily on the data they had collected. They buttressed their point with the statements of older residents about the river's depth long ago, before the Corps first began to dredge the channel.

## Traditional dispute settlement systems

In the normal course of environmental disputes the environmental interests would have begun a lawsuit with the object of delaying the Corps' dredging program. The Corps' authority to dredge the channel, even over local opposition, was clear. Congress had given that authority to the agency. Yet the Corps is a politically sensitive agency, and the environmental interests felt that they could get the agency to back down if they could apply enough pressure. One way of doing this was to go to court to restrain the Corps from going ahead with its project. The environmentalists knew they could not win a court decision (the agency's mandate was clear); but they felt they could, through delaying tactics, build a wider constituency against the project and thus pressure the Corps into abandoning it, or into undertaking ameliorative measures on the river itself. The Corps rejected such measures as much too expensive for the relative gain.

The local actors had another strategy. They contacted their Congressman and asked him to lobby the Corps to abandon the project. The Congressman moved carefully. There were other local interests—the local fishing industry, for example, —who might be on the Corps' side. It was indeed conceivable that the fishing industry would enter a suit against the environmentalists, in the hope of making them decide to abandon their suit against the Corps.

The case presented demonstrates certain typical features of environmental disputes. First, there were multiple parties with very different issues and interests. The primary parties were acting as agents for others as well as for themselves. Both sides claimed to seek the public interest, and the Corps, given its statutory mandate, claimed to represent the public interest. Yet the other side included elected officials from the affected local governments also representing the public interest. Second, one side used scientific and historical data to make its case, but the other side rejected the data and its relevance. The data that was available was used in an adversarial context. Third, the multiple parties to the conflict were not organized in an attempt to settle the dispute. Individual meetings between the Corps' representative and the Izzak Walton League took place, but not in a focused negotiating context. These *ad hoc* meetings allowed each party to state its position, but did not enable active negotiations. Fourth, the conflict was unregulated. Each party was free to pursue adversarial strategies, attempting to force their opponents to concede, while not conceding themselves. Each side was free to stall (the agency) or enter lawsuits (the environmental interests) with the object of sufficient delay to increase the incentives for the other side to capitulate. Each side configured its strategy to win, with the other side losing. The courts were used by the environmental group as part of their adversarial strategy and not as a settlement-seeking path.

Neither the courts nor the political process is well equipped to handle such multiparty complex disputes. The courts, of course, specialize in adjudicating cases, not in negotiating them. Yet in this case, as in many environmental disputes, the issues do not naturally fall into adjudicable categories. The issues can, of course, be framed as narrowly defined issues for court decision, but they lose their vitality in the process; in their essence they are questions of joint accommodation to a common course of action—in this case action by the Corps that would incorporate the points made by the environmental interests and the local officials. Further, in many cases litigation imposes its own requirements on the parties, and had the case gone to court, would have been fought on procedural grounds (for example did the Corps hold a proper public hearing) rather than on substantive grounds. Thus, litigation leads the parties away from consideration of their joint interests in settlement to a stylized and somewhat artificial adversarial context. Finally, litigation in many environmental cases is pursued as a strategy rather than in actual expectation of a positive court-ordered settlement. The strategic use of litigation to force opponents to grant concessions often backfires, however, by generating counter-adversarial actions. Thus litigation, far from settling complex disputes, may engender new rounds of litigation, delaying final decisions and increasing the costs of the dispute to all parties.

## A theoretical view

Figure 7.1, 'Conflict outcomes', maps the possible range of outcomes in a two-party dispute. In this hypothetical conflict (we may simplify our case by seeing the Corps of Engineers as Party A and the Izzak Walton League as Party B), each party's desired outcomes are found along one axis and each party's outcomes range from 0 at the origin to 10, complete satisfaction—winning the dispute on their own preferred terms. In the *joint outcome space* are four corner points which reflect different combinations of winning and losing by each party. Thus, in the upper left-hand corner we see a win-lose case where Party A wins and Party B loses, and in the lower right-hand corner we see the opposite situation, where Party A loses and Party B wins. Both of these outcomes are zero-sum solutions. The line connecting these two corners may be called the zero-sum distributive bargaining line. Any solution to the conflict falling along the line involves a pure tradeoff where one party wins only at the other party's expense. An outcome to the conflict in which the parties finish to the left of the zero-sum bargaining line results in a suboptimal settlement.

Our traditional dispute-processing system, the courts, institutionalize the win-lose, zero-sum distributive bargaining model. As a dispute settlement system the court's function is to decide cases based on the facts presented and the controlling laws that govern the factual situation. Courts make decisions, on the evidence and the applicable law, considering only what is presented to them by the parties in an adversarial context. They 'allocate' the decision (that is the impacts that flow from the decision) between the parties, usually along the zero-sum line but occasionally to the left of the line, the suboptimal negative-sum or lose-lose settlement.

Further study of Figure 7.1 shows that outcomes are possible to the right of the zero-sum line, in a positive-sum or win-win context. One of the major points here is that courts, as institutional dispute-settlement systems, only very rarely lead disputants into this zone. The very structure and operating rules of the courts prohibit them from enhancing the issues. They are set up, as noted above, only to resolve the issues before them, not to enrich the issues to the point where the dispute may turn from being an adversarial situation to one where win-win solutions may be found. What is missing, then, are mechanisms to move parties to the right of the zero-sum line. This is the role of the mechanisms of alternative dispute settlement—in particular, of mediation and (where conflicts are not formalized) facilitation techniques.

The line moving outward toward the win-win corner, the upper right, can be labeled the integrative-bargaining line. Movement along this line is a product of negotiation, where the aim of deal cutting (getting the best deal for one's side) is modified by the realization of possibilities for joint gains—of consideration of getting a better deal for the other side as well. Rather than simply focusing on the distributive-bargaining context (where Party A gains as Party B loses), in this model both parties gain. Integrative negotiation works not only by eliminating

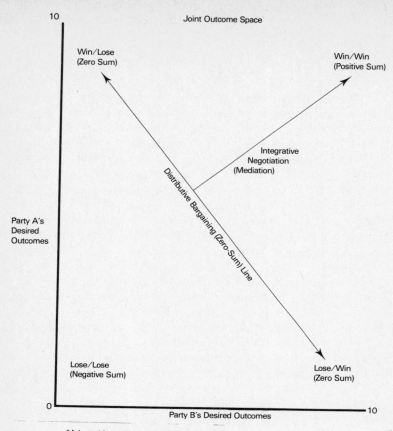

**Figure 7.1.** Conflict outcomes*

conflict but by channeling it into competition for mutual ends rather than for unilaterally conceived ends. In dispute situations integrative bargaining is difficult to achieve and may not last long, but it is essential to development of a jointly conceived solution. It may take some time at the stage of distributive bargaining, where parties are directly competing in a win-lose, zero-sum world to set the stage for transition to integrative bargaining, reaching beyond the zero-sum line.

There are certain requirements for dispute situations before integrative bargaining may be considered. The parties, for example, must be ready to negotiate directly with an end toward settling their conflict. This truism hides the requirement of true negotiations—that the parties organize themselves internally to negotiate, often by designating an individual or committee to represent their interests; that the parties lay out a set of negotiating positions that they will consider; that they will receive and make counter offers and will indeed move away from their original positions toward settlement. All of these conditions for negotiation can be met, and indeed often are, while the parties are in a distributive-bargaining, win-lose mode. This very movement toward substantive negotiation is a significant step for parties who might otherwise care to refer their dispute to their lawyers, their advocates, for execution—thereby distancing themselves from the stresses of negotiation and the challenges to their positions.

The essence of a true negotiation (that which goes beyond pure distributive bargaining) is that the parties—and this is particularly relevant in multiparty environmental disputes—create a temporary sense of the negotiation as an entity, a process, and a quasi-organization in which they are members and in which they have an investment. Pure zero-sum bargaining only requires that the parties state positions and attempt to manipulate their opponents into losing. It is essentially an adversarial and a conservative activity, where avoidance of risks to positions makes parties reluctant to innovate in proposals. Integrative negotiations, on the other hand, require parties to establish a relationship with one another that is based on some small measure of trust that both parties' interests can be addressed simultaneously. This modicum of trust, in turn, can only emerge from the process of direct exchanges between the parties, where each is able to observe the 'devil' across the table, take his or her measure, and through that process, find that they can deal with one another and that their interests are not mutually exclusive. To get to this point, the precursor to integrative negotiations, disputants must typically go through stages of adversarial contact in a series of meetings. The commitment to joint outcomes instead of unilateral outcomes typically only emerges after lengthy experience of testing one another in adversarial contexts.

Mediators act to create and to enhance the possibilities of integrative negotiation, where possible, but they first must deal with the earlier conditions described above. They form the center of the negotiation; they establish the negotiation as a quasi-organization. They are the advocates of the parties' joint interests, and in this role they push, test and probe for willingness to move to real negotiations. They help the parties form negotiating teams and develop negotiating positions; they also establish communications between the parties. They establish the negotiation by initially focusing on procedures (location and timing of meetings) and the development of ground rules as initial tests of good faith between the parties. The mediators then set up processes for position exchanges, team analysis and review of positions offered.

Mediators, of course, can only work through the parties; they cannot impose settlements. The parties define not only the issues but the state of the dispute. In many instances, as in our case study presented earlier, the parties are initially committed to an adversarial course, and are intent on limiting their contact to distributive bargaining along the zero-sum line. In these settings, mediators restrict their roles to one of keeping the negotiations going by assisting in communicating positions between the parties. In extreme cases in this mode, mediators may separate the parties and carry back and forth texts of positions. This type of bargaining will not by itself lead to the richer possibilities of integrative negotiation. Mediator interventions may be essential to find a basis from which the parties may be brought jointly to view one or more of the issues together at the negotiating table, to move toward collaborative negotiation.

In environmental disputes, mediation offers a path different from the traditional model of litigation. Mediators can help organize the complex of issues and multiple parties, and can offer themselves as advocates of an alternative path to settlement. The actions of the mediator are, as stated, tied to the approaches to the dispute situation taken by the parties. Even in the most adversarial cases, however, mediators are often able to get the parties to move, over time, away from purely competitive bargaining toward consideration of a wider range of positions and options than they were willing to consider originally. That movement, reflecting a shift from distributive to integrative negotiations, is the true test of the success of environmental mediation as an alternative dispute settlement system.

## Bibliography

Bacow, L. and M. Wheeler (1983), *Environmental Dispute Resolution*, New York, Plenum.

Bellman, H. *et al.* (1981), 'Environmental Conflict Resolution: Practitioners' Perspective of an Emerging Field', *Resolve*, Winter.

Bingham, G. (1985), *Resolving Environmental Disputes: A Decade of Experience*, Washington, DC, The Conservation Foundation.

Clark, P. and F. Cummings (1981), 'Selecting an Environmental Conflict Strategy' in *Environmental Conflict Management*, P.A. Marcus and W.M. Emrich (eds), Washington, DC, Council on Environmental Quality.

Colosi, T. (1983), 'Negotiation in the Public and Private Sectors: A Core Model', *American Behavioral Scientist*, **27**, no. 2, pp. 229–53.

Richman, R. (1985), 'Formal Mediation in Intergovernmental Disputes: Municipal Annexation Negotiations in Virginia', *Public Administration Review*, **45**, no. 4, pp. 510–17.

Schelling, T.C. (1960), *The Strategy of Conflict*, Oxford and New York, Oxford University Press.

Schein, E. (1969), *Process Consultation*, Reading, Addison-Wesley.

Susskind, L.E. (1981), 'Environmental Mediation and the Accountability Problems', *Vermont Law Review*, **6**, pp. 1–47.

Susskind, L.E. and M. Wheeler (1983), *Resolving Environmental Regulatory Disputes*, Cambridge, Schenkman.

# 8(i) Managing labor–management relations: a more complete approach

*Harold Davis*

At the onset, I want to make it clear that the ideas in this section do not necessarily reflect those of my employer. The views I am expressing here are my own and are, therefore, in no way official.

My topic is the management of labor–management relations or labor–management conflict. Other than nuclear disarmament, environmental management, human rights, and so on, labor–management relations is probably one of the most current of all issues. One reads or hears, for instance, such headlines as 'this is the year of the givebacks', or 'labor is in retreat' or 'can America catch up to the Japanese and to the Germans?' If we examine these headlines we can see that the essential thrust, as a whole, is somewhat negative. I have a list of recent wage concessions and it reads almost like a 'who's who' of American manufacturers. In automobiles, there are General Motors and Ford, where there have been reductions in starting wages, and cuts in vacations. In airlines, there is Eastern whose management employees agreed to a one-year wage freeze. In business machines, there has been an 8 percent cut in wages, plus delays in wage increases.

This list goes on for about ten pages and it does not cover all the concessions made by labor. If we look at it and consider some of the points of view expressed, we could say, or I have heard it said, 'well, maybe labor is finally getting its just deserts'. Indeed, that view has probably come down from the time when people thought that there was a lot of dictatorship at the bargaining table. Alternatively, we could say that perhaps this is just a natural down-phase in the win-lose kind of cycle which characterizes labor–management relations. We might also say that it is not just labor, but the whole of the United States that is going through such a downturn at present.

Among contemporary social commentators, we find that there are proponents of this idea that the current situation is just a temporary change and that there will again be an upturn. On the other hand, there are others who look upon the current situation in our economy and in labor–management relations in particular as a long-term, if not a permanent change. If I had to choose between these two points of view, I would probably tend towards the latter. Choosing one or the other at this point, however, would be premature and in fact, is really not necessary. In any case, no matter what the cause, and no matter how long the present situation will last, I think it represents a unique opportunity for participants in labor–management relations to change and improve their relationships permanently. I believe that this can be accomplished mainly by expanding the whole concept of collective bargaining but also our view of the labor–management relationship in its entirety.

For me, the best way to examine or explore these concepts is to look first at how the Federal Mediation and Conciliation Service (FMCS) currently handles labor–management relations and then to try to contrast that with how I think they could be handled. FMCS has been around since the early part of this century, becoming an independent agency in 1947. As an agency, it is very small, having fewer than 500 employees and with the current situation, that number is steadily diminishing. For instance, during the spring of 1982, there were approximately 260 mediators stationed in four regions throughout the country. During the autumn of 1986, there were about 220 mediators in two regions nationwide.

The FMCS is the chief governmental body that handles labor–management relationships, and within the FMCS, those relationships are currently handled in terms of two sections. One section deals with 'hot disputes', that is disputes or contract negotiations, while the other section deals with the technical assistance area, noncontractual negotiations or related kinds of activities.

Other types of disputes that arise within the labor–management context generally fall into the area of arbitration. In contrast to the mediators, the arbitrators we use are not federal employees. Many, however, are former mediators. They are outside people who meet our standards and whom we assign in response to the requests we receive for arbitration panels. Most of the arbitrations which occur through FMCS fall into the category of what might be called 'right' arbitrations, arbitrations which occur usually after contracts have been signed, when contracts are in effect. The form or the process by which these disputes come to arbitration is through the grievance process.

The main difference between arbitration and mediation is expressed in the kind of power possessed by the third party in each case. The mediator assists the parties in reaching a viable agreement, but does not have any authority to compel the parties to make an agreement. The arbitrator, on the other hand, is, in a sense, a private judge for the parties, and as such renders an award or decision which is final and binding on the parties. This is very crucial. There are real differences between the two processes and their functions, including the types of people who mediate and those who arbitrate.

In any case, most labor–management grievances which cannot be settled by the parties go to arbitration. In very rare cases, however, some do go to mediation, and in the majority of those cases, the mediators are federal employees.

Most of our mediators at FMCS have labor–management relations backgrounds, either as union representatives, management persons, or as educators or students specializing in labor–management relations. One requirement of our agency is that in order to become a mediator, a person has to have seven or eight years of bargaining-table experience. Hence, most of our mediators are not from academic training or student backgrounds. In addition, most of our mediators are middle aged, white males. When I entered FMCS, I did not have the seven years of bargaining–table experience, but I had attended law and graduate school and participated subsequently in an internship program. From that training I gained considerable insight into the psychological and communications aspects, the intrapersonal base, of labor–management relations. I also learned that to be an effective mediator, it was just as important to know something about psychology and communications as it was to know about labor–management relations in other, more direct ways. And this view has empirical support as well as theoretical value. When we have trained people in these insights—younger people, women, some minorities with no labor–management experience—they have subsequently proven themselves to be excellent mediators.

When I use the term 'technical assistance', I am including such areas as negotiation training and mediation training, as well as employee–employer training. For instance, we have training courses for foremen, stewards, as well as for an entire union and an entire management throughout the hierarchy of any organization. All this is relevant to another area which is becoming more current—labor–management committees. In these, both sides attempt to settle problems that are not amenable to standard contract negotiations. Normally, such problems are concerned with safety, health, pensions and so on—areas which in many cases cannot be dealt with during the relatively short intervals characteristic of most contract negotiations. In contractual negotiations, we usually have about thirty days in which to settle a dispute, whereas labor–management committees operate under much less constraining conditions.

Another area in which technical assistance is utilized is what is termed 'relationship by objectives' (RBO). What we attempt to do in RBO is get behind some of the problems which underlie the very essence of labor–management relationships. In my experience the demands which either side presents in contract negotiations are, in reality, their solutions to perceived problems. A worker might say, 'I think I am not being treated fairly. My solution to that is you give me a raise.' Management's view is, 'We think you are not working hard enough. Our solution is that you have to produce so many more widgets per hour.' What we would attempt to do via RBO in such a case is try to take that situation out of the category of demands, set that aspect aside, and then attempt to get at the underlying problems.

Let me present some statistics to provide a better understanding of the topics which I have been discussing. In a typical year, the Federal Mediation and Conciliation Service will receive more than 100,000 notices of disputes. About 25,000 of these will be handled by our mediators. Looking at this in terms of the 220 mediators at FMCS, we are talking about approximately 100 cases per year per mediator—a manageable but often exhausting workload. About 21,000 of these cases are contract disputes; FMCS mediators actually mediate about 10,000 of these, while monitoring the remainder. Among the remaining cases, about 2,000 involve technical assistance, and about 300 are grievances. Labor-management committees can exist at the plant, area or industry level. Conceivably, one labor-management committee could be involved with thousands of people. I have talked to some of the FMCS regional directors and they say that approximately 30 percent of our mediators get involved in these committees to some degree. An RBO is a highly structured situation. And if we handle more than ten or twelve of those per year, then I would say that we are doing very well indeed. On the arbitration side, there are approximately 33,000 panels submitted annually by the Federal Mediation and Conciliation Service. From these, 14,000 arbitrators are chosen.

I mention these statistics to make it clear that this is a very large ongoing situation. As Bryant Wedge has said, 'labor-management mediation is what defeated Karl Marx in the United States'. This situation almost expresses the genius of America, that is, being able to handle very volatile situations in a structured, institutionalized manner which leads in most cases to a peaceful resolution.

As an economics student, I was often told that in classical economic theory labor–management relations did not really matter, and that labor–management difficulties were 'sideline' aberrations that the laws of supply and demand would somehow take care of. Many economists still think that way, in contrast to what we are discussing here, which is very much concerned with the 'real world'.

In theory and practice the functions of dispute negotiations, technical assistance, arbitration and grievances are treated as if they were separate and distinct with respect to time, person, and organization. For instance, at FMCS, there are the offices of technical services, office of mediation, office of arbitration services and offices of administration. These are treated separately in terms of reports, training, and in terms of how the corresponding issues are dealt with. They are treated that way at FMCS partially to accommodate the prevailing view of the labor-management world.

One of the best training programs that I developed regarding the labor–management process was done for the National Aeronautics and Space Administration (NASA). Figure 8.1 represents part of that program—the sequence of events that characterizes the movement in a factory from the point of no union to that of a fully unionized plant with a contract. In a typical case of movement from the unorganized to the organized stage, a union organizer will come in to talk to the workers to interest them in the union. There are a lot of rules and regulations about when and how he can deal with them, and where he can deal with them. And when he gets a sufficient showing of interest, which is about 30 percent of the workforce, he can then petition for an election. There are many rules in an election, particularly those concerning unfair practices by either management or union. In any case, if 50 percent of the *voting* workers (no matter what proportion the voters are of the total workforce) vote for the union, then the union will be allowed in. After that, in the certification stage, the union begins to establish itself in the factory and begins to prepare for negotiations. It will send some demands to management, usually about sixty days before negotiations are to begin. Then both sides will enter into the negotiation stage, and attempt to resolve problems concerning wages, working conditions, working hours, and so on. About 95 percent of the contracts in manufacturing that result from this process will include a provision for arbitration. The contract administration stage is where the arbitration process occurs. Contracts normally run for one, two or three years. This process occurs throughout the life of the contract and then labor and management return to the preparation-for-negotiations stage.

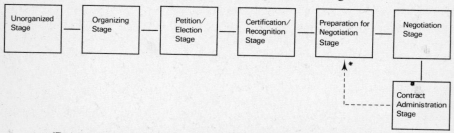

*The 'preparation for negotiation' and subsequent stages are repeated at each renewal of a contract.

**Figure 8.1.** Sequence of stages involved in the unionization of a business concern

I have used the chart in Figure 8.1 to help train many people. For example, I have trained many of our mediators at FMCS. I have also trained union and management personnel, and have conducted training in non-labor contexts, such as Housing and Urban Development (HUD), the Equal Employment Opportunity Commission (EEOC) and the Community Relations Service (CRS). I have also conducted joint training sessions with the American Arbitration Association, and I have taught in the area of family mediation and environmental mediation, among others.

I should point out that FMCS is concerned normally with the private sector, that is, mostly manufacturing and service concerns which are nongovernmental. But federal mediation is also involved in labor relations in the various agencies of the federal government. We are also involved in negotiating on the state and local level, but to a limited extent—only about 4,000 out of the 25,000 cases which we handle each year fall into this category. Another agency called the National Mediation Board handles labor relations within airlines and railroads.

In Figure 8.1, I have tried to illustrate the hierarchical breakdown of the functions in the labor–relations process, and how those functions are separated and viewed in linear terms. I believe that this kind of conceptualization of the labor–relations process is a primary cause of many of the problems that we have, including, for example, the win-lose syndrome which is characterized by a Hegelian-like struggle between thesis and antithesis to dominate the resulting synthesis (the contract).

Because of the downturn in the economy, management and labor are finally taking another look at the entire concept of labor–management relations, albeit, from some points of view, a very short-term look. We can see this occurring mainly in the automobile industry, which has been suffering the most. Also, for the first time in its history, FMCS has been given outside funds to help establish labor–management committees. Consequently, the current economic climate really gives us an opportunity to reassess the whole concept of labor–management relations, to reverse some of the linear thinking about labor–management problems and to put forward alternative ways of dealing with them.

One of the things I do when I teach negotiations is talk about what I call 'the dimensions of bargaining'. When we get down to the typical negotiation situation, as is abstracted in Figure 8.2, and ask the question, 'where do negotiations take place?', most people would say, 'negotiations take place between the union and the company'. However, in reality in many cases most negotiations actually occur among the members of each side, that is, more negotiations take place between the members of the union side and between the members of the company side separately (vertical negotiations) than between the union and the company together (horizontal negotiations).

Professionals often ask, 'how are negotiations affected by time?' In this regard, one of the points I make to our mediators at FMCS is that the most important thing is not so much what they do, but how and when they do it. In Figure 8.3, I have attempted to diagram the whole process of labor–management relations. The very center of Figure 8.3, the intrapersonal aspect, applies to processes within the individual. If we were to examine that, we could do so from a transactional point of view, that is in terms of conflicts which occur between the parent, the

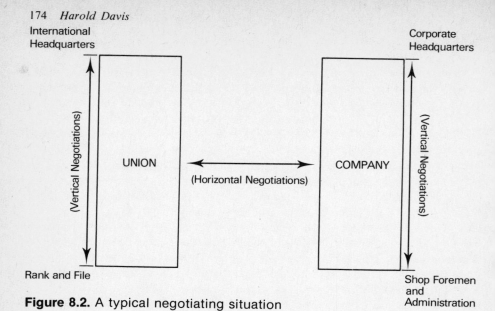

**Figure 8.2.** A typical negotiating situation

adult and the child (Harris, 1973); or from a Freudian point of view, conflicts between the id, ego and superego (Freud, 1961). A major source of all conflict is this area of intrapersonal conflicts. The intrapersonal dimension is constantly present and can flare up at any time. If there is a good mediation subsystem in place, however, then that can minimize the consequences of flare-ups. About some of the other levels, contracts are usually for a fixed period. Technological changes sometimes destroy an entire system; for instance, the development of rolled steel wiped out an earlier system of steel manufacturing. The same kind of development appears to be taking place in the computer industry. And some forecasters feel that, because of certain technological changes, the automobile industry will never recover to where it was.

Accordingly, we may look at the various levels or circles comprising Figure 8.3 as occurring at different points in time, but they are always interacting. Consequently, we need to look at the labor–management relationship in a new light. In effect, FMCS and the entire labor–management community need to change their perceptions and actions with regard to labor–management relationships. We need to stop thinking in terms of thirty days, sixty days, ninety days; or grievances, arbitration, fact-finding, and so on. We need to look at labor–management relations as they really are; as complex, multiparty, multifaceted, open-ended systems within other systems.

One statement which all my economics professors made while I was at college, which I will never forget, and which I now know was a massive falsehood was, 'other things being equal'. The main implication of that statement is that it is possible in life to hold things constant while we examine the effects of one factor at a time. There is no way that we can do that, yet in economics and other areas the experts still look at the world in that static kind of way, but we cannot deal with reality as if it were static, however, we must take into account its complex, dynamic nature.

I want now to address what I call 'synergistic systems mediation' (which will be the subject of a future paper). In this regard, let us examine the vast differences between environmental and labor–management negotiations. In the latter, there are usually only two parties with fixed issues. Sometimes there are twenty to thirty issues, but by the time a mediator becomes involved, there may be only ten or eleven issues. Also, the parameters of the case are usually well known. The National Labor Relations Board (NLRB) has set the standards for what constitutes fairness, each person in the process knows his role and so on. None of this applies to environmental disputes, where there are sometimes thirty to forty parties involved. The issues are not only unclear, but as one gets into them, they grow in number.

Some mediators in this field feel that we should not even attempt to mediate until all the issues have been defined and there is an impasse in the negotiations. That would be helpful to the mediator, but it is, in my opinion, nevertheless a shortsighted view of mediation. The function of mediation includes the solving of problems, but more than that, and of primary importance, mediation also involves uncovering or revealing previously unknown problems. Arbitration, by contrast, does not solve or uncover problems; it provides answers and decisions which may in themselves generate other problems.

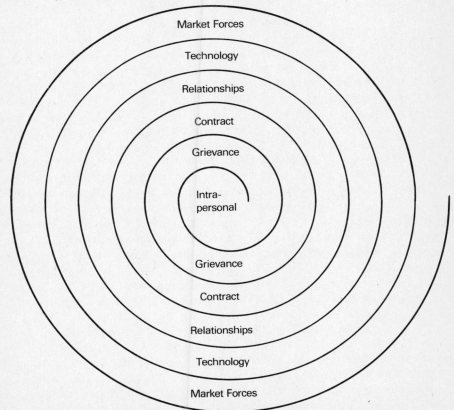

**Figure 8.3.** The process of labor-management relations (cyclical, circular and holistic)

Every three years or so, representatives of unions and companies sit down to negotiate approximately thirty days before their previously negotiated contracts are due to expire. And there they are, in many cases, at the last minute, pulling off their ties, staying up all night and generally exhausting themselves. One might ask, 'why do they go through this charade? Why don't they get smart, and instead of waiting until thirty days before the contract ends, why don't they get together a year before?' Hence, the concept of 'early-bird negotiations'. What happens when they do get together a year or so before? Do labor and management settle their problems any better? No! Their common attitude is, 'hell, we've got thirty days anyway. Why end it sooner?' This view is reinforced by the way labor and management negotiate, which is a typical American way of negotiating, that is, 'horse trading': 'you give me this and I give you that', or 'if you don't do that, I will do this to you'. The longer a party carries on with such behavior, the more chances it has of getting what it wants. Also, some parties conceive of this whole process as a kind of fixed-sum situation—'everything I gain is your loss, and everything you lose is my gain.' Even the new computerized models coming from some of the prestigious educational institutions continue this error.

If labor and management could look upon this situation as a whole process, and would not worry about when the contract was supposed to terminate, they might realize that they have a continual, dynamic relationship which is violated by the prevailing linear view, punctuated every three years by the zero-sum mayhem called contract negotiations. If they could undergo this transformation of vision, they would also realize that even the 'early-bird' approach would not be needed. Hence, when problems or grievances arise, instead of waiting for the contract stage, they could work on them as they occur. Some of the more progressive labor-management committees and 'quality circles' approach this ideal. Quality circles (QCs) are an approach to employee participation that has been used a great deal by the Japanese and is now widely used in the United States (see Marks, 1986 for a critical discussion).

Once when I was in the Philadelphia office of FMCS as a neophyte mediator, I overheard a conversation between a union representative and a management representative, and the former said to the latter, 'for three years, you have stuffed this contract down my throat and now I am going to make you eat it, page by page'. He then ripped the contract up and threw it in the management person's face, but there was nothing the latter could do about it because the old relationship had changed. Management was on top before, but now the positions were reversed. This lesson has stuck with me throughout my career in negotiations. If negotiators examined their situation in terms of Figure 8.3, they might say, 'hey, our relationship extends beyond the contract stage. So, let us not try to see who is on top, but instead, attempt to handle and improve our situation.'

The professional air-traffic controllers' strike provides a good example. I think that part of their problem was that they focused on the contract negotiations, but the problem which generated most of their grief occurred elsewhere in the overall process. They tried to deal with their conflicts only at the contract stage, when they should have dealt with them at the levels of technological change, market force change (change in the population of air traffic), and intrapersonal problems (fatigue, burnout, etc.). The conflicts manifested themselves in the outer circles, yet the parties tried to deal with them in the contract context.

Labor and management should not think, let alone talk in terms of winning and losing. People who are enlightened tend to say, 'what we really need to do is go from a win-lose to a win-win situation'. That would be a great improvement, but unfortunately, I also believe it is a short-run, limited point of view. What I am talking about—a state of being, a harmony in a relationship which goes far beyond winning and losing—may seem idealistic but it is immensely practical and necessary.

Let me provide an example of its practicality. In many of the negotiations in the automobile industry, labor–management had a win-win orientation and situation. They produced lots of cars, management made huge profits and the unions made fabulous amounts of money. They both were the so-called 'winners'. And who was the loser in that situation? The consumer! What this means is, even if win-win prevails among the parties directly involved, someone else, who is not directly in the process, may be losing. If we think about the situation as a relationship which needs to change, then we would not think in terms of 'us' against 'them'. Again, this may sound idealistic, but actually it is not. These ideas and corresponding processes have been around for a long time. They currently exist to a greater degree in Japan, though the Japanese did not initiate them. These ideas are not novel, but what is new is the fit between them and the prevailing economic conditions, a fit which might make Adam Smith redefine his 'invisible hand' so that people would find it in their best interests to adopt a problem-solving approach rather than the espoused selfish, individual interest idea.

My main point is that we should learn to view the labor–management relationship as a comprehensive, complex, dynamic, holistic and circular process. Our mediators should be trained that way, and the labor–management community should look at it that way, thus circumventing the objections many people seem to have when they say, 'we are not Japanese; we cannot do it like the Japanese.' What I have talked about here is truly an original American way of looking at things.

## Bibliography

Freud, S. (1961), *Civilization And Its Discontents*, J. Strachey (ed.), New York, Norton.

Harris, T.A. (1973), *I'm OK—You're OK*, New York, Avon.

Marks, M.L. (1986), 'The Question of Quality Circles', *Psychology Today*, **20**, no. 3, pp. 36–8, 42, 44, 46.

# 8(ii)  New directions in labor relations

*Kenneth Kovach*

I want to make some general remarks about labor–management relations, and the area I work in. It is important to remember that most of the structure for labor relations in the United States is set by law, unlike the situation in some European countries, and labor law in this country has had, at least during the last eighty years, the deliberate intent of fostering a certain amount and a certain type of conflict.

It is, however, conflict in a positive sense, not the kind that we had in labor relations before the National Labor Relations Act (NLRA) was approved by the Supreme Court in 1937, when people were effectively beating each other over the head. It is conflict in a checks-and-balances sense. Indeed, some of the preambles to the most significant pieces of labor legislation indicate that their intent is to promote labor conflict, but in such a way that neither party to a dispute can become stronger relative to the other and indulge in the kind of exploitation that we experienced earlier in this century.

Nevertheless, the government receives a lot of bad press about some of the laws it passes, and sometimes it deserves it. In the area of labor relations, however, I think they have done a very good job. If we compare labor relations now to the situation before the government became involved, I would prefer the current situation with its laws. If we look back at the late 1800s or early 1900s, we can see that there was no system of checks and balances. Management, the industrialists, the 'robber barons' had all the economic and political power up to World War I. This arrangement led to the very real exploitation of all labor, but primarily of the recently freed slaves and the newly arrived immigrants in what were once called the factory systems, the industrial centers. Eventually, this exploitation led to the passage of various laws: child-labor laws, the Clayton Act, the Fair Labor Practices Act. In this regard, states passed minimum wage laws long before the federal government did. And in general, all these laws have stopped some of the worst cases of exploitation.

The exploitation of labor in the past also led to the formation of labor organizations. People had nowhere else to turn. In fact, people in the most hopeless situations—the immigrants, people in the factory systems, the unskilled blue-collar workers—were even excluded from the unions during the first years of their existence. The unions were primarily a white, male, elitist kind of organization. In any case if one goes back to the early years of labor relations, one cannot only see why unions have come into existence, but also why they are located in particular geographical regions, and why they deal with certain kinds of issues in certain ways.

The development of the unions began to pick up momentum with the protection of the laws created primarily by the New Deal in the late 1930s under President Franklin Roosevelt. Since that time, I have read many labor-management texts which suggest, and have heard many people say, that unions have become too strong, particularly in the last twenty years; that they have acquired too much money, they have too much political clout, they are driving wages up, they are contributing to inflation and that they are 'run by a bunch of crooks'.

Be that as it may, I am a firm believer, like Harold Davis, in the cyclical nature of labor–management relations. I think it all evens out over time. Whatever we may say about union people today, we can say 'double' about the management side before the 1930s. Perhaps the unions have enjoyed periods during the last twenty years when they have had too much power, but I think there is evidence that that situation has been drastically reversed in the last three or four years, with labor experiencing the phenomenon of the 'giveback'.

In the auto industries, the United Auto Workers (UAW) have given up a certain amount of money to save Chrysler; then they were forced to do the same with Ford and General Motors. The United Steel Workers (USW) gave back almost as much as the auto workers, but that never received any publicity. Then there are the United Rubber Workers (URW), the Packinghouse Workers and the Meat Cutters Union at Armour & Company, the United Food and Commercial Workers, and it goes on and on. There have been many givebacks, and there will be even more over the next four or five years. Twenty years from now, however, this particular cycle will be forgotten; it will merely be a page in the history books.

As I read about these givebacks, I also read about people who are theorizing about the current situation as a new era in labor relations where everybody is going to treat one another differently. I do not agree with that assessment. What is more interesting to me as a labor negotiator is what concessions were made in return for those givebacks. As Milton Friedman has said, 'there is no such thing as a free lunch', and nowhere is that more apparent than in labor relations. Consequently, I am really interested in what the newspapers do not tell us: what did the company give up as a concession in return for the givebacks from the unions (for the wage cut, the freeze on the cost-of-living adjustment (COLA) clauses and so on)? Companies have given up many things. There are many guarantees in contracts now; for instance, at GM they will not shut down a plant for the next four or so years.

Many of the givebacks reflect what in Europe is called codetermination. This refers to the phenomenon whereby organized labor has more of a voice in making management types of decisions in determining the future of a company. It started in West Germany, where the Allies introduced it at the end of World War II. Since then it has spread. Currently, it characterizes labor–management relations in most of Western Europe, and now it is coming to the United States. If there is a trend in labor relations in the United States, it is not the givebacks, but the concessions for the givebacks.

The first dramatic step we saw in this country was a few years ago when, in return for the givebacks at Chrysler—which had also received a loan from the federal government—Frazier, the President of the United Auto Workers, was put on Chrysler's board of directors. It may or may not surprise some of us, but in West Germany that arrangement is part of the law: there must be certain numbers of people from the labor organizations on the company boards of directors. This is true for other European countries as well, but West Germany is the classic example. That same phenomenon is developing in the United States as well, for instance, there are people from the Meat Cutters Union and the United Food and Commercial Workers on the board of directors at Armour & Company.

Other changes are in the air, for example the profit-sharing plans. These have also not received much publicity. All the newspapers talked about was whether more plants were going to be closed down, about job security, and so on. Those issues are certainly part of the problem, but only in a short-term sense. Profit-sharing plans are indicative of the long term, and they are spreading. UAW, USW, URW, and so on, are all receiving profit sharing.

Both profit sharing and membership on boards of directors have put labor into typically management decision-making roles. Both are part of the codetermination trend that is going to be very evident in labor relations years from now as the United States moves towards the European model. If anything succeeds in reducing labor conflict, I think that it will be codetermination. Unions will be contributing input to levels of decision making higher in the organizational hierarchy than previously. Labor–management conflict will be minimized because by the time the conflict has filtered down to the bargaining table, the union will already have inputted concerns to the system.

When codetermination was forced upon Germany by the Allies after the war, the industrial sector did not like the idea at all. Because codetermination has been institutionalized there, however, a new attitude has developed. And even though there is still 'us' and 'them', it is not quite as antagonistic as the labor–management situation is in the United States. In Europe, there is now an attitude of, 'we are in this thing together. We both have input at the top level. And if we undermine the system, we blow it together.' The attitude is no longer that management makes all the decisions and unions exist solely to dig their heels in and protect people from an uncaring management. The new attitude in Europe, as I see it, involves a blurring and a reduction in 'them–us' antagonisms. Such a development can occur in the United States as well.

It has been suggested, however, that greater conflicts may ensue between labor leaders and the rank-and-file because the latter may perceive the union members of a codetermination arrangement as being far removed from the labor force and, in fact, as being closer to management. That is a sensitive issue for many union people who have already criticized some of the larger unions, including the UAW—supposedly the epitome of a democratic type of union, in contrast to the Teamsters and some others. Much of the criticism is, 'hey, we set you people up forty years ago under the NLRA to protect us from the big, bureaucratic, insensitive and dehumanizing companies, and now you are big, bureaucratic, insensitive and dehumanizing. You have become what we set out to fight against.' That is a legitimate comment.

What must be remembered here is that the wave of union leaders who came in under the NLRA in the late 1930s and early 1940s—Dave Beck, George Meany, Jimmy Hoffa and others—are beginning to withdraw from the scene. We are getting a different type of union leader who did not necessarily have to work his way up through the ranks. The new leaders are better educated, more articulate and they know how to get their point across without alienating quite as many people. They have a much better image. They can still sell themselves as union leaders even though they are working closely with management. A new breed of union leader is in the making with which the rank and file can better identify.

To recap a bit, labor laws foster a certain degree of conflict. But at the same time, they have a viable function. They have stopped management from treating workers as just another factor of production, and that was a step in the right direction. But speaking as one who negotiates for management, I still encounter the attitude among many management negotiators who deal with labor every day that the workers are still a factor of production. The law will not let management treat labor that way, but there is still that semi-elitist attitude which relegates labor to an inferior status.

This gives rise to the question that I am often asked, 'OK, I can see where the unions were once necessary, when children were working ninety hours a week in the mines, in the sweat shops, etc, but what about today? The law has taken over and institutionalized many aspects of labor–management relations. That has made the unions outdated. We no longer need the unions to protect us from child labor and unscrupulous employers. The law is doing it.'

Perhaps the law is doing that, but recalling the typical management attitude toward labor, the unions must exist as a deterrent. Suppose we all agreed that the unions had outlived their usefulness, that the government can successfully regulate labor relations with all its laws. Suppose we neutralized the unions. What would happen in the present economic climate with the givebacks and so on? Those people who are being laid off would be laid off a lot more unceremoniously. There would not be the consideration for the humane aspects that we see today, with the attrition clauses, the advance notice of lay off and retraining, and so on. These considerations would also be wiped out. Hence, we need the unions to push for them.

Unchecked power by anyone, management or labor, is not good. The law will certainly serve as a floor below which management cannot go, but in the present economic climate, if it were not for the unions, we would see a retreat, closer and closer to that floor.

I elicit a lot of argument when I say that we need the unions, because the people I say it to sit at the same side of the bargaining table as I, namely the management side. My fellow management negotiators will say to me, 'well, we are enlightened now; we have all been educated. We have read the books on job enlargement, job enrichment, and the human relations approach, and so on. We know the Hawthorne Studies, etc. We would not do that to people any more.' I disagree. Human nature has not changed since 1900, and it will not change over the next eighty years. There is still a certain percentage of people on the management side who, if the conditions are right, will take advantage of other human beings for the money. I have seen that time and time again. So unions are, at the very least, and in the words of Franklin Roosevelt, a kind of 'necessary evil'.

I have argued that codetermination will lead to a reduction of labor–management conflict in the United States, as it appears to have done in parts of Europe, but there are those, writing in rather influential labor publications, who do not share this view (Furlong, 1977 and 1979; Stokes, 1979; National Association of Manufacturers, 1975; US Labor Department, 1979). This is especially true regarding one expected end result of codetermination which is the improvement of the quality of work life. The people who do not share this view base their assessment on their reading of union goals over nearly fifty years of collective bargaining with management. For them, union objectives have not been about improving the quality of life at work; instead, they have been about economics. Quite simply, for these people, the unions have been, and still are pursuing the goals of more money and more leisure time. For them, the workers have been, and are demanding, 'I want more money for putting up with this horrible job, and more time away from it!' For these people, anyone who feels that codetermination is going to cause labor to shift its priorities from economic concerns to improving the quality of work life, is rather idealistic, but I do not agree.

To put everything in balance, let me conclude with a somewhat bizarre tale of an attempt to increase the quality of work life. Behavioralists have argued that the quality of work life can be improved and that one of the classic places where it needs to be improved is the American automobile industry: 'There the work is incredibly repetitive and boring, plus it drives people crazy. The industry, therefore, is characterized by high turnover, absenteeism, grievances, sabotage, etc. We should do something there if we want to stay competitive with Japan, etc.' To support their case the behavioralists have tended to refer to the Volvo experiments: 'this is how we should make cars because it takes into consideration the humane aspects of production.'

When Volvo switched from its more traditional to a new mode of production, the workers were put into small groups, they could take their breaks when they wanted to, they rotated jobs with one another, they could cover for one another when one of them took ill, etc. In general, they had far greater flexibility than their American counterparts who were still working on assembly lines. But then Volvo stopped, and returned to the old, more traditional ways. What had happened at Volvo?

When Volvo switched from the old to the new, all their indicators of job satisfaction went up, absenteeism and turnover went down, warranty problems went down, but production also went down. Production went down so much that the Volvo hierarchy said, 'to hell with this! We are in business to make a profit. We can absorb the turnover, the absenteeism, the recalls, the sabotage and still make more the old way because we turned out so many more units.'

Volvo lost millions of dollars in its attempt to increase the quality of work life. And Ford, GM, and Chrysler are aware of this 'experiment'. Consequently, we cannot expect them to be too eager to follow in Volvo's footsteps, but to stay where they are. The moral here is that we cannot blame the American car producers or Volvo for adhering to the old ways. They are, after all, in business to make a profit. The question is, of course, how much of a profit?

## Bibliography

Furlong, J. (1977), *Labor in the Boardroom*, Princeton, Dow Jones Books.
Furlong, J. (1979), 'Workers in the Boardroom', *Wall Street Journal*, 12 March. p. 18.

National Association of Manufacturers (1975), *Codetermination: Labor's Voice in Corporate Management*, Washington, DC.

Stokes, B. (1979), 'Answered Prayers', *Master of Business Administration*, December 1978–January 1979.

US Department of Labor, Bureau of International Labor Affairs (1979), *Industrial Democracy in Twelve Nations*, Monograph. no. 2, January.

# 9(i)  Terrorism and hostage negotiation

*Conrad V. Hassel*

In 1976 I was put in charge of a small group of agents at the FBI and told that we could observe terrorist incidents wherever they happened in the world, as long as we could gain access. We started with about five agents and experts in various fields—psychology, sociology, criminology, weapons and tactics, and so on. We were allowed to observe incidents in the United States as well as abroad. If the FBI had jurisdiction in a case, we could advise, provided the special agent or assistant director in charge of the incident asked for our advice. We could not make any operational decisions, but we could observe and occasionally advise.

As a result, we have been involved in several of the more spectacular hostage situations in the United States: the Hanafi Muslim confrontation in Washington, the takeover of the German Consulate in Chicago, the takeover of the Philippine Embassy and numerous highjackings, including the Croatian highjacking. Since we had done such a good job, it was decided to consolidate more operations within the unit. Currently, we are in charge of all special weapons and tactics training, all crisis management training, hostage negotiation training and all aircraft pilot training. The FBI does have pilots, flying everything from multi-engine jets to single-engine helicopters. We also have the liaison responsibility for most of the premier counter-terrorist units throughout the friendly world, for example the Israelis, the Special Air Service (SAS) Regiment in the United Kingdom, the British Royal Marines, the French GIGN and the GSG-9 in West Germany who took their initial training at the FBI Academy. The GSG-9 were involved in the famous Mogadishu operation. We are in contact with these people rather frequently.

Let me say some general things about terrorism before I present some CIA statistics. As a criminological phenomenon terrorism is not a great problem in the United States. In 1979–80, we lost about nine people in the United States as a result of terrorism, and six of those were killed in one incident—the bus that was machine-gunned in Puerto Rico. We probably had thirty to forty people injured during the same period. Hence, we cannot really say that terrorism is a great problem domestically. One 'good' week in New York City, Detroit or Philadelphia produces more casualties in killings than the last two or three years in domestic terrorism have produced.

Terrorism was brought to the public consciousness belatedly, in 1972, during the Munich massacre. At that time, everybody got excited about the problem and started to fund research into it. As a result, terrorism has become, over the years, somewhat of an academic cottage industry. Many people have approached the Law Enforcement Assistance Administration (LEAA) to do some kind of study. I have read some of the studies. One suggested that we ought to have orbiting satellites to observe terrorists; it was not clear, however, how from outer space we should identify terrorists. Another study suggested that we ought to have a death penalty for terrorists, that they should be summarily shot. Still another suggested that we should not mix convicted terrorists with the general prison population; we should put them into camps designed exclusively for terrorists.

All these recommendations, with the exception of the satellites, have been tried by other nations and, in my opinion, have been miserable failures. If we segregate people who have been accused of terrorism, they tend to take on a status as combatants, not as criminals. In Title Eighteen of the United States Code, there is no crime called terrorism. There is a law against murder, bank-robbery, extortion, but there is no mention of terrorism. Terrorists commit crimes and they should be treated as criminals, not as some special class that gives them greater status, and for the same reason, the death penalty option would be impractical.

How do we define terrorists? As so many have said in the past, one man's terrorist is another man's freedom fighter. Take for instance the incident of a Polish pilot who escaped from Poland and flew to Austria. Suppose he had shot and killed the aircraft's flight engineer before he got aboard and flew out. He could well have been accused of terrorism. I do not know whether the Austrian or the United States' Government would agree with that. What about the Russian pilot who flew his highly sophisticated MIG into Japan? The Soviet Union immediately demanded the return of the pilot and the aircraft. They did not get either. In our view, he was fleeing political repression. It is, therefore, difficult to know where to draw the line. At the United Nations, various conferences have been attempting for years to draw a line on terrorism. They have tried to define it and have been singularly unsuccessful. In general, 'terrorism' is not a well defined term. Though people worldwide have some understanding of it when it happens to them, there is very little international consensus on what it means.

There was a Gallop-type poll done in the United States, in about 1979, in which the respondents were asked about terrorism and about 80 percent of the people thought it was a very serious problem. This reflects not the success of terrorism as such, but the success of terrorism as a media event. It is a stage which sometimes presents an absurd play. If the experts are right, what terrorists want and demand more than anything else, is publicity. They certainly do get it. If they can capture the electronic media and get their manifesto across, whether it is meeting with some motion picture star or the freeing of prisoners and so on, then they will get their stage.

Terrorists get their stage, I think, from the media. This is not the media's fault. Terrorism, after all, really is a media event. It is a very interesting phenomenon, and by reporting it, the media are doing their job. I do object sometimes when the local disc jockey telephones the hostage-taker, and prevents us from getting through to negotiate; or when the TV cameras focus on the SWAT (Special Weapons and Tactics) teams running around in their camouflage uniforms and sniper rifles. Usually the hostage-taker has access to a television, and observing such scenes would not tend to lessen his stress. In any case, we are quite aware that we do not control the press, and that is exactly the way it should be. We do not even really make good friends with them: ours is an 'arms-length' relationship with the Fourth Estate.

There are many examples of publicity successes. Who ever heard of Black September before Munich? Who ever heard of the Moluccans before they seized the trains in the Netherlands? I knew there was a national ethnic group called Croatians, but I did not know that they were angry at anybody until they took over a plane (TWA 355) in 1976. They certainly made headlines that far outstripped their actual deeds.

This is not to say that terrorism is not a problem. What terrorism needs in order to be a problem is an issue. In the United States, in the late sixties and early seventies the issue of the Vietnam War went a long way to drive and fuel the domestic terrorists that we had at the time. That issue is no longer with us, and with its decline, we saw a decline in domestic terrorism. There are certainly issues today that could become rather severe. One of these is the economy. If the economic plans of our political leaders lead to positive results, then life will be beautiful; if they do not, there may be a problem.

Another issue is the world-wide anti-nuclear movement. This is an important issue in the United States as well as overseas. I am not saying that anti-nuclear people are terrorists. The great majority of them are not and by demonstrating, they are exercising their right to disagree with the policies of their governments. Any time a mass movement of that magnitude develops, however, it tends to attract some people who might not be too respectful towards the Constitution. For instance, there may be someone who says, 'It would be good to blow up nuclear plants because, though we might lose 10,000 to 15,000 people in the process, we will save the world; they will quit building nuclear plants.' The end justifies the means: we can see that in some of the writings of the 'gurus of terror'.

Although we have not had, and still do not have a really serious problem with regard to terrorism in the United States, it may be asked, 'how much of a commitment should the United States Government make to the solution of this problem?' There are various opinions on this from one end of the spectrum to the other. For instance, several years ago, I testified before a Senate committee which was holding hearings on the subject of establishing a cabinet post on terrorism. I said to the committee chairman, 'that is fine Senator, but what will you call him? The Secretary of Terror?' Ever since, the legislation in question has languished somewhere on Capitol Hill.

According to the most recent CIA statistics on international terrorism (1980), the United States has been one of the largest targets around the world. We are the 'belly of the beast', as the old SLA (Symbonese Liberation Army) used to call us. Looking at the figures for 1974–80, we can see that 1980 was almost a peak year, and that trend now continues. A dip occurred right after the Vietnam War, but now the incidence is increasing again. In 1980, the bomb was still the favorite weapon and quite a few American citizens were involved. In terms of the location of terrorist incidents, North America ranked as number four for 1980. However, much depends on how and what one interprets as a terrorist incident. As we know, all statistics can be interpreted in various ways. There are other sources of data besides the CIA whose figures would give us an entirely different picture.

To return to the CIA statistics, among American personnel who are targets of international terrorism, diplomats are ranked as number one, followed by business persons, government officials, military persons, and so on. Among the top ten categories world-wide, the terrorist threats that most concerned the FBI are number six, hijacking, particularly of aircraft and number seven, barricaded hostages. Many of the highjackings are not what would necessarily be considered terrorist in nature. There are homesick Cubans, ordinary criminals and other people who behave in this manner.

What kind of person generally becomes a terrorist? After the SLA case was closed, with many of the SLA members having been killed, we began to do background investigations on them, just to see what kind of people were attracted to the SLA—a left-wing, Marxist type of organization. Amazingly, many among the leadership cadre in left-wing terrorism in the United States were the sons and daughters of the upper-middle class. These were people, like Bernadine Dohrn, who belonged to the most favored group in society, yet they were attacking society. Why?

There are a lot of answers to that, and we have to see it in the light of the 1960s and 1970s—the years of protest in the United States which spawned many of these people. A colleague of mine, a psychologist (Strentz, 1981; also see Russell and Miller, 1977), compared them with the Red Army Faction in West Germany and with the Japanese Red Army, and found a similar pattern among many, but not all terrorist groups. Members of such groups tend to be recruited out of the university system, and are quite well educated. I must say that the great majority of those people who demonstrated in the 1960s and 1970s never became terrorists, but for some reason, some of the best and the brightest did.

Bernadine Dohrn, for instance, went to the University of Chicago Law School, which probably ranks as number three or four in the country. Yet she was rebelling against the government or the way she saw the country. Incidentally, these people tend to bring in the criminal element to support them. In the case of the SLA it was Cinque, who was recruited out of the prison system. The latter seem to give themselves high rank, in the case of Cinque it was 'field marshal'. For others, it may be 'information minister', and so on.

In any event, Bernadine Dohrn is a classic case. She has served her sentence, and has generally been forgiven. It is an interesting phenomenon to find people like her around the world. For instance, among the Palestinians, those who conduct the border incursions into Israel tend to be the basic front-line-troop types, but those who operate in Western Europe and in the United States are well educated. Generally speaking, they have at least one university degree, often more than one degree; often a professional degree. They speak at least two languages, are much more at home in Paris, Rome, London, New York, than they would be on the Gaza Strip in a refugee camp. They are highly motivated, highly intelligent people. And in my opinion, they are in no way mentally disturbed. I do not believe in the theory that terrorists are suffering from some mental disorder. They are dedicated people who believe in what they are doing.

Let me briefly mention the other side of the coin, the right-wing element. I was introduced to the right wing in 1964, when three civil rights workers (Goodman, Schwerner, and Cheney) were killed in Mississippi. Subsequently, I became involved in civil rights cases, many of the church burnings and bombings, the Liuzzo killing, the Selma and Montgomery marches. For some reason, none of these events was defined as terrorism in the 1960s, though they probably would be today.

The right-wing people were almost 180 degrees from the type of people we saw on the left; unskilled labor, service station attendants, and so on. I feel that they have a psychological problem. It may be 'pop' psychology, but I feel that they have an 'expectancy gap'. For instance, some were pumping gas for $40.00 a week in rural areas and they wondered why they had not done better in this world: 'it is not my fault, I am a good guy, it has got to be somebody else's fault.' And they picked out the normal scape-goats in all societies, Jews, blacks, Catholics, etc. In this regard, I do not think I have ever seen such pure hate, such pure, unadulterated, uneducated hate as I have seen in the Klu Klux Klan. They are very frightening people, associated with unimaginable damage and violence—lynchings, unsolved murders, etc.

One of the cases I worked on was the murder of Medgar Evers. The evidence in that case was the rifle which was used to kill Evers. We found the thumbprint of the prime suspect on the rifle. Also, a witness had located him in the area within a half hour of the commission of the crime. We went to court three times on that case, but each time ended up with a hung jury. One would think that we had rather good evidence, but it was not good enough. The prime suspect is a free man today.

Let me now briefly discuss international terrorism. There has been very little in the United States thus far. In 1973, for instance, the Israeli Air Attache to the United States was killed. Palestinians took credit, but the case remains unsolved.

In March 1973, two cars were parked in Manhattan, in front of banks which had Israeli connections. A third car was parked by the EL AL air terminal at Kennedy Airport. All three cars were packed with dynamite, and the time-fuses were set to go off at a certain time. But fortunately, for technical reasons, they failed to detonate. At the time that they were designed to explode, the man responsible would have been on a flight about halfway between the United States and Paris. He dropped out of sight in Beirut and has not been seen for a number of years.

Mr Busic, a Yugoslavian and a Ph.D candidate at Portland State College, highjacked TWA 355 in 1976. He claimed that he had plastic explosives, but what he really had was 'play-dough'. The copilot suspected it was 'play-dough', but the pilot thought it was genuine. The plane flew to Canada, Iceland and then to Paris. My psychologist colleague (Strentz, 1979) thought that this case presented an excellent opportunity to conduct some research. Passengers were let off in two stages; there were those who stayed on board for a short time, while others were on board for many hours. My colleague wanted to study the effect of the 'Stockholm Syndrome' on both groups of passengers.

The 'Stockholm Syndrome' refers to a phenomenon which was first observed in the early 1970s. A bank in Stockholm had been taken over by a man named Olsson, a Swedish criminal, and a kind of Robin Hood figure. He went into the bank, got everyone's attention by firing into the ceiling with an automatic weapon and demanded that a friend of his, Olofsson, be released from prison. Olofsson was released and taken to the bank. Olofsson then retreated into the vault with three or four hostages. He spent about a week in the vault, locked in with the hostages. Perhaps in defiance of conventional wisdom the hostages showed great affection for him and hatred for the police. They identified very closely with him. In fact, they even negotiated on his behalf. After the hostage situation was over, one of the women hostages even became engaged to Olofsson. This romance exists today, though Olofsson is still in prison. The 'Stockholm Syndrome', therefore, refers to the phenomenon whereby some—not all—hostages identify closely with their hostage-takers.

I would like now to discuss hostage negotiation. The priority in hostage negotiations is to preserve life. But whose life is more important? Sometimes those of us in law enforcement begin to argue about this point. Let us assume that the hostages are the most important, that the public are second, the police third and the hostage-taker fourth in priority. Some departments will put the hostage-taker even ahead of the police.

In the mid-1970s, there were two schools of thought on hostage negotiation. One of these was the Los Angeles theory. The Los Angeles Police Department is one of the finest departments anywhere in the world. They developed the SWAT program before the FBI did. They would not really negotiate, but instead, 'communicate'. That is—and they still do this—they would assign a member of the SWAT team to be the hostage negotiator. SWAT team members tend to be dressed in paramilitary fashion, accompanied by a variety of weapons. Their basic negotiation runs something like this: 'Look! At some time, you have got to come out; we do not have to go in. And if you hurt anybody in there, you are dead!' This was a highly successful theory of hostage negotiation; it worked brilliantly. Statistically, it was impressive.

On the other side of the country, the New York Police Department developed a different theory. In fact, the real innovator, the real developer of hostage negotiating theory was not the FBI, but Dr Harvey Schlossberg. At the time of the Munich incident, he was a uniformed policeman in the City of New York. A commissioner at the time said, 'this could happen in the United States'. He discovered Harvey Schlossberg, who has a Ph.D in psychology and is a psychoanalyst, and asked him to develop a hostage-negotiation program, which he did. And he really did seminal work. He developed the first hostage-negotiation theory, and he based it on what we might call a mental health model, the 'warm and fuzzy model', that is, everything is negotiable. What does that mean? Food, for example, is negotiable. Drinks are negotiable, but as items separate from food. What a negotiator must do is get into the mind of the hostage-taker the notion that the negotiator is not there just to communicate the hostage-taker's demands. For everything that the negotiator gives a hostage-taker, the hostage-taker must give something in return. It does not have to be a big item. It does not have to be a hostage, but it has to be something. That gets the negotiation going, and it works.

Transportation is negotiable as well. If there are seventy hostages held in a supermarket, and the hostage-taker says, 'Give me a car', I will give him a car. How many hostages can he take in a car? Perhaps four, and then sixty-six people will be released. On the other hand, if he is in a liquor store and has two hostages, he will probably take the two hostages with him. In this situation, a negotiator would not gain anything.

Freedom is negotiable, too. Of course, hostages should go free, but what about the hostage-takers? How many of us would say, 'OK mister hostage-taker, if you release the hostages, you will go free'? The Los Angeles Police would not do that, but the New York Police would. They would actually let a hostage-taker go, although to my knowledge, they have never yet had to go that far. They argue that,

'We can catch this guy next week, next month, next year, but we cannot replace a human life! And that is the most important thing—human life.' But not even New York will negotiate for weapons. They will negotiate for money, although the units involved, not necessarily the amount, should be reasonable. For instance, one person wanted five million one dollar bills, which presented formidable logistical problems.

The exchange of hostages is a very crucial point in negotiation. Though we advise against it, there are always people, police and others, who offer themselves in place of the hostages originally taken. Psychologically, hostage exchange is not a good idea. The young bank teller hostage is going to survive a lot better than the veteran police officer, FBI agent or military person.

We had a case in Minneapolis where a wealthy, suburban matron was kidnapped—not hostage-taken—and chained to a tree overnight. She had not been beaten, raped, or abused. The FBI swooped down, apprehended all the kidnappers and for some reason, the kidnappee and one of the kidnappers were facing each other. She ran over to the kidnapper, threw her arms around him and said in front of TV cameras, 'thank you for giving me back my life'. That is a difficult case to prosecute. FBI Director Kelly asked, 'why did she do this?'

This question was submitted to our unit at the FBI Academy, and I think that we found the answer. We had examined all the relevant case examples, and I think the most stirring was from World War I. In 1916, a German regiment and a French regiment were dug in, about 50–100 yards apart. Misinformation was passed down the line to both sides that the war was over, that the truce had been signed. A German soldier put his helmet at the end of his rifle, elevated it over the trench line, but nobody from the French line shot back at it. The French did the same, with no German firing back. One side then peeped over the trench and saw somebody else peeping back. On both sides they waited. They then yelled at each other, and finally met in no-man's land.

Here were rare scenes of Germans wearing French helmets and French wearing German helmets, looking over each other's family snapshots and in general discovering that they had experiences in common—the sergeant was just as much an s.o.b., the mud was just as deep, and the food was just as bad on one side as on the other. And then the colonel commanding the French regiment discovered what was happening. He ordered his men back into the trench line. He determined that the truce had not been signed and that it was only a false rumor. They complied, but they would not resume their lethal combat against the Germans. They were even transferred to another sector of the line. The Germans would not fight back either.

In every war fought by the United States or probably any liberal democracy, what have we done with the 'enemy'? Erich Fromm (1977) has answered this question: we dehumanize and depersonalize them. They become symbols, for instance, 'Gooks', something less than human. Then we are not killing people; instead, we are killing symbols. Once we get to know them, personally, and discover that they are human beings and not negative abstractions, then it becomes more difficult to continue waging eternal combat against them. This same phenomenon occurs in hostage situations. That is the gist of the Stockholm Syndrome; it is why one should not exchange one hostage for another—because the emotional cauldron that the hostage and the hostage-taker find themselves in is probably beneficial for the hostage. The longer that the hostage and hostage-taker remain together, the less chance there is that the hostage-taker will kill the hostage.

Hostage-taking is the only type of case that I am aware of in law enforcement or the military where 'doing nothing' is a positive thing. The problem is that throughout the military, government and police establishments, there are people who are characterized by the 'John Wayne Syndrome'; it seems to be an insult to their manhood that a hostage is being held. Furthermore, the press are sometimes not very helpful. For instance, if there is one hostage and one hostage-taker in an apartment building surrounded by fifty police officers, the press may say, 'There are fifty of you and only one of them; why do you not get the hostage out?' Here it would be very tempting to do something, but that something might backfire. Obviously, if shots are heard and bodies are coming out of windows, then 'something' has to be done, but that is not the typical situation. What is typical, once contact is established and the process begins, is that the negotiator will tend to succeed.

The last point to consider is the passage of time as a factor in hostage negotiations. For the sake of convenience, let us say that there are four types of hostage-takers. One of these is the terrorist. We have very few terrorist hostage-takers in the United States, but we have thousands of hostage-takings every year. The most dangerous hostage-taker, in my opinion, is not the terrorist, but the trapped armed robber. The terrorist has planned, he knows he is going to take hostages. This tends not to apply to the armed robber, who has planned only to rob a bank, liquor store, etc. In contrast to the days when bank robbers like John Dillinger had forty-five minutes to empty the contents of a vault, the police today, in most sophisticated cities, are on the scene within three minutes. This state of affairs encourages the taking of hostages.

Some people say that criminals are mentally disturbed, but I do not believe that the armed robber is mentally disturbed in any way. He may be sociopathic, antisocial to some degree, but even a perfectly normal individual does not act rationally at all times when he is under pressure. Anybody under severe stress acts irrationally. Hence, the first fifteen to twenty minutes in a hostage situation are critical. That is when we do not want flashing lights on top of police cars, and people running around with M16 rifles. Such posturing tends not to lower the stress level. Stress in a hostage situation is like pressure on a trigger finger: the more stress there is, the tighter the finger is pulled until the hammer finally drops, and somebody dies. Needless to say, we do not want the hostage-taker to fall asleep either. What we should aim for in such situations, in lieu of stress, is 'creative tension'.

There are several types among our third category, the mentally disturbed, who take hostages. There are, for instance, schizophrenics, psychotic persons who are out of contact with reality to some extent. The paranoid-schizophrenic type is probably one of the most out of touch with reality, or parts of it. The authorities deal with such persons a great deal. These are people who have written to their senator and their president; they have gone to their police department and FBI, but nobody has paid attention to them. Then they take one or more hostages, and say to themselves, 'By God, they are going to pay attention to me now. I have got an ambassador, I have got five people; they will listen to what I have got to say.' Perhaps if society had listened to them earlier, we would not have this problem.

How do we deal with the mentally disturbed hostage-taker? Exactly the same way we deal with the armed robber. Calmness. That a person is psychotic does not mean that he is not intelligent, that he does not reason from some base. If a person starts off with the basic premise that the moon is made of green cheese, he may nevertheless be very logical from that point on. The thing to do with that kind of person—which we find works well—is to allow him to ventilate, to indicate what his problem is.

It is not clear that the fellow who led the Hanafi takeover in Washington was mentally disturbed, but he was removed from the military because of 'dementia praecox'. He was an Hanafi Muslim: the Hanafi were a break-away sect from the Black Muslims. Many members of his family had been brutally murdered by the Black Muslims—his children had been drowned in a toilet bowl and his wives' throats had been slit. This had played on his mind for a number of years, culminating in his takeover of the B'nai B'rith, the District Building and the Mosque in Washington. From that background, he screamed out his vituperation, demanding that those people who were incarcerated for killing his family be brought to him. He also demanded that Muhammad Ali, the spokesman for the Black Muslims, be brought to him. We talked to Muhammad Ali, but he declined. Some District of Columbia council members offered to be substitutes for the hostages which he declined.

We had to make a decision whether to allow the leader to use the phone lines available to him at B'nai B'rith to talk only to the hostage-negotiators or to call anywhere he wanted to. We decided that he ought to be allowed unrestricted use of the phones. That was not a majority opinion. In any case, he called talk shows, and through them, was able to ventilate the venom that he had accumulated.

The hint of success in the Hanafi case was that no deadline was ever set. The leader did not say, 'I will roll heads out of the windows at ten o'clock tomorrow morning'. He never set a deadline, even though the press had queried him about this. Although he used the same words, over time we could see that he was calming down, looking for an honorable way out, without losing face. The DC Chief of Police at the time took much abuse because he allowed the primary hostage-taker to go directly to his home on bail. In my opinion, he saved lives. It was one of the best handled hostage cases we have ever had.

The fourth and last type of hostage-taker I want to mention is the antisocial or inadequate personality. Hubbard (1971) talks about this type in his book, *Skyjacker*. He believes that all aircraft highjackers are inadequate personalities. I think he is absolutely wrong about that, though some highjackers undoubtedly are inadequate personalities. In any case, what kind of person is the 'inadequate personality'? Let us imagine that a man grows up in a family of four or five siblings, and that in general, he is a failure. His brothers and sisters become successes, but he stays at home and cannot hold a job. There is nothing wrong with his intelligence. He just seems to have been what in the Marine Corps they call 'the ten percent'. He was always somewhat late doing things. He was not a very good athlete, his relationships with the opposite sex were not very in-depth or meaningful, and his father was a big hunter.

This actually happened. It was a typical case in New York. The father said, 'I want you out of here. You are twenty-six years old, you have not held a job for a month, you have flunked out of college. I want you out of here and never darken my door again.' So the son said something to the effect, 'I am going to do something to show the world that I am in fact adequate'. He decided to rob a bank, with the assistance of his father's twelve-gauge shotgun. He was going to rob a bank to show his father that he was a successful person, that he could be successful at something, but he was not going to rob just *any* bank.

He travelled by subway to Manhattan, walked into one of the largest banks in the city and got into the end of the line. The inadequate personality is generally a polite person. A teller pressed the emergency button when she saw the shotgun and two New York City police officers came rushing into the building. The man swung the shotgun towards the two police officers and demanded, 'I want a million dollars'. One of the officers reached into his pocket and said, 'hey, George, how much have you got? I have only a few bucks.' Then they looked up, gave him the big New York shrug and said, 'why are you asking us? You're in a bank!' That is basically an inadequate personality. Usually he can be negotiated out of the situation once he has made his 'statement' of defiance to an uncaring world which is constantly defeating him.

Although it is necessary for us to become more sophisticated in the skills of negotiation and all the other techniques of hostage rescue, what we must avoid at all costs is overreaction to terrorism. Overreaction by government generally means repression—which is exactly what the terrorists want. In fact, in my view, we might even need to accept a little terrorism which is preferable to destroying those principles so rare in today's world that are embodied in the first ten amendments to the United States Constitution.

## Bibliography

Fromm, E. (1977), *The Anatomy of Human Destructiveness*, New York, Penguin.

Hubbard, D.G. (1971), *The Skyjacker: His Flights of Fantasy*, New York, Macmillan.

*Patterns of International Terrorism, 1974–1980*, published annually by the CIA until 1980, thereafter by the State Department as *Patterns of Global Terrorism*, Washington, DC, US Department of State.

Russell, C.A. and B.H. Miller (1977), 'Profile of a Terrorist', *Terrorism*, **1**, no. 1, pp. 17–34.

Strentz, T. (1979), 'The Stockholm Syndrome: Law Enforcement Policy and Ego Defenses of the Hostage', *The Law Enforcement Bulletin*, April, pp. 2–12.

Strentz, T. (1981), 'A Terrorist Organizational Profile: A Psychological Role Model' in *Behavioral and Quantitative Perspectives on Terrorism*, Y. Alexander and J.M. Gleason (eds), New York, Pergamon.

# 9(ii) 'Terrorists' versus 'freedom fighters': the implications of alternative constructions of reality

*Arnold Sherman*

Conrad Hassel has raised some important points: (1) there is no commonly accepted definition of terrorism; (2) the incidence and impact of terrorism in the United States is still minimal; and (3) a good deal of terrorism in the United States can be viewed as crime. It may be a good idea to stop talking about terrorism, and terrorist groups, and deal instead with specific behavioral acts which violate a particular law.

Why is there no generally accepted definition of terrorism? Is it possible to get a definition of terrorism that would be generally accepted? To answer these questions we take the approach of the sociology of knowledge. Reinhard Bendix (1978) tells us that we live in an age in which governments have to try and act in terms of legitimacy, in terms of popular mandate. Such a view, however, is affected by the freedom fighter–terrorist dichotomy. There is no way around this; whether one is defined as a freedom fighter or a terrorist depends upon one's social location and allegiances. In this section the neutral term 'event' will be used to refer to any terrorist/freedom-fighting act. From the perspective of supporters, the event makes heroes of those involved. From the perspective of nonsupporters, the event is seen as something which could not be committed by civilized people. It is this perspective of noncivilized activity that I wish to explore in more detail.

Once any event occurs the battle over the definition of the situation ensues. This battle is critical because if we can define those responsible for an event as uncivilized, 'crazy' or nonhuman, the stage has been set for a certain kind of retaliation. Once those so defined become dehumanized, it is possible to do anything to them. The effort to dehumanize those responsible for an event has two important consequences. First is that all efforts to understand the objective factors which caused the conflict cease, and second, efforts to educate the population about the nature of the case are replaced by propaganda designed to support government policy.

If any particular event is supported, or acted against, because of how it is defined, then it is useful for governments *not* to aim for an objective definition. Since whether a group is labelled 'freedom fighters' or 'terrorists' is a matter of political perspective, no uncontested objective definition—one which pushes past our political presuppositions—may ever be achieved.

Accordingly, there is no seriously accepted definition of terrorism because, first of all, the construction of 'terrorism' is a political act; and second, words are important but the words that count in the definition and construction of terrorism are the words of people in positions of power. They have control and the capability to make words more meaningful than the people with less power. Given that point, plus some others (for example, questions concerning redistribution of wealth, pluralism and constitutionalism) I would like to consider: What is terrorism? What is a terrorist group? What is a terrorist act?

Let us imagine that some act has been committed by a certain person, and that another person has perceived the first in the commission of that act. Let us also assume that the observer has certain concepts in his mind, reference terms like 'terrorist', 'terrorist act', 'terrorist groups'. The question that then arises is, 'what was *that* act?' Another question is, 'what caused that label? What caused this concept in the observer's mind that was there as a reference term, available to be applied to the act without the observer really knowing what the nature of that act was?' Another question is, 'is it conceivable that there are certain types of actions in this world where the creation of a concept and the creation of the corresponding act are in fact related to the same basic set of factors, whatever those factors may be?' I would argue that in the case of the Kikuyu and Mau-Mau revolution and in other revolutions, those causes are, in fact, linked in an interesting kind of way, where terrorism is one particular type of tactic used by certain kinds of peasant revolutionary movements. I shall return to this later on.

What is 'terror'? It seems to be an intense emotional state of fear. It can be produced intentionally or unintentionally and in either case, it may or may not be produced for political purposes. Also, it can be produced in a few people or in large groups of people; and it can be produced by violent or non-violent means. It can be produced by governments, intentionally for political purposes, violently or nonviolently; or it can be produced by an oppositional group, intentionally or unintentionally, violently or non-violently.

For many situations, the terms 'terrorist', 'terrorist act' and 'terrorist group' are not useful. There are violations of the criminal law, and if we take the laws as given without asking why the law was created, which very often is a reasonable thing to do, then there are certain kinds of criminals involved, or at least people who violate criminal acts. There are also certain kinds of people who get involved for psychological reasons, and who should be treated in certain ways.

Where this leads to in terms of policy questions depends in part upon how much of their scarce resources authorities want to, or can, apply to managing the problem. It also depends on whether the 'problem' is an ambiguous criminal act or a psychotic or schizophrenic act where the objective is not to create terror in a large group of people for political purposes but to achieve a smaller purpose where the consequences may be minimal.

There has been a series of peasant revolutions going on for some time, including the Kikuyu, Mau-Mau revolution during 1952–6. The roots of that revolution go back to 1869, when the Suez Canal was completed. This changed the geopolitics of the world. One of the consequences was that it became necessary to create a link between the headwaters of the Nile River and Mombasa. A railroad was necessary and it was determined that the railroad had to go through the middle of Kikuyu land. British colonial policy required that colonies paid for themselves, but there were no real resources and minerals in Kikuyu land. Also, there was no industry that could easily take advantage of cheap labor. What happened was that head taxes, poll taxes and other kinds of policies were instituted in order to drive the Kikuyu off the land and transform it into plantations.

For a period of time, from 1920 to the late 1940s and early 1950s, the Kikuyu who had gone to England and learned democratic procedures and constitutional- ism tried to use the means of constitutional redress in order to win back some of their native rights over what they considered to be their own property, but they never won a single case in the courts of British colonial power. Almost a hundred years later, in 1952, for a number of reasons which we shall not go into, the Kikuyu switched to the use of political violence in an attempt to regain what they considered to be their land.

There have been similar actions in other countries. Some of the underlying causes which have sociohistorical backgrounds, for instance, the creation of the law by the British colonial power which outlawed the Mau-Mau was sociopolitically the same set of factors that created the Mau-Mau action. If we try to uncover such causes then we must realize that when we talk about prevention, two meanings are involved. One concerns the question, what do we try to do with a certain situation after the act has occurred? The other involves a broader sociological understanding of why these acts are likely to emerge time and time again in different locations. Sometimes, I think, we would do better by trying to understand the underlying, long-term, sociohistorical, geopolitical and economic causes. That way, we may be able to conclude that the cost of maintaining a certain geopolitical advantage is not worth the negative kinds of repeated behavior. If it is worth that cost, however, let us at least understand what the 'independent variables' are: what, in fact, is causing the system to operate the way it does.

Guaranteed retaliation may minimize 'terrorist' activity, but it will not deal with the underlying causes. The roots of the conflict will persist. Understanding those roots and providing a forum for education and inventing alternative means of managing conflict may in the future provide a more effective way of dealing with the persistent problems of intergroup conflict.

**Bibliography**

Anderson-Sherman, A. (1982), 'The Social Construction of "Terrorism" ' in *Rethinking Criminology*, H.E. Pepinsky (ed.), Beverly Hills and London, Sage.

Bendix, R. (1978), *Kings or People: Power and the Mandate to Rule*, Berkeley, University of California Press.

# 9(iii) Insurgents are not crazy or irrational— they are different!

*Robert Clark*

I would like to present a perspective which is derived from my having met and talked with members of insurgent organizations in Europe; from my observations of how they live and die, and how they get along with one another and with the imperatives of everyday life while they try to carry on a struggle that is very long, difficult and hazardous.

Conrad Hassel has suggested that it seems to be the policy of the Los Angeles Police Department to ensure that everyone connected with a hostage-taking event, particularly the insurgents themselves, understand that the incident has terminated in a failure for the insurgents. In other words, one of the objectives in dealing with any specific hostage incident is to make certain that the outcome does not ensure a repetition of similar events in the future.

My observation of admittedly a narrow slice of the insurgent world, is that this would be a very difficult task to achieve. It is very hard in the conduct of any specific incident to ensure that the people who are observing that incident, or the participants in the event themselves, understand that what has occurred has been a failure for the participants. One reason for this is that the feedback from each event is ambiguous. For most hostage-taking incidents, when the event has terminated, it is not exactly clear what the outcome has been from the point of view of the insurgent. Many times they do escape, not in the United States, but in Europe and in other areas of the world. They do manage to get away, or if they are caught, they spend a short time in prison and then they are released, sometimes as a result of other hostage incidents. Hence, over the long term, it is not clear in any given event what the exact outcome has been.

Second, in order to obtain a clear termination of an event, the consequences of it need to be predictable. That is, in order to make sure that every event terminates in a failure, we need to be able to communicate to every potential insurgent, hostage-taker or terrorist group, 'If you do this, then we guarantee that you will fail and you will suffer disastrous consequences.' My feeling is that this is probably not possible. There is such great variety in the way governments—and even within governments, specific agencies and law enforcement authorities—deal with incidents of this sort. Almost invariably, the insurgents receive a much different message: 'Maybe you will win and maybe you will lose, maybe you will get part of what you are after or maybe you will get all of it.'

An unpredictable, almost random kind of payoff schedule, almost like the outcomes of a slot machine or other kind of mechanical game, faces many insurgent groups around the world today. They do not have a 100 percent certainty that they will fail. It is more like 25, 30, or 50 percent, depending on the situation of the government involved, and so on.

There is something even more important than this having to do with the makeup of the people about whom we are talking. Here I am not referring specifically to people who are mentally disturbed, or who are caught in the act of a bank robbery, but to groups of people who have been involved in paramilitary revolutionary struggle for many years. Anybody who can endure that kind of life; who can risk his life day in and day out for twenty years or more, maintain some sort of a family under those circumstances and a more or less normal job, has to be a special kind of person. Anyone who can do that has to have a personality which enables him to reinterpret the world so that what appears to us to be a failure is turned into a success; what appears to us to be constant loss is reinterpreted or redefined by him as more opportunities.

Hence, even if we were, by some miracle, able to ensure that both the Los Angeles and the New York Police Departments dealt with hostage incidents in exactly the same way, that would be difficult enough. But imagine trying to get the governments of the United States, Canada, Italy, and Belgium, just to name four at random, to deal with similar situations in the same way. Even if we were able to achieve the certainty of response that would be necessary, we would still not be able to accommodate the peculiar makeup of insurgents. They are not crazy, or irrational; they are different. They have proven that they are different by leading a different life every day for 365 days a year. They have a special ability to reinterpret failure, to redefine loss in terms that make it rational and reasonable for them to continue the struggle. Any kind of policy aimed at dealing with hostage incidents or any other kind of insurgent incident for that matter must take that kind of reality into account.

# 9(iv) Terrorism: making the response fit the act

*Irwin Greenberg*

First, let me try to explain what my interests in mathematics, statistics and operations research plus a position in the Systems Engineering Department at GMU have to do with terrorism. This goes back to my days at MATHTECH, one of the better known consulting firms in the area. One of the things that I used to do there was to prepare proposals concerning 'risk analysis'. For example, the United States Department of Transportation might be looking for a study to determine whether or not it should be legal to transport explosives by air, a situation which is not now permitted. In risk analysis, one considers something with an extremely small probability of occurrence, but a very large penalty if it occurs. In effect, one is multiplying zero times infinity and trying to come up with a number in between. If there is a one-in-a-million chance that a catastrophe killing two million people occurs, then, according to risk analysis, it would be exactly the same as killing two people with certainty.

In the process of working in this field, it became clear to me that if there were to be one of these catastrophic occurrences—for example, if a liquified natural gas tanker were to explode in Boston Harbor—then in all likelihood it would not be an accident but a purposeful act: someone would do it deliberately. Terrorism involves such purposeful acts including those that border on catastrophe, hence, my introduction, however indirectly, to terrorism.

There are certain theories which would appear to have grown up in terrorist fiction but are now coming into some of the factual books on terrorism. Claire Sterling's book *The Terror Network* (1981) is an example of one in which the point is made that the terrorist is not necessarily an indigenous, home-grown, disaffected personality or disordered individual, but is often under the control of certain foreign governments. The result is terrorism for the benefit of the foreign governments concerned. There are various types of scenarios that could apply here. In one, the people involved in terrorist actions are essentially mercenaries hired by foreign governments to create situations which cause people to lose confidence in their own government's ability to protect them. Another scenario holds that terrorists are anarchists whose goal is to be so outrageous as to force reactions from democratic governments which are undemocratic in form—in effect, to create situations in which civil liberties and civil rights are reduced, if not suspended.

I think there ought to be differences in how we might deal with people who are behaving in 'terrorist' fashion depending on whether their behavior grows out of some personal grievance (as may have been the case in the Hanafi Muslim siege of the B'nai B'rith building in Washington) or whether they are working for a cause or as professionals in pursuit of payment for their services. It may very well be that in certain cases it is not media attention that people are interested in; rather, they seek the disruption of society as a means to achieve other goals. It would seem that the way one might negotiate in this type of situation or the way one would deal, in general, with this kind of threat to disrupt society would be qualitatively if not quantitatively different from the way one might deal with a homesick Cuban who is attempting to hijack a plane to his native land.

It seems that there will have to be a wide variety of approaches, a very flexible orientation to 'terrorism', depending upon the specific threat, the specific relationships among the people involved and their particular backgrounds.

## Bibliography

Sterling, C. (1981), *The Terror Network: The Secret War of International Terrorism*, New York, Holt, Rinehart and Winston.

# Part III: Conflict Management: The International Levels

# 10(i) East–West negotiations

*Adrian Fisher*

This section draws upon experiences I have had with negotiations, primarily of an international nature, including working together with Bryant Wedge on preliminaries to negotiating the Limited Test Ban Treaty of 1963. When discussing negotiations it is important to have an appropriate framework. Those without such a framework tend to view negotiations as a single, basic interest relationship between two single, rational self-contained units. My view is that negotiations are much more complex than that, particularly at the international level. For example, who are the actors involved in international conflicts? Is the United States a single decision-making entity? Were General Rowny and Paul Warnke a single decision-making unit when they represented the United States at Geneva? Not at all; they reflected entirely different constituencies: one against and one in favor of the SALT II Treaty. When discussing negotiations, therefore, and not only international negotiations, it is essential to fathom the complex of group decision making, to ascertain who represents whom. In the United States the situation is even more complex because of the separation of powers between the executive and the legislature. It would not, for example, have done the country much good if Bryant Wedge and I persuaded Khrushchev to agree to the limited test ban if we could not have subsequently pushed the treaty through the Senate.

The United States has been involved in a number of negotiations involving the Soviet Union. When I first went to Geneva to participate in one of these, it was to represent the United States at what was then the Eighteen Nation Disarmament Conference (ENDC). Actually, it was a seventeen-nation disarmament conference because France, although a member, did not participate. This has since been re-named the Conference of the Committee on Disarmament (CD) and consists of forty nations, including France and also China. (I was the one who negotiated the United Nations' resolution to extend an invitation to the Chinese to participate in the conference.)

Is it a negative or positive development that the international arms control negotiations moved from eighteen to forty nations? In a sense, it does not really matter because when there is a confrontation, the nations—whether eighteen or forty—are still working within a system dominated by two superpowers. If the United States and the Soviet Union are incapable of extinguishing all life on the planet, they certainly are capable, as indicated by Jonathan Schell (1982), of destroying civilization as we know it. Clearly, though each side must deal with its respective allies, and with the rest of the world, to evolve a decent global relationship, the Americans and the Russians have the major responsibility for preventing nuclear war.

But deal with their allies they must, even the Russians. Whenever the United States deals with its allies, it faces the problem of cosmetic versus real consultation. This is a common problem with any form of alliance relationship: to what extent is one's mind made up and to what extent is one still open to input from one's allies? Though we should be firm in our preferences, we should not be rigid, otherwise the consultation process would come to a grinding halt. If one of our allies is disturbed by a policy we are contemplating pursuing, we should not say, 'sorry, but we have already decided to go with this!' A second problem encountered in alliance relationships is 'leaking': if the United States is about to take a certain position with regard to the Russians, and discusses it with its NATO allies, will that position be published in *The New York Times* two days before the United States intends to present it to the Russians? It may be. How does one deal with this, especially since it is more difficult to prevent leaking in an alliance than in one's own government? The American president cannot threaten to dismiss the Icelandic foreign minister or, for that matter, force him or her to undergo a lie detector test.

Among other difficulties with international negotiation is the multi-party problem. For instance, underscoring the view that there is no such thing as a single decision-making entity, whenever the United States enters into a negotiating relationship with another nation, 'the delegation' and 'Washington' tend to be at odds with one another. Washington views the delegation as a group of 'softies' intent on wanting to return from abroad with something to show that the delegates were not wasting time, having fun in Geneva, and so on. The delegation, on the other hand, thinks that Washington is incredibly bureaucratic, characterized by interagency warfare waged at the expense of possible national interests. The limited test ban negotiations almost collapsed because Washington wanted the delegation, of which I was a member, to insist to the Russians that they not allow East Germany to sign the treaty, but if they did sign the treaty, that it would not affect the international status of East Germany. The Russians did not respond favorably to this idea. Consequently, the head of the United States' delegation, Averell Harriman, called President Kennedy from Moscow to argue that if Washington wanted the treaty, they would have to drop the East German issue. President Kennedy gave his approval and the Limited Test Ban Treaty was initialed on 25 July 1963 by Ambassador Harriman, Soviet Foreign Minister Gromyko, and Lord Hailsham of Britain.

In addition to problems characterizing the relationship between the United States and its allies, and between Washington and the delegation, there may be problems among the members of the delegation. American delegations to disarmament negotiations are usually made up of a few members of the military, a nuclear scientist, some people from the State Department and some from the Arms Control and Disarmament Agency. This seems to be a built-in basis for friction, as was the case between Paul Warnke and General Rowny during the SALT II negotiations. Interestingly enough, in most cases, there is a group *esprit* of living and working together that prevents this potential friction from rearing its ugly head. The Warnke–Rowny episode, therefore, seems to have been an exception to the rule.

The group *esprit* in American delegations is relevant to something we call 'back-channel communications'. These are the communications that occur between members of the delegation and their respective colleagues in Washington: for example, when a representative of the Joint Chiefs of Staff communicates directly with his colleagues back at the Pentagon. In my experience members of the delegation who wanted to send a back-channel communication would inform me of their intention to do so, and ask me what I thought its likely consequences might be, but not necessarily ask me for 'permission' to send the communication. I have never thought that this was a bad thing, nor have I ever objected to a member of my delegation sending a back-channel communication to his superiors in Washington without my permission. Back-channel communications will always occur, and indeed, must occur, but one must rely on the group *esprit* to prevent the back-channel communication from becoming a throat-cutting channel, which normally it is not.

One major problem area of negotiations at the international or any other level concerns the 'bargaining chip'. Bargaining chips are created for the sole purpose of being traded off for something else. For example, if one superpower wanted to reduce the number of missiles to 5,000, it might authorize the building of 10,000. The bargaining chip in this case would be the decision to build 10,000 missiles, designed to be traded for an agreement to limit missiles to 5,000. The Reagan Administration has sought funds for the production and deployment of binary chemical weapons. A leading argument for such weapons is that they are required as a bargaining chip for elimination or reduction of Soviet chemical weapons stockpiles. The assumption here is that the United States must threaten to go all-out with these weapons because that is the only way the Russians will know that the United States is serious about negotiating reduction of chemical weapons. Otherwise, if the Russians have an advantage over the United States in chemical weapons, why would they want to reduce their weapons unilaterally? For there to be some sense of a *quid pro quo*, the Soviets would have to undergo reductions of their chemical weapons in response to something the United States was doing; hence, the use of the bargaining chip approach in this case.

Though apparently an attractive option, there is a problem with the bargaining-chip approach to negotiation: the effect it may have on the other side. Would an American decision to go forward with binary chemical weapons increase the Soviets' incentive to negotiate the reduction of chemical weapons, or would it encourage the hawks in the Soviet Union to say to themselves, 'the Americans are not serious! They want to deploy binary chemical weapons, so why should we negotiate reductions in our own chemical forces?'

If the United States had a Constitutional Amendment stating that we would never again conduct nuclear tests, the Soviet incentive to negotiate a comprehensive test ban would be somewhat restricted. On the other hand, if we had a program in place for five hundred nuclear tests in the next year, the Soviet ability to negotiate a reduction or limitation would be restricted in this case as well. They have decision-making processes equivalent to our own. They have their hawks and their doves, as we do—again reinforcing the view that there is no such thing as a unitary decision-making entity. Hence, one has to evaluate the bargaining-chip option against the background of the question, what signal are we sending to which component of the other side? Are we saying, 'you had better negotiate with us', or 'we are going to do this, no matter what you do?' The bargaining-chip approach, therefore, although it has a certain validity, must be used with discretion, otherwise, it can be quite self-destructive.

Another major problem area in negotiations at the international and other levels concerns the so-called 'worst-case' doctrine: 'I don't care what you fellows think. I am interested in the security of the United States and if there is any doubt, we shall have to assume that the other side is cheating us!' In the context of the case that Bryant Wedge and I worked on, the Limited Test Ban Talks, we would ask the question, 'how do we know whether the Russians will adhere to the treaty?' The problem is that the worst-case view is nearly always one-sided; in the context of the limited test ban, it does not specify that there is an alternative to the worst case with an agreement, namely, a worst case without an agreement. 'Would we be better off with massive atmospheric testing, or would we be better off taking a chance on the treaty?' The simple answer is, there is no such thing, in any realistic sense, as a unidimensional worst case; there are, however, competing interests which have to be balanced. We should always examine the worst case of doing something with the worst case of not doing something, but as already indicated such a comprehensive formulation rarely, if ever, sees the light of day. Accordingly, bargaining chips and worst-case analysis should be placed in a proper perspective before either is 'let loose' to influence policy.

Let me discuss now the prospects for progress in the various negotiations involving the two superpowers. Would the chemical weapons program that the United States wishes to embark on make it more or less likely that the superpowers will reach an agreement on such weapons? I think less likely because there is nothing that the United States is going to do that will make its programs comparable to the fairly substantial Soviet chemical weapons programs.

What about theatre nuclear forces? The United States has an incentive to do something in this area as the West Europeans, who originally wanted American theatre weapons, have not subsequently always been so sure. The United States has put forward the zero option, which is to get all missiles out of the European theatre, but I do not believe that this is possible. The Soviets have more of these weapons in Europe than the United States has. They will be prepared to agree to a freeze, to proportionate reductions, but not to a zero option. The Soviets know that the Americans know this; consequently, I think that the Soviets expect that the United States will have a fallback position. This is especially likely given the European concern that they are in the line of fire, that if the 'balloon goes up', they are the 'theatre' within which these weapons would be used. I also do not see much happening at the Strategic Arms Reduction Talks (START) in Geneva, where General Rowny has been designated the American negotiator, nor at the United Nations Conference of the Committee on Disarmament (CD).

Although we may sometimes feel that we are skidding down the road to destruction, there is a basic limitation in the United States to fueling further the nuclear arms race, namely financial constraints. The Soviet Union seems to have the ability to squeeze their own people a bit more in this regard than we can, although that condition may change.

To conclude we will be going through some very difficult periods in international negotiations during the next few years until we make up our minds where we want to be. My own view is that we should favor the position that when our lives on this earth end, they should do so because of natural causes, not because of a thermonuclear exchange, and I am convinced that the Russians feel the same way. Although they hide this fact through all sorts of propaganda statements, and probably would take advantage of power asymmetries—hence, I am not a unilateral disarmer—they definitely do not want an all-out nuclear war, and with rationality on both sides, we can avoid that kind of catastrophe.

**Bibliography**

Schell, J. (1982), *The Fate of the Earth*, New York, Knopf.

# 10(ii) A marginal contribution to a safer world

*Bryant Wedge*

In his section Adrian Fisher comments generously on our working together on the Limited Test Ban Treaty (which was originally called the Three Environment Test Ban Treaty). It seems in order for me to report now that he was one of the first of the United States negotiation team to consider and test out a hypothesis that I put forward that the Soviet negotiators were attempting serious bartering to arrive at an agreement (Wedge and Muromcew, 1965). He helped spread this notion through the American delegation to the Eighteen-Nation Disarmament Conference (ENDC) and back again to Washington. This proved important in shaping the American response to Khrushchev's opening bid in May 1963 to exchange a partial test-ban treaty for a nonaggression pact. The bid could easily have been dismissed as a propaganda ploy as have so many other offers; instead, it was responded to by Ambassador Averell Harriman's historic mission to Moscow.

At the request of the Arms Control and Disarmament Agency I reviewed 5,743 pages of the record of the ENDC between March 1962 and April 1963. Among the impressions I gained was one of persistent efforts at quite simple bartering offers by the Soviet negotiators and their allies. Specifically, whenever the United States proposed a test ban, the record would soon show a Soviet suggestion of some such item as a nonagression pact. It was relatively easy for the American negotiators and analysts to dismiss this as a 'propaganda ploy', but when I described this as similar to 'Yankee horse-trading', Adrian Fisher and others confirmed the impression, at least as being worth testing. What had appeared to be extremely complex negotiations might actually represent a very simple, although covert, attempt to find agreement. So it proved to be; an agreement very much to American advantage (the United States had completed about 320 tests and the Soviet Union 159 when they were stopped) was rapidly negotiated in Moscow by Ambassador Harriman in July 1963.

Professor Fisher commented on the composition of the negotiating teams, very gently, it seems to me. The United States sent a heavy representation of technical specialists since seismic events and means of detection, including 'black boxes' (monitors of seismic events emplaced in the Soviet Union) were an important American concern. No wonder that the Soviets termed this, over and over, as 'a scientific screen for espionage', especially when the Soviet team was made up entirely of political specialists. No wonder, then, that the United States would consistently characterize Soviet interventions as 'propaganda'. How can a seismic physicist otherwise explain a penchant for 'nonaggression treaties'? Adrian Fisher, ever so gently, notes this sort of difficulty—the sort of difficulty that permits an independent analyst, sitting in a lonely office, to discover seriousness of purpose that had been missed at the negotiating table and missed by political analysts in Washington.

I am proud to have made a marginal contribution to the efforts of quite large teams, dedicated on both sides to a safer world, and I appreciate the work of a fine diplomat in translating analysis to reality.

## Bibliography

Wedge, B. and C. Muromcew (1965), 'Psychological Factors in Soviet Disarmament Negotiation', *Journal of Conflict Resolution*, **9**, no. 1, pp. 18–36.

# 10(iii) The other side of negotiations

*Alex Gliksman*

Ambassador Fisher discussed some difficulties involved in preparing for international negotiations, getting others in government in line, massaging the inevitable differences that emerge between 'Washington' and the 'delegation', and so on. What this assumes is that nations are, in fact, serious about the subject addressed in negotiations. This sometimes is not the case; sometimes there is another side to talks. Negotiations may not always be about what their formal titles would suggest is their purpose.

In 1973, for example, the United States and the Soviet Union entered into negotiations on Mutual and Balanced Force Reduction (MBFR) in Europe. Supposedly, these negotiations were to deal with reductions of conventional forces in the European region. Yet, MBFR as advertised was quite different than MBFR as practiced. For the United States, MBFR was a response to something all together different: the Mansfield Amendment, then before the United States Congress.

It may be recalled that in the late 1960s and early 1970s, the United States was undergoing a process of world-wide military disengagement. Vietnam had wounded America, physically and psychologically. Many in the United States did not want to be entangled with Asia's problems. The same attitude was also applied to Europe. Some said, 'Why have American forces there? All they are going to do is get us into somebody else's trouble.' The Mansfield Amendment, calling for cuts in the number of American troops in Europe, was a reflection of this desire for disengagement.

President Richard Nixon and his Secretary of State Henry Kissinger turned to arms control to forestall Senator Mike Mansfield and his supporters. The administration argued that if the United States wanted to disengage in Europe or anywhere else for that matter, it would have to proceed in an orderly and balanced fashion. The one way to maintain security was to match American reductions with a gradual process of cuts on the other side—the Warsaw Pact forces in Europe. Using the MBFR negotiations, the administration was able to argue that the United States needed its forces in Europe as bargaining chips to bring about reductions in Europe. This was an argument which even liberals could buy. Thus, at least at the start, mutual and balanced force reductions were a secondary concern.

It takes the mutual interests of two parties to make a negotiation. Given the fact that by agreeing to MBFR the Soviets helped sustain American troops in Europe, it seems a wonder that these negotiations occurred. If one looks at MBFR in isolation, Soviet behavior appears illogical. Beyond MBFR, however, we find that Moscow had ample reasons for helping the administration out of its dilemma with the American public and Congress.

What the Soviets wanted from MBFR was also not MBFR as such. Though they wanted to reduce American forces in Europe, they were less eager to reduce their own forces in the region. What they really wanted was a post-World War II peace treaty with the United States and the European powers, codifying the post-war status quo. Such a treaty would in essence recognize the Soviet's sphere of influence in Eastern Europe.

The Soviets had pushed for such a treaty since 1954. At that time, American officials, John Foster Dulles among them, talked about a concept called 'rollback', that is moving the Iron Curtain back to the Soviet border, an idea that made the Russians more than a bit nervous. The Soviets, too, had a concept of rollback, but their's was to ship the Americans back to North America. This provided the Soviets with two additional reasons for wanting such a conference. It would reduce the prospect of the United States giving effect to its rollback policy and it would give Moscow a special position as the key superpower on the continent.

It was these competing interests between the United States and the Soviet Union that created conditions for superpower cooperation. In exchange for negotiations which helped defuse Senator Mansfield's efforts, the United States endorsed the Soviet Union's call for a European conference which Moscow hoped would provide tacit recognition of its sphere of influence in the East. As a result, two sets of negotiations were born. Besides MBFR, the Conference on Security and Cooperation in Europe (CSCE) was started and eventually led to the 1975 Helsinki Accord.

MBFR was not a single-motive game; it involved other interests in addition to those just listed. For the Soviet Union, MBFR was seen as providing an opportunity to divide the United States from its European allies. One way to do this was to make enticing offers which the Europeans could accept but which the Americans could not, or vice versa. One technique, described in a book by Jeffrey Record (1980, pp. 60–1) was to use the 'backdoor': work out private arrangements with the United States which might be upsetting to the allies.

American motives and interests in MBFR changed over time. As was indicated, the United States looked to MBFR as a way to forestall the Mansfield Amendment. Later, the United States began to regard MBFR as a useful forum in and of itself. For one, the dialogue provided useful insights into Soviet and Warsaw Pact strategies, tactics and forces. For another, it also proved to be useful for the Alliance as a whole. Knowing of Moscow's interests, Washington at first feared Soviet successes in creating divisions between the United States and NATO. However, quite the opposite occurred.

Whenever discussions about arms control proposals take place, there is also talk about what constitutes essential defense requirements. In the process of this kind of dialogue between the United States and its allies, there emerged common definitions of the Soviet threat and of military requirements for meeting it. Since MBFR had this positive value for the Alliance, the American government kept MBFR alive, in the absence of any kind of agreement. Now, more than a dozen years later, the negotiations continue to take place.

This is not to say that serious arms reductions have never been considered. On several occasions the United States and some of its allies have agreed on the need to advance serious and specific proposals. On these occasions, agreement between the Alliance and the Warsaw Pact was possible. However, other participants in MBFR, a forum that involved nineteen states, twelve from the West and seven from the East, have had different interests. These worked against agreement being reached.

Occasionally, a source of resistance within Europe to an agreement on MBFR has been the Federal Republic of Germany (FRG). The FRG was interested in MBFR for several reasons. When the talks began, the Germans were pursuing *Ostpolitik*, their policy of détente with the East. Given Bonn's desire to demonstrate its commitment to *Ostpolitik*, engaging in arms talks was appropriate, but sometimes MBFR has been more an issue of style than of substance for Bonn. While this has been a source of criticism, the Germans have good reason to hesitate. Germany's position on the border with countries of the Warsaw Pact makes it painfully aware of the mass of Soviet force that could cross the border and come its way. They fear that if their forces were reduced or their freedom of maneuver constrained they could suffer terrible consequences. Bonn's ultimate fear is allied abandonment in war. Should that occur they would have to take care of themselves. Consequently, on occasions when an MBFR agreement was possible, the West Germans have had second thoughts. This runs counter to the intent of arms control.

The Conference on Security and Cooperation in Europe (CSCE), with its thirty-five participants, is also a mixed-motive game. Nations often enter into negotiations with specific goals. As noted, the Soviets wanted CSCE to obtain recognition of their place in East Europe; the United States came to CSCE to 'pay' for Soviet concurrence with MBFR, but the thirty-three other nations involved have their own interests which can alter the outcome radically.

In the negotiations that led to the Helsinki Accord of 1975, the American role was, at least initially, little more than that of an observer. This is understandable given the reason for American CSCE participation. The Europeans had totally different ideas. They saw more at stake than giving Moscow its desiderata. For them, CSCE provided an opportunity for all Europeans—not just the superpowers—to discuss peace and security in Europe, establish conditions for detente, create positive economic conditions and reduce barriers to trade, information exchange and human contacts between East and West. The Europeans were clearly not going to give the Soviets a peace treaty without extracting a price.

This was especially true for the neutral and nonaligned European states, in CSCE jargon, the NNAs, who remained outside both superpower and bloc-to-bloc discussions. The NNAs' concern was for what they saw as the overbearing influence of the superpowers in regional affairs; consequently, they wanted to use CSCE to reduce superpower interference in their business. In exchange for recognizing the Soviet sphere of influence, they sought constraints on the military forces of both blocs, NATO and the Warsaw Pact. From this evolved the package of confidence-building measures (CBMs) which constrained military exercises in the European region. These became part of the Helsinki Accord. Moreover, the NNAs also wanted to ensure that once the Helsinki meeting was over, the superpowers could not return to business as usual, settling the affairs of Europe on their own. Accordingly, the NNAs insisted that CSCE become a *process*. As a result assurances were given that the Helsinki negotiations would be succeeded by a series of follow-up meetings.

In many ways, the results of CSCE have not been to Moscow's liking. Through CSCE it obtained something more akin to a guide to proper conduct than a regional peace treaty. At the first CSCE follow-up meeting held in Madrid in 1977, the United States clashed with the Soviet Union over its human-rights practices. The preparatory sessions for the second follow-up held in Madrid in 1980 became an occasion for condemning the Soviet invasion of Afghanistan. Later, at the Madrid follow-up itself, the United States Secretary of State and the foreign ministers of West Europe used the Helsinki Accord as a yardstick to measure and then to denounce Soviet interference in the affairs of Poland.

The United States and the Soviet Union are not the only powers to seek talks for reasons extraneous to the subject matter of arms control. The ongoing Stockholm Conference on Disarmament in Europe (CDE) is a case in point. The CDE was first advanced by France in 1978 and the Stockholm conference was mandated by the Madrid CSCE meeting in 1983. CDE seeks to take the Helsinki Accord's confidence-building measures, make them more stringent and expand their scope to a far larger geographical area, extending from the Atlantic to the Urals.

Ambassador Fisher mentioned that France had abstained from the Eighteen-Nation Disarmament Conference (ENDC), thereby making it in reality a seventeen-nation conference. France's abstention reflected a broad French approach to arms control called the policy of the 'empty chair'. Paris extended this policy to MBFR, claiming that as an independent state it would not concur in any kind of alliance-to-alliance arms control arrangements.

France had always wanted to be seen as a world leader, but by abstaining from MBFR, leadership in West European security went by default to the United States. French absence from other negotiations involved similar costs. In the 1970s and into the 1980s, world leadership has come to be associated with leadership in arms control. To correct the situation, Valery Giscard d'Estaing, then President of France, came up with the idea of a Conference on Disarmament in Europe.

At first, the French seemed preoccupied with the idea that CDE was a French proposal. Its content seemed less important. There was very little substance to CDE initially. Later, the United States and its NATO allies, using the experience gained at MBFR, helped the French to make the CDE notion meaningful and substantial.

American endorsement of CDE provides another example of the influence of extraneous concerns on arms control. While President Jimmy Carter's State Department and Defense Department were instrumental in giving shape to CDE, once this work was done Jimmy Carter refused to endorse the French proposal. In the wake of the Soviet invasion of Afghanistan, the Carter White House feared that it might give the wrong impression to the American public, create a false sense of normalcy within the Alliance, and send a false signal of complacency and acquiescence to Moscow. Within three weeks of taking charge, however, Ronald Reagan came out in support of CDE. Again, the reason for this action had little to do with the specific merits of the proposal.

By early 1980, CDE had been endorsed by all other Allies and by several of the nonaligned states. It was soon evident to officials in Washington that the failure to endorse CDE was isolating America in Europe. This was confirmed by various reports prepared at the State Department, and at the Central Intelligence Agency. It was clear that the American refusal to endorse CDE was leading the allies to balk at cooperation in other areas and was an obstacle to improved relations with France. In the wake of Afghanistan, the State Department concluded that as a first gesture it would be a good idea for the United States to make concessions to something that France wanted in the hope of getting something that the United States wanted, particularly military assistance beyond the NATO area. The United States looked toward France as a potential key military ally in the Persian Gulf, especially in view of France's naval capabilities in that region.

European participants looked at CDE not so much as a disarmament proposal but as a means of getting away from a thorny issue, the human rights component of the Helsinki Accords. As mentioned earlier, at the Belgrade conference in 1977, the United States and the Soviet Union clashed over human rights. After the tensions of Afghanistan, Europe feared that a similar clash at the then forthcoming Madrid CSCE meeting would threaten what remained of détente. For Europe CDE provided a way of dealing with European security, while avoiding the pitfalls posed by discussions of human rights.

Epilogue: In the five years since the above was presented little has changed. If anything, it seems that nations have become more skilled at using arms control talks for purposes other than arms control bargaining. Without making judgments on the merits of the missile, it seems clear that the United States turned to arms control to sustain the MX program rather than to bargain about the future. The same seems true of the Strategic Defense Initiative (SDI).

Over the last few years the Soviets have used negotiations to draw attention away from their own military activities in order to scuttle the defense plans of the other side. This seems certainly true for two recent Soviet arms control campaigns, the first with regard to the cruise and Pershing-II missile deployments in Europe and the second with respect to the SDI. In terms of the first, the Soviets denounced the NATO missiles while ignoring the SS-20 deployments to which cruise and Pershing were a reply. As for the latter, while Moscow seems ready to decry the Reagan initiative, it seems unwilling to amend its own strategic defense activities which have led others to back the program.

This is a most unfortunate situation. Should it continue, the serious bureaucratic dynamics as described by Adrian Fisher could become of secondary importance to arms control.

## Bibliography

Record, J. (1980), *Force Reductions in Europe: Starting Over*, Cambridge, Massachusetts and Washington, DC, Institute for Foreign Policy Analysis.

# 10(iv) The pragmatic view

*Jonathan Dean*

As Alex Gliksman said people enter into complicated enterprises with very mixed motives and mixed objectives; however, I do not think that saying that by itself helps much to predict the final outcome of their activities, either in domestic life or arms control negotiations. These are not zero-sum transactions with 'winners' whose objectives are implemented versus 'losers' whose goals are thwarted; the opposite is true. A successful negotiation creates a new situation in which both sides benefit, otherwise they would not conclude an agreement (assuming, of course, that they have elected voluntarily to negotiate in the first place).

One of the points made by Ambassador Fisher struck me because it so closely parallels my own experience with the Mutual and Balanced Force Reduction (MBFR) talks in Vienna: the high number of groups and group interests involved in large transactions such as arms control negotiations, even when bilateral between the United States and the Soviet Union. In the United States, for instance, there are always at least five government departments involved in the steering group which is set up to run the arms control negotiations and they are all represented in negotiating delegations. Some systematic procedure is necessary for testing the quality of conclusions about the negotiating position of the other country and of suggestions for changing our own national negotiating position. There is distortion however, in allowing this degree of complexity in the operations of the executive branch on arms control. In practice we have a system of checks and balances not only among the three branches of our government, but within the executive branch as such. The constitutional division of powers seems to have been extended to the executive branch by a rather unrefined logic to the extent that each agency (or representative) has a valid vote on the United States position, regardless of whether a particular agency has a serious interest or a significant degree of responsibility regarding arms control. We have to keep in mind that government officials, bureaucrats if you will, very seldom are delegated authority to say 'yes' but nearly all can say 'no' and refer an issue to higher authority. No one is reprimanded for overtaxing the system in this way and each official has in practice a right of veto.

In effect then, we have a perfect confederation—a requirement for unanimity within the executive branch before any action is taken—in most of our arms control negotiations. This entails an effort to convince others that a given move is desirable which begins at home and never ends. This is especially true in multilateral negotiations where each of one's negotiating partners has a similar makeup. For instance, at the MBFR talks, I once estimated that there was a total of about two thousand senior officials involved from nineteen countries. In order to make any move, however small, we had to convince the large majority of them that the action intended was acceptable and desirable.

Ambassador Fisher mentioned a point on worst case analysis which I want to underscore. Professional government officials, especially those dealing with security matters, are indeed men whose job it is to figure out contingencies, to estimate the course of events. They generally consider what can go wrong in a given situation, not what can go right. For instance, a political leader will suggest an action or enterprise and his officials will tell him why he cannot do it and why it is risky. In a situation where there is a large number of negative votes in the hands of officials whose professional bent is to think of the worst case, there is a cumulative negative drag. If the participating governments want to move ahead, then negotiations must have the continuous direct interest and direct attention of their chief executive or at least of very senior officials cognizant of the political interests involved.

In addition to the often divergent motives involved in arms control and security negotiations, a further complication is divergence of opinion about the best approach to arms control. Should one, for instance, start with confidence-building measures, such as the exchange of information suggested in the French proposal for a Conference on Disarmament in Europe (CDE), or should we aim for reductions? Where should we enter on the subject matter? What is the ideal configuration? What is the best formula? In reductions, should we start with armaments or with personnel? Should we start with nuclear arms or with conventional arms? I follow such discussions with interest, but ultimately the conclusion has to be that there is no 'ideal' arms control, but only the pragmatic approach. We do what can be done, what is possible, regardless of what the ideal format or approach to arms control is, and regardless of particular motives. It is so difficult to gain agreement among governments on any aspect of this subject that we should accept what we can get when we can get it as long as the content makes intrinsic sense.

I would like to mention one or two reasons why we Americans, from the point of view of our own interests, should be thinking seriously about arms control in Central Europe. I want to mention a few facts which, although known, are seldom brought together. Ranged one after the other, they make a convincing case.

The first of these is that the current military confrontation in Europe is the largest ever to be assembled by human beings in any one place throughout peacetime history. At this moment, there are approximately three million men on each side confronting each other with the largest array of arms which has ever been assembled in any particular area. A military confrontation of this size, with these dimensions and number of personnel, entails, unavoidably and automatically, a high risk of misperception and miscalculation. This is a danger which we can clearly do without.

Another point is that the confrontation in Europe has been joined in recent years with other areas of confrontation. Hence, attempts to defuse tension, to reduce the risk of miscalculation in Europe, gain in logic if there is a possibility of conflict and confrontation in other areas which could spread to Europe.

A third factor is the expense involved. It is estimated that the nations of the world spend about one trillion dollars a year on military forces. My calculations are that the NATO and Warsaw Pact countries spend roughly two-thirds of that annual world total on their confrontation in Europe alone. Clearly, that is a lot of money, and the cost of the major items of equipment is mounting. A modern

American tank, for instance, now costs well over one million dollars, a fighter-bomber aircraft, up to fifty million dollars.

A fourth factor, which is a permanent feature of the problem, is the instability in Eastern Europe which we so dramatically witnessed in Poland in the early 1980s. Eastern Europe will not settle down; it will continue to be an area of repression and frustrated desire for change. In theory, however, an appropriate arms control agreement for Europe could provide a framework in which the Soviet Union might be somewhat more willing to permit, however grudgingly, social and economic change if it thought this would be without any significant change in the military balance. Fear of change in the military balance is certainly a major if not the strongest component of Soviet interest and actions in Eastern Europe.

A further group of reasons has to do with alliance relations. Our Western allies are strongly interested in arms control, and it is an act of wisdom on our part to seek at the MBFR talks in Vienna an agreement in which they can all participate.

These are serious reasons for arms control in Europe: they transcend tactical motivations and represent long-term, deep-rooted interests. Unfortunately, although the MBFR talks have been going on for some ten years at this point, they have not led to force reduction. Understandably, they have been criticized for not producing results. Many different motives may have played a role in creating that state of affairs, but, my view is that there is no ideal format, no ideal motive in arms control. We try to describe the whole of the 'animal' in any way we can, and lay hold of him where we can. Up to now, arms control, as suggested by its name, has been largely political, a means of reassuring the peoples and governments of the competing countries. It is not yet disarmament or real force reduction. We will ultimately have to move in that direction. In this relatively early stage, we have to take what we can, and the reassurance which comes from arms control makes a very important contribution to keeping the peace.

## Bibliography

Dean, J. (1986), *Watershed in Europe: Dismantling the East-West Military Confrontation*, Lexington, Lexington Books.

# 10(v) Towards a new rationality

*Dennis J.D. Sandole*

Ambassador Fisher discussed a number of aspects of international negotiations, two of which are capable of fueling action–reaction conflict spirals: the worst-case and bargaining chip orientations to conflict management. Although either could lead to unintended, negative outcomes, their interaction could exacerbate further the sources of tension, thereby hastening the development of an explosive situation.

Looking first at the worst-case approach, let us assume that an American foreign policymaker or negotiator defines the Soviet Union in negative, hostile terms: 'The Russians are about to develop a first-strike capability. Unless we are very vigilant, we will fall behind. Consequently, we must arm for all we can in order to protect ourselves.' This definition of the situation then leads to a corresponding American behavior with regard to the Soviets: a new round of American arming. It could also lead to the second part of the volatile combination, the use of the bargaining chip approach. After all, no 'rational' person really wants a nuclear war to occur. Therefore, at the same time that the Americans try to prevent the Soviets from achieving a first-strike capability, they also try to pressure them to come to the negotiating table. Hence, they must threaten to, and actually, arm for greater numbers and/or higher qualities of nuclear weapons in order to motivate the Soviets to negotiate nuclear arms control and ultimately, disarmament.

The logic here is interesting and for some, unassailable: in order to de-escalate, we must first escalate. The problem with this, however, is that there may well be a Soviet reaction, but not the one that 'logic' would have us expect. If the Americans have a worst-case definition of the Soviets which in turn leads to American extreme use of the bargaining chip approach, then, as Ambassador Fisher has said, the 'hawks' on the Soviet side may be strengthened, thereby increasing the probability that they will respond with their own extreme use of a bargaining chip approach. Once this has been done, the Americans will be confirmed in their worst-case definition of the Soviets, once more leading to an 'appropriate' American response. Then the whole cycle will begin all over again, from worst-case definition to worst-case response (which may ultimately lose its bargaining chip intent), to reciprocation by the other side, escalation, counter-escalation and so on *ad infinitum*.

The 'fascinating', if not deadly aspect of this process is its insidious nature. It sneaks up on its participants until, whether they discover what they have given life to or not, they are trapped by, and within the system. That system is the negative expression of the self-fulfilling prophecy. Everything that the Americans do with regard to the Soviets stimulates a Soviet response which confirms the original negative definition of the Soviets (which, at the outset, may not have been valid), and vice versa. After some time has passed, each *is* out to get the other!

Normally, the participants in this 'bite-counterbite' process do not see the role that they have been playing in creating and/or maintaining a hostile reality; they do not see that their actions have been leading to counter-productive outcomes. All that they see is that they have been 'right' all along about the 'enemy'.

Putting all of this into the context of the real world, the Reagan administration has talked a great deal about the necessity of the United States regaining its number one position with regard to nuclear weapons, the assumption being that the Soviet Union by virtue of its 'massive arms buildup', has forced the United States into second place (see Holzman, 1986). Even if President Reagan and his closest advisers did not believe their own public rhetoric, but, in class bargaining chip fashion, planned to engage in their own massive armament program to pressure the Soviets to negotiate, the Soviets might nevertheless believe it.

There is a great deal of distance, and not merely in geographical terms, between the United States and the Soviet Union. There is, for instance, a good deal of ignorance or 'anthropological innocence' on the American side about Soviet history and culture. Many are unaware of, or unable to appreciate the significance of Soviet sensitivities to penetration by the West. They have been invaded a number of times, brutally by Germany during World War II and, as their military presence in Eastern Europe indicates, they are not about to let that happen again. Given those sensitivities, an American extreme use of the bargaining chip approach could lead to disasterous consequences.

*Jonathan Dean*: One of the major problems with bargaining chips is that when the time comes to use them, to trade them off for the concessions they were designed to elicit, the trade-off does not occur because some of the negotiators, and/or their constitutents back home, want to retain them. In this case they cease to be bargaining chips and instead, escalation moves, pure and simple. This has occurred with great regularity on the US side of arms control negotiations.

*Alex Gliksman*: Also, to categorize people as hawks and doves is to oversimplify the differences between them. Instead of those terms, we might want to refer to people who, working in various ministries in the USSR as well as the US, have proprietary interests in maintaining certain systems.

I also have some difficulty with the notion that there is good and bad in every system. In my study of British policy towards Germany in 1938, British intelligence and others were arguing in favor of a soft line towards Hitler on the assumption that such a policy would influence him to adopt a softer approach himself; in effect, to reject war as an option. But they were clearly wrong. Hitler was *the* hawk in 1938 (and beyond).

*Adrian Fisher*: To refer to people as hawks and doves is clearly to oversimplify them. However, the terms do indicate a spectrum of opinion, one which we would observe if we sat in on any of the various inter-department meetings of the present government in Washington. We might also observe that the spectrum includes what we might call 'dawks' and 'hoves', i.e., people who are a bit of both extremes, perhaps with either dominating under different circumstances. But in any case, the spectrum does exist and not just in the United States. According to my own experience plus that of Averell Harriman, it exists in the Soviet Union as well.

*Dennis Sandole*: The hawk-dove spectrum is suggestive of a range of differences in orientation to conflict and conflict management, including differences in how rationality is viewed. This leads to my second point which concerns Ambassador Fisher's reference to 'rationality' as the basis for a belief that the Soviets and Americans can avoid nuclear holocaust.

But first, as a brief aside, it is an over simplification for us to talk about the nuclear dimension solely with regard to the United States and the Soviet Union when there are other states with various degrees of nuclear capability. In addition to the other permament members of the United Nations Security Council—Britain, France, and China—there are Argentina, Brazil, India, Israel, Pakistan, South Africa and others. It says something about the power of images that, even though these other nuclear and near-nuclear powers exist, and their numbers are growing, many people live in a bipolar world where in addition to 'us', there are 'them', and depending upon where one sits, 'them' are either the Soviets or the Americans.

One particular view of rationality has a long history, undoubtedly even a prehistory. Considering only the written record, it goes back at least as far as 416 BC when, according to Thucydides' history of *The Peloponnesian War* (1951, pp. 330–7), Athens attempted to negotiate the subjugation of the inhabitants of Melos. At one point in the deliberations, the Athenian negotiators said to the Melians:

> . . . We hope that you . . . will aim at what is feasible, holding in view the real sentiments of us both; since you know as well as we do that right, as the world goes, is only in question between equals in power, while the strong do what they can and the weak suffer what they must (Ibid., p. 331).

The negotiations failed: the Melians, pushing for fairness and justice, refused to accept Athen's 'might-is-right' position, and they were subsequently crushed.

The kind of rationality that is associated with this power-politics approach to conflict management has been labeled by game-theorists, some two thousand years after Thucydides, as 'zero sum': there are always winners and losers, and in some situations, what one wins, another loses. Gain plus loss equals zero; hence, 'zero sum'. What is significant about zero-sum thinking is not that one party's gain is equal exactly to another party's loss (which in the real world may not occur with much frequency), but that the people so characterized see the world in terms of winners and losers. Such a view tends to motivate them to pursue winning and to avoid losing, even at the expense of others.

While Thucydides and game theory may seem far removed from everyday experience, the rationality which both imply is part of the foundation of our own democratic system. For example, Jeremy Bentham and James Mill, 'the two earliest systematic exponents of liberal democracy', viewed society as 'a collection of individuals incessantly seeking power over and at the expense of each other' (Macpherson, 1977, pp. 24 and 26). Although the Soviets do not share the overall classical economics' assumptions that led Bentham and Mill to their view, but they nevertheless share that view, especially as a reflection of the capitalist epoch. Just like the Americans, the Soviets wish to 'prevail', to win or at least, not to lose, in the event of nuclear war.

This is not Ambassador Fisher's view of rationality. His is a more comprehensive, 'positive-sum' view, where both or all parties gain from their exchange. This is not to say that each gets exactly what it wanted originally, or gets exactly what the other has received, but only that each feels that it is better off with, rather than without, a particular agreement that prevents them from coming to blows. Clearly, an agreement to put into place the necessary infrastructure to prevent a nuclear holocaust would be a gain for all concerned (and in the nuclear sense, all are concerned).

But it is not Ambassador Fisher's sense of rationality that is influencing perceptions and behavior in much of the world—in Northern Ireland, Beirut, Sri Lanka, South Africa, between East and West, North and South, etc. Although John Burton (1979), Michael Banks (1984) and others (Sandole, 1984) have indicated that there is some evidence of a 'paradigm shift'—a movement away from what Morton Deutsch (1973) calls competitive processes of conflict resolution toward cooperative processes—zero-sum rationality, accompanied by the use of power to 'prevail', is still a key feature of human relations at all levels, including the global. The closer one is to the 'hawk' side of the spectrum, the more pronounced will be the expression of the zero-sum view: the more one will possess it and, in turn, be 'possessed' by it.

Finally, Ambassador Fisher has indicated that he does not expect too much from the Strategic Arms Reduction Talks (START). General Edward Rowny, who has been designated the chief American negotiator, came to George Mason University as a guest-speaker in a course on nuclear war given by Dr Robert Ehrlich, Chairman of the Physics Department. Although General Rowny expressed optimism that some kind of agreement could be reached, much of what he said reflected the bipolar view of the world where 'they' are clearly worse (if not also a bit more clever) than 'us'. For instance, in his dealings with the Soviets during SALT, he found that the United States was always out-negotiated by them. One reason for this are the cultural differences between the two countries, 'which Americans do not understand'. One of those differences is that 'the Soviets do not respect the letter of the law, whereas Americans do'. This, incidentally, prompted one member of the audience to enquire, 'But is the US all that different? What about all those broken treaties with the Indians?' General Rowny's response to this was that 'the Soviets are worse than us *by degree*'. Another American failing in these negotiations cited by General Rowny was a desperation to obtain an agreement which could lead the United States to show its hand prematurely. In his closing comments General Rowny said that the Soviets do not respect example, but strength, hence: 'We have to go up in order to go down'. This is a sentiment which not only supports the bargaining chip notion but also parallels a view often expressed in hostile, or near-hostile, encounters: 'The only language they understand is that of force!' This is the kind of view that makes the negative expression of the self-fulfilling prophecy more, rather than less, likely. It also implies that a unilateral arms control or reduction move by the United States would not be reciprocated by the Soviet Union. Though this may be true under some circumstances, there is evidence (see Etzioni, 1967) to suggest that, under other circumstances, it might not be.

*Adrian Fisher:* Do the Russians respect example? If we decided to disarm unilaterally, would we have a better chance of dealing with the Russians than if we did not? I think not. As I indicated before, I am not a unilateral disarmer. But this is not to say that the Russians will refuse to respond reciprocally to any and all unilateral moves. That is clearly not the case. For example, President Kennedy's American University speech of 10 June 1963, which included his unilateral decision to ban nuclear tests in the atmosphere, played an important role in bringing the Russians to the negotiating table. Had the President not made that announcement, I think the Russians would have behaved quite differently. So, with regard to the example versus strength issue, I think that General Rowny was oversimplifying a bit. But I also believe that, as a negotiator, General Rowny will be a bit more sensible than the model of the 'tough general' would have us believe.

*Dennis Sandole*: Unless the participants in the Soviet—American and other conflict relationships world-wide give some though to the merits of positive-sum rationality, plus ways of expanding and extending its influence, zero-sum rationality will continue to fuel and sustain conflict spirals which always contain the seeds of escalation beyond human control. 'Rationality', indeed 'realism', would seem to demand that we pay special attention to this problem.

## Bibliography

Banks, M. (1984), 'The Evolution of International Relations Theory' in *Conflict in World Society: A New Perspective on International Relations*, M. Banks (ed.), Brighton, Wheatsheaf and New York, St. Martin's Press.

Burton, J.W. (1979), *Deviance, Terrorism, and War: The Process of Solving Unsolved Social and Political Problems*, Oxford, Martin Robertson and New York, St. Martin's Press.

Deutsch, M. (1973), *The Resolution of Conflict: Constructive and Destructive Processes*, New Haven and London, Yale University Press.

Etzioni, A. (1967), 'The Kennedy Experiment', *Western Political Quarterly*, **20**, no. 2 (Part 1), pp. 361–80. Condensed and reprinted in *The Dynamics of Aggression: Individual, Group, and International Analyses*, E.I. Megargee & J.E. Hokanson (eds), New York and London, Harper and Row, 1970.

Holzman, F.D. (1986) 'What Defense-Spending Gap?' *The New York Times*, 4 March, p. A27.

Macpherson, C.B. (1977), *The Life and Times of Liberal Democracy*, Oxford and New York, Oxford University Press.

Rowny, E.L. (1982), Presentation at nuclear war course (Dr. Robert Ehrlich). Fairfax, Virginia, George Mason University, 3 February.

Sandole, D.J.D. (1984), 'The Subjectivity of Theories and Actions in World Society' in *Conflict in World Society: A New Perspective on International Relations*, M. Banks (ed.), Brighton, Wheatsheaf and New York, St. Martin's Press.

Thucydides (1951), *The Peloponnesian War*, Crawley translation, New York, The Modern Library (Random House).

# 11(i) Preventing nuclear war

*Ralph K. White*

Nuclear war is clearly a horrifying prospect. If we are not yet motivated to devote a good deal of energy doing whatever we can to prevent it, partly by thinking about how to prevent it, and then by acting; if we are not motivated to put it among the top, if not at the very top of the things that we think are worth thought and action, then I believe that we are either too hopeful or too hopeless. If we are completely hopeless about the possibility of preventing nuclear war, then, of course, there is no incentive to do anything about it, no matter how horrible it is. On the other hand, if we are very hopeful that nuclear war will never occur, then there is nothing about which we need to do anything.

I believe that there are more people who are too hopeful than those who are too hopeless. I have often talked with people who ask what I think the chances are of avoiding nuclear war. I usually say that, before the year 2000, the chances are about even. A lot of people are surprised that I think there is so much danger. And I would like to indicate why.

But first I want to indicate what I think is a much stronger basis for hope and optimism than most people think, at least those who take a hardline stance. In this regard, the Soviet Union is not the aggressive monster that most hardliners simply assume. The Soviet Union is, in some ways, a bad country; theirs is a bad system, one which is not really just or humane. It is backward in many ways. For instance, I think they have a good deal more propensity than we Americans to indulge in blatant lies when they feel threatened. That notwithstanding, I am convinced that they want peace even more than we do. In talking with Russians in Moscow and elsewhere I have often come up against their reaction to Americans saying that we need arms for self-defense. They say, 'self-defense? Who would attack you?' The American answers that a great many Americans are afraid that the Soviet Union would atack them or Western Europe. Their response to this is, 'How could we do a thing like that? That would be starting a war; we are the most peaceful country in the world. How could we be anything but the most peaceful country in the world, after what we went through in World War II?' At that point, I have to agree.

The Soviets went through such privations and tragedies during World War II, eating rats and cats during the siege of Leningrad, to mention but one of the many, many tragedies. If they did not hate and fear war more than we Americans did—who escaped with almost none of the horrors experienced by the Soviet populace—they would not be human. I think there is a very great lack of proper, realistic empathy on that point. Most Americans assume that because the leaders of the Soviet Union have an expansionist ideology in principle, their main purpose is to conquer the world. Perhaps that was true in the days of Lenin and Trotsky. Since the end of World War II, however, I think it is no longer valid. That is not their main purpose. It is perhaps priority number five. According to Bryant Wedge's (1963) ranking of Soviet priorities, the first purpose for the Soviet leaders is to stay in power. This is imperative—what they call the leading, dominant role of the party. Their second purpose perhaps is to maintain the integrity of their borders, including the borders of Eastern Europe—not letting the West gain any territory that it does not have already. Currently, they think that Afghanistan is within their sphere of control. Their third purpose is to avoid nuclear war. This is not to say they want to avoid any war. It is not a hatred of minor wars but it certainly is a hatred of major wars. The fourth purpose is economic progress: increasing productivity and living standards. The fifth purpose is expansion, piecemeal expansion, wherever it seems feasible without nuclear war.

If conquering the world is only the fifth priority, then we can say that it is *a* goal, but not *the* goal of the Soviet leaders, and certainly not one that they would pursue recklessly at the cost of a great war. This is very unconventional thinking from the standpoint of many Americans. But from the standpoint of the best informed Americans, the real Soviet experts, it is not unconventional thinking at all. In any case, plain, ordinary empathy should lead us to abandon this diabolical enemy image. This image, the assumption that one's enemy is inhumanly bad, and does not even have a human motive such as fear, is the dominant form of misperception. It seems to me that the Soviet Union has a great deal of fear and also touchy pride. Hence, it would be beneficial for us, who are also characterized by fear and touchy pride, if we could empathize with the touchy pride and fear (of us) in Soviet leaders.

All of this is a basis for hope. If we definitely want peace, particularly nuclear peace, and if they want it too, then why should there ever be a war? Why should there ever be a war if both sides really want to avoid it and really would pay a sizeable price in terms of other things in order to avoid it? That is the basis for optimism that goes beyond what many people think.

But there are at least six reasons for pessimism, reasons why I see a fifty-fifty chance of a major nuclear war occurring between now and the year 2000. First, we Americans are the ones who have not yet said that we would *not* be the first to cross the nuclear threshold, to cross the firebreak between conventional and nuclear war. Ever since the Stockholm Appeal in 1950, the Soviet Union has said that they would not start a nuclear war. They have even said, 'let us all agree whoever is first to do so is the war criminal, because that is the greatest crime of all—to *start* a nuclear war.' That has always made sense to me. If nobody starts a nuclear war, if nobody crosses that fateful line between conventional and nuclear war, then the horrors that Jonathan Schell (1982) has written about will not materialize. The earth itself, the human race, and the ecosphere will not be destroyed, at least not in our lifetime, if nobody is the first to use nuclear weapons. But we are the ones who have not said that we will not be the first. By our very deployment of tactical, theatre-nuclear weapons, and by our urging our West European friends to accept them, we are implying that if the worst came to the worst, if there were a real attack on Western Europe, then we would consider using nuclear weapons.

A second reason for my pessimism is what President Carter said in his announcement of the Carter Doctrine, which was applauded by Congress. He stated that if there were a foreign threat against the oil fields in the Middle East, we would use any means necessary, including armed force, to keep them out of foreign hands, meaning of course, the Soviet Union. Military people are nearly, if not completely unanimous in the view that we could not cope with an actual Soviet invasion of the Middle East unless we used the tactical nuclear weapons which we have implicitly threatened to use. We apparently care more about the oil in the Middle East—and we have plenty of good reasons to care about it—than we care about the fate of the Earth, *literally*!

To what extent would I go to protect our access to Middle East oil? We should arrange our goals in an order to priority. The oil fields are very important for the economy of others, particularly Western Europe and Japan, more so than for us. But how does that compare with the literal destruction of the human race? We should try to do both, we should use our best thinking and acting to keep access to the oil, especially for Western Europe and Japan, but not in a way that seriously endangers the survival of the human race and the environment.

A third reason for pessimism is that when we look at the situation logically, there is one circumstance in which one side or the other might well be motivated, despite its horror of war, to be the first to engage in a nuclear strike. And this concerns the combination of an intense crisis with equally intense emotion on both sides, coupled either with the misconception that the other side was starting to attack us or the fear that it soon would unless we attacked first. As long as there is a military advantage in a preemptive strike, and there certainly is at present, that kind of reasoning could lead rational people to start a nuclear war.

A fourth reason for pessimism is the proliferation of not only nuclear weapons, but the knowledge of how to make them. This has developed so far by now that it is erroneous to think merely in terms of the probability that we might start, or the Soviet Union might start a nuclear war. A number of other countries might be able to initiate such a war, and we could still get involved.

A fifth reason for pessimism is that both sides can play the 'game of chicken'. The idea in this game is that one fellow drives his car very fast and very close to the center of the road, while the other fellow with whom one is 'playing' drives his car also very fast and very close to the center of the road, so close that the players are scraping each other. The first one to veer in order to avoid a collision is the 'chicken'. This is very close to how World War I began. In the last days of July 1914, each side thought that the other was going to back down if it was just firm enough, and demonstrated that firmness. People can get committed in that manner, and they can gain great momentum moving in a certain direction. In the event they are on a collision course. If each side is confident that the other will back down, and neither therefore does, then it may be involved in a war that neither side wants.

My sixth reason for pessimism is that there is a characteristic of human nature, even in men and women of good will and intelligence, to rid our conscious minds of negative images of unpleasant possibilities. The very fact that so few Americans have since 1950 protested against our policy of being the first to use nuclear weapons, of holding such weapons in reserve at least, in case there is outright aggression of a non-nuclear sort; the very fact that I have heard so few protests among Americans since the 1950s, when the Soviet Union began to protest intensely against that policy, I think, is a sign of how we turn our minds away. Some psychologists call it selective inattention, the Freudians might call it repression. In any case, it is the phenomenon of not paying attention, of not thinking, of inhibiting our curiosity about what the causes of an event are, and consideration of what ought to be done. This condition is so prevalent in the United States that I do not rely on the American people to take the fairly obvious steps that would be necessary to avert a nuclear peril.

Jonathan Schell talks about a sort of schizophrenic, pathological reaction to the nuclear danger, a reaction consisting of, quite simply, not paying attention to it. He is absolutely right. I believe that the sanest people are the ones who are rubbing their noses in this horror, but even more, who are thinking about how to avoid it; practical, future-oriented, evidence-oriented thinking about how to prevent a nuclear war.

When I was a discussant for Dean Pruitt's contribution to this book (Chapter 3), I presented six ideas on how to prevent nuclear war. Let me now increase that number to eight, with four coming under the heading of *deterrence* and four under *tension reduction*. These all touch upon Pruitt's reference to 'firm but flexible'. We can be firm about our major goals, and not back down too easily, but we can also be flexible as to the means of achieving these goals. We can be conciliatory, cooperative in certain situations, without ceasing to be firm. We do not necessarily have to be too firm, just enough to get something which is much better than a mechanical compromise, and far better than just abandoning the negotiations.

The first item I am suggesting under the heading of deterrence is a relatively invulnerable second-strike capability: sufficient nuclear weapons deployed in relatively invulnerable circumstances (aboard submarines) to devastate at least most of the cities in the Soviet Union; a relatively invulnerable second-strike capability is vital, to put a wholesome fear into the enemy, to reinforce their verbal commitment to not be the first to use nuclear weapons; to make them realize that if they were the first to use nuclear weapons, even granting them all the advantage of striking first, many of their cities could still be destroyed.

A second item under deterrence is an emphasis on relatively defensive weapons. Long-range bombers, for instance, are essentially offensive weapons; but tactical fighter planes that might down enemy bombers over one's own territory are more defensive. Minefields are another form of defensive weapons. A third item is to improve not necessarily the quantity but certainly the quality of personnel and equipment in our conventional arms. A fourth item is collective deterrence through a democratic world federation.

Under the heading of tension reduction, my first suggestion is courteous communication under all circumstances with all actors, including our worst enemies. Being enemies is no reason for not communicating. A second is to renounce and denounce any first use of nuclear weapons, including tactical ones. We would continue to have nuclear weapons in some measure but we would pledge not to use them, unless the other side does. We would keep them *only* for deterrence. A third item is a drastic reduction of our nuclear weapons, down to the level and kind necessary for a relatively invulnerable second-strike capability. This includes, for example, George Kennan's (1981) proposal for a 50 percent reduction in strategic strength on both sides. I would go further and say we should do it unilaterally if the other side will not. A fourth item is scupulous avoidance of intervention anywhere, except, perhaps, if there has been clear, unambiguous aggression by our major opponent, the Soviet Union. There should be no more Vietnams. If there is a clear case of aggression—either against us, an ally, or a neutral—then some appropriate response could be argued for. In the case of Vietnam, it was very far from clear that the other side was the aggressor. In my considered judgment, we were more the aggressor than they were. If one superpower, for instance, the USSR, supplies another actor with arms, this would not be a clear case of aggression. The United States supplies arms to its favorite groups as well, without taking on the status of 'clear aggressor'.

Let us discuss further some of these ways for preventing nuclear war. What about the first item under deterrence, the notion of a relatively invulnerable second-strike capability, deployed primarily on submarines? Submarine-launched weapons are not yet that accurate and therefore they are primarily a second-strike weapon.

*Willard Matthias*: That is not entirely true, because I believe that the Trident II, which is now under development, will be about as accurate as the Mark 12A warhead on the MX missile so that we will have, in effect, a first strike weapon aboard those submarines. I think that the question of first strike versus second strike is also partly a question of numbers: that is, if we reduced the number of our warheads down to, say, 500, instead of the 10,000 or so we have now, then that would be a sufficiently reduced number that we would be unable to carry out a successful first strike, even with accuracy.

*Ralph White*: Except against cities.

*Willard Matthias*: Yes, but it would be impossible to knock out their retaliatory force with only 500 weapons. Therefore the Soviets would recognize that the only thing we could do with those 500 weapons would be to hit their cities. Therefore, the encouragement for them to engage in a first strike is eliminated.

*Ralph White*: The second item under deterrence is the preference for defensive weapons. We can liken this to the sword and the shield. Suppose that in ancient times there had been no swords and no spears but only shields on each side of any war. Would those wars have occurred? I think not. A shield is not threatening. It does not create the unhealthy, war-promoting type of fear, whereas a sword does. Long-range bombers: what could be more frightening to the Soviet Union, and more likely to make them think that we are aggressively hostile to them than our long-range bombers? Minefields are utterly different. The Soviet Union would have to attack us in order for our minefields to threaten them. It can only be wholesome to have them afraid to attack us, but it is thoroughly unwholesome to have them afraid that *we* would attack *them*. The fact that we think our motives are entirely pure and innocent does not mean that they will be perceived as such.

We have to be sensitive here to the mind set of the Soviet leaders and people concerning their suffering in World War II; to the fact that every child in the Soviet Union learns about World War II from the age of two on. It is everywhere: in their films and indoctrination in school; they hear it from their parents and their grandparents, and even from those who have never experienced World War II themselves, and they get it from the media. They are aware that their country has been invaded by the West, not once but at least twice during the twentieth century.

Regarding my third item under deterrence, I think we have allowed the quality of our military men, spare parts, amunition, and equipment to deteriorate. We do not frighten the Soviets and make them think we are diabolical if we concentrate on things like quality of armed forces, especially since they know that the United States' forces are less numerous than theirs. We do frighten them, however, with our nuclear weapons, especially the highly accurate ones. That is an unhealthy kind of fear, in contrast to the healthy kind associated with knowing that they would incur costs if they attacked Western Europe.

I do not think that the Soviet Union really wants to attack Western Europe. It is taken for granted by most of our hardliners that it does want to attack Western Europe. But why should they? They know that it would cause a war. They would lose very valuable trading partners if they attacked Western Europe. And why would they want to conquer and occupy France and West Germany when Poland is such a headache?

Perhaps this point about the Soviets not wanting to attack Europe, and how little it would take to deter them from doing so, is more obvious than I indicated. But there are other parts of the world. If, for instance, there were another Korean War or a war in the Middle East, and we wanted to keep it from spreading beyond the Middle East, a good conventional force would have a wholesome deterrent effect. Probably too late to save the oil fields if the Soviets wanted them, but I think it would not take very much to deter them from going into the Middle East if we did not threaten them from the Middle East and if we were willing to cooperate with them in that part of the world.

I have been asked how China fits into all this, where it seems to be a major factor, especially given the tradition enmity between the Soviet Union and China. China enters in very much in at least two ways. One is that since China has become an avowed enemy of the Soviet Union, the Soviets have some basis for feeling that they are encircled by enemies. The Soviets and their East European allies have 6 or 7 percent of the world's population. Most of the other countries around them are hostile, and that gives them that siege mentality which, I think, is one of the major causes of war and of the vicious circles that promote war. China enters also in another way. If we consider the military balance as a whole, we certainly should include our allies as well as ourselves. There has been a great deal of misleading talk by the hardliners who just compare the Soviet weapons with ours and ignore the weapons of our allies. As far as Europe is concerned, we and our allies have about the same number of troops as have the Soviet Union and its East European allies; hence, the balance is not nearly as much against us as some say. The same would be true in the Far East. The fact that China is more likely to be against the Soviet Union that for it gives the Soviet Union a very big problem. I can hardly imagine that they would start a war with both China and the United States. However, there is the Middle East, and I cannot see China or Western Europe fighting on our side if a war should start there, particularly if they would think, as most of the Europeans presently do, that we are partly responsible for the troubles in the Middle East. They would want to distance themselves from that. Such a war would result in a Soviet victory, I think, unless we used tactical nuclear weapons. In that case, we would both suffer terribly and it could well escalate to a major exchange.

At the beginning of this section I stated that nuclear war is clearly a horrifying prospect. Though I have discussed briefly some means for preventing nuclear war,

I have not exhausted the possibilities. There is a need, therefore, for further thinking about prevention. There is also a need, however, for appropriate action, lest that 50-50 probability really start to work against us.

## Bibliography

Kennan, G.F. (1981), 'A Proposal for International Disarmament', an address made in accepting the Albert Einstein Peace Prize in Washington, DC, 19 May. Reprinted by The Institute for World Order, New York.

Schell, J. (1982), *The Fate of the Earth*, New York, Knopf.

Wedge, B. (1963), *The View From the East: Soviet Perceptions of Disarmament*, Washington, DC, US Arms Control and Disarmament Agency.

White, R.K. (1984), *Fearful Warriors: A Psychological Profile of US-Soviet Relations*, New York, Free Press.

White, R.K. (ed.) (1986), *Psychology and the Prevention of Nuclear War: A Book of Readings*, New York, New York University Press.

# 11(ii) Perceptions of the 'Enemy' in United States foreign policy

*Willard Matthias*

There are two basic assumptions which have dominated American military and foreign policy since the late 1940s. The first is one which Dr. White discussed, the notion that the Soviet Government is basically an aggressive nation, determined to dominate the world by military force, if necessary. This idea has been around for a long time, and I agree with Dr. White that it is essentially erroneous. The Soviets are basically prudent, frightened and conservative.

This particular doctrine has been nurtured to a very considerable extent by the American military establishment who need something like this. Generally speaking, military organizations have to plan and think in terms of an 'enemy'. At least they think they do. Since 1945, the American military establishment has had control of the most horrific weapons that have ever been created by mankind. These men are, or will be, or theoretically could be responsible for pushing the button, flying the planes or arming the missiles which could dump these weapons onto other people. A decent human being who has to push the button can only come to the conclusion that those who will be targetted by these weapons must be some kind of devil, or otherwise really bad people. In this regard, I think that the American military establishment has a deep psychological problem and for this reason they are incapable of taking an objective look at the Soviets.

The second assumption is that our nuclear arsenal and strategy can save us from these alleged Soviet intentions; I think that this is also erroneous. For the most part, what we have done in terms of developing our nuclear arsenal and strategies over the years has been to increase, rather than to reduce the danger from any such alleged intentions. I do not want to discuss at great length what the intentions of the Soviets are because I am not even sure that it makes much difference. Even if they were as aggressive as it is alleged they are, I think there is a way to curb them which is much less dangerous to the United States than the approach which we have been pursuing.

There are, I think, two main problems with our military strategy and arsenal. First, our arsenal is too big; and second, we have developed a first-strike capability. The first-strike capability is an extremely dangerous thing to have, and I believe it is totally unnecessary. We have weapons that can only be useful for a first strike or for first use at a tactical level. This encourages the other side to develop the same capabilities.

I would like to say just one or two things about the threat on a conventional level; I do not think there is very much threat at any level, nuclear or conventional, from the Soviet Union to the United States. The principal threat to Middle East oil does not arise from the Soviet Union. It arises primarily from the Israeli problem, and secondly from the revolutionary situation in the Near East as a whole. In Europe, it is of course true that the Soviets can and do deploy substantial conventional forces and they are acquiring the capability to project their power around the world. They would like to have more influence, but the last thing they want to do is to take on any more Chinas. The last thing they want to do is expose their homeland to danger. I doubt very much if they are interested in carrying out aggression in the military sense, that is by going across borders with banners flying, with aircraft, infantry, tanks, and so on. This, I think, they regard as too dangerous and as unlikely to serve their interests in the longer term.

About nuclear strategy, I happen to be one of those people who believes that we had better recognize that our lives today are, and for the last twenty years have been, dependent on Soviet rationality. They could blow us up tomorrow if they wanted to; we could blow them up, but we simply must operate on a recognition that they have some good sense. If they depart from all rationality, then the game is up. Our policy with respect to nuclear strategy has to be one that encourages them to think in a rational fashion. The creation of a first-strike capability, which we are now rapidly developing, is therefore a very dangerous business. A Mark 12A warhead is very accurate. We are putting these on Minuteman missiles currently in place and are planning to put them on the MX. It can be argued that the only possible reason for putting such warheads on missiles in silos (which the Soviets can target) is that we are going to hit the Soviets first. There is nothing better designed to cause a Soviet first strike than to instill in them the fear of being struck first. The Trident II missile, which is going to be placed on the new Trident submarines, has essentially the same accuracy as the Mark 12A warhead.

It should not really matter to us whether our Minuteman forces are vulnerable so long as we can deliver some 250 nuclear weapons on the Soviet Union. I would suggest something in the order of 500 weapons, distributed among airplanes, submarines, and perhaps railroad cars in the desert, but we need nothing like the kind of force we possess today.

I am absolutely appalled at the mathematics-of-destruction industry, where people spin fine points about how many missiles it would take, and at what level of reliability to get a 90 percent chance of a hit, and so on. These considerations constitute retreats from reality. Indeed, this whole business suggests to some extent a self-destructive, lemming instinct on the part of the human race.

How did we get into the business of having such assumptions underlying our foreign policy, aside from the psychological problems of the military establishment? One reason is 'groupthink', a concept developed by psychologist Irving Janis of Yale, who wrote a very interesting book on this subject (1972). The idea is, once a particular view or assessment becomes current within the United States bureaucracy, and among the American political leadership and the media, it tends to stay in place, whether justified or not. There is a very strong tendency for people and particularly within the bureaucracy to set themselves up as thought-control types. Consequently, the individual who disagrees with the fashionable view or assessment has a very difficult time suggesting that what his/her colleagues are doing may be very stupid, or that it is wrong or that there is no evidence to support it. If he openly disagrees, he is going to find himself never promoted again; he is going to find himself shipped out to an undesirable location on the next assignment or in one way or another he is going to find himself out of the policy-making process. Groupthink, then, is a very important matter. It had a lot to do with our getting into Vietnam; it had a lot to do with some of the other crises with which we have been involved.

Now I would like to address something with which I have personal acquaintance, and that is what I consider to be the deterioration of the intelligence system in the United States over the last ten years or so. A great deal of what is said to be the threat to the United States, whether it is in El Salvador or the Soviet SS-18 missile, etc., is assessed and put into sacred script by the intelligence community in Washington. After consideration by the United States Intelligence Board such assessments are sent on to the White House and over to the Pentagon where they become the basis for military planning. There has always been a certain amount of calculated leak from the Pentagon in order to show that the Soviets are doing something of a 'threatening', dangerous nature. Nobody ever mentions the things that are done in the United States, however, the weapons that are built here, planned here, and so on which could destroy the Soviet Union; we only hear about what they could do to destroy the United States. This has been a practice for a long time. It is selectively designed to frighten the American people. These 'revelations' usually come out during the first three or four months of the year because that is when the appropriation bills for the Defense Department are under consideration.

What has happened more recently has been the politicization of the intelligence system to the point where it is now virtually delivering intelligence on order. Many people have developed the belief, as a result of the post-Watergate investigations, that the intelligence community is comprised of villains. This is not true. There were a great number of honorable men in this business. One of them was Richard Helms who refused to go along with the ruses and lies which the Nixon White House wanted him to carry out in order to divert investigation of the Watergate incident. Helms was dismissed at the end of the first Nixon Administration; he had not been a team player. His successors, in one form or another, have been political. They have been on the White House 'team'. President Ford, in particular, appointed a close political associate, now Vice President of the United States, who in one of his first acts after he became Director of Central Intelligence, decided that the assessments of Soviet threats made by the professionals in the Agency were insufficiently frightening. He appointed a special group, a 'team B', to check on the assessments of 'team A', the professional analysts. The 'team B' group consisted almost exclusively of people who were on record for the devil theory.

Since that time, I for one have not been willing to accept all of the intelligence assessments that have leaked out or been issued to the public. We may recall that in 1981 an assessment was made about how the revolutionaries of El Salvador were getting their military supplies from Cuba. This was known as a 'white paper'. The media accepted it full blown, without looking at it until several months later. Then they discovered that, in fact, the content of the paper justified a conclusion opposite to that which the State Department had alleged.

There is one other point I would like to make with respect to reasons why these misperceptions in the United States exist. The principal reason is ignorance. The history of what has gone on in America-Soviet relations since 1933 is not very well known. I think there is a great deal that is not even talked about in university courses. This ignorance about the Soviet Union is compounded by the nature of the political system in the United States which tends to bring into positions of power, in the Senate and the White House, people who are enormously ignorant about military matters, foreign policy matters and world affairs generally. The kinds of characteristics which it takes to get elected to the Senate or to the Presidency of the United States or to be selected for the staff of the President are not the characteristics that are helpful in running the kind of world we currently have.

In short, we have a constitutional system which was designed for an agricultural society of the eighteenth century that we are trying to use in the nuclear society of the twentieth century and it is not working very well. One of the reasons European political leaders, particularly those in France and Germany, have adopted much more sensible attitudes toward these matters is because they understand them better. For one thing, they are better educated; for another, they are in the center of Europe; and for still another, being in the parliamentary system over the years before they get into positions of leadership, they have had an opportunity to learn what is going on.

## Bibliography

Janis, I.L. (1972), *Victims of Groupthink: A Psychological Study of Foreign Policy Decisions and Fiascos*, Boston, Houghton Mifflin.

# 11(iii) A national case of jitters

*Dean Pruitt*

We are probably further away now from the adoption of the program that Ralph White has proposed than we have been since 1963. I think it might be worth analyzing why. Willard Matthias has suggested that there has been an exaggeration of the Soviet threat from the military and intelligence communities. I would like to add to this what I see as a national case of jitters and broaden the onus well beyond Washington.

America is now, and has been in the last five or so years, in a severe escalative process with the Soviet Union. This has strengthened the 'diabolical enemy' image of the Soviets in American minds. There is also decreasing empathy and an increasing fear which is leading to support for the people who are pushing heavy armaments programs. A president has been elected–and after all, this was a popular movement—who stands for an escalation of military preparedness, reduced cooperation with the Soviet bloc and increased efforts to undermine this bloc. There is also only lukewarm support for arms control negotiation. I know that such negotiations have begun, but the structure of this administration encourages serious doubts about whether they will succeed. When we decided to go into these negotiations, the clear word came from Washington, 'don't worry about it, we are going to propose something that they cannot accept anyway', and our proposal did indeed amount to a serious weakening of the Soviet Union. Publicly we ourselves became firmly committed to a rigid negotiation position from which it was hard to back down. This is not the way one would enter into genuine negotiations.

Furthermore, we have been insisting that our European allies also break their ties with the Soviet Union. We are so intent on furthering East–West conflict that we also interpret much of the Middle East situation in these terms.

It seems to me that many of these moves are very harmful to American interests; in fact, they undermine our interests. We have already heard about the many problems with a build-up that is, or can be interpreted as, a first-strike capability—the easily targetable nuclear missiles. The danger of not engaging in genuine arms control negotiations I think is quite manifest. The mounting federal deficit also endangers our strongest international tool, the vigor of our economy.

Now, how and why did we get into these questionable policies? It was partly because of Soviet behavior. The Soviets have built up conventional and strategic arms at a great rate. They have invaded Afghanistan and endorsed the suppression of the Solidarity union in Poland. There is some truth to each of these accusations, but part of our behavior is, it seems to me as a psychologist, due to considerations internal to the United States. I say this because it seems to me that we have overreacted to the Soviet threat.

What is the evidence of an overreaction? The strategic balance does not seem to be in the kind of danger that we have been told it is by President Reagan and by many military analysts. I am hard-put to understand any rationale for the 'window-of-vulnerability' theory which was used to justify the reactivation of the MX program and other such heavily escalative moves. The window-of-vulnerability theory said that there was a danger of a first strike from the Soviet Union to our land-based missiles which might conceivably be successful and that we then would be afraid to launch our sea-based missiles as retaliation. This theory assumes that the Soviets would know enough about our fears along these lines that they would then be emboldened to strike. This seems like a strange, unreal cuckoo-cloud-land to me, but this is apparently the basis for policy. It looks like worst-case analysis gone wild. It looks like overreaction.

The Soviet military action in Afghanistan is, of course, a serious matter—reprehensible, deserving to be denounced and opposed, but I think that we have greatly overinterpreted the implications of this action for Soviet intentions. After all, they were, in this case, defending a beleagured Communist regime on their borders. They have done this many times in the past—in Hungary, East Germany, Czechoslovakia and most recently, by proxy, in Poland. It does not look like a new policy to me, yet we have interpreted it as such and become very agitated. The result is counterproductive for our own interests.

The Soviet challenges in Angola, Ethiopia, and Cuba, which were the issues before Afghanistan came along, can hardly be viewed as severe, and yet we also became quite upset about them. The strangest episode of all, from my perspective, was the American reaction when a tiny Russian military force was found in Cuba. What possible danger could they have been to us? And yet, the whole country got overwrought.

Not only do we—the government, the public, the press—panic about trivia, but we also tend to ignore the evidence of our very real successes *vis-à-vis* the Soviet Union. Somehow these successes do not get factored into the equation. We note Soviet successes, but are not impressed with their profound loss of support from China. The Soviets have also lost their relationship with Egypt. Yet this does not seem like a gain for us—we still feel as if we are falling behind. What we have is a national case of jitters!

Why are we so jittery? Why do we so overreact? I have a hypothesis about this. I think it has a lot to do with loss of national self-confidence on the total world-scene. At one time we were the top dog. We were in control. I remember when we used to send our troops in whenever there was anything we did not like—in Lebanon, the Dominican Republic, Korea—and we were always successful. All of this came dramatically to an end with the loss of the Vietnam War, the first war that the United States has fought unsuccessfully. This led to a severe deflation of our national self-image. Then there was the Iranian imprisonment of American diplomats, and the oil crises, and so on. Events such as these have made it clear that we are no longer in control; we can no longer accurately view the world as our own private lake.

I am suggesting that we collectively feel 'one down' as a result of these incidents which have little to do with the Soviet Union. This is true of the people who put Reagan into office, that is, the majority—not just of the press or the Pentagon. We feel humiliated and confused; we know that we have been had, but are not sure why. So we focus attention on our age-old adversary, the Russians. They become scapegoats for our international uncertainties. Hence, we magnify the problems we have with them and the extent of our danger from them. We overreact. The election of Reagan fits into this picture because he stood for a view of the Soviets as an 'evil empire'.

Apart from the humiliation we experienced, Vietnam has shown us that we can no longer rely mainly on military methods; and we really do not know what else to depend on. One thing this leads to is reliance on linkage. That is, since we cannot count on military means to deter Communist political efforts, we have to link all other issues to these efforts. Hence, the Soviets have to reform before we will talk to them about arms control.

My suggestion that we are experiencing a severe case of national jitters may or may not be valid, but if it is true, it suggests some possible things that we can do, or tell ourselves, to try to avoid overreacting to every new Soviet move. One would be to try to analyze accurately the sources of the challenges we face, to try to understand better the vastly strengthened forces in the Third World that do not understand or appreciate us. This will make it less necessary to resort to scapegoating. Another would be to accept, to some extent, our declining power. I am not saying that we are not still on top, but we are not the pre-eminent top. We must also have some faith in our strength in general, and in particular our strength in the contest with the Soviet Union, for example, our extraordinary powerful second-strike capability, which has been alluded to a number of times here. Another thing to note is that Communist revolutions often do not translate into negative consequences for our policies. We have been able to get along quite well with Communist regimes in Yugoslavia and China. Also, Communist military relations often do not last. Egypt has withdrawn from such an arrangement. We are, I believe, better allies than are the Soviets. In effect, we ought to have more faith in our strength instead of being so frightened by the Communist shadow.

I also think it is necessary for us to redefine normal world politics. There is much turmoil in the Third World. There are bound to be Communist revolts. There is bound to be some Soviet military help for the revolts. If we call 'foul' everytime the Soviets develop a military relationship with another government, and dismantle détente as a response, then we are never going to get down to the major problems of our world. The most important of these is the one that Ralph White has alluded to—how are we going to prevent nuclear disaster? The fate of the SALT II Treaty is a clear case in point. We have been so concerned about deterring all Soviet moves, however small, that we have lost sight of the paramount necessity of moving away from world destruction.

# 12 (i) Surviving in the post-détente world

*Willard Matthias*

## The end of détente

May 1982 marked the tenth anniversary of the signing in Moscow of an important document—the SALT I treaty. On the same occasion, another document called 'Basic Principles of Relations between the US and the USSR' was also signed by Presidents Brezhnev and Nixon. It instituted what has been generally called 'détente'. We often tend to think about international agreements in terms of the symbolic words ascribed to them, rather than in terms of what those agreements actually contain. Let us look at what the main points of the 'Basic Principles of Relations' actually are.

The signatories declared that there was 'no alternative' to 'peaceful coexistence'. They did use, in this case, the Soviet terminology. They declared that this peaceful coexistence should be developed on the basis of 'the principles of sovereignty, equality, noninterference in internal affairs, and mutual advantage; that they would do 'their utmost to avoid military confrontations and to prevent the outbreak of nuclear war'; that they would be 'prepared to negotiate and settle differences by peaceful means'; that they would continue the practice, which they had begun shortly before, 'of exchanging views on problems of mutual interest', and they would try to do this at the highest level; that they would 'continue their efforts to limit armaments' with the objective of 'general and complete disarmament'; that they would strengthen their commercial and economic relations, develop cooperation in science and technology and expand exchanges and tourism. The word détente was not used at all.

Since 1972 a great deal has happened. It is widely believed in America that for all practical purposes détente is dead, that it benefited the Soviet Union more than it did the United States, and that a new cold war is upon us. However one might want to assess the detente period, one must recognize that the relationship which existed from 1972 to about 1977 has indeed substantially changed. President Brezhnev and Europeans generally, I believe, thought during the closing years of the 1970's that détente could somehow be restored and that a new cold war could be staved off. The Reagan Administration put an end to those hopes. The president's own rhetorical refrains and his vast new arms programs have raised serious questions aout what it is that America really is trying to do.

Put in national strategy terminology, we moved from a policy of containment *vis-à-vis* the Soviet Union which had characterized our policy during the 1950s and 1960s, to one of détente which lasted only about five years. After a transition period of about three years, while President Carter tried to decide what the Soviets were really like and what to do about them, the Reagan Administration acted as if it knew. Although the administration has talked as if it favors arms limitation, its unremitting hostility to the Soviet Union and continued vigorous pursuit of new arms programs has caused some observers, including the Soviets, to wonder if the

United States has not embarked upon a new national strategy of seeking military superiority over the Soviet Union and destruction of the Soviet regime. Whatever the real objective of the Reagan Administration might be, the fact is that as early as 1978 it had already become clear that a national policy called 'détente' and a military strategic concept called 'nuclear deterrence' had both become bankrupt. Are we now living in a post-détente and post-deterrence world which seems likely to terminate only in mutual destruction? Is there any alternative to an unmitigated enmity and an intensifying threat of nuclear war? I believe there is and that is what I want to talk about.

## Technology and military doctrine

The events of May 1972—the SALT I treaty, the signing of the Basic Principles of Relations, the decision to negotiate a comprehensive trade agreement and the improved atmosphere which accompanied these—were made possible, and in the view of many of the participants made necessary, by an emerging military balance between the United States and the Soviet Union. It was thought by the Soviets that, having achieved military parity with the United States, they could enter into a kind of partnership with the United States to head off dangerous confrontations. It was thought by many Americans that détente meant the world would settle down, that the Soviets would not cause so much trouble as they had, since it was widely believed also that they were the cause of most of the world's troubles. When these troubles persisted it was then concluded by these Americans that the Soviets were not playing fair, and they were succeeding because we were no longer properly respected in the world and that this lack of respect was due to a change in the balance of military power.

I do not believe that there was any shift in the balance of military power, and I believe the declining respect for the United States was a consequence of both bad American foreign policy and a fear of being dominated by American values and American economic power. It is a part of the American culture, however, that if something goes wrong, someone is at fault and something can be done about it. America's answer was to turn to its technology, and particularly to its military technology, to regain the respect which it believed it deserved.

Historically there has generally been a linear relationship between technology and military armament, between armament and military doctrine and between military doctrine and national strategy. Let me illustrate.

The industrial revolution of the eighteenth century made possible the equipping of a larger number of soldiers than in previous centuries. This enabled Napoleon to develop a new military concept, that is to shift from a small professional army to a mobile mass army. The new political situation which flowed from the industrial revolution also encouraged him to harness the nationalist fervor of the French Revolution to bring much of Western Europe temporarily under his control. The reaction to Bonapartism, manifested in the decisions of the Congress of Vienna, was the creation of a national security system in Europe based upon mass armies arrayed behind national boundaries. This concept persisted until the beginning of World War II.

The German generals and their Nazi overlords took advantage of the technologies that had developed during World War I and during the 1920s and 1930s. Rapid military transport, faster and stronger tanks, larger artillery and the fighter–bomber made it possible to pursue a new strategy of rapid movement and terror from the sky. The Germans lost the war when their opponents developed the means to pursue the same strategy which they had followed. The Western Allies did so before the Germans were able to produce nuclear fission, create a nuclear weapon and place it upon their fledgling rockets.

American leadership had recognized as early as 1940 that a nuclear weapon, if it could be manufactured, would probably prove decisive, and the United States ended World War II when it succeeded in doing so. The United States adopted a simple strategic concept for use of the nuclear weapon: use it against civilian populations as an instrument of terror. This was then converted into a national security strategy. We threatened 'massive retaliation' with nuclear weapons against anyone (that is, the Soviets) who engaged in any military action of which we disapproved.

After the Soviet Union exploded their first nuclear device in 1949 and then succeeded in deploying long-range aircraft and rockets in the 1950s, a new situation arose in which each side held the other side's population hostage, and this became known as 'the balance of terror'. In world politics, the result was that each side pursued policies designed 'to avoid military confrontation and to prevent the outbreak of nuclear war', as they stated in the 'Basic Principles of Relations', which I quoted earlier. This new situation became quite obvious in 1956, when the United States clearly disapproved of the Soviet invasion of Hungary, but was unable to do anything about it, lest it 'initiate', as one high administrtion official put it, 'World War III'.

## The current strategic situation

What was true in 1972, when the 'Basic Principles of Relations' were signed in Moscow, is not true today. We have entered into a new phase of global military history. Even as the two presidents inked the Moscow documents, military planners and technicians and their civilian coteries in both countries were establishing requirements and creating models of new weapons and weapon systems and drawing up plans for their use. These new plans and systems are now realities.

On the American side we have made significant progress in improving the accuracy of our missiles. We have placed the highly accurate MK12A warhead on many of our fixed-silo Minuteman missiles; we have the Trident submarine deployed with 240 warheads on board with highly accurate guidance systems; we are planning to deploy 100 MX missiles in fixed silos, each carrying ten highly accurate warheads; we are deploying cruise missiles in Europe which reduce warning time for attacks on the Soviet Union to ten to fifteen minutes. These weapon systems give us a first-strike capability against the Soviet Union, one which could theoretically destroy nearly all of the Soviet nuclear capability targeted against the United States. This is the case because 75 percent of the Soviet long-range nuclear capability is in fixed silos, and while the remaining 25 percent of the Soviet capability is in submarines, only about one-tenth of that submarine force is normally at sea at any one time. Indeed, the 20 to 25 percent of the American force which is silo-based can only be used for an American first strike because it could theoretically be taken out by a Soviet first strike.

The Soviets are similarly expanding and improving their strategic forces. Their SS–18 and SS–19 ICBMs are almost certainly being fitted with warheads of increased accuracy and larger payloads. In addition, the SS–20, which is mobile, poses a threat to Western Europe. Like the United States, the Soviet Union continues its research and development of missile-carrying submarines, bombers and space weapons. Nevertheless, the Soviet Union remains at a strategic disadvantage *vis-à-vis* the United States, since we have a very high probability of destroying a very large proportion of their capability in a first strike, while they have a much smaller chance of doing the same thing to us. Thus, if the Soviet leaders came to believe that we were planning to attack them they would have no alternative but to attack us in order to reduce the weight of attack upon them.

We have, then, arrived at the ironic condition that the nuclear forces which were designed to deter an attack by the other have in fact become forces which tend to provoke an attack by the other. Forces designed to deter have reduced their own capability to deter. In a situation of crisis—such as a new war in the Middle East, a breakdown of order in Eastern Europe, a Soviet–Chinese clash, American military action against a Soviet ally such as Cuba or Soviet military action against an American ally such as South Korea—there would be fear of an expanding conflict and of a nuclear first-strike by the other. What does this new strategic situation do to American–Soviet relations, and how do we get out of the dilemma we have provoked by expanding into technically possible new levels of nuclear armament?

## The political consequences of the new military situation

The first thing to do is to recognize that a new military situation exists and that it has quite different implications for American–Soviet relations and for the way in which we view, or should view, the Soviet Union. The simple fact is that—whatever we may think of Communism or the Soviet leaders or the peoples of the Soviet Union; whatever further development of military armament we might spend our energies upon; whatever we may say about our peaceful objectives and our commitment to world prosperity and Democracy—our lives and fortunes in the final analysis are dependent upon Soviet restraint and rationality as well as our own. There is a widespread view in this country, frequently expressed by responsible officials of the government, that the Soviet Union is an evil empire, that it cannot be trusted, that it is determined to destroy us by military force if necessary. However that may be, we have no alternative to relying upon their rationality and indeed their good will.

Aside from the fact that they have not blown us up yet, they have demonstrated, I think, a rather considerable capacity for being trustworthy and rational. The historical record shows, although there is always some debate about this, that whenever we have had a clear, unequivocal agreement with the Soviets, they have kept it. They have kept the two SALT agreements, even though they do not need to adhere to the second one. There are some seventeen other arms control agreements to which we are both parties. There are some seventy-five bilateral American–Soviet agreements on such matters as health, environment, energy, trade, aviation, and so on; as far as I know, they have kept them all.

There is no doubt that some Soviet actions in the international arena have been what can be properly described as expansionist, even aggressive. What is not so easy to describe objectively is why certain of these actions have taken place. A case can be made that many of these so-called aggressive actions were protectionist or opportunistic in origin. Whatever the Soviets have done, however, they have been careful to avoid provocations which might have resulted in direct military confrontations with the United States. They have been prudent, even frightened, whenever American interests have been directly threatened by their own actions or by those of one of their client regimes.

The history of our experiences with the Soviets is not really the point; what is, is that we have to count on them behaving in a rational way. That is why it is irrational for us to build a first-strike force and to level repeated rhetorical attacks on them. What is wrong-headed about this kind of American behavior is that it tells the Soviets that we are refusing to rely upon their rationality and that we are looking for a chance to destroy them.

Of course, the people who have been responsible for developing and expanding American nuclear forces continually say that the reason why we have not been attacked is that deterrence has worked: the fact that the Soviets have stayed on their side of the line proves that they are frightened of our nuclear forces. I do not think this argument makes historical or logical sense. We cannot know whether we have deterred them when we do not know what they intended to do. My own view is that the last thing they wanted to do was to get into a shooting war with any major power. The thing that struck me the most about a visit I paid to the Soviet Union a few years ago as an ordinary tourist, was the terrific impact—the terrible psychological and material effect—which World War II had upon them. They do not want to go through that again. But that is beside the serious point that we really have no way of knowing what they have intended, and therefore we cannot know whether deterrence has worked.

I do not mean to imply that wrong-headedness exists only in Washington. Moscow has its share of American-haters and capitalist-baiters. Its military establishment operates, as most military establishments do, with a devil image of its principal adversary. The Soviet *Officer's Handbook* (Kozlov, 1971, p.225) describes American policy in terms not much different from those used in America to describe Soviet policy, to wit:

In carrying out their aggressive foreign policy, the imperialists of the United States of America look upon their armed forces as the principal means of resolving international problems from a position of strength and of achieving their set military-political objectives, which, in the final analysis, amount to the achievement of world domination.

It is obvious that both sides need to look at their relations in more practical, survival-oriented terms and less in moralistic and ideological terms than they have in the past. Our problem and theirs is to recognize that both nations need to reciprocate rationality and respect without conceding principle or abandoning the field. This will require new military doctrines, new force structures and new national

national strategies both here and in Moscow. We can only indirectly affect how Moscow thinks and what it does, but the history of the arms race certainly shows that the two superpowers react to each other. Our first task is to review our own position.

## The bankruptcy of American military doctrine

In our modern-day rather self-righteous denunciations of terrorism, we Americans tend to forget that we actually carried out the greatest terrorist actions since Tamerlane, when we bombed Hiroshima and Nagasaki with nuclear weapons. Moreover, terror remained our sole military strategy for some years thereafter; we held the Soviet population hostage to assure the acceptable behavior of the Soviet leadership. The Soviets, of course, had a counter-terror capability even before they developed their own intercontinental nuclear capability; they held Western Europe hostage to their conventional force capability to seize it relatively quickly. Neither the United States nor its European allies were prepared to build up a conventional force to counter-balance that of the Soviet Union. Western Europe remained dependent upon the American nuclear unbrella and could only hope that the American leadership would act with restraint.

The mid-fifties, as I indicated earlier, saw a change; the Soviet Union developed the forces to bring North America under direct attack. This worried West Europeans who felt that the United States would not risk self-destruction on questions of interest to them, but only on questions vital to itself. This fear spawned the beginning of European nuclear forces (that is in Britain and France), and the deployment of tactical nuclear weapons to the American forces in Europe. This in fact helped the West Europeans only in a psychological sense; they felt more secure, but they wanted nothing of a limited nuclear war on their continent. This fear of nuclear war caused a new doctrine to emerge, the doctrine of graduated deterrence which said that, in the event of hostilities, the Western allies would not go directly and immediately to nuclear weapons, but would apply only such force as was needed to deal with the emerging military threat.

These developments in Europe and the improved technology of nuclear weaponry and of delivery systems were the main forces bringing about a new targeting philosophy for American military forces. We were getting so many weapons of varying sizes, and we were—theoretically at least—improving the accuracy and multiplicity of our delivery systems so much that we believed, or said we believed, that we could carry on nuclear warfare against an adversary's military capabilities without causing unacceptable civilian casualties. Nuclear war would become surgically neat, the cancer could be destroyed, humanity would be battered but it would survive and the awful scourge of Communism banished from the earth. I doubt that very many practical military thinkers believed all that, nor did many people outside the military planners and their civilian coteries.

The doctrine nevertheless had an appeal. We could tell ourselves we were no longer terrorists; we could deal with military forces and installations. Additionally, it justified what we had already been building in the way of weapons and delivery systems for at least a decade. This doctrine received its most sophisticated treatment and defense by Secretary of Defense Harold Brown in the closing days of President Carter's Administration. This was PD 59, a top-secret document leaked by the White House in August 1980 to show that the Carter Administration was not 'soft on Communism'. Once it was leaked, it had to be explained and Brown did this in a speech at the Naval War College (Brown, 1980, p.9).

'Deterrence remains', he said, 'our fundamental strategic objective.' But more interesting things followed:

But deterrence must restrain a far wider range of threats than just massive attacks on US cities. We seek to deter *any* adversary from *any* course of action that could lead to general nuclear war. . . . It is our policy—and we have increasingly the means and the detailed plans to carry out this policy—to insure that the Soviet leadership knows that if they [sic] chose some intermediate level of aggression, we could by, selective, large but still less than maximum nuclear attacks, exact an unacceptably high price in the things the Soviet leaders appear to value most, political and military control, military force both nuclear and conventional, and the industrial capacity to sustain a war.

Now, if we were Soviet leaders reading this, what would we think? What does Brown's speech tell us to do? 'It tells us that we should not engage in any military action at all, or that if we contemplate any major military action, we better damn well hit the United States first. Secretary Harold Brown has told us that if there is any major military action on our part, the US will do everything it can to destroy our military capability and our political system.' In short, Secretary Brown's strategy is really an all-or-nothing game. Either there is no military action by the Soviets at all, or *we* blow us all up. Since Secretary Brown himself has said that he does not believe a limited nuclear war could be kept limited, one must assume that he himself saw the alternatives the same way—despite his prescription for beginning at a limited or selective level.

The same thing—in fact, it may be a worse thing—was said by Secretary Weinberger during his confirmation hearings in January 1981:

We should never enter a war we do not intend to win, or in which we do not expend every single effort of every single weapon and every facility that we have to win. If troops are committed, if we are in an active engagement, we have every obligation and every duty then to go all the way forward and win. I do not want to be misunderstood about that. (US Congress, 1981, pp. 38–9).

Again, this is an all-or-nothing declaration. We have put ourselves into a position where we had better not engage our forces anywhere because if we do, then we have to go ahead and run the ultimate risk of nuclear action. What this in effect also says, is that we no longer have the military establishment to play a role in international affairs but we have one for fighting a nuclear war. We are caught by our own doctrines and weaponry in a hopeless situation; we are caught between a paralysis of power and nuclear destruction. Unless something is done about our military doctrine, we are going to have an extremely expensive military establishment which is of no practical use, one which by its own declarations we cannot utilize in international relations in any combat capacity without running an immediate risk of nuclear destruction.

We may recall that the US Marines were deployed to Beirut in a non-combat role as guardians of the airport. The terrorist attack which caused the deaths of some 250 Marines proved that such a non-combat role was impossible to sustain. Given our doctrine, we either had to withdraw or greatly expand our force and be prepared for large-scale combat with the possibility of nuclear exchanges. We ignominiously withdrew.

### Toward a new military doctrine

An important opening toward the construction of a new doctrine was made by McGeorge Bundy, George Kennan, Robert McNamara and Gerard Smith in the spring of 1982 in an article in *Foreign Affairs*. The article was an examination of the desirability of revising existing NATO military doctrine by giving up American NATO plans to make first use of nuclear weapons to defend Europe.

One of America's doctrinal problems is that we have sought to make our threat of first use credible by devising plans and creating nuclear capabilities for a continuing escalation of nuclear conflict. This has led our planners to believe that, in order to become really credible, we had to be prepared to escalate up to general nuclear war and to be capable of 'winning' such a war. What Bundy and company argue is that this sort of increase is unnecessary in order to make our nuclear deterrent credible. They argue, quite correctly I believe, there is no current or prospective Soviet degree of 'superiority' which would tempt Moscow into nuclear adventurism. What does 'superiority' mean in this sense? It means a virtually 100 percent assurance of not receiving an enormously costly retaliatory strike. All we would need to prevent that assurance is a moderately sized and invulnerable capability for a second, or retaliatory strike. A second-strike force of, say, five hundred weapons deployed in a survivable mode (several such modes are conceivable at reasonable expense) would almost certainly be sufficient to convince any possible enemy to adhere also to a no-first-use policy.

A no-first pledge would have an immediate advantage in making our European allies more disposed than they are now to resist Soviet aggression should it come. At present they are more prone to avoid nuclear destruction by accommodation to the Soviets than to resist the Soviets and accept destruction. In any event European conventional military capabilities have very substantially improved from what they were thirty years ago, so that the Soviet Union could not think it could sweep easily over Europe. Also, Soviet leaders could not be certain that a large-scale military adventure could be carried out with impunity to its system and their physical safety even with an American no-first-use pledge.

There would be many other advantages to a no-first-use pledge which I shall not discuss here, but only mention: it would render technological improvements and the fear of them meaningless; except in the means of making the small second-strike force invulnerable; it would reduce military expenditure and lead to a sounder economy; and it would free our military forces for duties in support of foreign policy without the fear of military engagement leading to nuclear destruction.

Of course, in order for a no-first-use pledge to be meaningful we would need to restructure our forces, dispose of nuclear warheads and of carriers for such weapons which could not effectively be converted to conventional use. We would need to revise our tactics and our field manuals. We would need to restrain our forces and to reindoctrinate our officer corps. We probably would have to improve the conventional capabilities of some of our forces. We would need to do these things not only to convince our adversaries that we meant business, but to make our forces fit for some useful purposes in the modern world, that is, for something other than frightening the Soviets into believing they could not win a nuclear war, which they do not want to fight anyway and which would, if it occurred, be a war without any winners.

## Peaceful competition—a new national strategy

When referring, as I have just done, to the need for a new military doctrine, I have no expectation that this will be developed in the near future. What I am hoping to do is to contribute to a debate which I hope will come increasingly into the open as the political and economic costs of our present course become more manifest. We might wish to start by trying to escape the dangers and dilemmas presented by our present military doctrines and capabilities. We should want to proceed thereafter or concurrently to a debate about a national strategy designed to replace détente.

A change of military doctrine along the lines I have described would provide the United States with a much greater capability than it now has to carry on a competition with the Soviet Union for world leadership. Reducing the threat of nuclear war on our initiative would restore a moral character to American leadership which has been deeply lacking in the eyes of the world since our adventure in Vietnam, but, more importantly, it would free our diplomacy for a more active and decisive role. It would allow us to use our military forces whenever their use would be helpful and appropriate; would free resources for more effective overseas aid and investment programs, would permit an effort to resolve some outstanding world problems; it would, in short, encourage conflict resolution.

What I am describing is a national strategy I call 'peaceful competition'. This is not a new or exciting title, but I believe it is likely to be a more accurate description than any other phrase for the kind of world we are bound to be living in if we can substantially reduce the threat of nuclear destruction. The world is much too dynamic a place to expect it to settle down or to be divided into zones of hegemony among the great powers. There will still be revolutions, ethnic and religious conflicts, struggles over territories and attempts by some to impose their social, religious, economic, political and ideological systems upon others. In many of these our adversaries will be communists, some perhaps allied with the Soviet Union. We will lose some and we will win some. The important thing is that these conflicts be kept isolated, that they be screened whenever possible from big-power involvement, that diplomatic efforts for resolution of them be chosen before military action is taken.

Without a fear of immediate escalation into general nuclear war, without American forces so completely dominated by the nuclear option, with objectives established at somewhere less than the 'win' level, American military forces would from time to time need to be deployed to clarify the existence of a United States interest or to enforce a negotiated agreement. Used sparingly, with clear objectives, without breast-beating or provocation and accompanied by negotiation, the use of military force can be constructive and can contribute to peaceful change. If, however, American military forces are used to prevent revolutionary change where it is clearly desired or to keep in power a small oligarchy, as in Vietnam, such action tends to isolate the United States, encourage international alignments destructive of American long-term interests and even lead to prolonged and self-destructive engagement.

I would like to add a judgement upon a subject which, as a long-time intelligence officer, I have thought a great deal. This is the arena of covert action. I think we should give it up as an instrument of national policy. In all the years that I have been observing these operations I cannot think of a single one which in the last analysis was of benefit to the United States or to the people who lived in the area. For years it was said what a great operation it was when we overthrew Mossadegh in Iran and re-installed the Shah. We would in fact, have had the best of all possible worlds in Iran if we had kept Mossadegh. We tried to overthrow the government of Syria and we earned the undying enmity of the Baath regime. The CIA overthrow of the government in Guatemala in the 1950s has resulted in thirty years of murder, at times at the rate of 500 to 1000 people a month. The killing has dropped off lately; there are few political activists left to kill.

The Soviets have not been particularly successful in their covert operations either. The number of places that they have been kicked out of over the years in Africa and Asia is quite substantial and, to a very considerable extent, this has been because of mismanagement of their covert operations. Indeed, I believe it was their covert operations which set off the 1967 war in the Middle East which resulted in such great damage to their political position in that area.

Most important of all, we should reopen a wide range of contacts with the Soviet Union. These should of course be carried out on a regular basis, perhaps once a month, at the highest levels in order to make progress on major issues such as arms control and in order to explore ways of finding solutions to other problems such as those involving Afghanistan, Kampuchia, Angola, Ethiopia, South Africa and the Near East. We would do well to try again to get a trade agreement. We have little influence over another nation if the only instrument of influence we possess is the ability to bomb it out of existence. With greater trade we would garner greater influence. Indeed, we ought to help to enhance Soviet consumerism. There is nothing more conducive to peace or more resistant to war than a stake in the comforts of life.

I believe, in agreement with some of the more distinguished scholars in the United States, that a slow but sure transformation of Soviet society is underway, a change toward greater pluralism and decentralization. Our military and foreign policies should be directed toward the encouragement of that transformation. Each time we move to a new level of armament or rhetoric, we retard that movement by stimulating the siege mentality lying deep within the Russian personality.

We need to monitor Soviet society carefully and objectively. After all, we depend upon them for our continued life and health. I would be a great deal more comfortable about our Soviet-watching had I not seen the politicization of our intelligence system during the past ten years. We need to return to professional control of the intelligence apparatus, and we need to maintain outside monitoring, not by a presidential panel as at present, but by public panels representing academic, journalistic and political communities.

There is a chance we will survive in the post-détente world. We will not survive. however, unless as a nation we change some of our ideas about the world we live in. If we are prepared to look clearly at some of the myths we have lived by, some of the military concepts we have never really examined, some of the weapons we think give us safety, then we have a much better chance than we have now of living through this century.

## Bibliography

Brown, H. (1980), 'Excerpts from Address on War Policy', *The New York Times*, 21 August, p. 9.

Bundy, McG, G.F. Kennan, R.S. McNamara, and G. Smith, 'Nuclear Weapons and the Atlantic Alliance', *Foreign Affairs*, **60**, no. 4, pp. 753–68.

Kozlov, General-Major S.N. (ed.) (1971), *Officer's Handbook*, Moscow. English translation by Secretary of State Department, Government of Canada, Ottawa; published in English by the United States Air Force.

United States Congress, Senate Committee on Armed Services (1981), *Hearings on the Nomination of Casper W. Weinberger to be Secretary of Defense*, 97th Congress.

# 12 (ii) What makes the Russians tick?

*Leo Hecht*

I want to address Russian reaction and beliefs toward possible involvement in a nuclear war, and why they think the way they do. Though the Russians make up somewhat less than half of the population of the Soviet Union, they are the most important people; hence, I will restrict myself to them.

There is among Russians a definite national paranoia which has existed for centuries. Historically, it is understandable. Starting with the ninth century, they were invaded by the Vikings; later by the Tartars, Swedes, and Turks; and during their revolution in 1917 they were invaded by thirteen nations, including the United States, which they have never forgotten. They refer to it all the time. They were also invaded by the Germans during World War II. Consequently, they are extremely sensitive to potential threats.

When Americans converse with Russians, they are likely to hear, 'look at our history, you Americans have never really experienced this. No one has ever come onto your territory to do you harm.' And of course, basically, there is some truth to this. Unless we have experienced a war on our own territory, then we have never really experienced a war. In every generation, the Russians have had one or two major conflicts. When people have lost so many members of their families, their society and their society has been ruined economically time and again, then there is no desire for further war. The Russians, therefore, abhor the idea of another war.

There are, however, other sides to the Russian psyche which also have a long history. The most important one for me is the 'messianic complex', that is, Russians feel that they have something which they must bring to the rest of the world. Anyone who has read Dostoyevsky of 120 years ago, or has read Solzhenitsyn recently will feel that there is something that the Russians have which the rest of the world must also have, 'something' which suggests that there is a much greater degree of purity in the Russians than there is in most nationalities. It is not unusual, therefore, to find a very strong patriotic, nationalistic and to some extent, xenophobic posture among Russians.

In addition, they adhere, at least officially, to Communist philosophy which is a doctrine of constant revolution: there must always be a thesis, an antithesis and a synthesis on a higher plane which then becomes a new thesis which enters combat with the new antithesis. It is an upward curve: one cannot stand still. One cannot say, 'we have achieved something and this is where we are going to be'. There must be an ingrained desire to achieve new goals, new heights, which may, in part, account for the expansionist ideas of the Soviet Union, though this desire can take various forms, nonbelligerent as well as belligerent.

The average Russian citizen is generally very well read. He reads a great deal more than the average American citizen, and the average Soviet intellectual plays a much greater part in the life of the Soviet Union than the average intellectual plays in the life of the United States. This well-read person is constantly looking for information about what the United States is doing. The Russian does not think about an entire people, however, only about leaders, and the only thing that he sees, with regard to the United States at present is President Reagan. What does Reagan intend to do? He does not look at the priorities of the American public. He has to centralize his ideas as to who is leading.

How do the Russians determine what Reagan's intentions are? They read *Pravda* or *Izvestia*, but reasonably intelligent Russians definitely do not believe their own media, newspaper, or radio; hence, they read between the lines. No matter what they read and what they listen to, whether it is 'Voice of America' or Soviet broadcasts, they are impressed with the fact that there is no tangible American foreign policy with regard to the Soviet Union. The person whom they dearly loved was Kissinger, not because Kissinger was a friend of the Soviets, but because his was an orderly system which they could understand and relate to. They certainly could not relate to anything from the Carter administration, and since the only thing they hear from the Reagan administration is saber-rattling with no tangible information, they are worried.

How do they feel about the United States? Russians are in awe of the United States. They feel that the United States is still the strongest, most important country in the world. They feel that much more strongly than we do, in fact. They fear us. They want to have a chance to catch up with us economically, and they hope to have a period of peace during which they can accomplish this goal.

There are other problems in the Soviet Union. For the past several years they have been faced with problems of succession which have led to conflicts which have been fought out in the Central Committee. Since elites like Suslov and Brezhnev have passed on the Central Committee has gained additional power. The probability is that power will be concentrated in the Central Committee which contains many 'younger' people. These are people in their fifties who are well educated and represent the military, technocracy, industry and the economic sphere. They want some kind of stability. Their conflict is with the old guard who does not really want to change anything.

The Russians do not want to engage in any kind of conflict which may lead to a nuclear war, but they still have to deal with the United States. They cannot compete with the United States economically. The United States often conducts foreign politics in terms of economics, but this possibility is not available to the Russians. What is left for them to do? Subversion! Sometimes this succeeds, and sometimes not. In any event, their main intent is to cause as much instability as possible within the Western bloc, to avoid being caught off guard.

Those Russians who do not particularly delve into the philosophy of communism want peace. But even those who are dyed-in-the-wool communists will say, 'we do not want a war, because we are going to win anyway. We are going to win on the economic level, so there is no sense in having a war. War would only be to the benefit of the United States. If you look at what is happening, we Soviets are on the rise, while you Americans are on the economic decline. Your markets are shrinking, ours are expanding. There is no sense, there is no need for war.' In either case, the Soviets, and the Russians particularly, do not look forward to another war. The situation in Afghanistan, even though it is a very small war, has had a tremendous psychological effect upon the average Russian citizen. He does not want it, he does not want anything like this to be escalating. He would like very much to have some kind of meeting of the minds with the United States, which he respects a great deal.

# 13(i) International conflict resolution and problem solving

*John W. Burton*

Why is importance attached to conflict resolution processes? It seems that the present situation we face internationally is one in which two great powers are virtually locked in conflict and, as part of this power-politics conflict, the West must respond to invitations by governments in its sphere of influence to give support when these governments are under threat. Consequently, on many occasions the United States seems obligated to defend the indefensible, perhaps against its better judgement. On the other side, the East has to respond to invitations by minority, 'liberation' or other groups that seek such help. In the power-politics framework in which the Soviets also operate, they do not have much alternative but to respond.

Both sides, having given support, then lose control over their clients. If a nonlegitimized authority is guaranteed the support of the United States, for example, then no pressure from the United States on it to reform its ways is likely to have any effect—it knows that its survival is strategically important, no matter how ruthless its domestic policies. The Third World countries that do not seek great power support also become pawns in this power-politics game. One can already see some disillusionment in movements toward neutralism in all regions.

If this is a reasonable description of what is going on, then it would seem that some process of resolving conflicts, bringing about political and social change peacefully in the areas outside the main thermonuclear relationship, is important. The conflict resolution process must go on in tandem with the power-politics exercised by the great powers. It cannot be a substitute for long-established, traditional diplomacy and the normal processes of power bargaining and deterrence at that thermonuclear level. This process of resolving conflicts in the spheres of influence of the great powers is not something that can be carried out on a government-to-government basis. What is happening in the countries of the Third World is a matter for the peoples in those countries to decide, and great powers have no role in trying to determine or impose constitutions or particular political and social structures. If there is going to be a resolution of this type of conflict, if there is going to be peaceful change, then probably there is a need for a third party, a nonofficial facilitator, perhaps with official blessing. However, if such an endeavor is mounted it must be as realistic, politically, as the power-politics in which the great powers are engaged. It is not a 'do-goodism' endeavor. The process must be one track running parallel to the power-politics track that dominates relationships in the international field.

If we intend to resolve conflict within this wider power-politics framework, we must also take into account the domestic aspect. If a thermonuclear power is feeling insecure internally, for any reason, this is an additional reason for being concerned about power relationships. If a great power feels secure and not vulnerable internally, then its potential for external aggression or external intervention is lessened. Currently both sides have their own serious internal problems. The same processes of conflict resolution seem to be appropriate in respect of these domestic issues: both sides have an interest in helping to overcome internal problems.

Any conflict resolution approach must be well-founded, that is it has to be unchallengeable in its epistemological, theoretical and applied aspects. It is these that I want to examine at this point.

First of all, let us stand back from any particular interest we have, academically or in practice and perceive this situation more broadly, as a whole. We are familiar with the exponential rate of population growth. The same, almost vertical curve applies to consumption of energy, to technological developments, to communications growth and to many areas in which there is largely empirical knowledge involved. Perhaps the same exponential rate applies to phenomena related to population and technological increase such as movements of populations to cities, industrialization. If it were to apply to these then one could deduce that it applies also to levels of violence, the erosion of authority and many other social and political conditions that characterize developed as well as underdeveloped political and economic systems. Accompanying this exponential growth in so many areas of human activity, has been a similar outpouring of research findings, articles, books, theses on aspects of problems experienced in societies and in the international system.

The rate of increase in empirical knowledge—one could calculate it by written works produced—is on this same exponential scale. The great bulk of this outpouring is analytical and empirical in kind, relying frequently on the collection of and reference to empirical data, highly specialized and descriptive. Foreign-policy studies, historical studies, area studies, comparative political studies, strategic studies, institutional studies, regional studies and studies in other areas such as sociology and psychology—the bulk of these is within this descriptive and empirical set.

We therefore appear to have an explosion of empirical knowledge about problems which are themselves increasing on this ever increasing scale. However, this does not seem to be accompanied by any similar explosion of theory, explanation, predictive power and policy insights, related to the problems being described. There appears to have been no significant increase in our conceptual knowledge and in our abilities to answer our key questions in political theory. If one had any doubt, one would only have to look at our teaching syllabuses and the traditional notions employed in policy making. Notions such as national interests, balance of power, rights and obligations, sovereignty and legality, socialization are all still anchored in the classics, from Aristotle to Marx. Students must have the impression that there has been no twentieth-century thinking. Our political models, both free enterprise and the centrally planned systems, are models of past centuries. The problems we face, especially problems arising out of demands for political participation at all levels from the family to industry to the international system, are increasing at the same compound-interest rate while our ability to solve them, even to think about them, is largely static.

Our experience has been that our amassed empirical knowledge is from time to time subject to a paradigm shift. The gap between knowledge and reality may then be narrowed and a great deal of this amassed empirical knowledge becomes irrelevant. In this way we manage to some degree to cope with this exponential increase in knowledge. Antibiotics made irrelevant a body of knowledge and experience in the treatment of many diseases, however, no such paradigm shifts have been experienced in political science; no general theories seem to have appeared; no dramatic breakthroughs seem to have occurred in the whole history of classical thought. We have a mass, a tremendous mass of empirical knowledge, most of which is not very valuable.

Let us take a cluster of problems: crime, terrorism, community conflict, industrial conflict and so on. Each has been studied separately. Each has its own separate literature, based on particular disciplines. At the applied level, each is dealt within a separate department of government and separate agencies. In the United Kingdom, the Northern Ireland situation is dealt with by one department in one particular way. A similar conflict in Cyprus is dealt with by another department and dealt with differently. Each is analyzed from different points according to some model or theory that focuses on some particular aspect.

In relation to rebellion, Gurr (1970) has a deprivation theory. Davies (1962) bases his thinking on expectations. Johnson (1966) seems prepared to regard such phenomena as part of the rational processes of change. There are aggression theories, theories about economic structures and others. The various schools of thought have spawned even more specialized studies. There are no synthesizing theories, there is nothing that is pulling knowledge together. Essentially, empirical studies are analytical. They describe and deal with symptoms; they are limited; they reduce complex problems to puzzles. Let us be clear on the difference. A puzzle, whether it be a mechanical puzzle or some other puzzle, can be worked out. When we come to the end of it, we know we have come to the end of it. When we come through a maze we know we have come to the end of it. When we work out a mathematical problem—which should not be called a problem for it is a puzzle—we know that we have come to the end of it. We tend to make puzzles out of our problems by removing the complex variables. In political life we can do this readily by the use of coercion in one form or another.

Northern Ireland is conveniently defined as a minority rebellion in a democratic state. It is as simple as that, a political definition. The remedies are accordingly to send the army in or to coerce the minority. The identity, ethnicity, participating aspects are not within the definition or the label given and, consequently, are not taken into account in the policy that flows from the definition. These studies are all carried out within a traditional state-centric model of society that assumes that societies are integrated wholes or, if they are not, that they should be and that it is the duty of governments to see that they are. The assumption is that the general good is also the individual good; that there are those with a right to rule and those who have a moral obligation to obey, to be socialized into obeying. The focus of attention, the unit of explanation, the explanatory variable, have been, in all our classical studies, institutions and structures.

The great Kuhn (1962) and Popper (1974) debate has not led to any change from these traditional analyses and descriptions. The advice of Popper to refute rather than to find confirmation does not touch the main problems. It is merely advice about how to conduct the analysis of a situation and to arrive at a theory that relates to some aspect of the problem. The inductive-deductive debate did not seem to touch on the problem of synthesis. The problems associated with dealing with the phenomena that occur on different social-system levels, such as violence, are not touched by this debate. We have to ask ourselves whether crime, terrorism, class conflict, racial conflict, communal and minority conflict and war are separate phenomena, as has been assumed, or may they be overt symptoms of some common phenomenon or sets of phenomena?

Now, clearly, it is not possible to move from one social-system level to another if the unit of analysis, the explanatory variable, is institutions or structures. Small groups, communities, nations are wholly different in organization and structure. A separate disciplinary approach is convenient in psychology, economics, sociology and in international relations, where divisions are based largely on organizational size, because structures have been taken as a focus of attention. The problem may be overcome by taking the individual as the independent or explanatory variable. This is not the malleable and invented individual, known as Economic Man, who conveniently behaves in such a way as to conform with the free enterprise system. Nor is it Legal Man, who conveniently costs his behavior in relation to penalties and conforms. Nor is it Psychological Man, who is conveniently socialized and pliable. Nor is it Ideological Man, who conveniently fits into the system or the model being employed. We are not talking about the Classical Man whose interests are identical with that of the common good. We are concerned—if we are taking the individual as the unit of explanation—with the individual who acts at all systems levels, maximizing his or her satisfactions, by any means that come to hand, legal or illegal, moral or immoral, by the use of power. It is the individual who is involved in the various types of conflicts we listed from crime to war. It is the individual who is not deterred by threats and sanctions, when acting separately or in a group of nations, if his or her basic needs are at stake. It is this individual who is being revealed more and more by our experiences of crime, terrorism, cooperation and conformity at all social levels. It is the individual who has evolved over millions of years and has characteristics, motivations and needs that are universal both over time and space. It is this inconvenient individual who does not fit into and cannot be socialized into any system, merely because others think it is suited to their needs, because others try to socialize or coerce, because others create structures that are in their view just. It is the individual who has a learning capacity that is genetic and who requires, and will pursue, regardless of consequences to self or society, those conditions needed for learning—consistency of response, recognition, identity, control or participation—as a means of ensuring these needs. It is an individual who does not fit into any form of serfdom, slavery, colonialism, capitalism or socialism. It is an individual who finds positive law and elite systems unacceptable: a very difficult, objectionable and sometimes aggressive and violent individual in any system that is not constructed by and for him. The question arises whether a synthesis is possible with this individual as an explanatory variable and the unit of analysis.

There now seems to be a representative body of scholars, including Barrington Moore (1978), McGregor Burns (1977) Lord Scarman (1977), Herbert Kelman (1977), Paul Sites (1973), Cynthia Enloe (1973), and many others who are moving toward the individual as the unit of explanation. The various disciplines of law, politics, sociology, anthropology and psychology have been forced to hypothesize some universal ontological human needs that will be satisfied by fair means or foul. This literature, which is in fact an exploding one, does seem to suggest that, for the first time in our thinking, a paradigm shift is taking place. A paradigm shift of this order cannot take place in the absence of an alternative methodology that enables movement from one system level to another, nor in the absence of a synthesizing theory. Let me first turn to methodology.

There was a gentleman born in Cambridge, Massachusetts in 1839 who later on did not conform with Harvard norms, but who as a review writer, contributed many papers to the problem of methodology: Charles Sanders Peirce. Peirce, a contemporary of William James, came up with a view which is totally at variance with our current conceptions of methodology (see Levi, 1980), for instance, those of Popper. Popper argues conveniently that a hypothesis is a matter of personal concern, of no scientific interest, that the only scientific interest is in the testing and in the conclusions that may be drawn. Hypothesis is a personal matter; the whole inductive-deductive argument has been on this basis. We were left, in this framework, with either of two options: either we operated deductively and talked about swans being white, and so on which is not very productive or we operated inductively and we invented a scientific method to make amends, to compensate for the problems of induction. For Peirce, however, hypothesis formation is the major point of scientific interest. He called his approach abduction, sometimes retroduction, because he was emphasizing the need to go back and find out how hypotheses have been arrived at. Popper had a great deal of difficulty in explaining how we made any progress at all in science because out of an infinite number of hypotheses, we seem to have picked many of the correct ones. Peirce tried to explain this, emphasizing the need to query our assumptions at all times, until our hypothesis has been reduced to something almost axiomatic and from which deductions could be made. He claimed that abductive logic was the only method for generating a syllogism in which, in the second proposition, we could introduce new material.

Within a framework of analysis that enables us to operate at all systems levels, we have the possibility of behavioral analysis at all levels. We can consider whether deterrence deters without having to have a third world war, without having to see if NATO deters the Warsaw Pact. We can analyze deterrence at different systems levels. Similarly, we can analyze conflict at different systems levels. So much then for methodology.

We are also seeing the beginning of a theoretical synthesis, one based on some fairly self-evident hypotheses, as Peirce would have favored. The synthesizing theory emerging in the literature has been labeled control theory, deriving largely from those concerned with deviance. One-half of this theory hypothesizes certain universal needs which, as I have suggested, are derived from learning theory: needs such as stimulus, security, identity, control, consistency of response and so on. This theoretical framework of analysis removes any ideological basis of policy. There are certain givens, certain laws of behavior, which are not probablistic statements. All people, in all cultures, at all times and in all circumstances have certain needs that have to be, that will be fulfilled; not should, or ought, but will be fulfilled, regardless of consequences to self or system. It is a synthesis of theories that deals both with covert behavior and motivations and has an application at all systems level. It clearly subsumes power theories in the sense that the individual will pursue these needs either separately or in conjunction with others by fair means or foul and regardless of consequences. In the exposition of one control theorist, Steven Box (1971), it explains the use of legal norms where these are functional and the intervention of others if these do not appear appropriate to circumstances. That is one-half of control theory: the pursuit of certain ontological human needs.

The other half is related to bonding. Clearly, if the individual is going to behave in this way, society is going to be caught up in a condition of anarchy. The constraint that prevents this happening in practice is not the constraint of deterrent strategies and the coercion of central authorities. The only constraint in this view is concerned with bonding, the constraints which arise out of values attached to relationships. As I have suggested, this theory originated in deviance studies. It was pointed out that if there are no valued relationships with authorities in particular, or parents and schools, then there are no constraints. The individual is free to pursue his or her needs by any means that come to hand. Let us remind ourselves that this is a theory that can be applied at all systems levels.

If we isolate the state so that it has no valued relationships then no norms will be observed. When Japan was cut off from raw materials and markets during World War II, the cabinet met. To a man, the cabinet thought it was stupid to bomb Pearl Harbor; to a man, they voted to bomb Pearl Harbor because there were no options, there was nothing to lose. We can easily put states in this position. On the other hand, if there are valued relationships, then the constraints operate. The Icelandic-British dispute over fisheries, for instance, at no stage really got out of hand.

In this control theory framework the conforming and the dissident, the normal and the abnormal, are comprehended within the one theoretical framework. Control theory applies at different systems levels. It directs our attention to conceptions and assumptions that are not usually subject to reexamination. For example, it obviously directs attention to size of institutions, for which reason scholars in many areas now are turning back to traditional society to find out what were the controls. Size was an important consideration. It casts doubt on the assumption that societies are or could be made to be integrated wholes because of the need for identity. Why should we assume that members of society want to be integrated in the culture, or in the social norms of that society? It provides us with a framework in which concepts otherwise ill-defined such as freedom, justice and legitimacy, can be given meaning. It provides some navigation points and given as a basis of a policy, as a means of assessing whether declared goals can be achieved and whether the goals, in any case, are appropriate.

On the applied side—and we have dealt already with the methodological side and theoretical side—our attention is directed away from reactive decision making, in a hierarchical process, towards interactive decision making, in which the decisions take place only after interaction has occurred with all those affected by them. Decision-making theory, in the literature, started in the 1950s with a model which depicted only certain inputs and certain outputs (See Modelski, 1962). There was no place in the model for the decision-making process.

Subsequently, somewhat more interest was shown in process and the 'black box' came to be spelled out in more and more detail. Karl Deutsch (1963) came along with the experience of wartime cybernetics in aircraft and dealt with feedback into the decision-making process. We have been provided with more and more complex and more sophisticated decision-making models applying to industries, governments and authorities generally. However, we cannot go any further with this model; it is reactive.

We could go through the same process of model development on a different basis by using an interactive model whereby parties interact before producing an output. Our attention seems to be directed both by the empirical world and by theoretical analysis to this shift in the decision-making process. If we take this to its logical extension, then we are right into the heart of problem solving. One very good example of the way in which such a process could work are the Rhodesia–Zimbabwe talks. I have heard it said on many occasions in the United States, including at the annual conference of the International Studies Association conference, what a good model this was. To my mind, it is a disastrous model. What happened was that the parties came to London and they confronted the Foreign Secretary (Lord Carrington) and said, 'We do not want to discuss the Constitution at this point. We have a problem, which we have to work out, a tribal problem, or however you might describe it. It could be that the constitution we need is a devolved one or maybe we need three states—we do not know yet, we have to sort this out first.' The reaction of the Foreign Secretary was, 'You are invited to a constitutional conference, you can make some amendments to the Constitution, but that is all you can do. This is the basis on which you are given your independence.

This occurred within a reactive decision-making framework. It was bargaining and negotiating. It was not problem solving, though the main parties to the dispute were asking for a problem-solving framework in which the dispute could be considered prior to a constitution being drafted. There is a difference between, on the one hand, traditional bargaining, negotiating, and settlement of disputes and, on the other, the analysis and interaction of parties with a view to resolving a conflict.

It would seem, therefore, that if we are looking for the right framework—and this is relevant to the Conflict Management Program at George Mason University—then we should have the following components: (1) methodology: I suggest that the literature on abduction is worth looking at; (2) theory, particularly of needs and bonds; and (3) application of interactive decision-making or problem-solving processes. We can insert into such a framework the necessary components of teaching courses.

I would like to reiterate that this is an endeavor—a 'scholarly', 'scientific', 'academic' endeavor—that has to be pursued within the existing political realities. There is no suggestion here that conflict resolution processes can, at any point in the forseeable future, be a substitute for the normal processes of power bargaining, strategic processes, deterrence and so on. There will not be arms control and disarmament until the need for arms is no longer felt. However, the two can go in tandem, the two can operate together; but they will only operate together if we can come up with something that is, in theoretical terms, hard; that is politically realistic; that is well tested. For this purpose we do need to make sure we have got the right methodology, theory and practical application.

The beginnings of a problem-solving approach have already appeared, in the United States. In some states, I understand that certain categories of the majority of first-time offenders do not necessarily appear before the courts. They are dealt with instead by a variety of people—authorities, teachers, parents, or social workers—who are concerned with behavior. The same kinds of developments are taking place in matrimonial disputes and in industrial relations to a larger and larger extent. Though little progress has been made in international relations the Conflict Management Program at George Mason University could well be part of the answer that the great powers are looking for when they confront each other; when each is supportive of one party or another to a dispute which is of mutual concern to each. I would hope not merely that this program flourishes, but that the idea of a United States Peace Academy will be taken up by the Reagan administration as an essential ingredient of their fundamentally power-political approach to the struggle which preoccupies them much of the time.

## Bibliography

Box, S. (1971), *Deviance, Reality and Society*, New York, Holt, Rinehart and Winston.

Burns, J.M. (1977), 'Wellsprings of Political Leadership', *The American Political Science Review*, **71**, no. 1, pp. 266–75.

Davies, J.C. (1962), 'Toward a Theory of Revolution', *American Sociological Review*, **27**, pp. 5–19.

Deutsch, K.W. (1963), *The Nerves of Government*, New York, Free Press.

Enloe, C. (1973), *Ethnic Conflict and Political Development*, Boston, Little Brown.

Gurr, T.R. (1970), *Why Men Rebel*, Princeton, Princeton University Press.

Johnson, C. (1966), *Revolutionary Change*, Boston, Little Brown.

Kelman, H.C. (1977), 'The Conditions, Criteria and Dialectics of Human Dignity', *International Studies Quarterly*, **21**, no. 3.

Kuhn, T.S. (1962), *The Structure of Scientific Revolutions*, Chicago, University of Chicago Press.

Levi, I. (1980), 'Induction in Peirce', in *Science, Belief and Behaviour*, D.H. Mellor (ed.), London and New York, Cambridge University Press.

Modelski, G. (1962), *A Theory of Foreign Policy*, London, Pall Mall.

Moore, B. (1978), *Injustice: The Social Bases of Obedience and Revolt*, New York, Pantheon Books.

Popper, K.R. (1974) 'Norman Science and its Dangers' in *Criticism and the Growth of Knowledge*, I. Lakatos and A. Musgrave (eds), London and New York, Cambridge University Press.

Scarman, L. (1977), 'Human Rights', *University of London Bulletin*, 39.

Sites, P. (1973), *Control, the Basis of Social Order*, New York, Dunellen.

# 13(ii) Four conceptions of peace*

*Michael Banks*

To be invited to think aloud about the nature of peace is not just an appropriate way to mark the inauguration of the program in conflict resolution here at George Mason University; it is also a stimulating opportunity. It invites us to lift our gaze from the customary task of scholarship which in conflict studies—as in any other field—mostly consists of what has been accurately described as 'the painstaking examination of the obvious'. For once, we can attempt to be hopeful and visionary and consider the global context in which the new enterprise of applied peace research must be developed.

Why is there a felt need for programs in international conflict resolution? The reason, I suggest, is that it is a very nasty world out there. It contains murderous terrorists, brutally invading armies and gigantic famines which are largely man-made. It contains great numbers of dreadful things called, variously, SS and MX missile systems. It contains rioting mobs, kidnapped businessmen and diplomats and political prisoners. Not all those prisoners are the victims of tyranny, though many are, in Tibet or Siberia or South Africa or Chile. Some are incarcerated by democracies because responsible governments can find no other way to curb the desperate acts of ordinary people caught up in a protracted communal conflict which, in the present state of knowledge, appears to have no solution. In the prisons of Northern Ireland in recent years people have felt so passionately about the political conditions around them that they have smeared the walls of their own cells with excrement or even starved themselves to death. That sort of political intensity exists in the world; the problems are on that scale.

If we look ahead, at the implications of the exponential growth curves computed by the futurologists, we can see that unless corrective action is taken now, the future may well be worse. It is not just that ecological considerations, resource shortages and population growth are important in themselves—obviously they are—but for social scientists, their importance is increased by what we know about the deterioration of human behavior under conditions of resource shortage, fears and overcrowding. With steadily increasing interdependence, the threat of violent conflict looms over the rich and comfortable people of the world, as well as over the much more numerous poor and deprived who have never been strangers to it.

What contribution can an academic undertaking offer in the hope of alleviating these problems? To explore the possibilities, I wish to set out four competing answers to the question, 'what is peace?'—for peace, ultimately, is the condition that education in conflict management is designed to achieve. My argument will be that peace consists of a new way of thinking and acting. What is involved is often described as a 'paradigm shift' (Vasquez, 1983, Chapter 1), rightly in my view, because peace is an intellectual matter. It is not the result of cultivating goodwill or of being pious on Sunday mornings. It is a matter of ideas and institutions, as John Burton (1982) has suggested.

The first step is to move beyond our traditional understanding of peace and war. In the past, we have thought of peace as merely the absence of war: a condition in which the army is not engaged in combat against foreigners and not engaged in violence against people at home either. That is a negative, limited conception and we need to move away from it towards an alternative view which includes the presence of something positive. To achieve the shift, we must be creative. What we have to create is a new profession, made up of new people, with new training and new ideas, doing new things. What all these novelties will be like, we do not fully know. We have to invent them; that is what an innovative program in conflict resolution is for. We can see the shape of what is needed if we contrast that way of thinking with some of the traditional ideas about conflict and peace.

## Peace as harmony

First, there is the utopian conception of peace as a life of harmony, from which conflict itself has been banished. In such a condition, not only is violence unknown, there is not even any disagreement. This view describes people, individually and collectively, as living in a state of self-absorption, enjoying a mystical existence. It cannot help us to think of peace in such terms. It was briefly fashionable to do so in the 1960s, an age that seems so long ago, when many people 'dropped out', took psychotropic drugs and even attempted to find self-sufficiency on the basis of subsistence farming. That was, however, never anything more than self-indulgent diversion. Peace interpreted as personal tranquillity does, of course, form a plan of life for that distinguished minority of people who are able to retreat to a monastery. It may perhaps be just within the reach of persons who were born to sainthood or who have benefited from first-rate psychotherapeutic care.

Most of us, however, cannot live in a world without conflict, physically or even mentally. Nor would we wish to do so, for conflict is both inevitable and necessary. It is inevitable because both people and groups have basic needs, expressed in society through competing values and clashing interests. It is necessary in order to provide the catalyst for social processes without which life would hardly be worthwhile: stimulus, challenge, change and progress. In the language of social science, conflict itself is functional, but its functional benefits can and sometimes are accompanied by disfunctional costs: hostility, rigidity, violence and destruction. In the world as a whole, and often in domestic society as well, we lack the things that we need to maximize the benefits of conflict, and to minimize its costs: appropriate understanding, relevant institutions and the personnel to staff them.

In consequence, we live in a world in which conflicts are rarely understood and often mismanaged. Realistic peace education must start from a recognition of these facts. Its aim must not be to abolish conflict, but to facilitate its healthy expression and to bring it under societal control. The techniques of conflict management must be developed in ways which permit conflicts to yield constructive, rather than destructive, outcomes; which guide political relationships towards moderation rather than extremism; and which help progressively to create less threatening conditions for the continued existence of the human race. Set against this task, the idea of 'peace' as a life without any conflict at all, important as it may be for spiritual and cultural purposes, is at best irrelevant and at worst a badly misleading conception.

## Peace as order

Second, there is a conception of peace as stability: life made predictable and relatively safe by a minimum of political order. Peace seen in this perspective is the product of an efficient political system, both at home and in the relations between states. This is how peace is conventionally analyzed within the international relations discipline. With sadness, in the context of peace research, we must note that this view is highly persuasive. It is persuasive not only because it is widely held, among theorists and practitioners alike, but also because it fits so neatly into the prevailing general theory of world politics and into the historical facts as that theory interprets them.

Peace, from this view, is to be measured not by the relatively small amount of violence and risk that actually occurs, but by the much greater amount that would occur if responsible political leadership were to permit the dismantling or mismanagement of the structures that maintain what order and stability we have achieved. The emphasis is always upon the need to preserve the best of what we already have. Radical change is quite easily capable of producing, not progress towards some higher and more desirable condition, but degradation, anarchy and mayhem. We must, therefore, be extremely careful to protect those institutions and policies which time and testing have proved to be effective. The task of intellectuals is, from this point of view, not to dream dreams of what life could be like if only people were nicer and politics less cruel, but rather to analyze the conditions of peace realistically, in the light of history and current circumstances.

The reasoning behind this mental scheme is equally familiar to those with doctorates in international relations, and to those who only read the newspaper accounts justifying cruise missile deployment, describing the latest terrorist bomb outrage or detailing the collapse of decent life in Lebanon. We live, it suggests, in a world of states. States provide the basic guarantees of security and predictability that make everyday life possible. Domestically, there is a regime of law and order, backed always by force. Internationally, there is a twin structure: on the one hand of balanced deterrence between major power centers, both regionally and globally; and on the other hand of an ordered hierarchy which maintains a rudimentary form of world government whereby the affairs of the smaller and weaker states are directed by the larger and more powerful ones.

The mechanisms for this management by the powerful are less clearly visible (and far less legitimate) than they are under the constitution of a well run state, but they nevertheless do exist for the world as a whole and they are effective. In military and political affairs, most of the direction takes place within buffer zones, security blocs or spheres of influence generated by the balance-of-power mechanism. In economic affairs, core states exercise hegemony across wide swathes of international economic activity. This process in turn creates stable relationships, or regimes, for each economic sector. Although both hegemony and sectoral regimes are based on power, and extend an ideological sway as well, they do produce some of the benefits of peaceful relationships: mutual (if grossly unequal) profit, habits of cooperation and a stable framework for everyday life.

In all these things the competition and occasional open hostility, including even warfare between the great powers are continually tempered by their shared interests both in maintaining their topdog status in the hierarchy and in imposing a sufficient degree of order among the weaker states to prevent disruption of the world system as a whole. They therefore act in concert, notably in the nineteenth century but also today in such areas as the control of the spread of nuclear weapons, restraint upon the growth of their own defense systems and the limitation of the influence of such bodies as the office of the UN Secretary-General of the Group of 77, which might otherwise threaten those shared interests. The people of the world have lived under this system of international politics since the seventeenth century, and most of us, for most of that time, have survived. To tamper with the conditions of peace, for example by replacing a power balance with unilateral disarmament, or negotiation from strength with appeasement or hegemonial economic management with a new international economic order, is to threaten us with something worse.

Given the unimaginative character of this conception of what peace is about, it is not surprising that its exponents have always held an equally restricted view of what is involved in education and training for peace. Peace education has been thought to consist of the orthodox study of international relations; peace training has been thought to consist of preparation for the practice of diplomacy. That is why the proposal for a United States Academy of Peace met with firm resistance, from several established academic centers of international relations, when it was discussed in nationwide hearings by the US Congress and US Peace Academy Commission during 1978–80 (US Congress, 1978; US Department of Education, 1981). Clearly, many scholars and diplomats do sincerely believe that the best that can be done is already being done. It is appropriate, therefore, to consider what they recommend as measures to preserve, and where possible improve, the fragile peace that they perceive in the international system.

On these issues of research ('which aspects of world politics are crucial to its functioning?') and policy ('what suggestions do scholars have for practitioners?') there has always been a division between conservative (realist), and liberal (idealist) strands of thought. While sharing assumptions about the immutability of the state system within a general conception of peace as order and stability, the two groups differ in many ways. Within the international relations discipline itself, much has been made of the issues at stake between them (Alker and Biersteker, 1984). From a peace research perspective, the sharpest distinction is to be found in their respective attitudes toward the use of force as a means of conflict management. Conservatives accept it and seek to refine it, direct it rationally and minimize it. Liberals try to escape from it, seeking refuge in law, international organizations and a great variety of piecemeal modifications.

The distinction between the two groups is best illustrated by the question of what should be done with the world's immense stockpile of weapons. Liberals favor disarmament; the conservatives, arms control. It is a frequently repeated debate and the conservatives always win it. Logically, it makes no sense to remove armaments from states if one holds the view that order is the prime value and force is the principal instrument by which to achieve that order. It makes a greal deal of sense, however, to insist that changes in arms levels, downwards or perhaps upwards, should never be permitted to destabilize the balance which produces order. To take a second example, liberals have proposed collective security: the scheme whereby states would promise, long in advance of an outbreak of aggressive war, to pool all of their armed forces so as to produce a massive superiority and thereby deter all acts of aggression forever. Conservatives have rightly treated this idea either with scepticism or derision, according to temperament. They point out that states are by nature and function selfish organizations, willing enough to risk force in their own defense or that of an ally whose defeat would threaten them directly, but hardly likely to do so in support of a small state, far away, just as a matter of principle.

These examples show that the liberal side of the debate with the conservatives is basically flawed by its inability to step outside the peace-as-order conception of world politics. For that reason, the literature of the liberal-idealist tradition has always been inferior to the conservative-realist literature. Conservative writings have greater coherence, offering more trenchant advice to decision makers. Students of the field have therefore learned that international relations, much more than economics, is a dismal science. In international relations, a critical pose is applauded while progressive insights are fashionably dismissed.

This situation is most unfortunate. If we examine more closely the research interests of the two groups, it becomes clear that the conservatives have nothing to offer, beyond more of the same old prescriptions. Their vision of the future is that it should resemble the past and often an idealized past at that. The liberals, in contrast, have persistently sought to transcend the basic dilemmas of power politics and in doing so have thrown up a whole array of ideas which point directly to the paradigm shift that the discipline so badly needs. As I have argued at greater length elsewhere (Banks, 1984, pp. 3–21), however, they have been intellectually timid and few of them have followed the logic of their own argument towards its rather disconcerting conclusion. The point can be demonstrated by a closer examination of contemporary activity on the two wings of the mainstream international relations discipline.

The conservative wing, which was fashionable in the 1950s and is again in the 1980s under the new banner of 'structural realism' (Little, 1985), has always stressed the purest form of peace-as-order doctrine. Order is seen to rest upon power, especially in the form of the threat and intermittent use of military force, which must be harnessed to the most prudential interpretation of the responsibilities of statecraft. Much realist energy is therefore devoted to the systematic critique of everything that might interfere with the natural workings of the power-political mechanisms. The radical theory of imperialism is dismissed as reductionist, liberal programs of institution-building are termed legalistic and moralistic, arguments for economic cooperation are subordinated to national interest concerns and attempts to interpret the whole system of world politics in an ideological framework are rejected as mere mist on the eyeglasses.

In place of these false leads, realism argues that our research and practical experimentation should concentrate only upon buttressing the hierarchies of power in the world and stabilizing the balances. Negotiation by the powerful states is a prime research area; open multilateral diplomacy is frowned upon. There is extensive work on the technicalities of arms control and continuing debate about alliance unity and the crucial arcana of military affairs: intelligence assessment, the doctrine of launch on warning, the implications of emerging technology for conventional warfare. Rational control of policy is seen as central, exemplified by studies of decision making and a focus upon crisis-management techniques. The affairs of minor states are judged in terms of great power interests, as candidates for economic pressure, political manipulation and armed intervention. Much attention is paid to the search for means to suppress acts of terrorist violence by small groups of the dispossessed despite the fact that the damage they do is quantitatively trivial by comparison with the damage that the great powers have wrought in the world. None of this research is capable of changing the system. It is designed only to enable individual states to preserve their interests, given the world that we live in.

In contrast, the liberal wing has concentrated its efforts on finding reforms which might lead to evolutionary change. They have argued for the liberalization of international trade, so that economic growth in poor states can be accelerated and some of the inequalities of the system thereby reduced. They have exposed the misperceptions in policy formation which could lead to the outbreak of war and asserted the beneficial role which can be played by United Nations peacekeeping forces in areas of severe (but small-power) conflict. Many liberal campaigns have actually brought about changes in the conduct of international politics. The European Communities have been extensively integrated. A rudimentary world public opinion has emerged within the extensive family of United Nations institutions. Principles for the restraint of warfare have been developed and to some extent have proved effective. Human rights have been firmly established on the international agenda, famine and disaster relief have been promoted and international law has been codified. Across a wide range of issue areas, liberal programs of the interwar period and again in the 1960s and 1970s have offered suggestions and modifications consistently.

There is material here on which a program of education in conflict resolution should devote some of its time and effort. It was, after all, partly by just such halting and patchy reformism that today's advanced democracies withdrew the fangs of despotism from the absolute monarchs who so ruthlessly exploited the peoples of Europe as recently as two centuries ago. However, we have to face the raw truth that reformism within the framework of a peace-as-order conception of society and politics has severe limitations. Ultimately, liberals and conservatives face the same constraining facts of sovereignty and the security dilemma. The essential difference between them is that conservatives fall back upon intellectual retrenchment, whereas the liberals persist in the attempt to move forward despite the impossible odds.

The real tragedy of the liberals in international relations is that their effort has always been designed to make the system of world politics more civilized, rather than either to break the system as the revolutionary thinkers would advocate or to rethink it from first principles as the peace researchers suggest. In trying to reform the system, they merely reinforce its inner logic and ensure that their proposals run into sand. Any attempt to strengthen international law, for example, must be self-defeating in the long term whether it is designed to equalize the rights of states or to promote rule by a concert of the strong. This is because public international law takes the state as its subject and a stronger law makes for an enhanced status for the state. That contradiction can be broken only by changing the subjects recognized by the law, and substituting, say, individual persons, corporations, communal groups, municipalities and the like. The law has taken some steps in that direction, but they are of negligible impact. Similarly, any attempt to foster an international organization which is comprised of states (rather than of some other constituency such as industries, ethnic groups, social classes, professions or even people) must remain forever subject to the crippling veto of a powerful state member. Again, all the research on decision processes and perceptions, based on the well intentioned effort to reduce error in the outbreak of war, may ultimately succeed in improving decision making—and in doing so, render warfare itself a far more efficient and dependable instrument of policy.

In summary, a conception of peace merely as the product of an ordered international political system can never help to achieve a future for the world which is substantially different from the past. Even on the liberal wing, its prescriptions consist at best of tinkering with the system, in an attempt to make old institutions work better to fit new circumstances. Research conducted within its set of assumptions, while occasionally of value in peace research, is likely on the whole to perpetuate the characteristics of world politics as we have known them in the past, rather than to usher in progressively beneficial changes, first in the climate of opinion and then in policy and in institutions. A program of studies in conflict resolution cannot prosper, intellectually, if it accepts either of this perspective's two most basic tenets. One is the doctrine that objective conflict between states is the inevitable, overriding and permanent tendency of international politics. The other is the related argument that because national politics takes place under government, whereas international politics takes place between governments, we cannot draw upon domestic experience to illuminate and ameliorate the problems of international relations.

These issues go to the heart of the 'paradigm shift' referred to earlier. An effective academic program in conflict resolution must provide its clientele with a framework of ideas which will enable them to think constructively and act with a good chance of success when eventually they reach positions of influence. The curriculum, therefore, must be founded upon a single, integrated set of theories about society and politics in the world as a whole. This will show not only that conflict is universal and exists at all levels, but also that it can be managed appropriately at all levels. It will show too that it actually is managed appropriately—routinely within some states, often in many states and occasionally within international relations as well. The peace research movement has already begun to build an alternative international relations theory which demonstrates how to do this. For example, the work of Kenneth Boulding, who is one of the most persistently optimistic of social scientists, takes a long stride in the right direction (1978a, 1978b).

**Peace as justice**

There is a third, and very different, conception of peace. It is one which my radical students at the London School of Economics, especially those from the Third World, keep urging upon me. This is the view that peace consists of justice. Now justice is not a simple matter, as is well known to anyone who has sought to mediate between children disputing possession of an attractive toy, or has allocated an assortment of offices to staff in a building or has made the rash commitment to initiate an affirmative action program without first assessing all the implications. On the one hand, justice can consist of substantive human rights, or on the other hand of procedures which conform to given constitutional and legal principles. It can stipulate retributive punishment for past offences, or the opposite: relief from punishment in certain instances. It can mean absolute equality of treatment in respect of everything that matters to people, or it can mean unequal shares according to a specific principle of proportionality which is considered to be fair. Often, debate about it is tinged by the influence of some ideological formula which is regarded as sacrosanct by people living in one society although hateful to those who live in another society.

But the complexity of the matter does not, of itself, constitute a ground for rejecting a normative view of what is involved in the construction of a peaceable world. It is all too easy to bow to the dominance of cultural relativism, disregard the moral dimension, stick to a supposedly value-free perspective and concentrate in positivistic style on what are alleged to be the salient, objective 'facts' of any given situation. Students of conflict resolution cannot afford to assume such a posture, for three compelling reasons. First, the state of political feelings in the world will not permit the systematic neglect of the demands for justice which are now so widespread because they are the fuel upon which violent conflict feeds. Second, the pure theory of justice is a required ingredient for the pure theory of society and politics, a point long taken for granted in the normative tradition of political philosophy, but long neglected, with inevitably damaging effects, in the empiricist tradition of modern social science. Third, the development of conflict research in recent years has begun to suggest ways in which considerations of justice can be successfully incorporated in scholarly analysis—'successfully', that is, in the sense that academic detachment is not compromised. The study of mediation provides the leading example of this (Folberg and Taylor, 1984; Mitchell, 1981a; Banks, forthcoming).

Of these considerations in relation to justice, political feelings in the world must be our point of departure. These feelings are aroused, today, by at least three problem areas which give rise to passionate demands that wrongs be set right: poverty, ethnic oppression and political weakness.

Poverty is the most decisively unjust of these issues, and it has been the subject of a useful literature in recent years, thanks to the activism of UNCTAD (Jones, 1983), the sober reports of the World Bank (1980) and the Brandt Commission (1980, 1983) and the debates between right and left in the international relations community. All this attention has meant that 'social justice' has become an everyday term, specifying the redistribution of the world's material resources so as to extend the provision of goods and services to all those in basic need. It does not matter, morally, whether a North–South transfer which would eliminate absolute poverty is carried out to absolve Western and Arab guilt over past centuries of trading the peoples of Africa in slavery or whether it is done on the same impulse that brings aid to the victim of a road accident from a passing driver. Where a moral imperative exists, knowledge of it is alone sufficient to create an obligation.

The obligation is, of course, one that could easily be met. As the World Bank has pointed out (1980, p.61) in its somewhat coy discussion of 'malnutrition', there is no shortage of food stocks to satisfy the needs of the quarter of the world's people who are starving; the obstacles are all in the areas of politics, money and the logistics of distribution. Our understanding of these obstacles is plainly inadequate and that must partly be seen as the responsibility of the international relations discipline, which has concentrated its research elsewhere, on great power policies and national security studies. Here, then, is a theme that must be added to the list of items on a conflict resolution syllabus.

Grievances about injustice are felt with equal intensity in relation to the oppression of ethnic groups and the political weakness of the majority of the states and peoples of the world. Although most of the rich and powerful states in the world are democracies and their peoples genuinely favor such ideas as self-determination, human rights, fair play and freedom, the international system nevertheless violates those principles with remarkable consistency. Since Plato published *The Republic* more than twenty centuries ago, we have understood in the abstract, and practised in Western society, the explicit distinction between rights, on the one hand, and powers, on the other. We agree with Plato's injunction: justice does not consist of the interests of those who hold power, but we do not apply it to our foreign policies, nor to the theoretical doctrines which inform our conventional textbook wisdom about international relations. A good, though subtle, example is the widespread failure in the West, even among intellectuals, to grasp the purpose and importance of the 1970s' UNESCO campaign for a 'new international information order'. Had that campaign succeeded, it might at least have begun to mitigate the imperialism of news and entertainment that now imposes an alien media culture on the peoples of the Third World (see Richstad and Anderson, 1981).

Comparable problems are raised by the frustration of ethnic needs for group identity and the more general marginalization of many of the peoples of the world. In the terminology of conflict theory, the problems are both latent and manifest. Most serious among the latent conflicts are those where continuous and severe injustice is combined with the exclusion of suffering peoples from participation in the political process. Consider, for example, the condition of the black peoples of southern Africa today or the Kurds in the Middle East; or the population of Poland, victimized by the exigencies of international politics over several centuries; or the alienation of the scattered remnants of the Armenian people left behind after the twentieth century's first great act of genocide. Other cases have become more prominent as they have moved from the latent to the manifest stage of conflict dynamics and open violence has appeared. It is tragically evident now in Sri Lanka, in Ulster, in Lebanon, in Eritrea, in the Basque country and among the exiled Palestinians.

Does peace, then, consist of yielding to the claims of these groups and the many others like them? The answer must be no. Certainly it is the case that the savagery of political conduct in these situations can never be constrained until the international political system provides institutions to deal more justly with them. That is the key point: we do need new institutions and that need will be met only after the production of a better understanding upon which the institutions can be designed. No long-term progress can be made simply by removing specific grievances, however justified they are. To do so would merely extend the practices of existing politics, where politics is defined as the struggle between different groups for causes which they regard as just. Peace is a political matter, of course, but there is far more to it than submission to the demands of IRA hit men, Shi'ite suicide bombers or Sikh murderers of innocent tourists. It is the framework within which the demands of aggrieved groups are expressed that must be changed.

Justice, then, is of crucial importance. But awareness of that should not induce the kind of emotional involvement that leads peace researchers into taking sides. Nor should it deflect our analysis from its proper focus on ideas and institutions. The fundamental need in a program of studies on conflict resolution is to examine violent conflicts, not as problems in themselves, but as features of an international political system which is failing to meet the needs of the world's peoples. In conventional analysis economic deprivation, ethnic claims and demands for participation are usually treated as 'domestic' problems, even though they visibly spill over into world politics in ways which are often complicated and sometimes disruptive. This is because our studies of international relations are largely empirical. They are concerned with showing how the world came to be the way it is and how it works now. This is archaic and inappropriate. Would a medical school present its students only with pictures of malformed and diseased bodies while ignoring both the model of perfect health and the procedures of treatment?

We need, therefore, studies of world politics which show what is wrong with the system, 'wrong' in the sense of being inefficient; also, studies which show just how wicked it can sometimes be, and why that happens; and above all, studies of ways to improve it. It is encouraging to note that in some respects the international relations literature has begun to meet these needs in the past generation (Smith, 1985, pp. 1–28). The dependency theorists have explored the problems of unequal exchange in the political economy of world affairs. The world system theorists have probed into history to show the ways in which the system has developed via a process of exploitation. The peace researchers have set out alternative models of a normatively based world order. The conflict analysts have begun to unlock the mysterious process whereby violent conflicts, ostensibly the result of rational choices by responsible decision makers, sometimes take charge and consume those who seek to use force as an instrument of policy, but there is a very long way yet to go.

## Peace as conflict management

What, then, of the fourth conception of peace? It is, as academics are fond of saying, very much a matter of research in progress and not something yet susceptible of fullscale description. As I have attempted to argue in this section, traditional views of peace are inadequate, especially for the purpose of conveying to students of conflict resolution a clear impression of what it is that they are trying to achieve. In the past, we have been accustomed to think of peace as a fixed condition, a particular state of affairs to be brought about by specific means: turning our swords into plowshares or setting up a world government under the slogan of peace through law. Now we can see that although these conditions may be highly desirable, they are the products of peace, not elements of its definition.

We can see too that some of the more sophisticated conceptions of peace, often pursued with vigor in philosophy or in the theory and practice of international relations, also fall short of the target. Peace is not a state of general tranquillity, but rather a network of relationships full of energy and conflict which is nevertheless kept under societal control. Nor is peace either solely a matter of imposing order, or the achievement of any particular vision of justice for all. These values are relevant, both in themselves and in the trade-off between them, but neither of them alone can provide a sufficient framework.

Even if we are as yet a long way short of being able to fill in all the details, we can certainly sketch out some of the outlines. We need to think of peace not as a condition, but as a process, a dynamic state of affairs in which the essential properties arise from how we do things, not what we do. That is why there needs to be a paradigm shift in our thinking about peace before we begin effectively to construct it. Its positive elements, where they can be described with any confidence, have been indicated at relevant points in the argument of this section. Of necessity at this stage in the development of our understanding, my closing summary must be generalized and tentative.

The theory of peace is based upon a recognition that the point of departure must be the needs and values of ordinary people: what they require of society for physical survival and spiritual self-fulfilment, what possessions they aspire to own, what activities they enjoy, what groups they belong to and which relationships they cherish. These things give people their identity; with them they will be likely to live in some contentment, without them they will be spoiling for a fight. As Christian Bay has put it, 'natural communities are the prime instrumentality' (1981, p. 202). At times when it is necessary to define a precise content for all or any of these needs and values, the people involved must do the defining for themselves, for participation is itself a human need which is universally felt.

If this observation is thought to be bland, it can be contrasted with any standard text on international relations. That volume will be found to comprise an account of the worship of false gods; not real human needs, but reified institutional values like the state and the perpetuation of its armed forces; nationalism often cultivated to secure an established elite against its rivals; the traditional glories of territorial ownership, prestige and privileges in relation to foreign peoples; and a whole array of perceived threats and insecurities piled up over time by past policies and also generated by the very institutions designed to reduce them. These things exist and cannot be denied, but they describe world politics as it is; they are not a theory of peace. As the behavioralists argued a generation ago in defense of abstract theorizing in international relations, the cause of the disease is not always to be found at the scene of the epidemic.

The peace researcher's conception of peace, having begun with values, proceeds directly from there to conflict analysis. This might seem odd. The objective, after all, is to build a general theory—general in the sense that it deals with society and politics, portraying a situation in which conflicts are expressed and resolved rather than suppressed or settled coercively. Can that general theory be derived from analysis of just one phenomenon? What about that process which is often thought to be the antithesis as well as the antonym of conflict, namely cooperation? If we look at other disciplines, do we not find that they describe stable structures as well as dynamic processes: government in addition to politics in political science; the economy in addition to exchange in economics; the personality in addition to behavior in psychology?

The justification for plunging straight into conflict analysis is that it provides our most powerful source of understanding for the study of peace. Other sources do exist, certainly, and I would not wish to understate their value in the peace research enterprise. There is much to be learned about the nature of peace from an examination of the thoughts and actions of outstanding people like Mahatma Gandhi, William Penn, Karl Marx, Bertrand Russell and Dag Hammarskjold and outstanding organizations like Amnesty International, the International Committee of the Red Cross and the Society of Friends (Bailey, 1985). Every branch of social science has something to offer, especially where scholars have taken pains to synthesize the findings of a particular field and demonstrate their relevance to peace. Some examples are Simon Robert's study of order and dispute in legal anthropology (1979), F.H. George's summary of operational research on problem solving (1980), Charles Beitz's examination of the relevance of philosophy to the problem of distributive justice (1979) and work on international jurisprudence by Terry Nardin (1983) and Julius Stone (1984). Within international relations itself, there is now an impressive selection of useful books. Their authors attack the policies and assumptions that damage peace (Halliday, 1983; Burton, 1984); set out either partial (Wilson, 1983; Fischer, 1984) or comprehensive (Galtung, 1980) accounts of the faults of the present system of world politics and the characteristics of a better one; and describe ways to disentangle the integrative strands of society and community from the divisive hostilities of power politics (Mayall, 1982; Banks, 1984).

I have mentioned only a few studies, among a large number which can assist in building models of stable structures that might evolve in a peaceful world—a world, that is, in which conflicts are successfully managed without violence and rigidity. Valuable as they are, they cannot form the core of peace research. Many of them are speculative or normative or in extreme cases apocalyptic, as when Jonathan Schell points out that 'if we ask what it is that we would have to give up in order to resolve the nuclear predicament we find that it is nothing less than the whole present structure of international affairs' (1984, p.25). Even when these works have an empirical base, they can at best only form a necessary background to the serious business of peace research. Their function, which is an essential function if peace research is to succeed, is to educate public opinion, alter the climate of informed thought and influence decision makers to steer resources towards research on peace instead of research on war. The point has been forcefully stated in James Rosenau's presidential address (1984, p.300) to the International Studies Association.

The serious business of peace research, then, is conflict research. Only in the concrete task of analysing actual conflicts (preferably including current, ongoing ones so that the mutual feedback between theory and practice is immediate) can we build up the body of knowledge that is required. To extend the medical metaphor employed earlier, the responsibility of the conflict analyst begins with recognition of symptoms and proceeds through diagnosis and prognosis to methods of treatment. Fortunately, a substantial amount is already known about each of the phases of conflict dynamics and is reported in a steady flow of scholarly works: Deutsch (1973), Moore (1978), Burton (1979), Wehr (1979), Gurr (1980), Mitchell (1981b), Kriesberg (1982), Zimmermann (1983) and others. The core of peace theory is to be found in them, in the contrasts between conflicts that are managed well and those that are handled badly.

It is the function of other chapters in this book, not this one, to spell out in some detail the substance of what we already know about conflict dynamics and to suggest which paths towards further understanding are likely to prove the most useful. Here it is only necessary to point to the major features of conflicts as they are described in social science. They follow patterns which can be mapped and to some extent predicted, despite the nearly universal impression of those involved in them that each conflict is unique and uniquely intractable as well. They are extremely complex, although they often convey a superficial image of simplicity. Within their complexity lies a whole set of opportunities for changing course, and thereby restraining a given action from worsening the situation. There are always more parties involved in a given conflict than seems to be the case at first sight and more issues too; and furthermore, as the conflict develops, both parties and issues spread out, change and multiply.

At every stage in the growth of a conflict, choices are made. The function of conflict research is to illuminate those choices, which are literally vital ones. Peace will come about when the choices made are consistently benign rather than malign. Injustice is a warning signal; legitimized regimes have a greater chance of secure survival. Polarization is dangerous; multiple loyalties are relatively safe. Negative sanctions harden attitudes; positive inducements soften them. Homogenous issues exacerbate confrontation; fragmented issues reduce it. People trained in adversarial techniques (lawyers, diplomats, the military) tend to advocate policies which build walls between parties; people trained in problem-solving techniques (businessmen, psychologists, technical experts) are more likely to advocate policies which build bridges between parties. Reliance upon a single channel of communication foments misperception; multiple channels give more opportunity to perceive the opponent realistically. Isolationism puts an actor at risk; interdependence, if encouraged, generates a network of criss-crossing relationships which can ultimately become impossible to tear apart.

Every conflict, therefore, potentially contains both the symptoms of malady and the possibility of switching behavioral choices to health-promoting activity. In conflict, nothing is inexorable, however strongly the parties may feel that events are in the saddle and ride mankind. It is undoubtedly the case that the task of conflict management becomes progressively more difficult as conflict dynamics ride forward on their own momentum. As Kenneth Boulding pointed out in his classic monograph, 'the biggest problem in developing the institutions of conflict control is that of catching conflicts young' (1962, p.325). That remains an unsolved problem which must be overcome for peace to be established, but, in common with all the other choices facing parties in conflict, it is a matter for them to decide. A stable structure of peaceful relationships cannot be imposed on the world by peace theorists. Peace research is not in the business of designing utopias. It is in the business of clarifying the options for people and their decision makers in conflict situations.

*I am grateful to the Economic and Social Research Council of Great Britain for the award of a research grant, reference number E00242020, for support while this paper was in preparation.

## Bibliography

Alker Jr, H.R. and T.J. Biersteker (1984), 'The Dialectics of World Order: Notes for a Future Archeologist of International Savoir Faire', *International Studies Quarterly*, **28**, no.4, pp. 121–42.

Banks, M. (ed.) (1984), *Conflict in World Society: A New Perspective on International Relations*, Brighton, Wheatsheaf and New York, St. Martin's.

Banks, M. (Forthcoming), *Resolution of Conflict: A Manual on the Problem Solving Approach.*

Bailey, S.D. (1985), 'Non-Official Mediation in disputes: Reflections on Quaker Experience', *International Affairs*, **61**, no.2, pp. 205–22.

Bay, C. (1981), *Strategies of Political Emancipation*, Notre Dame and London, University of Notre Dame Press.

Beitz, C.R. (1979), *Political Theory and International Relations*, Princeton and Guildford, Surrey, Princeton University Press.

Boulding, K.E. (1962), *Conflict and Defense: A General Theory*, New York and London, Harper & Row.

Boulding, K.E. (1978a), *Ecodynamics: A New Theory of Societal Evolution*, Beverly Hills and London, Sage.

Boulding, K.E. (1978b), *Stable Peace*, Austin and London, University of Texas Press.

'Brandt Commission' I (1980), Report of the Independent Commission on International Development Issues, *North-South: A Programme for Survival*, London, Pan and Cambridge, Massachusetts Institute of Technology Press.

'Brandt Commission' II (1983), Report of the Independent Commission on International Development Issues, *Common Crisis—North-South: Co-operation for World Recovery*, London, Pan and Cambridge, Massachusetts Institute of Technology Press.

Burton, J.W. (1979), *Deviance, Terrorism and War: The Process of Solving Unsolved Social and Political Problems*, Oxford, Martin Robertson and New York, St. Martin's.

Burton, J.W. (1982), *Dear Survivors—Planning After Nuclear Holocaust: War Avoidance*, London, Frances Pinter and Boulder, Westview.

Burton, J.W. (1984), *Global Conflict: The Domestic Sources of International Crisis*, Brighton, Wheatsheaf and College Park, University of Maryland, Center for International Development.

Deutsch, M. (1973), *The Resolution of Conflict: Constructive and Destructive Processes*, New Haven and London, Yale University Press.

Fischer, D. (1984), *Preventing War in the Nuclear Age*, London, Croom Helm.

Folberg, J. and A. Taylor (1984), *Mediation: A Comprehensive Guide to Resolving Conflicts Without Litigation*, San Francisco and London, Jossey-Bass.

Galtung, J. (1980), *The True Worlds: A Transnational Perspective*, New York, Free Press and London, Collier-Macmillan International.

George, F.H. (1980), *Problem Solving*, London, Duckworth.

Gurr, T.R. (ed.) (1980), *Handbook of Political Conflict: Theory and Research*, New York, Free Press and London, Collier-Macmillan.

Halliday, F. (1983), *The Making of the Second Cold War*, London, Verso Editions.

Jones, C.A. (1983), *The North-South Dialogue: A Brief History*, London, Frances Pinter.

Kriesberg, L. (1982), *Social Conflicts*, 2nd ed, Englewood Cliffs and London, Prentice-Hall.

Little, R. (1985), 'Structuralism and Neo-Realism' in *International Relations: A Handbook of Current Theory*, M. Light and A.J.R. Groom (eds), London, Frances Pinter and Boulder, Lynne Rienner.

Mayall, J. (ed.) (1982), *The Community of States: A Study in International Political Theory*, London and Winchester, Massachusetts, Allen & Unwin.

Mitchell, C.R. (1981a), *Peacemaking and the Consultant's Role*, Farnborough, Hants, Gower and New York, Nichols.

Mitchell, C.R. (1981b), *The Structure of International Conflict*, London, Macmillan and New York, St. Martin's.

Moore Jr, B. (1978), *Injustice: The Social Bases of Obedience and Revolt*, London, Macmillan and New York, Pantheon Books.

Nardin, T. (1983), *Law, Morality and the Relations of States*, Princeton and Guildford, Princeton University Press.

Richstad, J. & M.H. Anderson (eds) (1981), *Crisis in International News: Policies and Prospects*, New York and Guildford, Columbia University Press.

Roberts, S. (1979), *Order and Dispute: An Introduction to Legal Anthropology*, Harmondsworth and New York, Penguin Books.

Rosenau, J.N. (1984), 'A Pre-Theory Revisited: World Politics in an Era of Cascading Interdependence', *International Studies Quarterly*, **28**, no. 3, pp. 245–306.

Schell, J. (1984), *The Abolition*, New York, Knopf and London, Picador (Pan).

Smith, S. (ed.) (1985), *International Relations: British and American Perspectives*, Oxford, Basil Blackwell.

Stone, J. (1984), *Visions of World Order: Between State Power and Human Justice*, Baltimore and London, Johns Hopkins University Press.

US Congress, House Subcommittee on International Operations of the Committee on International Relations (1978), *Hearings on the National Academy of Peace and Conflict Resolution*, 95th Congress, 2d session.

US Department of Education (1981), *To Establish the United States Academy of Peace*, Report of the Commission on Proposals for the National Academy of

Peace and Conflict Resolution to the President of the United States and the Senate and House of Representatives of the United States Congress, Washington, DC, US Government Printing Office.

Vasquez, J.A. (1983), *The Power of Power Politics: A Critique*, London, Frances Pinter and New Brunswick, Rutgers University Press.

Wehr, P. (1979), *Conflict Regulation*, Boulder, Westview.

Wilson, A. (1983), *The Disarmer's Handbook of Military Technology and Organization*, Harmondsworth and New York, Penguin Books.

World Bank (1980), *World Development Report 1980*, Washington, DC, The World Bank.

Zimmermann, E. (1983), *Political Violence, Crises and Revolutions: Theories and Research*, Cambridge, Schenkman.

# 13(iii) Problem solving: some lessons from Europe

*A.J.R. Groom*

George Mason University has been involved in establishing a program in conflict management including developing a framework for the United States Peace Academy. This is not the first time that such efforts have been made; they have been made in Europe, and we have not done a very good job of it. However, some good results have come out of it, for instance the development of problem-solving techniques which have actually been applied to ongoing conflicts, both intercommunal and international. John Burton (1969) in Britain as well as Herbert Kelman (1972) in the United States have been very innovative in developing these, which on occasion have moved seemingly intractable conflict towards a resolution.

Another insight generated by our experiences concerns organizational frameworks. We tend to look at problems from a vantage point determined by hierarchies; very often we define problems in terms of our position in the hierarchy—a government person will see a problem from one point of view, a pressure group person from another point, a United Nations Security Council person from still another point, and a multinational corporation person from yet another point of view. In effect, we tend to make the problem fit our role in the hierarchy. What we in Europe have learned is the importance of attempting to conceive problems in terms of their own characteristics, independently of our positions in various hierarchies. We have also learned, however, that this is very hard to accomplish. Perhaps the Conflict Management Program at George Mason University can profit from, and contribute further to this awareness.

## Bibliography

Burton, J.W. (1969), *Conflict and Communication: The Use of Controlled Communication in International Relations*, London, Macmillan and New York, Free Press.

Kelman, H.C. (1972), 'The Problem-Solving Workshop in Conflict Resolution', in *Communication in International Politics*, R.L. Merritt (ed.), Urbana, IL & London, University of Illinois Press.

# Part IV: Conflict Management: Generic Theory, Research, and Practice Revisited

# 14(i) Conflict management: the state of the art

*Bryant Wedge*

One of the fundamental ideas that has emerged from most, if not all of the sections in this book is that conflict is a process; it always involves movement through time. In any analysis of conflict, therefore, one must always include the dimension of time, but there are other dimensions as well, for instance, that of level: where, in terms of some framework, a given conflict happens to be at a particular time. One such scheme, borrowed from the work of John Lovell (1974), appears in figure 14.1.

Still another dimension is that of unit, or actor: the identification of the parties to conflict. The parties may be individuals, groups, organizations, nation–states. There are many potential parties who are not in conflict with each other at all; they may be too far apart, too deeply isolated or simply have no contact with one another. However, as soon as actors initiate contact, a condition of latent conflict, which is labeled 'fermentation' in Figure 14.1, comes into being. Any relationship, no matter who the actors are, is always in a state of latency, of fermentation of conflict potentiality, because at some point in the development of the relationship, the actors become aware that, on various issues, their interests appear to be incompatible. The perception of incompatible interests is the essence of conflict: what one party wants, the other has, and so on. Even at this inchoate level, a sort of 'peace' or 'resolution' can occur, at least temporarily.

As a relationship develops further, one or more of the parties may become aware of some sense of 'relative deprivation' (see Gurr, 1970), and perceive that the 'other side' is somehow preventing their experience of some preferred state of affairs. At this point, fermentation may rise to a point of challenge, of 'confrontation', where the parties are 'eyeball to eyeball' and where they may do a number of things: one side may back down; they may adjust their differences, that is divide the 'pie' in ways that are at least temporarily satisfying (hence, achieving a resolution of sorts); they may move up to the next level of 'violence'; or they may return to fermentation.

At each level on the scale, the parties may stay put, move up or move down. Many conflict relationships, for instance those in the Middle East, are characterized by this upward and downward movement. Upward movement, incidentally, may have little to do with 'deep, driving forces', which conflict analysts tend to look for, but instead, with quite accidental developments. In this regard, I agree with Montesquieu that 'great events are not necessarily preceded by great causes; on the contrary, the least accident produces a great revolution, often as unforeseen by those who cause it, as by those who suffer from it' (cited in Rapaport, 1966, p. 58). Hence, violence, which is always latent in conflict relationships, may, in the normal course of events, appear to erupt suddenly.

This has occurred in the Falklands/Malvinas dispute. This conflict, in my view, is between the Falkland islanders and the government of Argentina. The islanders

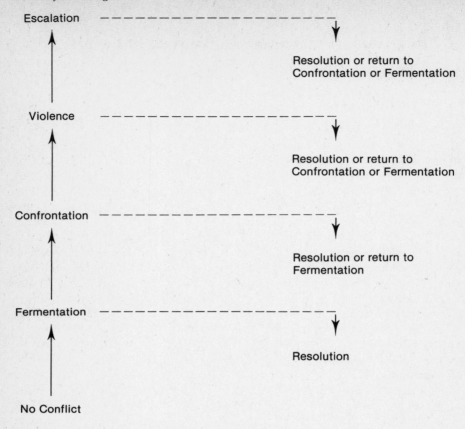

**Figure 14.1.** Levels of manifest conflict

do not want Argentina to take over because they envisage a foreign dictatorship being thrust on them. Hence, they have engaged Great Britain in their defense, and Britain is clearly caught up in it. The Falklands, with their 1,800 inhabitants and some 60,000 sheep, may not appear to be too significant in the overall scheme of things. As a consequence, some of us have felt that had the dispute been handled differently, it could have moved from confrontation to fermentation, but instead, as is often the case, it moved up to violence.

There are other conflict relationships—serious conflicts, domestically and internationally—that do not move up to violence but simmer down. Some situations, like street riots, may move up to violence, but as the participants return home, the underlying conflict moves down to confrontation or even fermentation.

Needless to say, the street riot is not likely to lead to resolution. What is likely to do so, according to many of the discussions in this book, is certain diplomatic or mediated action. Resolution is best pursued when some 'honest broker', an impartial third party, intervenes in such a way that the parties find if possible to talk with each other without beating each other over the head. The third party must first determine the right 'excuses' for, and mechanisms of intervention, plus the right parties and venue and then intervention becomes almost a magical process. Resolution, even of serious and violent conflicts, becomes possible because the parties are encouraged to reanalyze and reassess whether the opponent is really so much of an 'enemy'.

This kind of third-party intervention and constructive, direct contact between the parties did not occur during the course of events leading up to the Falklands War of 1982. Both before and after hostilities began, however, efforts were made to offer mediative services. As I have spelled out in 'Toward Resolving The Malvinas–Falkland Islands Dispute: A Proposal' (see Appendix), John Burton, Roger Fisher, James Laue and I were prepared to intervene. Though we were not called upon to do so, after the cessation of hostilities, mediation activities between Britain and Argentina were undertaken under the direction of John Burton to contribute to resolving the postwar state of hostilities.

We live in a time in which global changes are taking place at every level of human existence. It is not a secret that nuclear weapons have changed our environment forever. As Einstein said, the atom has changed everything about man except the way he thinks, and he predicted that it might destroy us if we did not catch up with it. We are also familiar with the notion of the population explosion, that by the year 2000 we may have created a living Hell on Earth. There are also the general technological advances, if we can call them that, which have created interdependencies so great that people world-wide are locked into massive power–, energy– and communication-grids which transcend national boundries.

These kinds of changes have been occurring in the last two or three decades, and few of us have changed in response in the way we think about the shape of the world and the way we should live together in it. In addition to these changes of a scientific and physical kind, there have been sociological, political and behavioral changes, where our thinking has also lagged behind. For example, an important change has occurred in the locus of sovereignty. Sovereignty is a significant issue in the Falklands dispute, but it is an eighteenth-century kind of sovereignty with sovereigns, or kings and queens, and the ambassadors who represent them. This is the world of the Congress of Vienna of 1815, about which Henry Kissinger is an expert, but there are few heads of state in that sense anymore. Sovereignty, or the capacity to make decisions, no longer resides in any single locus but on a scale somewhere between the leadership and the people. Thus the old concept of sovereignty is a myth. Nevertheless, when governments are undergoing crisis and stress, they tend to revert to that old notion. The heads of state and of government start behaving like the kings of old, dispatching troops and fleets, manipulating 'truth', and so on. The problem is that the people may not always support such action taken in their name. The response of many Americans to the Vietnam War, for instance, influenced President Johnson not to seek another term. Similarly, the response of many Americans to Watergate influenced President Nixon to resign. In neither case did the sovereignty of the individual person survive the perceived transgressions of that person.

This relates to another area of change: with few exceptions, the days are gone of honoring greatly our 'crowned heads' or leadership in general. We can, and often do, get rid of our presidents, prime ministers and dictators rather quickly. At some point even dictatorships have an increasingly difficult time suppressing the genuine, legitimate needs of their people. Even in the family sovereignty and the capacity to suppress have changed remarkably: parents with regard to children and husbands with regard to wives. The children and wives are no longer willing to accept the *status quo ante*. In familial as well as political and other systems, therefore, we are faced with fragmentation, and we can respond with either incoherence or transformation. I prefer the latter, and one of the instruments of transformation is conflict management: skills and capacities to intervene at various levels and in various ways which will allow us to live together more comfortably.

Most of the ideas in the previous chapters can be located within the matrix outlined in Figure 14.2. The matrix has two axes: levels of analysis and methods of analysis. 'Levels' here refers to the organizational context of conflict, as defined by the actors involved, whereas in Figure 14.1, it refers to the location of conflict in terms of intensity: is it moving up or down, or stabilizing at one 'level'? For purposes of illustration, the matrix contains only five levels: interpersonal, small group, large-interest group, nation and international system. Many of us can relate immediately to the first two of these, starting from the bottom. Firstly, many of our quarrels are at the interpersonal level, though they may also involve larger contexts as well (for example, the family/small group in the case of divorce). Secondly, most of us live most of our lives and experience most of our conflicts at the small-group level: within the family, the neighborhood, and so on.

Moving up the scale we have, thirdly, the large-interest group, which includes the interpersonal and small-group levels but also relations between large groups. Hence, in the United States there is electoral conflict between the Republican and Democratic Parties which is managed by an established conflict-management mechanism called the political party system. Ethnic groups are large-interest groups. People identify with others of the same race, culture or some other background and pursue their interests in terms of the interests of those groups. In the United States, for instance, this has occurred with regard to Hispanics, blacks, and native Americans whose conflicts with the dominant culture have sometimes turned violent. The large corporations and trade unions are also in this category, with their conflicts, at least in the United States, being managed successfully most of the time by the collective bargaining system.

The fourth level, that of the nation, is the largest coherent grouping within which people live. The nation is where all the power lies nowadays which may be a bit unfortunate. As the holder of the monopoly of power, it is the only legitimate killer of people, including its own citizens. Indeed, if we applied the same ethical criteria to nations that we apply to individual persons, we would have to conclude that nations are the most murderous organizations in all of human history, but those kinds of ethics are obviously not applied. Clearly, as we move up the scale to the nation, the rules change.

There are two faces to the nation. One is the face it turns toward its citizens, acting as the Great Father, pointing its majestic finger at the errant ones. The second face it turns toward other nations, hence, the fifth and final level of analysis in our scheme: the international system. At that level, relations can become quite confused and chaotic, even dangerous, especially since many statesmen act in

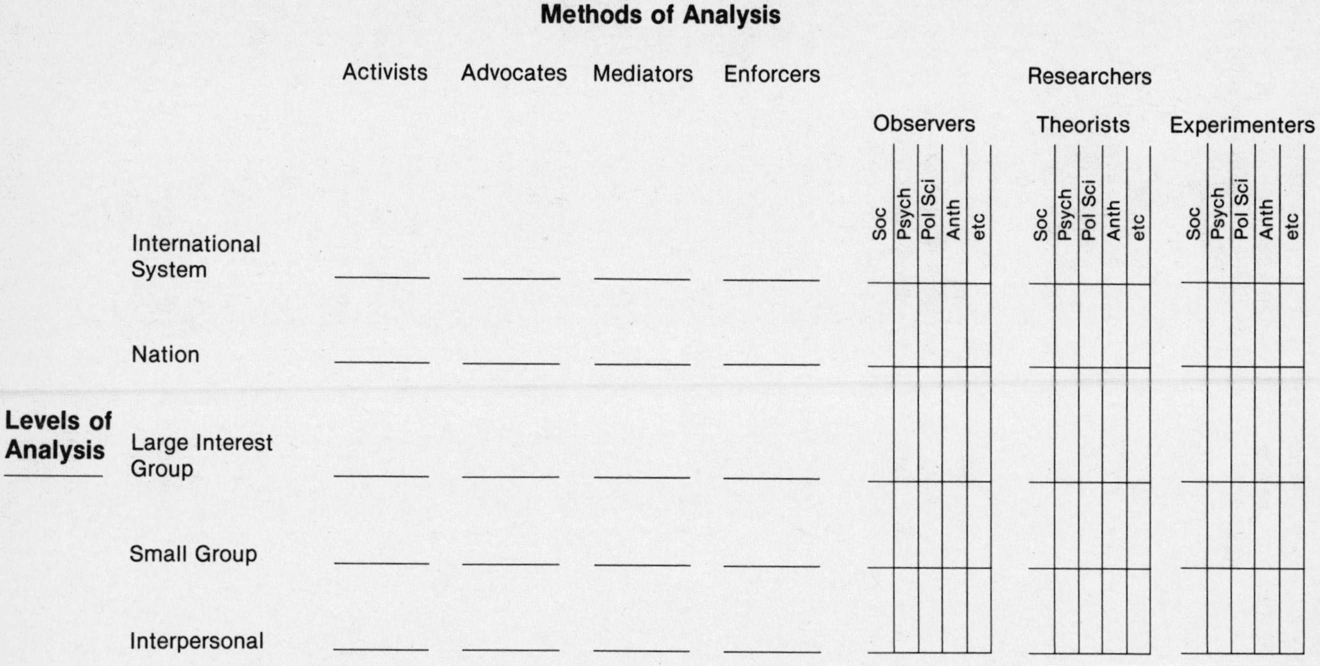

**Methods of Analysis**

| Levels of Analysis | Activists | Advocates | Mediators | Enforcers | | Observers | | | Theorists | | | Experimenters | |
|---|---|---|---|---|---|---|---|---|---|---|---|---|---|
| International System | | | | | Soc | | | | Soc | | | | Soc |
| | | | | | Psych | | | | Psych | | | | Psych |
| Nation | | | | | Pol Sci | | | | Pol Sci | | | | Pol Sci |
| | | | | | Anth | | | | Anth | | | | Anth |
| Large Interest Group | | | | | etc | | | | etc | | | | etc |
| Small Group | | | | | | | | | | | | | |
| Interpersonal | | | | | | | | | | | | | |

**Figure 14.2.** Integrative conflict/conflict management matrix

terms of what has been called the 'billiard-ball' model. According to this view, which has been described by Arnold Wolfers (1962, pp. 19–24) and John Burton (1972, pp. 28–9), states are the only significant actors at the international level. Moreover, they are all the same in the sense that they are closed and impermeable systems in full control of all that exists within their frontiers. The only interactions of significance are those that take place between states, specifically, between state governments. And just like billiard balls, 'only the hard exteriors touch, and heavier or faster moving ones push others out of the way' (Burton, p. 28). Though 'this obviously is not an accurate portrait of the real world of international politics' (Wolfers, p. 19), our foreign offices continue to view it that way. The diplomacy in the Falklands dispute has certainly been conducted as if this were the case.

The methods-of-analysis part of Figure 14.2 comprises James Laue's typology of intervenor roles: activists, advocates, mediators, enforcers and researchers (see chapter 1 and Laue, 1982). How one analyzes a particular conflict depends on which of these five roles one is playing: analysis, therefore, is role-dependent. For the moment, I will address only the researcher role which I have subdivided into three parts: observer, theorist and experimenter.

Some researchers tend to be inductive: they initate the research process by making observations of cases or situations within a natural, laboratory, and/or archival setting. From such observations they may develop a theory which they or others might then subject to rigorous testing. Other researchers tend to be deductive: they begin the process with a theory which they or others might then test through real-world observations, laboratory experimentation and/or statistical analysis of existing data.

In either the inductive or deductive case, the subroles of observer, theorist and experimenter are apparent and interrelated. There may be a division of labor across members of a research team with each specializing in one function or the three subroles may be found in one and the same person. In addition, the various disciplines have their own preferred approaches to observation and experimentation, as well as their own theories. Thus the social psychologist who is concerned with theories of perception knows that certain things happen with great regularity whenever groups enter into conflict. One of these is the phenomenon of the 'black-top enemy-image': the notion that among the enemy the leadership is the villian while the people are basically good. According to Ralph K. White (1970, pp. 310–19), this is merely one dimension of a larger phenomenon known generally as the 'devil image' or what he calls the 'diabolical enemy–image'.

Perceptions may have exceedingly little to do with what actually exists, but they are nevertheless of great importance, particularly in conflict situations, because they influence our actions. We act in terms of what we believe to be true, of what we think the other side may be doing and why it may be behaving the way it is and we may be horribly wrong. One of the first things my colleagues John Burton, Roger Fisher, James Laue and I might have done if we had had the chance to intervene in the Falklands dispute, would have been to explore with the Falkland Islanders and the Argentinians whether there was any validity to the former's perception that the latter wanted to impose a Spanish-speaking dictatorship on the island.

In addition to social psychology's emphasis on perception, there is anthropology's emphasis on culture, political science's emphasis on power politics and power balances, plus others, all part of the theorist subdivision of the researcher role. The point is, when we as researchers anaylze any particular conflict, we should be aware, and be able to make use, of the most relevant tools.

I now want to address some changes that are taking place that I think might suggest remedies to the 'world circumstance'. There is a feeling among many people that a significant shift is occurring in orientations to, and processes of, conflict management. One of the earliest to make that observation was Carl Jung (1968) who talked about the spiritual transformation in mankind. Teilhard de Chardin (1961) maintained that the slow convergence of events will lead ineluctably toward the transformation of our minds. I hear the same kind of message from others, that some major change in our perceptions is in process, and that it is a correction for our earlier habits of thinking which are no longer functional, a correction to accommodate some of the changes I mentioned earlier.

Included in this 'paradigm shift' is a change in our views of conflict. I was brought up to believe that conflict was pathological, an abnormal phenomenon, something to be avoided, suppressed or held down. Now, conflict is regarded as normal, inevitable, often productive. Change is also occurring in our views of peace. Earlier in my life, I had the notion that peace was a passive state of quietude, where people were soft-spoken and kind. Even my earlier psychotherapeutic work reflected this notion: I was to bring about pacific states in that quiescent sense. In effect, I was teaching people to avoid fights and instead, I should have been teaching them to fight better, though not—I should hasten to add—in the sense of using force. I should have been teaching them that peace is a disputatious state and that there are ways for working toward positive solutions of those disputes. Peace in this sense, therefore, is both a state of affairs which may be rather rocky at times and the techniques and skills for moving that state of affairs toward positive outcomes.

Those skills and techniques are, of course, what this book has been about: the identification and examination of mechanisms by which conflicts can be surfaced and analyzed; mechanisms by which the parties can undertake a common search for areas of mutuality. Part of those skills and techniques is the self-control of aggression. As Arnold Goldstein and his associates (1982, 1981) have argued, a good deal of the violence in the world comes about because people 'sit on themselves' for too long and then 'detonate'. Rather than suppressing anger, they argue, it should be expressed as nonviolent assertiveness, and they suggest ways for achieving that. The Falklands dispute, incidentally, is an example of a conflict that was 'sat on' for a long time before it, too, exploded.

There has been some degree of institutionalization of these mechanisms (see Wedge and Sandole, 1982), including the idea in the United States and elsewhere of academies, institutes or universities of peace. Even this book has contributed to that process, conferring additional legitimacy on the arts and sciences of conflict management. The lecture series that lead to the book was launched to determine what the state of the field was. I must say, after meeting each week for three hours over a four-month period with some forty presenters, plus a loyal audience of between 50 and 70 persons, that something is definitely out there. Though hardly any of the pieces may appear to fit together, I feel a certain integration, a certain fitting together of the sections, suggesting that we are, in fact, dealing with a genuine disciplinary field. I also feel that, with amazing speed, people are grasping that something helpful resides in what we have gathered together.

## Bibliography

Burton, J.W. (1972), *World Society*, London and New York, Cambridge University Press.

Goldstein, A.P. and A. Rosenbaum (1982), *Aggress-less: How to Turn Anger into Positive Action*, Englewood Cliffs and London, Prentice-Hall.

Goldstein, A.P., E.G. Carr, W.S. Davidson, II, P. Wehr *et al* (1981), *In Response to Aggression: Methods of Control and Prosocial Alternatives*, Oxford and New York, Pergamon Press.

Gurr, T.R. (1970), *Why Men Rebel*, Princeton, Princeton University Press.

Jung, C.G. (1968), *The Archetypes and the Collective Unconscious*, 2d. ed., Princeton, Princeton University Press.

Laue, J.H. (1982), 'Ethical Considerations in Choosing Intervention Roles', *Peace and Change* (Special Issue on Conflict Resolution, M.A. Dugan (ed.)), **8**, no. 2–3, pp. 29–41.

Lovell, J.P. (1974), *The Search for Peace: An Appraisal of Alternative Approaches*, International Studies Occasional Paper no. 4, Pittsburgh, University of Pittsburgh, University Center for International Studies.

Montesquieu, *The Persian Letters* (1966), cited by D.C. Rapaport, '*Coup d'etat*: The View of the Men Firing Pistols' in *Revolution*, C.J. Friedrich (ed.), New York, Atherton Press.

Teilhard de Chardin, P. (1961), *The Phenomenon of Man*, New York, Harper & Brothers.

Wedge, B. and D.J.D. Sandole (1982), 'Conflict Management: A New Venture into Professionalization', *Peace and Change* (Special Issue on Conflict Resolution, M.A. Dugan (ed.)), **8**, no. 2–3, pp. 129–38.

White, R.K. (1970), *Nobody Wanted War: Misperception in Vietnam and Other Wars*, rev. ed., Garden City, Anchor Books.

Wolfers, A. (1962), *Discord and Collaboration: Essays on International Politics*, Baltimore and London, The Johns Hopkins University Press.

## Appendix: toward resolving the Malvinas–Falkland Islands dispute—a proposal

*Purpose*: It is proposed that a team of experienced impartial mediators, unconnected with any government, be designated (possibly as a Special Commission of the United Nations) to assist all the parties to the Malvinas–Falkland Islands dispute to arrive at agreements among themselves and satisfactory to each through impartial mediative intervention. A group of scholars and practitioners of international dispute settlement has been organized and is prepared to offer its services should the parties and/or the United Nations Security Council or Secretary General so request.

*Sponsorship and organization*: This proposal is sponsored jointly by the Harvard Negotiation Project and the Center for Conflict Resolution of George Mason

University. The fiscal agent is the George Mason University Foundation, 4400 University Drive, Fairfax, Virginia 22030. Some private contributions and pledges have been made to fund the organization of the project.

Project Directors are Professor Roger Fisher of Harvard University Law School and Dr. Bryant Wedge, Director of George Mason University's Center. The General Coordinator if the proposal is acted on will be Professor James Laue, Director of the Center for Metropolitan Studies of the University of Missouri at St. Louis and former Vice-Chairman of the Commission on Proposals for a United States Academy of Peace and Conflict Resolution. Several experienced scholar-mediators from other universities in the United States and Great Britain have agreed to participate as needed.

*Proposed Procedures*: The general purpose is to assist the disputing parties to freshly analyze the context and substance of the disputes, their own interests in finding an acceptable solution, and various options and alternatives open to them in an atmosphere of minimal coercion. Flowing from this is the negotiating process itself, moving toward direct contact in a mutually acceptable venue with facilitation by the mediation team or Commission. The entire process would build on the achievements of the governments of Argentina and Great Britain in moving toward interim settlements with the support of the United Nations and the official representation of Secretary of State Alexander Haig of the United States.

As presently organized through consultation among the proposers and associates and with offices of the several governments and United States officials, three coordinated levels of action are visualized. First, mediation between the inhabitants of the Malvinas–Falkland Islands and the government of Argentina would be organized under the direction of Dr. John Burton, former Permanent Head of the Australian Foreign Office and presently Director of the Centre for the Analysis of Conflict at the University of Kent, Canterbury, England. He would form a team of British and American scholars of problem-solving communication processes to assist representatives of the Falkland Governing Council and the government of Argentina in examining the issues and images between them, and seeking mutually agreeable proposals to present to their governments.

Secondly, Professor Roger Fisher and Dr. Bryant Wedge would undertake to formulate a single-text negotiating memorandum in close consultation with each of the concerned governments and the Office of the Secretary General of the United Nations; they would circulate the memorandum in sequential order among the parties with a process of refinement and elaboration of articles that would prove acceptable to all the parties.

Finally, the Project Coordinator would maintain close and continual contact with the international political processes and initiatives at the United Nations, seeking counsel and providing information on progress of the negotiating teams to the staff of the Secretary General and Security Council. This would be designed to maintain close linkage and reconciliation with the international political process.

*Implementation*: The first steps are to acquaint interested governments with the availability of the technical resource; if such a Commission is considered potentially valuable, these governments may introduce a resolution in the Security Council or other appropriate international bodies directing the Secretary General to establish the Commission with such consultative bodies as are deemed appropriate. It is assumed that the Political Affairs Office of the Secretariat would provide review and counsel to the Secretary General and to the Project Directors. Costs would be modest, in the neighborhood of $120,000, for a two to three week effort. These could be borne by private subscription as have the costs of organizing this team and proposal or direct compensation by Secretariat funding mechanisms.

*Comment*: This proposal was inspired by private United States citizens who are aware of the recent emergence of technical advances in mediation activity in tens of thousands of cases at many levels of social dispute; it is they who asked the Directors to formulate a technically elegant approach. As always, an early question is who would be the most effective and appropriate mediators? In the present dispute, it is considered that credible and impartial mediators could best be drawn from private and scholarly sectors of the United States and international society, mediators wholly free of any political commitment or dependency and able to deal directly with established officials of national and international government institutions. It is considered likely that all the parties would respond favorably toward such a mission and would find advantages in moving toward a comprehensive resolution that satisfies the basic interests of each.

# 14(ii) Conflict management: elements of generic theory and process

*Dennis J.D. Sandole*

We have chapters in this book on family and divorce mediation, community relations, environmental mediation, labor-management relations, hostage negotiation, international relations, and conflict and conflict management generally. Having thought about these, as well as Bryant Wedge's concluding chapter, it is my impression that there is a generic quality to conflict and conflict management in spite of the apparent differences between the various levels. I want to discuss some of these cross-level commonalities, particularly those that relate to movement along the scale presented by Wedge.

Biologists make use of a distinction that I also use in my work: the 'genotypic' versus 'phenotypic' levels. For my purposes, the phenotypic refers to observables, to 'symptoms' of underlying processes, while the genotypic refers to those underlying processes which may not be visible. Typically, it is the interaction between the genotypic and some aspect of environment that leads to phenotypic phenomena.

What most of us see or think of when we observe conflict situations are phenotypic phemonena: the claims and demands of the parties; their behavior (of an attack by one side on the other); the results of their behavior (casualties) and the level of their interaction (interpersonal, intergroup, interorganizational, international). It is also on the phenotypic plane where we observe differences among the specific manifestations of these abstract levels: family, community, environmental, labor–management, insurgent, and inter-state conflict and conflict management.

What most of us cannot see, and indeed, have some difficulty conceptualizing, are the underlying processes, the genotypic phenomena; and it is at the genotypic level that I believe cross-level commonalities exist. What might some of these be?

First, let me state a simple generic truth: fundamental to conflict and conflict management at all levels are perception and behavior. One of the major assumptions underlying perception and behavior, at least in the Western World, is what I call the 'assumption of cross cultural homogeneity'. This is the belief that, in spite of apparent cultural and other differences, most, if not all of us basically perceive things in much the same way—we live in the 'same world'.

If this assumption is true, then the methodology necessary for us to understand the perceptions and behavior of any actor is straightforward. We must attempt to achieve identification with the individual(s) concerned and then introspectively inquire 'What would I do?' or 'What would I have done if I were actor X in situation Y?' Consequently, we should have little, if any difficulty establishing empathy with any given actor.

Armed with the beliefs associated with the cross-cultural assumption (CCA) and using this methodology (explicitly or implicitly), many Americans, including President Reagan, and others elsewhere probably had little if any difficulty concluding that the Soviets knew what the Americans knew in September 1983, namely that the South Korean flight which had violated Soviet airspace was, 'in fact', an innocent civilian airliner which had lost its way; moreover, that by knowing this, and then shooting down KAL Flight 007, the Soviets were guilty of brutality and barbarism.

That many Americans, including President Reagan, and others could come to this conclusion does not mean that they were necessarily right (see Hersh, 1986), but it does mean that they all share certain beliefs which suggests that the CCA is alive and well.

This should not be too surprising. For about three hundred years, the beliefs of men and women, at least in the Western World, have been influenced by a dominant philosophical tradition associated with the French philosopher René Descartes—namely, the view that sensory experience is fixed and neutral, that we all live in the same world. In the language of Thomas Kuhn (1970), Descartes' ideas have had the status of a paradigm: a set of beliefs and values which has come to dominate, for a time, the perceptions and behavior of some group of people.

We can perhaps better visualize Descartes' view—the Cartesian view–by glancing at Figure 14.3. There we have what I call the 'four-worlds' model of the perceptual-behavioral process, comprised of internal and external elements. Following, and extending, the work of Karl Popper (1972), we can see that the external domain of the actor is comprised of two parts, the world of nature (Popper's World I) and the world of human-made things, processes and systems (Popper's World III). The natural world consists of all givens in nature, extraterrestrial as well as terrestrial—earth, water, air, fire, space, and so on. The human-made world is comprised of guns and butter, money and stock markets, Shakespeare in print and Shakespeare on stage, the invasions of the Soviet Union, Afghanistan, Lebanon, Grenada, and so on.

The internal domain of the actor is also comprised of two parts: the mental world (Popper's World II) and the biological/physiological world (my extension of Popper—World IV). The former consists of all the beliefs, values and expectations that the actor has learned and internalized over time as a consequence of his or her interactions with the external environment. The latter consists of the senses, neurons, brain, muscles, glands and so on of the organism which are involved in the processing of and reactions to stimuli.

Putting these pieces together, when something occurs in an actor's environment (natural or human-made), physical energy generated by the event (for example light, sound) may trigger one or more of the actor's senses. If that happens, then the energy will begin to be transformed—encoded—into information. In effect, the stimulus will begin to make its way up to the brain, from neuron to neuron, via electro-chemical processes. Once in the brain, the stimulus should arrive in that part which we have labelled the mental world where, against the background provided by the beliefs, values and expectations stored there, it either does or does not become identified as something. If the stimulus does not decode, it 'dies' in the system. It it does achieve identification, in effect, leads to a 'definition of the situation' (see Pruitt, 1965), it may do so in terms of either, or some combination of the following: (1) a bare sensation—the idea that something is out there, but the actor cannot quite put his or her finger on it; (2) recognition—the idea that a

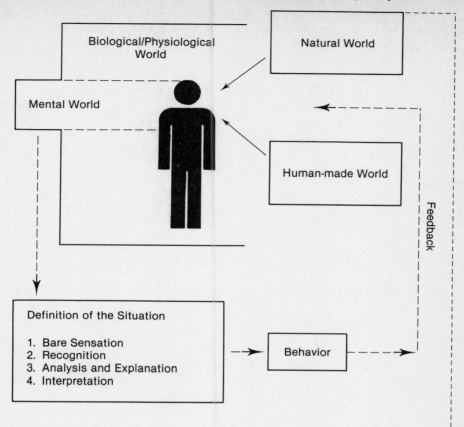

**Figure 14.3** A four-worlds' model of the perceptual-behavioural process

certain something is definitely there; (3) analysis and explanation—a 'cause' or a reason for that certain something being there and/or (4) interpretation—some idea of what that certain something means in terms of some larger scheme of things, coupled with an idea of how to respond to it.

According to the Cartesian view, although we may have different 'explanations' or 'interpretations' for things, we should nevertheless experience the same 'recognition' of them. If we do not, then some of us are either mentally disturbed, lying or otherwise misguided. From the point of view of President Reagan and many others, the Russians were plainly lying about KAL Flight 007. Additionally they were, and are misguided and something is probably wrong with them as well; there is after all, all that talk about Soviet 'paranoia'. But without getting into the specifics of Flight 007 and its destruction, how well does the CCA stand up to critical analysis?

There is a growing theoretical and research literature in many fields which supports what anthropologists have been trying to tell us for years, namely, that inference is involved at all stages of the perceptual process, that we can live in different worlds with regard to bare sensation and recognition long before we enter different worlds with regard to explanation and interpretation. As Kenneth Boulding (1956), Thomas Kuhn (1970), and others have argued, this applies not only to 'mere mortals' but also to the 'high priests of truth', those who make the strongest claim that they are the paragons of objectivity—scientists.

A major consequence of living in different worlds with regard to bare sensation and recognition is that we can talk past each other. If we hold incommensurate images of space, time, the physical or social universe, then we are clearly not thinking and communicating about the same things in the 'same way'. And for any one of us, 'those other people' are either lying, psychologically disturbed or otherwise misguided.

But there is something else here as well. Depending upon our thresholds for tolerance of differences, of ambiguity, of what Festinger (1962) calls 'cognitive dissonance', some of us may perceive those others as frustrating. They have, in effect, refused to accept our perceptions as valid. Depending upon the importance of the beliefs and values which underlie those perceptions, whether they have what Boulding (1962) calls 'inner-core' status—in which case they are not simply something we have but something we are—the frustration level may be rather high.

The frustration–aggression nexus, as conceptualized, for instance, by John Dollard and his associates (1939), suggests that within families, other groups, or society in general, frustration leads to increases in the incidence of various forms of aggressive behavior. This relationship may be even more intense between sovereign states in the Hobbesian international system, the world of the Machiavellian practitioners of power politics. There, the frustrations generated in part by incommensurate world views, by talking past each other, could lead not only to frequent and perhaps more intense displays of violent behavior but also, via the insidious mechanism of the negative self-fulfilling prophecy, to the development or perpetuation of violent conflict systems (see Sandole, 1984, 1986).

If we glance at Figure 14.4, we can get some idea of how the negative self-fulfilling prophecy might operate with regard to two actors. Let us assume that at a particular point in time, 'time-1' ($t_1$), something is occurring in either the natural or human-made environment of Actor 1—for example an increase in the frequency or intensity of violence in the international system. At 'time-2' ($t_2$), energy from this 'happening' triggers Actor 1's visual sensor, where the stimulus starts to become converted into information. By $t_3$, the information has passed through the central nervous system, arriving at the part of the brain where the mental world is located. At $t_4$, the stimulus has been 'recognized', and Actor 1 experiences a definition of the situation, a perception—for example violence in the system is on the increase. Actor 1 further defines this as a threat to its security. At $t_5$, Actor 1 behaves in accordance with the perception: it invests in a new military system for *defensive* reasons.

From the perspective of power politics, what Actor 1 has done makes sense. There is a problem here, however, which Actor 1 may not discern, part of which is that Actor 1 does not operate in a vacuum. Its behavior—its decision to invest in a new weapons system—feeds back into the human-made world at $t_6$ and by $t_7$ has

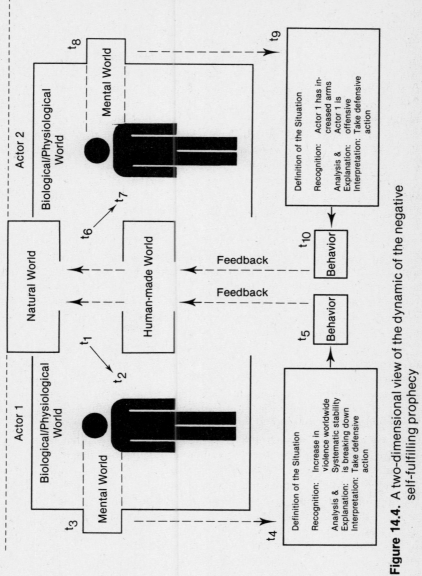

**Figure 14.4.** A two-dimensional view of the dynamic of the negative self-fulfilling prophecy

triggered Actor 2's visual sensor. By $t_9$, Actor 1's behavior has been defined by Actor 2 as an offensive move, to which Actor 2 must respond appropriately. Hence, by $t_{10}$, Actor 2 has also invested in a new weapons system, one which is intended to be a counter to Actor 1's system. Actor 2's behavior is subsequently perceived by Actor 1 as offensive, influenceing it to behave in yet another defensive manner which is subsequently perceived by Actor 2 as confirmation of its original definition of Actor 1 as offensive, and so on. Thus we go back and forth.

As I mentioned in my commentary on Adrian Fisher's chapter (Chapter 10), what is fascinating, if not deadly about the negative expression of the self-fulfilling prophecy is not merely the condition of misperception on the part of the actors at some point in time, but the process whereby those misperceptions generate behaviors which bring about the very realities which the actors perceived to exist in the first place. In other words, misperceptions lead to, and are eventually replaced by accurate perceptions. After a while, those whom we have been defining as aggressive, hostile, and so on—and toward whom we have been behaving accordingly—*are* 'out to get us'. What is even more interesting and fascinating about this is that few, if any actors, even realize the nature of what is taking place around them. All they seem to experience is progressive reinforcement of their expectations, a sense that they have been right all along about the 'enemy'.

Hence, without lying, or being mentally ill or otherwise misguided, the Soviets and Americans can point to real evidence concerning the hostile intentions of one another. They can do so without even being aware that they have played—and continue to play—a role, if not in the creation, then certainly in the maintenance and perpetuation of the hostile environment which concerns them both. The same applies to conflicts at other levels.

But what is the nature of the process by which actors are prevented from discerning the role they play in these insidious processes? Why is it that people in conflict situations, once they reach, in Bryant Wedge's scheme (Chapter 14 (i)), the 'confrontation' stage and beyond, tend to perceive themselves as merely 'reacting' to the provocations of others, as merely 'defending' themselves against the 'offensives' of others?

I have argued elsewhere (1984) that perceptual stability, that is, resistance to change, is comprised of cognitive, evaluative and affective dimensions. 'Cognitive blindness', for instance, is the condition of not perceiving something that is one's perceptual field—or of not perceiving it in a certain way—because the actor lacks the appropriate 'handle' (concept, hypothesis, model, theory) in terms of which he or she could grab a hold of the thing. 'Cognitive resistance' is prolonged 'blindness' or resistance on the part of the actor's belief/value system to detect the thing in his or her perceptual field. It is, in effect, resistance to undergo the conceptual changes necessary to detect the thing. The essential difference between cognitive blindness and cognitive resistance is that the former refers to the initial condition of nonperception which is due to the absence of appropriate conceptual 'lenses' through which efficient perception could be made, while the latter refers to persistence in retaining the old lenses in the continued presence of the novel phenomenon.

We tend to internalize those images that make 'sense' to us, that is, have worked for us in the past. Given the nature and pace of our phylogentic evolution (as contrasted with our cultural/technological evolution: see Rapoport, 1974), once we have internalized successful survival models, then something in us, perhaps our 'homeostatic', life-sustaining processes (see Cannon, 1939) is very reluctant to give them up. We are, in effect, very slow to detect, and then to respond to, changes in our environment. Hence, Bryant Wedge's (Chapter 14 (i)) reference to perceptual and behavioral lag.

Nevertheless, change is possible. As a consequence of remaining in an actor's perceptual field for a time, a novel stimulus may eventually begin to approach the status of a 'bare sensation'. As this begins to happen, however, something very interesting occurs, and it concerns cognitive dissonance. When we start to experience the bare sensation that something is not quite right, that something is 'out there' that we cannot quite put our fingers on, then we are, in effect, experiencing dissonance and it comes across as psychological discomfort, as anxiety. Festinger (1962) tells us that we respond to dissonance, to anxiety, in two possible ways: (1) we act to reduce the dissonance we are already experiencing and/or (2) we avoid new situations of dissonance. We can attempt to do either or both of these consciously or unconsciously. Attempting to do so unconsciously seems to be a contradiction: to attempt something surely we must be aware and therefore conscious of it. Again, 'we' is not a unidimensional term. There are many parts to 'we', unconscious as well as conscious, biological as well as psychological, and so on. It is the unconscious part of 'we', perhaps directed by the homeostatic properties of organisms, which can lead to a kind of resistance beyond the previously mentioned cognitive resistance.

When dissonance starts to be experienced through anxiety, this is an emotional signal that something important to the actor is under attack. For instance, the more intensively we relate to a certain value, that is, the more it has 'inner-core' status, then the more intense will be our sense of anxiety when that value is threatened. The more intense the anxiety associated with an assault to a cherished value, the more likely it is that something in the body, perhaps associated with homeostasis, will come to the defense of that value. Value defense in this sense takes place through the *defense mechanisms* (for example rationalization, displacement, dissociation, projection, reaction-formation) which disguise or deny the threat to the value. The 'purpose' of these mechanisms is not so much to prevent change, though that is their consequence, at least for a while, but to protect the actor from the anxiety that would normally flow once certain values come under attack. Often, however, these mechanisms linger in their operation, and during their duration, we do not 'see' what it is that is assaulting our most fundamental values (see Hilgard, *el al.*, 1971, pp. 454–62).

Thus, in addition to cognitive blindness and cognitive resistance, both of which operate at the unconscious level but are concerned with cognitive structures, there may be unconscious resistance involving values and affect—what I call 'evaluative-affective resistance I' (EAR I).

Resistance, however, does not necessarily end with the defense mechanisms. If they are overwhelmed by an assault to particular values, then what was previously an unconscious form of value defense becomes a conscious form: 'evaluative-affective resistance II' (EAR II). When value defense in this sense occurs, then the more important the value to the actor, the more likely it is that it will be defended passionately, aggressively, perhaps violently. 'Role defense' (Burton, 1979) and 'narcissistic rage' (Wedge, 1986) are relevant here.

Accordingly, Americans and Soviets, and parties to other conflicts, may not see the full complexity of the linkages between their own behaviors and the hostile environments against which they are constantly defending themselves, because of (1) cognitive blindness, (2) cognitive resistance, and (3) EAR I. There seems to be a natural progression from (1) to (2) to (3) which may correspond to the progression from 'no conflict' to 'confrontation' in Bryant Wedge's scheme (Chapter 14 (i)). Once actors move from (3) to (4), from EAR I to EAR II, then, because they are preoccupied with conscious, often violent defense of their respective positions and corresponding values, they will probably never see the full connection between their behavior and their hostile environments. In such cases, conflict systems may terminate because of suicide, homicide or genocide or, through 'positive feedback', by collapsing under their own weight. Alternatively, they may stabilize over time in terms of some range of intensity–fluctuation, that is, they may become 'protracted' (see Azar and Burton, 1986).

I have discussed here only a small portion of what might be considered generic about conflict and conflict management. A more comprehensive treatment must await a later time. In the meantime (see Burton and Sandole, 1986, 1987; Avruch and Black, 1987), I conclude by mentioning briefly one additional generic aspect, something which is implicit in this chapter, and in some of the others as well: the intrapsychic effects of and contributions to conflict at other levels. Once individuals in conflict—whether at the interpersonal, intergroup, interorganizational, international or any other level—start to express themselves through the conscious defenses (through 'violence' and 'escalation' in Wedge's scheme), they may become brutalized, unable to view their 'enemies' as anything but despicable subhumans. Under such circumstances, which can lead to an extension of the conflict beyond the lives of its original participants, potential third parties who wish to intervene effectively must be able to operate at the intrapsychic as well as interparty levels. Unless the first is dealt with adequately, the second may only worsen. This is a challenge for all concerned.

## Bibliography

Avruch, K. and P.W. Black (1987), 'A Generic Theory of Conflict Resolution: A Critique', *Negotiation Journal*, 3, no. 1, pp. 87–96.

Azar, E.E. and J.W. Burton (eds) (1986), *International Conflict Resolution: Theory and Practice*, Brighton, Wheatsheaf and Boulder, Lynne Rienner.

Boulding, K.E. (1956), *The Image: Knowledge in Life and Society*, Ann Arbor, University of Michigan Press.

Boulding, K.E. (1962), *Conflict and Defense: A General Theory*, New York and London, Harper & Row.

Burton, J.W. (1979), *Deviance, Terrorism and War: The Process of Solving Unsolved Social and Political Problems*, Oxford, Martin Robertson and New York, St. Martin's Press.

Burton, J.W. and D.J.D. Sandole (1986), 'Generic Theory: The Basis of Conflict Resolution', *Negotiation Journal*, **2**, no. 4, pp. 333–44.

Burton, J.W. and D.J.D. Sandole (1987), 'Expanding the Debate on Generic Theory of Conflict Resolution: A Response to a Critique', *Negotiation Journal*, **3**, no. 1, pp. 97–9.

Cannon, W.B. (1939), *The Wisdom of the Body*, rev. ed. New York, Norton.

Dollard, J., L.W. Doob, N.E. Miller, O.H. Mowrer and R.R. Sears (1939), *Frustration and Aggression*, New Haven and London, Yale University Press.

Festinger, L. (1962), *A Theory of Cognitive Dissonance*, Stanford, Stanford University Press.

Hersh, S.M. (1986), *'The Target is Destroyed': What Really Happened to Flight 007 and What America Knew About It*, New York, Random House.

Hilgard, E.R., R.C. Atkinson and R.L. Atkinson (1971), *Introduction to Psychology*, 5th ed, New York, Harcourt Brace Jovanovich.

Kuhn, T.S. (1970), *The Structure of Scientific Revolutions*, 2d. ed, Chicago and London, University of Chicago Press.

Popper, K.R. (1972), *Objective Knowledge: An Evolutionary Approach*, Oxford and New York, Oxford University Press.

Pruitt, D. (1965), 'Definition of the Situation as a Determinant of International Action' in *International Behavior: A Social Psychological Analysis*, H.C. Kelman (ed), New York, Holt, Rinehart & Winston.

Rapoport, A. (1974), *Conflict in Man-Made Environment*, Harmondsworth and New York, Penguin Books.

Sandole, D.J.D. (1984), 'The Subjectivity of Theories and Actions in World Society' in *Conflict in World Society: A New Perspective on International Relations*, M. Banks (ed), Brighton, Wheatsheaf and New York, St. Martin's Press.

Sandole, D.J.D. (1986), 'Traditional Approaches to Conflict Management: Short-Term Gains vs. Long-term Costs'. *Current Research on Peace and Violence* (Special issue on Conflict and Conflict Resolution, ed. J. Käkönen), **9**, no. 3, pp. 119–24.

Wedge, B. (1986), 'Psychology of the Self in Social Conflict' in Azar and Burton, op. cit.

# Bibliographic Epilogue: For Further Reading and Beyond

*Dennis J.D. Sandole*

In my introductory chapter, I suggested that conflict and peace studies (CAPS), of which conflict management is an integral part, is 'a field whose definition is being stretched to include social movement as well as "metadiscipline" and profession'. Bryant Wedge (Introduction and Chapter 14(i)) has talked about 'the science-based profession of conflict management' which is 'a genuine disciplinary field' as well as 'a new professional field'. James Laue (Chapter 1) has said that 'the field of conflict intervention is not yet a fully developed social science or a discipline or a profession . . . but an embryonic field worthy of further study and systematization'.

As Laue's reference to part of the 'Report of the Commission on Proposals for the National Academy of Peace and Conflict Resolution' makes clear, there are criteria to determine whether or not a field, or a discipline, or a profession exists:

the Commission has established that peace studies is a distinct and definable field of learning for three reasons: it has a literature, courses of study, and professional organizations; it has some well-defined assumptions and definitions, and a variety of research methodologies; and it has a strong applied component in the practice of conflict intervention.

Kenneth Boulding (1978, p. 343) also talks about criteria, arguing that 'conflict and peace studies can certainly claim to be a discipline', because it has a subject-matter for teaching and examinations, a bibliography and specialized journals.

Whatever one's views on the exact disciplinary or professional status of CAPS, or any of its subfields, the various indicators of status do exist to some extent. Moreover, the present volume does contribute to one of them: the literature. In addition, many of the contributions to the volume make references to the literature, especially on family, environmental, international, and generic conflict and conflict management. These, however, constitute only a fragment of the total relevant bibliographic domain. Accordingly, I have assembled the following supplementary bibliography, covering many, if not all of the aspects and levels of conflict management, plus other subfields of CAPS (conflict analysis, peace research and peace education) touched upon in this volume. For purposes of manageability, it consists only of some of the books, monographs and articles published during the 1980s, with four exceptions (Boulding, E., *et al.*, 1979; Boulding, K., 1978; Smith, 1971; and Zawodny, 1966). Although not an exhaustive listing it does provide additional opportunities and directions for further reading, thinking, research, practice, and teaching.

## Supplementary bibliography in conflict and peace studies

Alker Jr, H.R. and M.I. Midlarsky (1985), 'International Disputes Data: A Comparison of Approaches and Products', *International Studies Notes*, **12**, no. 1, pp. 1–9.

Anderton, C.H. (1985), 'A Selected Bibliography of Arms Race Models and Related Subjects', *Conflict Management and Peace Science*, **8**, no. 2, pp. 99–122.

Ashley, R.K., P.L. Lauderdale, P. McGowan and S. Walker (eds) (1985), *International Studies Quarterly* (Symposium: Methodological Foundations of the Study of International Conflict), **29**, no. 2.

Axelrod, R. (1984), *The Evolution of Cooperation*, New York, Basic Books.

Baur, E.J. (1983), 'College Curricula in Conflict Regulation, The Emergence of a Discipline', *Peace and Change*, **IX**, no. 1, pp. 81–92.

Bendahmane, D.B. and J.W. McDonald Jr. (eds), (1984), *International Negotiation: Art and Science*, Washington, DC, Center for the Study of Foreign Affairs, Foreign Service Institute, US Department of State.

Bendahmane, D.B. and J.W. McDonald Jr. (eds), (1986), *Perspectives on Negotiation: Four Case Studies and Interpretation*, Washington, DC, Center for the Study of Foreign Affairs, Foreign Service Institute, US Department of State.

Bialer, S. (1985), 'The Psychology of US–Soviet Relations', *Political Psychology*, **6**, no. 2, pp. 263–73.

Bidol, P., L. Bardwell and N. Manring (eds) (1986), *Alternative Environmental Conflict Management Approaches: A Citizen's Manual*, Ann Arbor, Environmental Conflict Project, School of Natural Resources, University of Michigan.

Bolz, F.A. (1983), 'The Hostage Situation: Law Enforcement Options', in *Terrorism: Interdisciplinary Perspectives*, B. Eichelman, D.A. Soskis, and W.H. Reid (eds), Washington, DC, American Psychiatric Association.

Brock-Utne, B. (1985), *Educating for Peace: A Feminist Perspective*, Oxford and Elmsford, New York, Pergamon Press.

Brookmire, D.A. and F. Sistrunk (1980), 'The Effects of Perceived Ability and Impartiality of Mediators and Time Pressure on Negotiation', *Journal of Conflict Resolution*, **24**, no. 2, pp. 311–27.

Boulding, E., J.R. Passmore and R.S. Gassler (1979), *Bibliography on World Conflict and Peace*, 2d ed., Boulder, Westview Press.

Boulding, K.E. (1978), 'Future Directions in Conflict and Peace Studies', *Journal of Conflict Resolution*, **XXII**, no. 2, pp. 342–54.

Buntz, C.G., J. Hartley and H. Liberato (1981), *Conflict Management: A Working Bibliography*, Stockton, California, Center for Research and Development, School of Business and Public Administration, University of the Pacific.

Burton, J.W. (1987), *Resolving Deep-Rooted Conflict: A Handbook*, Lanham, Maryland, University Press of America.

Carbonneau, T.E. (1984), *Resolving Transnational Disputes Through International Arbitration*, Charlottesville, University Press of Virginia.

Carroll, B.A., C.F. Fink and J.E. Mohvaz (1983), *Peace and War: A Guide to Bibliographies*, Santa Barbara and Oxford, ABC-Clio.

Colosi, T.R. and A.E. Berkeley (1986), *Collective Bargaining: How It Works and Why*, New York, American Arbitration Association.

Compa, L. (1986), 'To Cure Labor's Ills: Bigger Unions, Fewer of Them', *Washington Post*, 16 November, pp. K1-K2.

Coulson, R. (1986), *Arbitration in the Schools*, New York, American Arbitration Association.

Deutsch, M. (1983), 'The Prevention of World War III: A Psychological Perspective', *Political Psychology*, **4**, no. 1, pp. 3–31.

Drake, W.R. and T.A. Fee (1985), 'Court-Ordered Arbitration: A Report on the First National Conference', *Dispute Resolution Forum*, August, Washington, DC, National Institute for Dispute Resolution.

Dugan, M.A. (ed.) (1982), *Peace and Change* (Special Issue on Conflict Resolution), **VIII**, no. 2–3.

Dunlop, J.T. (1984), *Dispute Resolution: Negotiation and Consensus Building*, Dover, Massachusetts, Auburn House.

Duvall, R.D., P.T. Hopmann, B.L. Job and R.T. Kudrle (eds) (1983), *International Studies Quarterly* (Special Issue on the Economic Foundations of War), **27**, no. 4.

Elkouri, F. and E.A. Elkouri (1985), *How Arbitration Works*, 4th ed., Washington, DC, Bureau of National Affairs.

Evarts, W.R., J.L. Greenstone, G.J. Kirkpatrick and S.C. Leviton (1983), *Winning Through Accommodation: The Mediator's Handbook*, Dubuque, Kendall/Hunt.

Ferencz, B.B. (1985), *A Common Sense Guide to World Peace*, New York and London, Oceana.

Finn, M.E. (ed.) (1984), *Peace and Change* (Special Issue on Peace Education for the Nuclear Age) **X**, no. 2.

Fischer, D.D. (1982), 'Decisions to Use the International Court of Justice: Four Recent Cases', *International Studies Quarterly*, **26**, no. 2, pp. 251–77.

Fisher, G. (1980), *International Negotiation: A Cross-Cultural Perspective*, Chicago, Intercultural Press.

Fisher, R. and S. Brown (1985), 'Building a US–Soviet Working Relationship', *Negotiation Journal*, **1**, no. 4, pp. 307–15.

Fisher, R.J. (1983), 'Third Party Consultation as a Method of Intergroup Conflict Resolution: A Review of Studies', *Journal of Conflict Resolution*, **27**, no. 2, pp. 301–34.

Fogg, R.W. (1985), 'Dealing with Conflict: A Repertoire of Creative, Peaceful Approaches', *Journal of Conflict Resolution*, **29**, no. 2, pp. 330–58.

Folger, J.P. and M.S. Poole (1984), *Working Through Conflict: A Communication Perspective*, Glenview, Scott, Foresman.

Folger, J.P. and J.J. Shubert (1986), 'Resolving Student-Initiated Grievances in Higher Education: Dispute Resolution Procedures in a Non-Adversarial Setting', *NIDR Report No. 3*, Washington, DC, National Institute for Dispute Resolution.

Forsberg, R., *et al.* (1985), *The Peace Resource Book 1986: A Comprehensive*

*Guide to Issues, Groups, and Literature*, Cambridge, Massachusetts, Ballinger.

Fraser, N.M. and K.W. Hipel (1984), *Conflict Analysis: Models and Resolutions*, Amsterdam and New York, North-Holland.

Frei, D. (1986), *Perceived Images: US and Soviet Assumptions and Perceptions in Disarmament*, Totowa, New Jersey, Rowman and Littlefield.

Friedland, N. (1986), 'Hostage Negotiations: Types, Processes, Outcomes', *Negotiation Journal*, 2, no. 1, pp. 57–72.

Fuselier, G.D. (1981), 'A Practical Overview of Hostage Negotiations', *FBI Law Enforcement Bulletin*, June–July.

Galtung, J. (1985), 'Twenty-five Years of Peace Research: Ten Challenges and Some Responses', *Journal of Peace Research*, 22, no. 2, pp. 141–58.

Gantzel, K.J. and P. Wallensteen (eds) (1981), *Journal of Peace Research* (Special Issue on Causes of War), XVIII, no. 1.

Goldberg, S.B., E.D. Green and F.E.A. Sander (eds) (1985), *Dispute Resolution*, Boston, Little, Brown.

Hall, L. (1986), 'Preliminary Thoughts on Graduate Programs in Dispute Resolution', *Negotiation Journal*, 2, no. 2, pp. 207–11.

Hassel, C.V. (1983), 'Preparing Law Enforcement Personnel for Terrorist Incidents' in *Terrorism: Interdisciplinary Perspectives*, B. Eichelman, D.A. Soskis, and W.H. Reid (eds), Washington, DC, American Psychiatric Association.

Heckscher, C. (1986), 'Multilateral Negotiation and the Future of American Labor', *Negotiation Journal*, 2, no. 2, pp. 141–54.

Herrman, M.S. and E.S. Weeks Jr. (1984), *Final Report of the National Conference on Peacemaking and Conflict Resolution, March 4–6, 1983*, Athens, Georgia Center for Continuing Education, The University of Georgia.

Herrman, M.S. with K.K. Covi (1986), *Final Report of the National Conference on Peacemaking and Conflict Resolution, September 18–23, 1984 (University) of Missouri-St. Louis)*, Athens, Carl Vinson Institute of Government, The University of Georgia.

Hill, B.J. (1982), 'An Analysis of Conflict Resolution Techniques: From Problem-Solving Workshops to Theory', *Journal of Conflict Resolution*, 26, no. 1, pp. 109–38.

Himes, J.S. (1980), *Conflict and Conflict Management*, Athens, The University of Georgia Press.

Høivik, T. (1983), 'Peace Research and Science: A Discussion Paper', *Journal of Peace Research*, 20, no. 3, pp. 261–70.

Honeyman, C. (1986), 'Bias and Mediators' Ethics', *Negotiation Journal*, 2, no. 2, pp. 175–7.

Houweling, H.W. and J.G. Siccama (1985), 'The Epidemiology of War, 1816–1980', *Journal of Conflict Resolution*, 29, no. 4, pp. 641–63.

Huelsberg, N.A. and W.F. Lincoln (eds) (1985), *Successful Negotiating in Local Government*, Washington, DC, International City Management Association.

Intriligator, M.D. (1982), 'Research on Conflict Theory: Analytic Approaches and Areas of Application', *Journal of Conflict Resolution*, 26, no. 2, pp. 307–27.

Isard, W. and C. Smith (1982), *Conflict Analysis and Practical Conflict Manage-*

*ment Procedures: An Introduction to Peace Science*, Cambridge, Massachusetts, Ballinger.

Isard, W. and Y. Nagao (eds) (1983), *International and Regional Conflict: Analytic Approaches*, Cambridge, Massachusetts, Ballinger.

Johansen, R.C. (1983), 'How to START Ending the Arms Race', *World Policy Journal*, **1**, no. 1, pp. 77–100.

Johnson B., R. Jones and J.A. Corbin (1984), *Dispute Resolution Directory*, Washington, DC, National Institute for Dispute Resolution.

Jones, R.M. (ed.) (1986), 'Regulatory Negotiation', *Dispute Resolution Forum*, January. Washington, DC, National Institute for Dispute Resolution.

Jones, R.M. (ed.), (1986), 'Dispute Resolution in Higher Education', *Dispute Resolution Forum*, April. Washington, DC, National Institute for Dispute Resolution.

Käkönen, J. (ed.) (1986), *Current Research on Peace and Violence* (Special Issue on Conflict and Conflict Resolution), **IX**, no. 3.

Katz, N.H. and J.W. Lawyer (1985), *Communication and Conflict Resolution Skills*, Dubuque, Kendall/Hunt.

Keating, Jr. J.M. (1985), 'Public Ends and Private Means: Accountability Among Private Providers of Public Social Services', *NIDR Report No. 2*, Washington, DC, National Institute for Dispute Resolution.

Kelman, H.C. (1981), 'Reflections on the History and Status of Peace Research', *Conflict Management and Peace Science*, **5**, no. 2, pp. 95–110.

Kelman, H.C. (1985), 'Overcoming the Psychological Barrier: An Analysis of the Egyptian-Israeli Peace Process', *Negotiation Journal*, **1**, no. 3, pp. 213–34.

Kemp, A. (1985), 'Image of the Peace Field: An International Survey', *Journal of Peace Research*, **22**, no. 2, pp. 129–40.

Kidder, R.M. (1986), 'Unmasking Terrorism' (Five parts), *The Christian Science Monitor*, 13–16 and 21 May.

Kilpatrick, A.O., *et al.* (1983), *Resolving Community Conflict: An Annotated Bibliography*, Athens, Institute of Community and Area Development, The University of Georgia.

Kohn, A. (1986), *No Contest: The Case Against Competition*, Boston, Houghton Mifflin.

Kressel, K. and Pruitt, D.G. (eds) (1985), *Journal of Social Issues* (Special Issue on the Mediation of Social Conflict), **41**, no. 2.

Krippendorff, E. and H. Wiberg (eds) (1981), *Journal of Peace Research* (Special Issue on Theories of Peace), **XVIII**, no. 2.

Lake, R.W. (ed.) (1986), *Resolving Locational Conflict*, New Brunswick, Transaction Books.

Laszlo, E. and J.Y. Yoo (eds) (1986), *World Encyclopedia of Peace*, vols 1–4, Oxford and Elmsford, Pergamon Press.

Lemmon, J.A. (ed.) (1983), 'Dimensions and Practice of Divorce Mediation', *Mediation Quarterly*, **1**.

Leng, R.J. (1983), 'When Will They Ever Learn? Coercive Bargaining in Recurrent Crises', *Journal of Conflict Resolution*, **27**, no. 3, pp. 379–419.

Levy, J.S. (1982), 'Historical Trends in Great Power War, 1495–1975'. *International Studies Quarterly*, **26**, no. 2, pp. 278–300.

Lewicki, R.J. (1986), 'Challenges of Teaching Negotiation', *Negotiation Journal*, **2**, no. 1, pp. 15–27.

Lewicki, R.J. and J. Litterer (1985), *Negotiation: Readings, Exercises and Cases*, Homewood, Illinois, Richard D. Irwin.

Lichbach, M.I. and T.R. Gurr (1981), 'The Conflict Process: A Formal Model', *Journal of Conflict Resolution*, **25**, no. 1, pp. 3–29.

Lopez, G.A. (1985), 'A University Peace Studies Curriculum for the 1990s', *Journal of Peace Research*, **22**, no. 2, pp. 117–28.

Lukov, V. (1985), 'International Negotiations of the 1980s: Features, Problems and Prospects', *Negotiation Journal*, **1**, no. 2, pp. 139–48.

McCarthy, J. with I. Ladimer (1981), *Resolving Faculty Disputes*, New York, American Arbitration Association.

McCarthy, J., I. Ladimer and J.P. Sirefman (1984), *Managing Faculty Disputes: A Guide to Issues, Procedures, and Practices*, San Francisco and London, Jossey-Bass.

McCarthy, J. with A. Shorett (1984), *Negotiating Settlements: A Guide to Environmental Mediation*, New York, American Arbitration Association.

McDonald Jr, J.W., (1984), *How To Be A Delegate*, Washington, DC, Center for the Study of Foreign Affairs, Foreign Service Institute, US Department of State.

Maas, J.P. and R.A.C. Stewart (eds) (1986), *Toward a World of Peace: People Create Alternatives*, Proceedings of the First International Conference on Conflict Resolution and Peace Studies, Suva, Fiji, University of the South Pacific.

Mack, A. (ed.) (1986), *Peace Research in the 1980s*, Oxford and Elmsford, Pergamon Press.

Marquand, R. (1986), 'Teaching for Peace', *The Christian Science Monitor*, 31 January, pp. B1–B12.

Marshall, T.F. and M.E. Walpole (1985), 'Bringing People Together: Mediation and Reparation Projects in Great Britain', *Research and Planning Unit Paper No. 33*, London, Home Office.

Meschievitz, C.S. (1986), *Annotated List of Teaching Materials*, Madison, Dispute Resolution Clearinghouse, Institute for Legal Studies, University of Wisconsin Law School.

Mirabella, R.W. and J. Trudeau (1982), 'Managing Hostage Negotiations', *Police Chief*, **45**, no. 5, pp. 45–7.

Mitchell, C.R. (1980), 'Evaluating Conflict', *Journal of Peace Research*, **XVII**, no. 1, pp. 61–75.

Mitchell, C.R. (1985), 'Conflict, War and Conflict Management' in *International Relations: A Handbook of Current Theory*, M. Light and A.J.R. Groom (eds), London, Frances Pinter and Boulder, Lynne Rienner.

Mitchell, C.R. and K. Webb (eds) (1988), *New Approaches to International Mediation*, Westport, Greenwood Press.

Modelski, G. and P.M. Morgan (1985), 'Understanding Global War', *Journal of Conflict Resolution*, **29**, no. 3, pp. 391–417.

Moore, C.W. (1986), *The Mediation Process: Practical Strategies for Resolving Conflict*, San Francisco and London, Jossey-Bass.

Most, B.A. and H. Starr (1983), 'Conceptualizing "War": Consequences for Theory and Research', *Journal of Conflict Resolution*, 27, no. 1, pp. 137–59.

Muncaster, R.G. and D.A. Zinnes (1982–3), 'A Model of Inter-Nation Hostility Dynamics and War', *Conflict Management and Peace Science*, 6, no. 2, pp. 19–37.

Murray, J.S. (1986), 'Understanding Competing Theories of Negotiation', *Negotiation Journal*, 2, no. 2, pp. 179–86.

Neale, M.A. and M.H. Bazerman (1985), 'Perspectives for Understanding Negotiation: Viewing Negotiation as a Judgmental Process', *Journal of Conflict Resolution*, 29, no. 1, pp. 33–55.

Newcombe, H. (1984), 'Survey of Peace Research', *Peace Research Reviews*, IX, no. 6.

Parker, P. (1983), 'The Role of the Advisory, Conciliation and Arbitration Service (ACAS) in British Labor Relations', *Occasional Paper No. 83-3*, Washington, DC, Society of Professionals in Dispute Resolution.

Patton, B.M. (1985), 'On Teaching Negotiation', *Working Paper No. 85-3*, Cambridge, Program on Negotiation, Harvard Law School.

Pearson, J. and N. Thoennes (1985), 'Mediation Versus the Courts in Child Custody Cases', *Negotiation Journal*, 1, no. 3, pp. 235–44.

Pillar, P.R. (1983), *Negotiating Peace: War Termination as a Bargaining Process*, Princeton, Princeton University Press.

Pompa, G.G. (1985), 'Public Agencies' Roles and Capabilities—Community Relations Service and State and Local Agencies', in *The Elements of Good Practice in Dispute Resolution*, Proceedings of the 12th Annual Conference of the Society of Professionals in Dispute Resolution (SPIDR), C. Catrona (ed.), Washington, DC, SPIDR.

Pruitt, D.G. and J.Z. Rubin (1986), *Social Conflict: Escalation, Stalemate, and Settlement*, New York, Random House.

Raiffa, H. (1982), *The Art and Science of Negotiation*, Cambridge and London, Harvard University Press.

Reardon, B.A. (1985), *Sexism and the War System*, New York, World Policy Institute.

Reich, R.B. (1985), 'Toward a New Public Philosophy', *The Atlantic Monthly*, May, pp. 68–79.

Rikhye, I.J. (1984), *The Theory and Practice of Peacekeeping*, New York, St. Martin's Press.

Ross, M.H. (1985), 'Internal and External Conflict and Violence: Cross-Cultural Evidence and a New Analysis', *Journal of Conflict Resolution*, 29, no. 4, pp. 547–79.

Rubin, J.Z. (1985), 'Third Party Intervention in Family Conflict', *Negotiation Journal*, 1, no. 3, pp. 269–81.

Sandole, D.J.D. (1985), 'Training and Teaching in a Field Whose "Time Has Come": A Postgraduate Program in Conflict Management' in *The Elements of Good Practice in Dispute Resolution*, Proceedings of the 12th Annual Conference of the Society of Professionals in Dispute Resolution (SPIDR), C. Cutrona (ed.) Washington, DC, SPIDR.

Sandole, D.J.D. (1988), 'Simulation as a Basis for Consciousness Raising: Some

Encouraging Signs for Conflict Resolution' in *Communication and Simulation: From Two Fields to One Theme*, D. Crookall and D. Saunders (eds), Clevedon, Avon, Multilingual Matters.

Shea, G.P. (1980), 'The Study of Bargaining and Conflict Behavior: Broadening the Conceptual Arena', *Journal of Conflict Resolution*, **24**, no. 4, pp. 706–41.

Simowitz, R.L. and B.L. Price (1986), 'Progress in the Study of International Conflict: A Methodological Critique', *Journal of Peace Research*, **23**, no. 1, pp. 29–40.

Singer, J.D. (1982), 'Confrontational Behavior and Escalation to War, 1816–1980: A Research Plan', *Journal of Peace Research*, **XIX**, no. 1, pp. 37–38.

Singer, J.D. (1985), 'The Responsibilities of Competence in the Global Village', *International Studies Quarterly*, **29**, no. 3, pp. 245–62.

Singer, L.R. and E. Nace (1985), 'Mediation in Special Education', *NIDR Report No. 1*, Washington, DC, National Institute for Dispute Resolution.

Singer, L.R. and R.A. Schechter (1986), 'Mediating Civil Rights: The Age Discrimination Act', *NIDR Report No. 4*, Washington, DC, National Institute for Dispute Resolution.

Small, M. and J.D. Singer (eds) (1985), *International War: An Anthology*, Chicago, The Dorsey Press.

Smith, C.G. (ed.) (1971), *Conflict Resolution: Contributions of the Behavioral Sciences*, Notre Dame, University of Notre Dame Press.

Sobakin, V. and R. Fisher (1985), 'Ground Rules for *Entente*: Respectful Attitudes Can Improve Soviet–US Relations', *Negotiation Journal*, **1**, no. 3, pp. 211–12.

Sørensen, B. (1985), 'Security Implications of Alternative Defense Options for Western Europe', *Journal of Peace Research*, **22**, no. 3, pp. 197–209.

Soskis, D.A. (1983), 'Behavioral Scientists and Law Enforcement Personnel: Working Together on the Problem of Terrorism', *Behavioral Sciences and the Law*, **1**, no. 2, pp. 47–58.

Steinberg, G.M. (1985), 'The Role of Process in Arms Control Negotiations', *Journal of Peace Research*, **22**, no. 3, pp. 261–72.

Stephenson, C. (ed.) (1981), *Peace and Change* (Special Issue on Alternative International Security Systems), **VII**, no. 4.

Stoll, R.J. and W. McAndrew (1986), 'Negotiating Strategic Arms Control, 1969–1979', *Journal of Conflict Resolution*, **30**, no. 2, pp. 315–26.

Sullivan, T.J. (1984), *Resolving Development Disputes Through Negotiations*, New York and London, Plenum Press.

Susskind, L.E. (1986), 'Evaluating Dispute Resolution Experiments', *Negotiation Journal*, **2**, no. 2, pp. 135–9.

Thompson, W.R. (1982), 'Phases of the Business Cycle and the Outbreak of War', *International Studies Quarterly*, **26**, no. 2, pp. 301–11.

Tracy, L. and R.B. Peterson (1986), 'A Behavioral Theory of Labor Negotiations—How Well Has It Aged?' *Negotiation Journal*, **2**, no. 1, pp. 93–108.

United Nations Educational, Scientific and Cultural Organization (1986), *UNESCO Yearbook on Peace and Conflict Studies*, Westport, Greenwood Press.

Ury, W.L. (1985), *Beyond the Hotline: How Crisis Control Can Prevent Nuclear*

*War*, Boston, Houghton Mifflin (Penguin Books, 1986).

van den Dungen, P. (1985), 'Peace Research and the Search for Peace: Some Critical Observations', *International Journal on World Peace*, **II**, no. 3, pp. 35–52.

van der Wulp, P. (ed.) (1986), *Coming to Terms with Conflict: Third Party Intervention and Aspects of Culture*, Amsterdam, Royal Tropical Institute.

Väyrynen, R. (1985), 'Is There a Role for the United Nations in Conflict Resolution?' *Journal of Peace Research*, **22**, no. 3, pp. 189–96.

Volkan, V.D. (1985), 'The Need to Have Enemies and Allies: A Developmental Approach', *Political Psychology*, **6**, no. 2, pp. 219–47.

Ward, M.D. (1982), 'Cooperation and Conflict in Foreign Policy Behavior: Reaction and Memory', *International Studies Quarterly*, **26**, no. 1, pp. 87–126.

Ward, M.D. and U. Luterbacher (eds) (1985), *Dynamic Models of International Conflict*, London, Frances Pinter and Boulder, Lynne Rienner.

Weede, E. (1981), 'Preventing War by Nuclear Deterrence or by Detente', *Conflict Management and Peace Science*, **6**, no. 1, pp. 1–18.

Weihmiller, G.R. and D. Doder (1986), *US–Soviet Summits: An Account of East–West Diplomacy at the Top, 1955–1985*, Lanham, Maryland, University Press of America.

Weingarten, H.R. and E. Douvan (1985), 'Male and Female Visions of Mediation', *Negotiation Journal*, **1**, no. 4, pp. 349–58.

Weiss-Wik, S. (1983), 'Enhancing Negotiators' Successfulness: Self-Help Books and Related Empirical Research', *Journal of Conflict Resolution*, **27**, no. 4, pp. 706–39.

Wesselius, C.L. and J.V. DeSarno (1983), 'The Anatomy of a Hostage Situation', *Behavioral Sciences and the Law*, **1**, no. 2, pp. 33–45.

White, R.K. (1983), 'Empathizing with the Rulers of the USSR', *Political Psychology*, **4**, no. 1, pp. 121–37.

Wien, B.J. (ed.), (1984), *Peace and World Order Studies: A Curriculum Guide*, 4th ed. New York, World Policy Institute.

Work, L. (ed.) (1984), 'Family and Divorce Mediation', *Dispute Resolution Forum*, December. Washington, DC, National Institute for Dispute Resolution.

Zartman, I.W. (1985), *Ripe for Resolution: Conflict and Intervention in Africa*, Oxford and New York, Oxford University Press.

Zartman, I.W. and M.R. Berman (1982), *The Practical Negotiator*, New Haven and London, Yale University Press.

Zawodny, J.K. (ed.) (1966), *Man and International Relations*, vol. I: *Conflict* and vol. II: *Integration*, San Francisco, Chandler.

## Notes on Contributors

*Michael Banks* is Lecturer in International Relations at the London School of Economics.

*Charles Bethel* is an attorney and Director of Accord Associates, a firm specializing in dispute resolution services.

*Kenneth E. Boulding* is Professor Emeritus, University of Colorado and was Distinguished Visiting Professor at George Mason University in Fall, 1985.

*John W. Burton* is Distinguished Visiting Professor of Conflict Management and International Relations at George Mason University.

*Robert P. Clark* is Professor of Government and Politics at George Mason University.

*Thomas R. Colosi* is Vice President of the Office of National Affairs, American Arbitration Association.

*Harold E. Davis* is a Commissioner and mediator with the Federal Mediation and Conciliation Service (FMCS).

*Jonathan Dean*, currently Arms Control Advisor to the Union of Concerned Scientists, was United States Ambassador to the Mutual and Balanced Force Reduction (MBFR) Talks in Vienna.

*Morton Deutsch* is Edward Lee Thorndike Professor of Psychology and Education at Teachers College, Columbia University.

*A. Bruce Dotson* is Associate Professor and Assistant Director, Institute for Environmental Negotiation at the Unversity of Virginia.

*Daniel Druckman* is Principal Study Director of the National Research Council, National Academy of Sciences and Adjunct Professor of Conflict Management at George Mason University.

*Maire A. Dugan*, formerly an Assistant Professor at Kent State University's Center for Peaceful Change, is Vice President of Agreements That Work, Inc., a firm engaged in mediation, training and consulting in all conflict areas.

*Adrian S. Fisher* was Deputy Director of the United States Arms Control and Disarmament Agency and, in that capacity, was involved in negotiating the Limited Test Ban, Nuclear Nonproliferation and Seabed Treaties. He was also United States Ambassador to the Committee on Disarmament in Geneva. Prior to his death in 1983, he was Professor of Law at George Mason University Law School.

*Lawrence D. Gaughan* is Professor of Law at George Mason University Law School and Professional Director of Family Mediation of Greater Washington.

*Joseph B. Gittler* is Distinguished Visiting Professor of Sociology, George Mason University.

*Alex Gliksman*, formerly Staff Director of the Arms Control Subcommittee, United States Senate Foreign Relations Committee, is Director of Strategic Defense Studies for the United Nations Association of the USA.

*Irwin Greenberg* is Professor of Systems Engineering at George Mason University.

*A.J.R. Groom* is Professor of International Relations at the University of Kent at Canterbury.

*Conrad V. Hassel*, an attorney, was formerly Chief of the Special Operations and Research Unit of the Federal Bureau of Investigation.

*Leo Hecht* is Professor and Head of Russian Studies at George Mason University.

*Elizabeth Janssen Koopman* is Associate Professor, Department of Human Development at the University of Maryland.

*Kenneth A. Kovach* is Professor of Management at George Mason University.

*James H. Laue* is Professor of Sociology at the University of Missouri-St. Louis, and President and Executive Director of The Conflict Clinic, Inc., an independent, not-for-profit corporation that works in collaboration with Harvard Law School's Program on Negotiation toward improving the practice of conflict resolution in areas of public concern.

*David C. McGaffey*, a United States Foreign Service Officer, is Deputy Chief of Mission, United States Embassy, Georgetown, Guyana.

*Willard C. Matthias* was formerly an Intelligence Officer with the Central Intelligence Agency and Member of the Board of National Intelligence Estimates.

*Gilbert G. Pompa* was, until his death in 1986, Assistant Attorney General and Director, Community Relations Service (CRS) of the United States Department of Justice.

*Dean G. Pruitt* is Professor of Psychology at the State University of New York at Buffalo.

*Larry Ray* is Director of the Special Committee on Dispute Resolution of the American Bar Association.

*Roger Richman* is Associate Professor of Public Administration at Old Dominion University.

*Dennis J.D. Sandole* is Associate Professor of Government and Politics and Faculty Associate in Conflict Resolution at George Mason University.

*Joseph A. Scimecca* is Professor of Sociology and Head of Department of Sociology and Anthropology at George Mason University.

*Arnold K. Sherman*, formerly an Assistant Professor of Sociology at George Mason University, is President of Agreements That Work, Inc.

*Ethan T. Smith* is Chief of Plans and Programs of the United States Geological Survey.

*Ralph K. White* is Professor Emeritus in Social Psychology, George Washington University.

*Bryant Wedge*, formerly Director of the Center for Conflict Resolution at George Mason University, is Medical Director, South Community Mental Health, District of Columbia.

# INDEX

(NOTE: *passim* means that the subject so annotated is referred to in scattered passages throughout these pages of text. Page numbers in *italics* contain an article by the person indicated.)

interests of 100
marines 243–4
negotiations with Soviet Union 8,
    60, 210
negotiator for 100–3
Office of Management and
    Budget 133
Peace Academy 1, 5, 258, 262,
    275
political system 233
racial disorders in 19, 21–2
racial history 21
State Department 120, 204, 213
Steel 24
United Steel Workers (USW) 179,
    180
University
    George Mason ix, 1, 4–5, 10,
        30–1, 119–21, 199, 221
    North Western 50
    of Chicago Law School 187
    of Northern Virginia 1–2
    of Virginia 8
    Yale 231
Urban League 141
Ury, William 112, 114

Value structure 151–2
vertical hierarchy 102
Vienna 215, 217
Vienna, Congress of 281
violence
    and terror 195
    definition of 17
    levels of 279
    political 197
    potential for 134
    threat of 141
Virginia
    Council on Higher Education 2
    Environmental Endowment 158
    University of 8
Volvo 181

wage laborers 35
Walton League, Izaak 162–5
war
    Cold 9, 237
    course on 221

Korean 228
nuclear 9, 81, 221, 242, 244–5,
    248
preventing nuclear 223–9
Vietnam 186, 210, 227, 232,
    235–6, 245–6, 281
weaponry in 36
World I 190, 225, 239
World II 211, 219, 223, 227, 238,
    241, 248, 256
Warnke, Paul 203, 204
Warsaw Pact 210–12, 216
Washington 130, 143, 184, 192, 198,
    204, 205, 208, 210, 219, 232, 234,
    241
*Washington Post, The* 120
Watergate incident 232, 281
Wayne, John, syndrome 191
weapons
    binary chemical 205
    cruise missiles 261
    defensive 47, 83, 226
    nuclear 218, 223–9, 230, 239,
        242–3
    stockpile of 262–3
Wedge, Bryant *1–2*, 5, 8, 10, 11,
    82, 171, 203, 206, *208–9*, 223,
    *279–88*, 289, 294–5, 298
Weinberger, Caspar 243
wells, drilling of 152, 154
West Germany (German
    Democratic Republic) 179–80,
    184, 219, 228, 233
White, Ralph K. 6, 9, *81–5, 223–9*,
    230, 234, 236, 284
Wilson, Woodrow 67
'Window of vulnerability, the' 54
Wood, Harlington 138, 140
World Bank 286–7
worst case doctrine 206, 215–16,
    218, 235
Wounded Knee 132, 138–40

xenophobia 248

Yugoslavia 236

zero sum outcome 114, 115, 117,
    165–6, 206, 215, 220, 222